Radiohead FAQ

Radiohead FAQ

All That's Left to Know About the World's Most Famous Cult Band

Dan Caffrey

Backbeat
Books

Guilford, Connecticut

Backbeat Books
An imprint of The Rowman & Littlefield Publishing Group, Inc.
4501 Forbes Blvd., Ste. 200
Lanham, MD 20706
www.rowman.com

Distributed by NATIONAL BOOK NETWORK

The FAQ series was conceived by Robert Rodriguez and developed with Stuart Shea.

Book design by Snow Creative Services

British Library Cataloguing in Publication Information available

Library of Congress Cataloging-in-Publication Data available

ISBN 978-1-61713-712-9 (paperback)
ISBN 978-1-4930-5397-1 (e-book)

This book is dedicated to my wife, Susan Myburgh. You pushed me through, gave me tough love (and sheetcake) when I needed it, and are my favorite human being on this planet or any other. I love you—even if you despise Radiohead.

Contents

Acknowledgments

This book wouldn't exist without Robert Lecker, who sought me out after reading some of my articles about Radiohead on *Consequence of Sound*. Thanks, Robert, for taking the chance. Thanks to my editor Bernadette Malavarca for shepherding me through the process and answering all of my pesky questions. And Dan Bogosian, where would I be without the advice and morale support on our text thread? Can't wait to read *Red Hot Chili Peppers FAQ*.

Also, a huge thanks to the other *CoS* writers who also worked on those lengthy Radiohead pieces: Sean Barry, Nina Corcoran, Justin Gerber, Wren Graves, and Mary Kate McGrath. It was an honor to work alongside such fine writers.

When I was deciding whether or not I could take on *Radiohead FAQ*, only two people knew about it outside of my family: Audrey Polinski and Daniel Mutis. Seeing as the three of us were devising a play that involved a lot of discussion about the band, taking the leap and writing this thing seemed meant to be. Thanks for the encouragement, collaboration, and being ace human beings.

Speaking of shows about Radiohead, my good friend Chris Acevedo convinced our old theatre company, Tympanic, to produce an entire short-play cycle inspired by *OK Computer*. Thanks, Chris, for the vinyl and steering me away from an evening based on *Yankee Hotel Foxtrot*. And thanks to everyone who worked on the project, which we named *Today We Escape* after a lyric from "Exit Music (For a Film)." Thanks, Jon Patrick Penick, for playing Terry and covering "A Punchup at a Wedding" in our band a couple years down the line.

Reaching the bottom of the rabbit hole that is Radiohead's music is no easy task, and several people were instrumental in getting me information, merchandise, and music I couldn't track down on my own. Thank you, Alex Young, for the press contacts (and for writing many of the articles that I referenced for the book), Mae Shults for the endless well of music knowledge and those *OKNOTOK* tapes, Sami Jarroush for some trivia I didn't know about, Brent DiCrescenzo and Max Tannone for so generously offering their time for interviews, and Jeff Blehar—not only for compiling the best Radiohead bootlegs out there, but for giving several of the chapters a thorough fact-check (sorry/not sorry about "How to Disappear Completely").

Endless gratitude to every last one of my friends and family members simply for being you. If I could list all of you here, I would. But I do want to call out my parents, Drew and Janine Caffrey, who have always fostered creativity in their children. I know not every parent loves hearing that their kid wants to be a writer, but they've always viewed it as something to be celebrated. So thanks,

Mom and Dad, for letting me be me, always putting your children before you, and for just being incredible and supportive people—not just to me, but for everyone you encounter. I love you both.

Keeping it in the family for a bit, a big hug to my sister Alison Drew Balletta—the Jonny Greenwood to my Colin. While I've only ever really learned bass guitar, Alison can play just about any instrument she picks up. She's one of the most talented people I know, and yet still finds the time and energy to be a selfless force in this world. She's also married to an equally selfless person, my best friend and brother-in-law Mike Balletta. Now would also be a good time to mention my (and Mike's) other best friend, Dan Pfleegor. We've been a triumvirate since middle school and I expect it'll be that way the rest of our lives. Thanks for the love, support, and friendship.

Thank you, Peg and Owen Caffrey, or as they shall eternally be known in my heart, Dram and Obie. Obie, if those pearly gates are indeed a thing, I know you've already walked through them. Equal thanks and love to Howard Walker III and Adele Walker (Grammy and Poppy) for completing the cube of amazing grandparental role models. Grammy, I wish "A Reminder" was a real device. Maybe it is. I love you all.

I already thanked my wife and soulmate, Susan Myburgh, in the beginning of this book, but her love, patience, talent, and all-around wonderfulness deserves another mention. I hope I'm not keeping you up in the other room with my keyboard-klacking, and I hope you're having pleasant dreams scored by Kurt Vile songs. You're probably next to Hank, who remains the best dog and writing buddy out there. Thanks, Hank.

Finally, a hat-tip to my fellow Radioheadz; Randall Colburn, Justin Gerber (again), McKenzie Gerber, and Michael Roffman. We'll get to that *OK Computer* episode someday.

Introduction

The World's Most Famous Cult Band

I used to hate Radiohead.

I still remember reading their *Rolling Stone* cover story from 2001 (this was right after the release of *Kid A*) and groaning at the title alone: "In Order to Save Themselves, Radiohead Had to Destroy Rock & Roll." It was hard for me to dive deeper into the music when I couldn't get past the pretension of the musicians themselves, especially the singer—some guy named Thom Yorke. Whenever he did interviews, he seemed so serious; so self-important; so moody.

What I didn't realize at the time was that just because someone's serious doesn't mean they can't have a sense of humor, too. As it turns out, Radiohead has a *great* sense of humor. It's why this book has an entire chapter dedicated to the comedy inherent in their work. And even if the band was as pretentious in real life as they came off in the *Rolling Store* story, so what? Artists can be difficult, just like the rest of us.

Unsurprisingly, my eventual gateway into Radiohead's music—at least in the comprehensive sense—came from that very thing: the music. In March of 2016, rumblings of a new Radiohead LP (their ninth) had already been quietly shaking the internet for months. A release date would be announced any day. Since this was going to be one of the biggest releases of the year, I did my duty as a music critic and started making my way through their back catalog—something I had attempted several times before. I decided to start with *Amnesiac* since it had always been the hardest work of theirs for me to get through. Best to get it out of the way first.

Maybe it was the frigid Chicago weather, still caught in the dying gasp of winter. Maybe it was the noise-canceling headphones—something I had never worn when listening to Radiohead's music in the past. Or maybe it was just my time. Whatever the case, as I walked from my neighborhood of Albany Park to a fellow music critic's apartment in Avondale, something about Radiohead's music suddenly felt warm to me. This sensation occurred as soon as the opening track, "Packt Like Sardines In a Crushd Tin Box," starting playing. Under the sterility of Yorke's pitch-corrected vocals, a thick organ and drum loop exuded heat. These were disparate musical elements taking care of each other; mechanized sleekness mixed with soul; an automaton warming up by a fireplace.

From there, the floodgates opened. With all of Radiohead's music on my phone, I now had a portable space heater that I could take with me wherever I went that winter. The molten flow of "15 Step," the trashcan-fire percussion of

Radiohead performing at the Comcast Center in Mansfield, Massachussetts in 2012.

Tim Bugbee/Tinnitus Photography

"There there," and the crackling fuzz of the bassline on "The National Anthem" all made it easier to brave the cold.

It turns out the music was just the beginning. As any Radiohead fan knows, there's a whole separate universe to their artistry that goes beyond the sounds—one filled with breathtaking artwork, revolutionary methods of distribution, crackpot (or maybe not!) conspiracy theories, and so much more.

That's what I've tried to capture with *Radiohead FAQ*—not so much the tale of the band (Mac Randall already nailed their biography long before me with his book *Exit Music: The Radiohead Story*), but the endless flow of material, research, tangents, and conversations that come with being a fan. How many other musical acts have an audience so dogged and obsessive? This isn't *Radiohead: The Movie*, but *Radiohead: The World's Most Famous Cult Band*.

Looking back on that *Rolling Stone* article, I begrudgingly admit it was at least half right. Radiohead really did destroy themselves, or at least their general aesthetic, to reach the next level as artists. It's a realization I could have only come to after becoming a fan. It's a realization I could have only come to after joining the cult.

"Take Me on Board Their Beautiful Ship"

OK Computer

It's May 14, 2017. As I sit down to write the first chapter, *OK Computer* is about to celebrate its 20th anniversary, and the internet is already bursting with retrospectives on the band's landmark third studio album. By June 23, a reissue called *OK Computer OKNOTOK 1997 2017* will emerge fully loaded with a brand-new remaster and a bonus disc packed with B-sides and three previously unreleased tracks.

And that's just the digital version. There are also physical double-CD and triple-LP editions, as well as a box set that contains a hardcover art book, 104 pages of frontman Thom Yorke's notes, a 48-page sketchbook of "preparatory work" from band artist Stanley Donwood and Tchock (Yorke's visual-art alias), and a mixtape of demos.

While all of this forms a treasure trove for any Radiohead devotee, it's also a daunting reminder for someone about to write what's meant to be an encyclopedic book about the band. There's a lot to explore with Radiohead—so much that, in the wake of the *OKNOTOK*, this chapter will probably have to be heavily revised before I'm even done writing it. It's a hell of an album with which to start this book.

But it's also the *only* way to start this book. Outside of *Kid A*, *OK Computer* is Radiohead's biggest contender for Best Album Ever, and because it falls more easily into the genre of rock with a capital "R," it appeals to a wider audience. In a *Pitchfork* retrospective reflecting on what it was like to review *OK Computer* for *Spin* when the album came out in the United States on July 1, 1997, critic Barry Walters remarked that, while interpretations of the subject material varied, there was no denying that *OK Computer*—love it or hate it—was a watershed moment for the band.

Not that Radiohead initially set out to record anything with such an enormous impact, which seems crazy in 2017, a time when every album the band puts out is considered a cultural event. In fact, *OK Computer* was originally

Album art for *OK Computer*.

envisioned as nothing more than a negative reaction to the band's previous album, 1995's introspective and emotionally straightforward *The Bends*.

Guitarist/multi-instrumentalist Jonny Greenwood insisted that the only concept at play was for the band—burned out at this point by the *Bends* tour—to record the album by themselves, preferably somewhere tucked away.

With sessions beginning in July of 1996, Radiohead attempted to self-produce their new album at their own Canned Applause studio, near Didcot in their childhood stomping ground of Oxfordshire. But the remoteness soon led to frustration, squabbling, and only being able to finish just four songs: "Subterranean Homesick Alien," "No Surprises," "Electioneering," and "The Tourist."

The lack of productivity prompted Radiohead to hire an actual producer in Nigel Godrich, who, at that point, was no stranger to the band. In addition to engineering *The Bends* under producer John Leckie and producing 1994's *My Iron Lung* EP as well as the already recorded "Lucky," he made gear recommendations to Radiohead when they decided to purchase their own equipment for *OK Computer*.

Under Godrich's guidance, the band would find a more suitable recording environment that September in St Catherine's Court, a 16th-century manor house in the English countryside, just north of Bath, Somerset. Then owned by actress Jane Seymour, St Catherine's was far more accommodating than the cramped Canned Applause, which the band has described as little more than an apple shed with no restrooms. Still, they would return there in October to rehearse and fine-tune songs during the *OK Computer* sessions, before revisiting St Catherine's off and on from November 1996 until March 1997.

Another second wind came from their German-British record label, Parlophone, who encouraged them to go on tour in August 1996. Across 13 dates opening for Alanis Morissette, Radiohead was able to flesh out many of the remaining songs into something close to their final versions before returning to St Catherine's Court in the fall. As much as this seems to contrast with *OK Computer*'s dense sonics, it's also in line with one of its big ideas: the conceit of embracing technology while simultaneously lamenting the chronic alienation it can cause. Yes, the members of Radiohead create their music with complex machinery. But the machinery also requires flesh and blood.

The same idea pops up in Douglas Adams' seminal science-fiction satire, *The Hitchhiker's Guide to the Galaxy*, when a spaceship's computer says it can't

Much of *OK Computer* was recorded at St Catherine's Court—pictured here in 2006.
Adrian Sherratt/Shutterstock

defend the passengers from incoming missiles. "OK, computer," orders one character. "I want full manual control now." The passengers are saved and an album title is born.

It's unclear when this mini-thesis of human-meets-machine—or any of the other thematic ideas for the album—began to crystalize. But at some point, Radiohead realized they had something special. They realized they were consciously leaving behind everything they had done up until that point and shattering the preconceived notions of their own future.

The Songs

"Airbag"

Another musical idea on *OK Computer* is reluctant harmony—the idea of sonic elements that are seemingly at odds (at least prior to 1997) blaring away until they reach something cohesive. That's how "Airbag" begins, and it's an aesthetic that becomes a throughline for the rest of the album.

Even in the opening seconds, Jonny Greenwood blends a riff that sounds leftover from *The Bends* with the jingle of sleigh bells. Electricity intertwines with an instrument that's existed for centuries. Then Phil Selway's drums enter as the backbone—albeit one with several missing vertebrae. As noted by the band, they were trying to recreate the feel of a DJ Shadow song.

To achieve that effect, Selway pounded away for 15 minutes while the rest of the band recorded him on an Akai S3000 sampler. They ended up using only a three-second portion, then manipulated it on a Macintosh and looped it to give the song a danciness, with strategic dropouts where there's no percussion at all. It's not trip hop per se, but Radiohead's *version* of trip hop. Similar to the gaps in the drumming, Colin Greenwood deliberately leaves out bass notes here and there.

Much like everything else on *OK Computer*, "Airbag" started off in simpler fashion, performed acoustically in concert as early as 1995. A performance at British radio station Xfm on October 28 of that year has a dreamier feel to it than the final product, stripped of the rhythm section and lulling along at a cloud's pace. The momentum is harder to track, nudged along by Yorke's acoustic strumming and a stargazing lead from Jonny.

Lyrically, Yorke starts a trend that pops up on many of *OK Computer*'s songs: filtering everyday events through a science-fiction filter. In 1987, he and his girlfriend at the time were involved in a car accident. Although she received whiplash, Yorke walked away unscathed, prompting him to consider how lucky we all are any time we survive a trip in an automobile, as he told *Select* in 1997.

In "Airbag," he takes that sentiment to the extreme by having a car accident be a means of rebirth. Making the event even more miraculous, the car crash—sung about in Yorke's clearest mid-range—is accompanied by larger-than-life events such as another world war and explosions of stars. The slightly varied lyrics in an early demo from *OKNOTOK* have a more realistic bent, with some of the wilder phrases such as "jackknifed juggernaut" traded out for straightforward language ("the world you left behind"). The central statement of "An airbag saved my life" also appears more frequently, drawing further attention to the original title of "Last Night an Airbag Saved My Life," itself a playful riff on Indeep's 1982 post-disco hit "Last Night a D.J. Saved My Life."

Yorke may be poking fun at the self-aggrandizing in the lyrics. When he proclaims that he's "back to save the universe," it's never clear if he actually means it or is criticizing his own vehicular survival. Perhaps it's miraculous that there aren't *more* fatal car accidents, but does the mere act of survival make someone exceptional? "Airbag" leaves the question open-ended, asking the listener to ponder it as the song leaves us with four mechanized beeps in its final seconds, counting us down into a song that relies more heavily on science fiction.

"Paranoid Android"

The imagery on *OK Computer*'s second track may be grotesque and morose, but the song's origins are rather random—almost a parody of an epic, dramatic song rather than the real deal. Divided into three distinct sections, many critics have dubbed "Paranoid Android" as a "Bohemian Rhapsody" for the '90s. The band dismissed this comparison to *Melody Maker* on May 31, 1997, citing "Paranoid Android's" relative simplicity when compared to Queen. It's the same approach as "Airbag": Radiohead trying to imitate a musician with an inimitable style and ending up with something inimitable of their own.

Even before Yorke wrote his fractured lyrics, "Paranoid Android" began as three different songs that the band tried to drunkenly mash together at Canned Applause, knowing they were goofing around and would likely never reach the operatic grandiosity of "Bohemian Rhapsody" or the Beatles' "Happiness Is A Warm Gun," another classic-rock epic and occasional reference point. As a result, the shifts between the song's four sections are jarring, perhaps intentionally so—the sound of a band trying to ruin their own joke, but creating something wondrous.

The first section has an almost Latin flavor to it, the handheld percussion of rhythm guitarist and effect-unit extraordinaire Ed O'Brien's claves and cabasa sprinkled over a fingerpicked acoustic riff from Yorke that, in G minor, seems harmless enough at first. But from the moment the electric guitar and Yorke's vocals creep in, there's a sense of foreboding that continues to grow. Everything becomes more synthesized—the monotone voice of the Macintosh SimpleText application uttering the words "I. May. Be. Paranoid. But. Not. An. Android." A cro magnon predecessor to Siri, the SimpleText app has a doom-laden flatness that would be featured more prominently on the second half of the album with "Fitter Happier."

The destruction is stalled, at least for a time, as the SimpleText's countdown-like inflection leads not to apocalypse, but the most straightforward rock portion of the song. While it mostly keeps the same rhythm as the first section (occasionally launching into ⅞ time), part two of "Paranoid Android" moves into the key of A minor, with Colin Greenwood's bass as the engine underneath.

Then, an explosion.

As with "Creep," Jonny Greenwood deliberately disrupts the softness with clanging distortion, which soon ascends into a solo backed by Selway's furious drum fills. The comedown arrives with the third section, which slows down the previous tempo of 84 BPM to 63 BPM. Written mostly by Jonny, this segment of "Paranoid Android" is lifted by a makeshift choral arrangement (most likely created by multi-tracking Yorke and O'Brien's vocals). The fourth and final section brings back the second with a new guitar solo from Greenwood and a chromatic descension that abruptly ends the whole mess.

Perhaps because the music for "Paranoid Android" was so intentionally fragmented from the get-go, Yorke took the same approach with the lyrics. A large chunk of the text comes from a real-life experience, when he was out at a bar in Los Angeles, surrounded by several people high on cocaine. As he told Q magazine in 1997, one woman flipped out at her friends after someone spilled a drink on her. Decked out in Gucci apparel, her tantrum haunted Yorke and inspired the lyric "Kicking squealing Gucci little piggy."

But like "Airbag" before it, reality ballooned into a more abstract take on bigger themes. The image of a prospective tyrant threatening to pin someone against the wall could easily be about the oppression of any suffocating institution, from the media to Parliament to the British monarchy. The "chicken voices" Yorke describes in his head are obviously a manifestation of paranoia, and Marvin the Paranoid Android—the namesake character from *The Hitchhiker's Guide To The Galaxy*—is chronically depressed because his creators rarely give him full access to his formidable brain.

Then again, maybe all of those random images are just that: random images, filtered through the sound of five talented musicians getting sloshed, making jokes, and experimenting with form. But that doesn't mean fans and critics should feel prohibited from drawing their own conclusions about the song and thinking about how it relates to some of the oppression and fear in their own lives.

If one needs further proof of "Paranoid Android's" more comedic origins, they only need to watch footage of its original live incarnation. Here, the song has a drawn-out, woozy Hammond organ outro from Jonny Greenwood in the third section (the band has erroneously said that this extended "Paranoid Android" to 14 minutes, though in reality, it was only 15 seconds longer than the album track). Radiohead would also bring out glockenspiel, as if trying to pile on as many prog-rock tropes as they could before the song ended. During these performances, it's not the band's riff on the Beatles or Queen, but Iron Butterfly. The joke does grow old after a while—as jokes between bandmates often do—showing that Radiohead was wise to simplify the song.

Despite "Paranoid Android" not being as deadly serious as many fans would like to believe, it will always be an ideal place to start for any novice of Radiohead. "Airbag" marked a shift in tone from *The Bends*, but "Paranoid Android" is undeniable proof of how big Radiohead's ambition had gotten, even if they considered such a thing to be pretty ugly.

"Subterranean Homesick Alien"

If we consider "Last Night An Airbag Saved My Life" to be the unofficial full name of "Airbag," then "Subterranean Homesick Alien" marks the third song in a row on *OK Computer* where the title derives from another piece of pop culture.

This time, the band is of course riffing on Bob Dylan's "Subterranean Homesick Blues." And just as "Airbag" sounds nothing like Indeep, "Alien" sounds nothing like Mr. Zimmerman. Rather, Radiohead drew musical inspiration from Miles Davis' *Bitches Brew* when writing the song during *The Bends* sessions; premiering it acoustically with Yorke and Jonny Greenwood on KCRW's *Morning Becomes Eclectic* on April 4, 1995; and eventually laying it to tape at Canned Applause (of the four compositions recorded there, "Alien" is the oldest).

Although the song is nowhere near as complex as anything on *Bitches Brew*, the influence is still obvious, particularly in Jonny's extended use of an electric piano (*Bitches Brew* featured two to three electric piano players on all six of its tracks). It contributes to the dreamlike feel of the song as Yorke's narrator fantasizes about being abducted by the extraterrestrial beings of the title. But is the title referring to the literal aliens? Probably not. Unlike the narrator, they feel very much at home in their own environment, laughing together at home movies of human beings and their repressive habits. No, it's the human who's the actual homesick alien.

The clever role reversal came about during Yorke's time at Abingdon School as a boy, where he met the other members of Radiohead. While there, he received an assignment to write his own piece of Martian poetry, a popular literary movement in England where human activity is viewed through the lens of alien life. The idea alchemized years later when, while driving down a country lane, he hit a bird that he believed to be a pheasant and began thinking about what it would be like to get abducted by aliens.

This may have contributed to the song's pastoral atmosphere. While many would describe Jonny's piano, O'Brien's Rickenbacker 12-string, and Yorke's woozy Fender Rhodes as spacy, the arrangement feels much more earthbound, capturing the solitude of driving down a country road at night.

"Exit Music (For A Film)"

Radiohead recorded *OK Computer*'s fifth track, "Let Down," in the ballroom of St Catherine's Court at 3 a.m., but "Exit Music (For A Film)" is the song where the presence of Jane Seymour's mansion is most obviously felt—a haunted house trying to expel its paranormal forces into the listener's ears.

The effect comes from Yorke recording his vocals in a stone staircase, giving his performance a natural reverb. But it isn't just the stones of the 16th-century staircase that contribute to "Exit Music"'s seemingly advanced age. Yorke also used a text from the same time period as inspiration: William Shakespeare's *Romeo and Juliet*, a story that had a profound effect on him at a young age and made him question why the title characters didn't just run away from their families.

While on tour with Alanis Morissette, Australian auteur Baz Luhrmann was putting the finishing touches on his own version of Shakespeare's romantic tragedy, the 1996 film *Romeo + Juliet*. Set in the modern Verona Beach, the adaptation reframes the Capulets and Montagues as rival mafia empires. Swords become pistols (emblazoned with the fictional gun brand "Sword" so the text can stay intact), Queen Mab is literalized as an ecstasy tablet, and the film has Luhrmann's trademark smash-cut editing—more reminiscent of a 1990s music video than a traditional adaptation of the Bard's work. Polarizing as it may be, there's no denying *Romeo + Juliet*'s bratty flair.

Luhrmann's production team sent Radiohead the last half-hour of the film while the band was opening for Morissette, asking if they could write a song for the closing credits. Radiohead happily obliged, with Yorke honing in on the image of Juliet pressing a handgun to her head in the movie's final moments.

Yorke originally tried to write lyrics using only lines from Shakespeare's play, but found the effect to be too esoteric. As a solution, he wrote the song from the young lovers' point of view in contemporary language, giving them the happy ending he had always envisioned for them.

The final result is surely more relatable than Yorke's original, iambic pentameter vision would have been. As Romeo and Juliet plan their doomed escape, it could be the POV of any teenage couple around the world. Resenting one's family, being overwhelmed by love and lust, and longing to flee a hometown are feelings that most folks have experienced at one point in their life.

Ultimately, "Exit Music" lived up to its title by playing over *Romeo + Juliet*'s end credits, although it wasn't released on the soundtrack. Doing so would have meant unveiling it to the world on October 29, 1996, almost seven months before *OK Computer* hit shelves in Japan.

The song has more indirect ties to the film's aesthetic, too. Because Luhrmann mixes the holy with the hedonistic—a youth choir sings Prince songs; angel imagery swarms at a drug-fueled masquerade—there's a sacred yet passionate vibe to *Romeo + Juliet*. Radiohead adopts this contrast as well, gradually introducing more earth-shaking elements to Yorke's lonely voice and acoustic guitar.

By the time the song ends in apocalyptic rumbling, the full band and another ghost choir (this time created by Jonny Greenwood on a newly acquired Mellotron) have both made appearances. And if "Exit Music" has the same entitled me-against-the-world mentality as *OK Computer*'s next song, "Let Down," the lyrics aren't nearly as eye-rolling. Remember, these are teenagers. And feeling entitled is just as big a part of being a teen as fighting with one's parents.

"Let Down"

The best way to describe *OK Computer*'s second single, "Let Down," is deadpan prettiness. Sure, the guitar arpeggios from Jonny, O'Brien, and Yorke twinkle, but the actual playing sounds numb, matching Yorke's lyrics of feeling apathetic toward the rest of society.

Likewise, Yorke's high-register delivery is soothing yet detached, a result of him deliberately performing the song with as little emotion as possible. Even when the band adds more bricks to their wall of sound—they've confirmed that they were going for a Phil Spector vibe—one can almost hear each player sighing with resignation. Yorke's dual vocal lines stay in unison during the verses before he harmonizes with himself during the chorus, but there's no sudden surge of exuberance. Selway matches this by switching from the floor toms to the snare during the final build. It's such a subtle shift that it feels like a reduction—not an amplification—of power.

The juxtaposition of shrug and shimmer was novel in 1997, but despite "Let Down" growing into a consistent fan favorite since Radiohead premiered it in 1995 (possibly at a November 14 performance at Paris' Virgin Megastore), the lyrics do come across as overly sulky today—the one time on the album where the imagery hints that Yorke might actually feel superior in his apathy towards others. That's not to say it isn't an accurate descriptor—apathy always has a certain snobbishness about it—but it does strip the song of some of its likability.

The more fascinating lyrical elements are reminiscent of Franz Kafka's *The Metamorphosis*, exploring the gross-out details of humans discovering they're nothing more than insects. As they get obliterated by the whirlwind of urban life, their shells smash, their juices spill onto the pavement, and their legs give away. When their broken bodies start to grow wings, it appears there could be some salvation for their physical beings, but Yorke quickly dismisses the new change as nothing more than a useless chemical reaction. Insects become a central metaphor again four songs later on "Climbing Up the Walls."

There might be one final glimmer of hope, however. In the song's closing moments, beeps from a ZX Spectrum computer add an excitement and chipperness. All of the band members used ZX Spectrums while growing up in the 1970s, so does that mean their use here is a sign that the narrator may reclaim the happiness of their youth? Or is it a cruel tease, an instance of nostalgia that ultimately comes up empty?

Much to listeners' shock, O'Brien revealed in his online *Kid A* diary that "Let Down" almost didn't make it onto *OK Computer*. The constant shuffling of tracklists would become a staple of the Radiohead recording process (they had already practiced this to some extent with *The Bends*), but due to its high regard amongst Radiohead fans (if not this particular writer), it's hard to imagine "Let Down" not appearing on the record.

"Karma Police"

Compositionally, the two songs may not many have similarities, but "Karma Police" could easily be considered a companion piece to "Paranoid Android." Both served as singles for *OK Computer*, and both sound deadly serious, despite starting off as goofs. No, the law agency of the title isn't from some fascist organization in a George Orwell novel, but an in-joke between the band members.

"It was a band catch phrase for a while on tour—whenever someone was behaving in a particular shitty way, we'd say, 'The karma police will catch up with him sooner or later'," Jonny Greenwood told *Melody Maker* in 1997.

Nonetheless, "Karma Police" (road-tested on the tour with Morissette) sure *sounds* menacing with its A Dorian key and thundercloud piano, and some of the comic imagery seems to have been repurposed to be more Orwellian. In the song's final version, the Karma Police spirit away anyone who makes the narrator feel uneasy.

There's another piece of literature that connects to "Karma Police," even though the band may not have been aware of it when they wrote the song. Halfway through, the key switches to an even darker B minor, and by the end, Ed O'Brien has warped his guitar notes into white noise. By distorting them through one of Nigel Godrich's digital rackmount delay units, he allows the fridge-buzzing to overtake everything else. Even if the song's nebbish man has been arrested, his presence still haunts the narrator, a sign that he—or any of us, really—will always be vexed by our fellow humans. As Jean-Paul Sartre posited in his 1944 existential drama, *No Exit*, "Hell is other people." That's the sickest joke of all, and one that Radiohead would probably have a good laugh at.

"Fitter Happier"

The second half of *OK Computer* starts off esoterically, and the recording process was as unconventional as the final product. During a three-month period of being dogged by writer's block, Yorke found himself only able to come up with lists of words, as opposed to actual songs. One night when he was drunk, he wandered into Radiohead's rehearsal room, plunked out several discordant sequences on the piano, and recorded random phrases from one of the lists (this one hastily scribbled in 10 minutes) using Macintosh's SimpleText application.

The mechanized voice behind the spoken-word line of "Paranoid Android," SimpleText—affectionately dubbed "Fred Cooper" by its creators—came installed on Macintosh LC computers in the 1990s. It sounds similar to Call-Text 5010, the device that allowed that allowed deceased theoretical physicist Stephen Hawking to vocalize his thoughts during this time period, leading many fans to falsely believe that it was actually the renowned physicist reading Yorke's disturbing phrases.

It's interesting how, despite Hawking and Yorke using a similar voice to communicate, the emotional effects are vastly different because of the writing. Hawking was articulate, logical, and empathetic—his complex thoughts honestly connecting with others, even though they were being spoken with little variation in tone and inflection.

Yorke, on the other hand, crafted purposely alienating phrases with "Fitter Happier," and the disconnect is obvious as soon as "Fred" starts speaking. When taken in the greater context of the rest of *OK Computer*, statements such as "regular exercise at the gym, three days a week" become cult-leader commands rather than healthy mantras.

And because of the robotic narrator's descent into nonsense language, there's a sense of them having been unhinged the entire time. "A pig in a cage on antibiotics" (a line taken from Jonathan Coe's 1991 satirical novel of British politics, *What a Carve Up!*) is the exact opposite of an engaged, physically fit individual. To make the whole affair even more disorienting, a clip from Sydney Pollack's 1975 political thriller, *Three Days of the Condor*, plays underneath.

Yorke has since admitted that he no longer enjoys the absurdly bleak words—many of them also inspired by self-help books—despite their creepy effectiveness.

"Electioneering"

In the 2017 documentary *Get Me Roger Stone*, the disgraced political strategist describes politics as "show business for ugly people." As despicable as Stone is as a human being, it's an observant statement coming from the man who was instrumental in getting Donald Trump elected as the 45th President of the United States.

Even without the Trump connection, Stone's declaration still rings true. Is show business really that different from politics? According to "Electioneering," the members of Radiohead would think not. On its surface, the song critiques several different political figures, ideologies, and movements by speaking from the point of view of a glad-handing politician. George H.W. Bush's term "voodoo economics," London's poll tax riots, and the International Monetary Fund all get referenced in one way or another. While the politician never outright disagrees with any of these things, the music underneath conveys anger and unease: Yorke and O'Brien's guitars—tuned to drop D and distorted to the point that they resemble warped banjos—may as well be the squall from a protester's megaphone; Selway's cowbell is a trash can smashing onto the hood of a police cruiser.

But "Electioneering" goes deeper than just critiquing those in power. Because at the end of the day, don't the members of Radiohead—one of the most popular rock bands in the world—have a certain amount of unspoken power? By singing in the first person, Yorke makes them complicit in the manipulation of their fans.

"After a while you feel like a politician who has to kiss babies and shake hands all day long," O'Brien told *HUMO* in 1997. "If Tony Blair can behave as a pop star, why shouldn't we feel a bit like politicians?"

"Electioneering" had such multiple layers from the beginning, with most of the lyrics intact from its earliest live performances in 1996. One interesting change, though: In its original incarnation, it ended with Yorke and O'Brien harmonizing the words "Doin' it all" over a joyous chord progression. The politician/rock star may be a scumbag, but, to quote another Radiohead song, they're happy to serve.

On the album, the band bypasses this refrain to get straight to the chaotic finale. Instruments drop out, percussion crashes, and synthesizers squelch. Regardless of how someone feels about politics (or show business), one thing's for certain: It's a true circus, and "Electioneering" captures a life under the lobbyist big top.

Radiohead, however, does not hold such a high opinion of the song. They claim to have included it on *OK Computer* only to mix up the pacing, and it's the album's sole track to not be revived after the initial tour cycle. Even then, the band only played it three times.

"Climbing Up the Walls"

By the time Radiohead recorded *OK Computer*, rock music already had a long relationship with orchestral music. Everyone from the Beatles to Pink Floyd to Neil Young had employed string quartets or even full orchestras to add something distinct to their sound.

But, as is usually the case with everything in rock, the novelty eventually became the cliche. By 1997, any band interested in maximalism had penned a song that involved a mounting cascade of strings—lushness for lushness' sake. U2 had done it. Even Guns N' Roses had done it. With "Climbing Up the Walls," Radiohead wanted to do something different.

"I got very excited at the prospect of doing string parts that didn't sound like 'Eleanor Rigby'," Jonny Greenwood told the *Guardian* that year.

So he turned to a more unexpected source for the string section of "Climbing Up the Walls": *Threnody to the Victims of Hiroshima* by Polish composer Krzysztof Penderecki—itself a rebellion against the stereotypes of classical music. Composed in 1960 as a tribute to the victims of the Hiroshima bombing of 1945, *Threnody* relies not on conventional melody and changes in notes, but an aleatoric approach. That is, the variations come from slight yet effective changes in timbre and texture, sustaining then bending the notes in a way that conveys a sense of slowly building catastrophe. It's no coincidence Penderecki's composition has been used to pile on the dread in several horror films, including Stanley Kubrick's *The Shining* and Wes Craven's *The People Under the Stairs*.

Fittingly, "Climbing Up the Walls" is Yorke's own version of a horror movie, drawn from a *New York Times* article about serial killers and his own time spent working as an orderly in a mental hospital. This was shortly after the Care in the Community policy was introduced in the United Kingdom. Enforced by Margaret Thatcher's government in the 1980s, it was designed to ensure that as many mental patients as possible could be taken care of in their homes instead of hospitals. Though the policy may have been noble in intent (or maybe not), Care in the Community's detractors have argued that the initiative resulted in many mental patients being released into the streets, left to fend for themselves when they don't have the means to. Yorke was among these critics.

Radiohead conveys his feelings of unease with a repetitive, almost monotonous Bm, G, Em chord sequence, each one seeping out of the speakers like a freshly pressed Rorschach blot. It helps that the band recorded "Climbing Up the Walls" in the library of St Catherine's Court, amplifying the gothic mood of the song. They further ratchet up the tension with insect noises, an ominous sequence from Colin Greenwood's Novation Bass Station synthesizer, a series of broken radio transmissions, and of course, those strings.

Jonny instructed the 16 members of the string section to play a quarter note apart from each other, giving their part the feel of an off-kilter, never-ending cycle. The strings begin underscoring the rock elements of the song about a minute-and-a-half in, then lock into a more traditional ascent at the 3:33 mark. In the last 20 seconds, Jonny and the classical instrumentalists fully embrace Penderecki by coming together for a tortured squeal with slight variations from each player.

This wouldn't be the last time Jonny would draw inspiration from Penderecki. The two masterminds would collaborate in a more direct sense in 2012 with the album *Jonny Greenwood/Krzysztof Penderecki*. In addition to new, original music from both musicians, the project also included "48 Responses to Polymorphia," itself a reactionary composition from Greenwood to one of Penderecki's earlier works.

If "Climbing Up the Walls" has one shortcoming, it's the point of view in the lyrics. There's no denying the unsettling nature of Yorke's imagery—eyeballs in cupboards and a madman burying themselves in someone's brain. At the same time, the first-person vantage point lessens the blow, falling victim to the literary trope of the villain who relishes being a villain. Dangerous people—especially those suffering from mental illness—don't always have this kind of self-awareness. If Yorke had written "Climbing Up the Walls" from the third person, the protagonist would seem more like a legitimate threat and less like a mustache-twirling cartoon.

"No Surprises"

"No Surprises" is the most lyrically straightforward song on *OK Computer*, a trait that can be attributed to the time when it was written. Originally penned as an acoustic encore titled "No Surprises, Please" in 1995 when the band was opening for R.E.M. and recorded as the first track during the first day of the Canned Applause sessions, the words read like remnants of *The Bends*—rife with the type of self-loathing discontent that could be found in a diary. This is even truer of the original version, where more intimate lyrics describe a man and woman's relationship souring in grotesque detail.

But where *The Bends* mostly revelled in romantic unhappiness, the final version of "No Surprises" stays in line with *OK Computer*'s overall distrust of the government, corporations, and modern comforts. And because it was one of the earliest songs written for *OK Computer*, one could argue that it ignited Thom Yorke's desire to further explore those more all-encompassing themes.

It also remains somewhat of an anomaly on the album in that it sounds resigned. Even the other "pretty" songs on *OK Computer* have a defense mechanism, a refusal to accept one's circumstances, regardless of whether or not it results in actual change. But on "No Surprises," Yorke is placated. While he lists off the misery-inducing forces of a life in the suburbs—a soul-crushing job, the automotive pollution—by the end of the song, he prefers the quietness. He could bring down the government, or he could settle for a life of redundancy. At least his expectations are fulfilled, if only because he sets them so low.

Many Radiohead fans have posited online that the lyric "a handshake of carbon monoxide" implies that the narrator isn't being inactive—that he's actually going to kill himself through carbon monoxide poisoning in his garage—but it's likely much simpler than that. Most people that give up on their dreams *don't* kill themselves. They merely settle for a life that's different from what they envisioned for themselves as children. But it's a life nonetheless. That somehow feels like the more emotionally devastating truth.

To reinforce the atmosphere of somnambular pleasantness—of people driving around suburbia in a dopy yet content stupor—the band treats the arrangement like a lullaby, gently nudged along by O'Brien's twilight guitar line and a glockenspiel played by Jonny Greenwood. Nigel Godrich even instructed the band to play the song faster than normal when they recorded it, so he could slow it down significantly for Yorke's vocal and give the entire affair a narcotic haze. According to Yorke, they ended up going with their first take for the album.

"Lucky"

Radiohead has collectively acknowledged "Lucky" as being the catalyst for the rest of *OK Computer*, even though they didn't decide to include it until they were almost done putting together the album.

In fact, the band didn't compose it for placement on any proper Radiohead album at all. Birthed from a scraping guitar noise that O'Brien would tinker with during a summer 1995 tour of Japan, "Lucky" was originally recorded for *The Help Album*, a charity collection put together by War Child. The record's benefits would go on to aid children disenfranchised by the Bosnian War. Unlike most of the other British and Irish bands appearing on the compilation, Radiohead opted for an original song rather than a cover. Their decision had less to do with one-upmanship than it did with inability.

"It was "only because we're so bad at covers," O'Brien told *Melody Maker* in 1997.

"Lucky" begins with O'Brien's metallic scraping effect, picks up some momentum with a cymbal click from Selway, then becomes a fully developed ballad when Yorke enters with an Em chord and a comfortable mid-range vocal.

We know that "Lucky" was a lynchpin for the rest of *OK Computer* because, well, the band has said so. But even if they hadn't, there are clear elements that signal it as a building-out point. The central story of someone being reborn as a superhero after a plane crash connects it to "Airbag," and the idea of a love so strong it transcends death ties back to "Exit Music (For a Film)."

"Lucky" could also be seen as the reverse image of "No Surprises." While both songs are melancholy in pace and tone, the narrator of "Lucky" refuses to be a slave to the government. With such a bounty of lyrical and thematic ideas, it's no wonder Radiohead opted not to use a newly recorded version of "Lucky" when they finally decided to use the song for *OK Computer*. As with "No Surprises," the original take, recorded with Godrich at Surrey Sound, was also the best.

"The Tourist"

OK Computer covers a lot of ground in its examination of 20th-century life: the chaos, the alienation, the tension, the technology. So it comes as somewhat of a surprise that it ends not with a message of anxiety, but of peace.

Or maybe that's just the logical response to a record that, if we distill it into one rapidly descending elevator pitch, is about the speed of modern life and the pitfalls that come with it. Perhaps it's necessary to close with the band asking the world at large—and themselves—to slow down.

Jonny Greenwood wrote the music for "The Tourist" when he was in a picturesque square in France, stricken by all the American visitors rushing around, trying to see all the sites instead of soaking everything in naturally. Yorke embraced this exact theme when writing the lyrics, directing the refrain of "Hey man, slow down" toward himself after a restless night in Germany.

"I walked out to find something to eat, but I couldn't find anything, and this fucking dog was barking at me," he told *Rolling Stone* on May 31, 2017. "I'm staring at this dog, and everyone else is carrying on. That's where 'hey, man, slow down' comes from. It sounds like it's all about technology and stuff, but it's not."

When Yorke was frantically trying to decide the sequencing of *OK Computer*'s final tracklist, he once again turned to this message. After all the chaos, it was the only way to conclude the album. Fittingly, the band had only decided to include "The Tourist" at the last minute when they had time to breathe, despite having recorded it during the Canned Applause sessions.

And so, *OK Computer* ends on a note of comfort, letting the listener know that, if we all take a moment to breathe, maybe everything will be alright. My colleague at *Consequence of Sound* (and Radiohead superfan), Justin Gerber, has always found this kind of solace in the final moments of *OK Computer*, an album that otherwise offers few moments of respite. And, in the spirit of any true Radiohead superfan, he has a theory about the lyrics that would make the song even deeper than it initially appears.

"It all goes back to Cameron Crowe's 1989 film *Say Anything…*" he posits in his video retrospective on the album for a *CoS* series called *Masterpiece Reviews*. Right before the credits, the film's two young lovers, Lloyd and Diane, are about to take off on a plane. Diane worries that the aircraft will crash. Lloyd tells her that most plane crashes occur within the first five minutes of takeoff. So when they hear the smoking sign go off once the plane is at a certain altitude, they can rest assured that their flight will go smoothly. Everything will be okay.

"So what do *Say Anything* and *OK Computer* both end on?" asks Gerber. "A ding." He's referring to the album's final note, a crystalline bell played by Jonny. "Maybe everything will be okay for Lloyd and Diane. And Thom. And maybe for all of us."

That theory seems more relevant—and comforting—than ever. The world is a lot faster, tenser, and more claustrophobic than it was in 1997. It's like we're living in the embodiment of *OK Computer*'s first 11 songs. But if we're lucky, maybe we'll soon get closer to the tone of its final track.

B-sides

"Lull"

There are only two B-sides from the *OK Computer* singles that weren't included on one or both of the compilation EPs *Airbag / How Am I Driving?* and *No Surprises / Running From Demons* (covered in the next chapter).

"Lull" was originally released as the final B-side on CD1 of the "Karma Police" single. It's possible that Radiohead withheld it from the two EPs out of distaste for EMI's practice of releasing singles with slightly different track listings in order to make more money. However, EMI did eventually include it on the 2009 "Collector's Edition" reissue, along with "How I Made My Millions," which originally appeared on the "No Surprises" single after the *No Surprises / Running From Demons* EP.

It's easy to see why Radiohead might have held it in such high regard. The glockenspiel from "No Surprises" makes a return, sprinkling the rather miserable lyrics about anxiety with childlike innocence (the line about disappearing into a keyhole is particularly imaginative). It's hooky, rife with nocturnal majesty, and at under two-and-a-half minutes, it's an easy pill to swallow. Only later does one realize how bitter it is.

"How I Made My Millions"

Radiohead doesn't usually aim for a low-fi quality, but "How I Made My Millions" makes a case for them recording an album on a four-track a la Bruce Springsteen's *Nebraska*. Actually, make that a MiniDisc.

As O'Brien told BBC Radio 1 on January 6, 1998, Yorke recorded the song at home on a piano. At first, a quiet clanking suggests that we're hearing the pressing of the keys and pedals, but it was actually someone—probably Rachel Owen—doing the dishes in the background. When the band was struggling to come with a new song in the studio, Yorke showed them his scrappy home recording. They were, in O'Brien's words, "blown away by it." Fans were, too.

Conclusion

At this point, what else is there to say about *OK Computer*? Most of it was covered in the immediate aftermath of its release. There was no slow-building appreciation in the United States as there was with *The Bends*. Even if the album took several listens to sink in, it was almost universally heralded as a masterpiece. The one somewhat amusing outlier is *Rolling Stone*, who originally slapped *OK Computer* with a three-star rating, only to revise it to five stars in 1998.

The acclaim also extended to fans around the world. To list out all of *OK Computer*'s overall chartings and certifications would take up more page space than this book allows, but it's sold 4.5 million copies worldwide to date, and in 2015, was added to the Library of Congress' National Recording Registry. That comes in addition to being nominated for Album of the Year and Best Alternative Music Album at the 40th Annual Grammy Awards (it won the second category), and being shortlisted for the 1997 Mercury Prize.

2

"An Empty Space"

The *OK Computer* EPs

In the family of music formats, the extended play (EP) has always been the odd middle child, never as short and brisk as the single, but rarely achieving the significance and attention of the full-length album. Part of this is due to its convoluted history.

Publicly released in 1952 by RCA Victor, the EP was designed to compete with Columbia Records' long play format (LP)—itself a means of offering more music than a traditional 45 single. Because the LP had a 33 ⅓ revolutions-per-minute (rpm) speed and larger size of 10 or 12 inches, it was able to hold up to 20 minutes of music per side.

The problem was, the LP's size and speed prevented it from being played on a traditional 45 rpm phonograph. Thus, the EP was born. At seven inches and with narrower grooves, it could hold seven-and-a-half minutes of music on each side, but still be played on a 45 phonograph.

Unlike a 45 or LP, there has never been a preconceived notion as to what should live on an EP. With a single, the definition lies in the name of the format: It's meant to showcase one song. Even when the disc contains a handful of extras (as is often the case), it's all built around that central track and billed as such. And with an LP, it's meant to be a self-contained larger work, ideally listened to front to back.

Different musicians have used the more flexible format of the EP for different reasons. Radiohead's contemporaries Pavement, for instance, tended to treat their EPs as mini albums, recording songs specifically for a smaller collection rather than throwing a handful of B-sides together that didn't make the cut for a larger work. Their 1989 EP *Slay Tracks (1933–1969)* was recorded in a single day, then distributed as their first official release as a band. Likewise, they used their 1992 EP *Watery, Domestic,* as a means of introducing new band members Bob Nastanovich and Mark Ibold in recorded form (they had previously only played on tour).

On the flip side, many of the Beatles' EPs were more or less cash grabs—ways for their record label, Parlophone, to make a quick buck by releasing compilations of songs that had been released elsewhere, with no new material included at all. All four tracks on 1963's *Twist and Shout* and *The Beatles (No. 1)* were already available on the band's debut, *Please Please Me*; 1964's *All My Loving* had two songs apiece from *Please Please Me* and *With the Beatles*; and everything on *Extracts From the Film a Hard Day's Night* appeared—duh—on the album of (almost) the same name.

Radiohead's EP Dilemma

Radiohead has followed a similar approach as the Beatles with their EPs, which is somewhat surprising given both acts' reputations as true album bands. Then again, maybe that's the exact reason why most of their EPs have often been little more than compilations of already released material. Maybe, as an album band, Radiohead prefer to focus on that very thing: the album. Why waste time recording new material for a disc of four or five songs when it could be saved for a disc of 10 or 12 songs unified by a larger theme?

Or, maybe it wasn't even the band's decision at all. Maybe it simply came down to their record labels wanting to make more money, as was the case with the Beatles (until 2007's *In Rainbows*, Radiohead was signed to Parlophone in the United Kingdom and Capitol in the United States, just like the Fab Four were until their self-titled LP, a.k.a. the "White Album"). If that sounds unnecessarily distrustful, just look at how Capitol, Parlophone, and British conglomerate EMI released singles from Radiohead (and countless other acts) throughout the 1990s and early 2000s.

To capitalize on a single, record labels wouldn't just later compile them on EPs—they would distribute different versions and reissues of a hit, supplementing the same track with a different set of B-sides, remixes, and/or live recordings. Case in Point: The rollout for Radiohead's debut single, "Creep," all the way back in 1992. It would go on to be distributed as a cassette promo, the UK original release, a UK re-release on CD, a UK re-release on vinyl, and eventually, a digital re-release.

No Surprises / Running from Demons and *Airbag / How Am I Driving?*

All of this is important to consider when examining the two EPs of the *OK Computer* era, *No Surprises / Running From Demons* and *Airbag / How Am I Driving?* As the titles suggest, each EP is more of a B-sides compilation and glorified single for *OK Computer*, and they should be analyzed as such.

There's no great unlocking to be had here; just two collections of songs, most of which had already appeared as B-sides to previous singles on *OK Computer* and *The Bends*. Also, four of the songs appear on both EPs, thus further taking

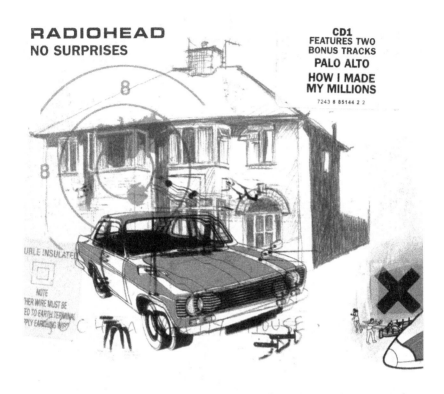

Album art for CD1 of "No Surprises."   *Author's collection*

away their respective identities as whole musical works. It's no wonder why Radiohead intentionally withheld two of their best *OK Computer* B-sides, "Lull" (originally on the "Karma Police" single) and "How I Made My Millions" (originally on the "No Surprises" single) from both of the EPs until they could release the songs on their own terms with *OKNOTOK*.

But are the EPs completely dispensable? Not quite. *Airbag / How Am I Driving?* (released April 21, 1998) is at least sequenced in a way that suggests the band moving in a more musically complicated direction. Whether or not this sequencing was decided by the band or the label, it gives the collection more substance than *No Surprises / Running From Demons*, which was released quickly and without the same kind of curation on December 10, 1997 in Japan to promote Radiohead's upcoming Japanese tour.

In what seems like a cynical cosmic joke, *Airbag / How Am I Driving?* got nominated for a Grammy Award for Best Alternative Music Album in 1999, showing that the music-buying public hardly realized it was a compilation EP at all. Its competition? Full-length albums by the likes of the Smashing Pumpkins, Beastie Boys, PJ Harvey, and Tori Amos (the Beasties won for *Hello Nasty*). Ironically, *OK Computer* had won that very award just one year before. While no hardcore Radiohead fan would put what's been hailed as the band's greatest LP in the same class as one of its accompanying EPs, the Recording Academy apparently doesn't take slightness into consideration when doling out awards in the often misguided "Alternative" category.

Ultimately, a Grammy nod doesn't change the fact that, of the seven non-*OK Computer* songs spread across *No Surprises / Running From Demons* and *Airbag / How Am I Driving?*, several are throwaways, a couple are decent, and one gives the listener a dramatic foreshadowing of what's to come on Radiohead's next album, 2000's *Kid A*. So instead of dissecting two EPs filled with 75 percent of the same mediocre material, let's break down all of the non-*OK Computer* material track by track.

The Songs

"Pearly*"

Appears on: CD1 of the "Paranoid Android" single and *Airbag / How Am I Driving?* EP (original); *No Surprises / Running From Demons* EP (remix)

A remixed version of "Pearly*" appears on *No Surprises / Running From Demons*, and the altered production does indeed make all the difference. In addition to the guitar squelching being higher in the mix, Phil Selway's floor toms are louder and the song has a slightly different ending.

Outside of that, both versions suffer from the same flaws: a clumsy start, faux grunge wailing that feels more akin to the *Pablo Honey* era, and cryptic lyrics that often get debated on Radiohead message boards. One theory is that the song is a comment on English culture's fetishization and mistreatment of black women, as seen through the eyes of the bigoted narrator. If that's the case, Thom Yorke's heart may be in the right place with "Pearly*", but lines like "that's where she got her sweet tooth for white boys" still read as problematic today—further proof that "Pearly*" lacks any kind of finesse.

"Melatonin"

Appears on: CD2 of the "No Surprises" single, *Airbag / How Am I Driving?* EP, and *No Surprises / Running From Demons* EP

At 2:09, "Melatonin" is slight, even when compared to some of the slighter material Radiohead was producing during this era of heavy experimentation.

But what it lacks in length and weight, it makes up for in adventurous spirit. Floating along with muffled drums and a synth drone, it's a hint at the farther reaches of space that would be explored on *Kid A*. And with lyrics about two parents reassuring their son that no harm will come to him, it plays like a lullaby for a nursery in a space station—emitting from a tinny-sounding music box rather than a stereo. Maybe it's these themes that made it one of Yorke's personal favorites, even if the rest of the band wrote it off.

"Meeting in the Aisle"

Appears on: CD1 of the "Karma Police" single, *No Surprises / Running From Demons* EP, and *Airbag / How Am I Driving?* EP

Regardless of its content, "Meeting in the Aisle" was destined to be remembered fondly among Radiohead fans because it's the band's first-ever (officially released) instrumental track. This makes it a natural predecessor to *Kid A*, which would only have one instrumental track, but still place a much greater emphasis on the sonic environment as opposed to the clarity of Yorke's words and voice.

So does "Meeting in the Aisle" sound like *Kid A*? Not exactly. Since the programming is executed by Henry Binns and Sam Hardaker of British chill-out duo Zero 7, there's a club-ready vibe that sets it apart from *Kid A*'s colder soundscapes. It's no wonder Radiohead used it as entrance music to warm up the crowd at their 1998 shows.

"Meeting in the Aisle" also signaled the band's new foray into danciness—a trait that would touch every album of theirs from here on out.

"Bishop's Robes"

Appears on: CD 1 of the "Street Spirit (Fade Out)" single and *No Surprises / Running From Demons* EP

Recorded during the same sessions that yielded "Lucky," "Bishop's Robes" is another deep cut that dies by its lyrics. Although there's an interesting contrast between the drunken guitar and futuristic synths, Yorke's trying too hard here to be sinister as he describes the nefarious "bastard headmaster" of a school. Critiques of authoritarian educators are best written with more atypical imagery (see Pink Floyd's "Another Brick In the Wall").

It's widely accepted that Yorke wrote "Bishop's Robes" as a dig toward Michael St. John Parker, the strict headmaster at Radiohead's alma matter, the Abingdon School in Oxfordshire. While Yorke has never directly mentioned Parker's name in connection with the song, he introduced it at a 1995 Stockholm gig as being "about an old headmaster that we had ... The guy was a fascist idiot." That's a fittingly blunt introduction for a song that, outside of their standalone single "Pop is Dead," might be Radiohead's most blunt and uninteresting composition.

"A Reminder"

Appears on: CD2 of "Paranoid Android," CD1 of "Karma Police," *No Surprises/Running From Demons* EP, and *Airbag/How Am I Driving?* EP

With "A Reminder," Yorke created a mnemonic device for the most dire of mental circumstances.

"I had this idea of someone writing a song, sending it to someone and saying, 'If I ever lose it, you just pick up the phone and play me this song back to remind me,'" Yorke told KRCW's *Morning Becomes Eclectic* on June 9, 1997. The song's leisurely pace caters to this idea of swimming upward in a sea of memories until breaking the surface—perhaps the only way to conquer amnesia.

So for a while, "A Reminder" is enchanting, lulling the listener through time and space with the the gentle murmur of a Czech crowd recorded on a train and Jonny Greenwood's twinkling organ line. But as the lyrics grow more frustrated, with Yorke imploring his lover to bludgeon him if he one day can't get his mind back, the arrangement gets more disorienting. There's no abrupt change, but the organ notes grow wilder; the guitars escalate into frantic harmonics. In less than a minute, "A Reminder" captures the helplessness of watching a loved one's personality slip away.

According to Yorke, the idea for "A Reminder" just came to him while sitting in a hotel room with nothing to do. Despite its humble beginnings, the concept and instrumentation makes for a heartbreaking depiction of age and senility. Of course playing an old, self-written song to someone with Alzheimer's or dementia won't bring their memory back to full capacity. But wouldn't it be wonderful if it could?

"Polyethylene (Parts 1 & 2)"

Appears on: CD1 of "Paranoid Android" and *Airbag / How Am I Driving?* EP

In 1997, Radiohead had three types of songs: acoustic haunts, Brit-grunge guitar workouts, and sonic explorations of deep space. With *OK Computer*, it became the norm to mash up these different styles.

"Polyethylene" accomplishes this over two distinct parts, starting with a briefly sketched acoustic ballad that ends in a countdown and launches into blown-open stadium rock. For the final moments, the synthesized strings and cavernous space effects that have served as underscoring become the dominant theme. Given its tonal shifts and that it was recorded with the rest of *OK Computer* at St Catherine's Court, it's not a shock that "Polyethylene" almost made it onto the album. Along with "A Reminder," it's one of two great songs on the *OK Computer*-era EPs.

"Palo Alto"

Appears on: CD 1 of "No Surprises" and *Airbag / How Am I Driving?* EP

What would *Pablo Honey* sound like with the subject matter of *OK Computer*? That's the question answered by "Palo Alto."

Not that the song has the depth of *OK Computer*'s best moments. The lyrics go for fairly low-hanging fruit, taking aim at the California technological mecca of the title, where the band played in 1996. The words are a bit too literal to rank with Radiohead's best tech-critiquing work, which means that the most interesting trait "Palo Alto" has going for it is a guitar descension that ends up resembling Julius Fučík's ubiquitous circus theme, "Entrance of the Gladiators."

"Palo Alto" has, however, had a few short-lived brushes with contextual greatness. It was briefly titled "OK Computer" and its drums were laid down at Abbey Road Studios in November of 1997 during the very same sessions where York finalized the recording of preliminary bass track for "The National Anthem" from *Kid A*. Prior to that, the band recorded the rest of the song's tracks on mobile equipment in the back of their tour bus, as seen in the documentary *Meeting People is Easy*.

3

"I Resent Your Voice"

Live Transmissions From the
OK Computer-Era Tours

I t goes without saying that *OK Computer* was a game-changer for Radiohead both in the scope of their audience and the press surrounding them as a band. But for a quintet of modest lads from Oxfordshire—especially frontman Thom Yorke—the increased visibility took some getting used to. To chart this mood-shift, it's best to go backwards and examine recollections of two separate tours—one that mostly took place after the album was released and one that took place during its genesis.

The *OK Computer* (a.k.a. "Against Demons") Tour/ *Meeting People is Easy*

Radiohead's detractors usually hang their criticisms on the supposedly depressing nature of the band's music. "Serious," "sad," and "music to cut your wrists to" are all adjectives that frequently come up in conversation with Radiohead haters.

That last phrase was coined by British newscaster Kay Burley while reviewing the music video for "No Surprises" on the United Kingdom's *Sky News*. The clip pops up in the 1998 tour documentary *Meeting People is Easy*, and to Burley's credit, the band members' demeanor in the film doesn't exactly dispel her callous description.

Directed and mostly recorded by the band's frequent cameraman Grant Gee, *Meeting People is Easy* follows Radiohead as they slog their way through the Against Demons tour in support of *OK Computer*. The massive jaunt began on May 22, 1997 in Barcelona, Spain, then wrapped up 104 shows later at New York City's Radio City Music Hall on April 18, 1998. The marathon nature of the tour shows on the face of each band member, who exude varying degrees of irritation, moodiness, exhaustion, and bewilderment toward the onslaught of reporters and fans enraptured by Radiohead's newfound fame.

They're unsure of their success; unsure if they'll come out on the other end of it; unsure if they'll continue to put out quality work or retain their artistic integrity on their next album—if that album ever gets recorded at all. This uncertainty manifests itself in general unpleasantness, causing Radiohead to act exactly like their critics accuse their music of sounding. Gee also pulled most of the footage from the Japanese leg of the tour, when the shows were nearing their end and the band was at their most ragged.

That's not to say the band members are being outright jerks in *Meeting People is Easy*. They're more worn out by the speed and volume of the hype. And that's the documentary's greatest feat: accurately depicting the numbing whirlwind of being in a hugely popular, touring rock outfit. Comprised of handheld footage from a Sony PC-100 camera, sound clips, news bites, and grainy concert footage, the film runs like a disorienting collage. That it has no discernible timeline—nor a clear beginning, middle, or end—is very much by Gee and Radiohead's design.

But accuracy doesn't necessarily make for an easy watch. At 95 minutes, *Meeting People is Easy* is an exercise in patience, forcing the viewer to feel as strung-out and distant as the band. In that way, it serves as a visual companion to *OK Computer*, exploring the feeling of always being in transit and unable to communicate in a world that's moving faster than human beings have the capacity to handle. Many of the band interviews take place in hotel rooms with reporters who speak a different language. The questions are asked in French or Japanese, recited to a band member in broken English so they can give their (usually tired) answer, which is then translated into the interviewer's language so they can publish it somewhere in written form. It's like a never-ending game of telephone, only adding to the disconnect of being on tour.

The band's answers range from terse to polite to nonsensical to smartass, depending on who's talking. Yorke tends to be the most difficult, often burying his head in his hands at hearing the same, somewhat unanswerable questions over and over: "What does music mean to you?" "Are you related to the Britpop scene?" etc. In a 2017 *Rolling Stone* retrospective on *OK Computer*, Ed O'Brien admits to playing babysitter to Yorke during that time as the band collectively fretted over their frontman's mental health.

Of all the members we see interviewed in *Meeting People is Easy* (Jonny Greenwood and Phil Selway are usually nowhere to be seen), Colin Greenwood comes off as the most sympathetic and self-aware. At one point, he apologizes to a reporter for not being more forthcoming with his answers.

Every now and then, the completely zonked out Yorke does have an endearing moment when talking to reporters, usually when he's reflecting on the positive effect Radiohead's music has on people around the world. At one point, while riding in a cab in New York City, he describes being moved whenever he

RADIOHEAD

JAPAN TOUR 1998

Lost Child

ニルヴァーナを失った９０年代のロックシーンで 英・米を中心にユース・カルチャーの
オピニオン・リーダーとして 今、最も信頼され、熱狂的な支持を受けているレディオヘッド！
'９７年を代表する傑作をひっさげて、'９８年１月、松本社会文化会館で 衝撃のライブ！！

1998 / 1 / 15 (祝)

松本市社会文化会館

Open 18:00 / Start 19:00

オールスタンディング（入場整理番号付）
¥6,300（税込み）

チケット電話予約・問い合わせ：メディック　0266-28-3496

●主催：Ｐ４Ｄ／長野朝日放送／ＦＭ長野　●協力：東芝ＥＭＩ　●企画制作：クリエイティブマン プロダクション
◆協賛：ラスティックシェイカーフィールド
■インターネットホームページアドレス：http://www2m.meshnet.or.jp/~peoples/p.htm
プレイガイド 平安堂（長店・南松本・諏訪・伊那・鹿光寺）・アベレコード・MIDORI長野・冨光堂・池田楽器パラス店・アルピコカウンター
井上プレイガイド・ライオン堂・TSUTAYA南松本店・笠原書店（本店・長池店）・諏訪プラザチケットカウンター・チケットぴあ各店

Poster for a concert on the Japanese leg of Radiohead's 1998 tour. *Author's collection* hears how much his songs mean to a teenage fan. It's a rare moment of appreciation in a film that still buzzes with hatred—and thus a perceived unappreciation—of fame, preventing Yorke from coming across as totally unlikable.

The other saving grace of *Meeting People is Easy* is the music itself. While much of it is heard in fleeting snippets of live recordings—more broken radio transmissions than full-on performances—a few of the fully shown songs are sublime. Most notable is an early version of "Nude," which would later pop up on *In Rainbows*, and a soundcheck take of "Follow Me Around." The yet-to-be-released gem starts with Yorke singing to a completely empty auditorium, then takes on more weight when the rest of the band joins him.

Despite the behind-the-scenes malaise, the Against Demons tour was, by all accounts, an astounding success in terms of performance. Many longtime Radiohead fans insist it's the best the band has ever played, and the tour cycle included some of their most celebrated concerts, such as a landmark set at the Glastonbury Festival on June 28, 1997.

The stakes were high for Radiohead during that particular performance, considering it was their tour's first stop in the United Kingdom and *OK Computer* had been released in their homeland only 12 days prior. Also, Glastonbury—a festival that all of the members of Radiohead had grown up attending—was making a triumphant return after a year-long hiatus.

There's a decent recording of Radiohead's entire Glastonbury performance on YouTube, cobbled together from a variety of amateur and professionally shot footage. If much of the set is marred by a disgruntled Yorke—frustrated at the blinding stage lights and monitors that keep cutting out—it makes the second half that much sweeter, the shift from frustration to adoration allowing the performance to become the stuff of legend.

After nearly walking offstage during "Talk Show Host," Yorke becomes reinvigorated once the equipment recovers on "Bones." From that point on, the band gets a collective shot in the arm—the majesty of "Fake Plastic Trees" drowns out the whininess instead of the other way around, "High and Dry" moves from despairing to anthemic, and O'Brien's backing vocals on closer "Street Spirit (Fade Out)" may as well be the lead.

"This gig obviously means a fucking lot," Yorke tells the crowd when the band returns onstage for the encore.

Watching the Glastonbury set makes *Meeting People is Easy* easier to handle, as does the ultimate outcome for Radiohead. When viewing the film today, anyone with the most casual knowledge of the band knows that their fears didn't come true. Their career didn't flounder. They didn't become sellouts. They retained their agency and—for the most part—their privacy, at least in the context of how famous they are. They have the exact career they always wanted to have. In Gee's documentary, the band just has a hard time admitting that, yes, this is actually something they want.

And that's the rock-star paradox, isn't it? One doesn't get to be as famous as Radiohead without some part of them wanting that kind of status, and that's what makes *Meeting People is Easy* frustrating at times. The success is self-imposed, and to hear the band trash their own worth and the process that comes with it rings false.

As exhibited in the *Rolling Stone* retrospective, they already know this.

"Lighten the fuck up," Yorke laughs when asked what he would tell his younger self. "'You need to step away and learn to love why you love it and remember why you did it.' It took me a long time."

Alanis Morissette's Can't Not Tour

Ironically, Radiohead had a more enjoyable experience playing their *OK Computer* material before the album actually came out, on a tour where they weren't even performing for their usual fans.

In 1995, Canada's Alanis Morissette, who, in the preceding year, had risen to superstar status with her own third album, *Jagged Little Pill*, asked Parlophone if Radiohead would fill the opening slot on her Can't Not tour. Frustrated by their lack of productivity while recording *OK Computer* at Canned Applause, Radiohead obliged after some encouragement from their label.

In retrospect, it may seem like a strange pairing given the two acts' ultimate career paths. Morissette would go on to further explore the sound she forged on *Jagged Little Pill*, easily her most successful and defining album. While there would be variations in tone, imagery, and the level of musical aggression, she would always work in the singer-songwriter mold. Conversely, Radiohead would go on to dismantle the defining traits of their first three albums on *Kid A*.

But in 1996, Radiohead and Morissette were taking somewhat similar career trajectories. All of the musicians started in a genre they would soon disown (in Radiohead's case, grunge; with Morissette, dance-pop), wowing their critics with landmark albums that proved they had more versatility than many of their contemporaries. People thought they were one thing, and they ended up being another. Morissette was impressed by Radiohead early on, covering "Fake Plastic Trees" on three different concert dates before the band joined the bill in August 1996. For their part, Radiohead wasn't quite as taken with Morissette's recorded work.

"Her music's pretty terrible, but she's a lovely person," O'Brien told *Melody Maker* on May 24, 1997.

Mutual personal—if not musical—respect aside, Radiohead still recognized that Morissette's fan base was much different from their own. After opening for her on August 12 in Darien, New York, Yorke and Jonny Greenwood recalled the crowd throughout the tour being, at best, indifferent. With nothing to lose, the band used the dates to road-test some of the material that would go on to make up *OK Computer*, including "Paranoid Android."

"My main memory of that tour," Greenwood told *Rolling Stone*, "is playing interminable Hammond organ solos to an audience full of quietly despairing teenage girls."

Others from the Radiohead camp remember the run of shows differently. Clark Staub, who worked for Capitol Records at the time, insists that fans went wild, remembering that "if they'd been allowed an encore, Radiohead would have got an encore."

Whether that's true or just record-label PR speak (Capitol was Radiohead's American distributor at the time), it's certain that the Can't Not tour played an important part in the genesis of *OK Computer*. Because they weren't in front of their usual crowd and their fan base hadn't reached the astronomical level it would after their third album, there was little pressure put on Radiohead to do any one specific thing. They were free to experiment and create, continuing to perfect the already released "Lucky" and find their footing with over half of *OK Computer*: In addition to "Lucky" and "Paranoid Android," "Let Down," "Electioneering," and "No Surprises" all made appearances on their short opening stretch of the Morissette tour, with "Karma Police" and "Climbing Up the Walls" making their live debuts.

4

"Ice Age Coming"

Kid A

Today, it's become somewhat of a cliche for Radiohead to redefine themselves with each album. That's not to say they've reached a place of creative stagnancy (their most recent LP, *A Moon Shaped Pool* is still different from anything else in their catalog), but with every record, there's been a pattern of tearing down what came before so the band can reemerge as something new. At this point, the most shocking thing they could do would be to revert back to the simpler sound of *Pablo Honey* and *The Bends*.

That wasn't the case in 2000. While there's no denying that 1997's *OK Computer* was a milestone, it was still, for all intents and purposes, a proper rock album. Even if it elevated what the medium could accomplish, this was AOR with experimental touches, not vice versa. And, like any game-changing piece of art, it birthed a string of imitators.

"After the *OK Computer* tour we felt we had to change everything," Colin Greenwood told the *Chicago Tribune* on October 20, 2000, 18 days after the release of their fourth studio album, *Kid A*. "There were other guitar bands out there trying to do similar things. We had to move on."

It's easy to understand that mindset, but at the same time, the bands frequently accused of being Radiohead clones—Coldplay, Travis, etc.—weren't aping *OK Computer* at that point in their careers. If anything, they were drawing more from the heart-on-the-sleeve histrionics of *Pablo Honey* and *The Bends*.

Still, Colin's statement is a testament to Radiohead's—and, more specifically, Thom Yorke's—desire to push themselves to the next creative plane. In 1997, Yorke had an epiphany that led to the creation of *Kid A* immediately after the band finished their show at NEC Arena in Birmingham, England. Fatigued from the hype and locomotive tour of *OK Computer*, he collapsed in a chair in the dressing room, realizing that the band had taken their most recent album as far as it could go.

As was the case with *OK Computer* (and every Radiohead album since), the band was unsure of where to go next. Ed O'Brien thought the most surprising move would have been a back-to-basics guitar record, but Yorke quickly shot that down, despite not having a clear vision of his own. In the spirit of experimentation, he and the band just began trying things out.

While the approach was similar to their last album, *OK Computer* at least had somewhat of a foundation. Before recording, a handful of songs were already in place, and Radiohead committed to developing further compositions by playing together as a traditional band setup. With *Kid A*, however, everything was built from the ground up, grown from the soil of a still-forming, prehistoric earth.

For Yorke, that meant listening exclusively to electronic artists on Warp records such as Autechre and Aphex Twin. Having DJ'd while studying art at Exeter University, he already had some remedial experience with electronic textures and beats. But he was far from an expert in the genre. Wanting to take himself further into unfamiliar territory, he immersed himself in electronica, pulled to music that "was all structures with no human voices in it," as he described to *The Guardian* on August 31, 2000.

Album art for *Kid A*.   *Author's collection*

To continue pushing himself, Yorke bought an isolated house in Cornwall, filling up his time with hiking through cliffs, drawing, and playing a baby grand piano—an instrument he had little experience with.

"I'm such a shit piano player," he said in *Rolling Stone*'s People of the Year profile on December 14, 2000. "I remember this Tom Waits quote from years ago, that what keeps him going as a strong songwriter is his complete ignorance of the instruments he's using. So everything's a novelty."

When the band reconvened at Paris' Guillaume Tell recording studio in January of 1999 (their own brand-new studio back home was still under construction), Yorke still didn't have any songs fully formed. In retrospect, that was probably the point. It wasn't as much about creating a body of work that could be fleshed out, but getting into a more flexible mindset that would eventually produce exceptional and adventurous results. Ready to experiment, the band took further inspiration from Tom Waits, equipping themselves with unfamiliar instruments such as modular synthesizers and the ondes Martenot, an early-20th-century predecessor to the theremin that soon became favored by Jonny Greenwood.

That's not to say the recording sessions were particularly easy once everybody locked into mad-scientist mode. O'Brien, in particular, was still unsure of how he felt about a fragmented approach that led to so many songs without guitars, especially in a band that had three guitarists. At one point, he even considered asking Dr. Dre to come in and offer assistance, although he quickly abandoned the idea. Maybe Dre's presence could have actually helped the band work faster. For several months, Radiohead just kept noodling, doing away with melody in an attempt to come up with something that involved more glitch and rhythm.

But the Paris sessions yielded few satisfactory results, and in March, Radiohead took their sonic laboratory to Medley Studios in Copenhagen, Denmark. This resulted in 50 reels of tape, each containing 15 minutes of music. Although some of these fragments would eventually be used in the final product that was *Kid A*, at the time, they were just that—fragments, sometimes nothing more than a loop on a drum machine brought in by Yorke.

In their continuing search for a new direction, Radiohead next went to an old, empty mansion near the Batsford Arboretum in Gloucestershire, England. At this point (it was already April), the band began to wonder if they might benefit from some structure.

"It's taken us seven years to get this sort of freedom, and it's what we always wanted," wrote O'Brien in an online diary he started keeping on the band's website in summer of 1999 to update fans on the recording process. "But it could be so easy to fuck it all up." A deadline from their record label, Parlophone—something so many major-label bands would love to do without—would have perhaps been a good thing at that time, forcing Radiohead to finish something that seemed unfinishable.

It didn't help that there was constant infighting—so much that Radiohead held a series of meetings to discuss the future of the band. Since the group is so notoriously private, they've never revealed the exact source of the tension (a similar situation occurred during the recording of *The Bends*), only that they needed to work out "personality issues" and how each of them could, according to O'Brien, "be a participant in a song without actually playing a note."

Some stability finally did arrive in September of 1999, when the band's own studio in Oxfordshire's Sutton Courtenay village became fully operational. Being at their home base made it easier to focus, as did some guidance from producer Nigel Godrich, who split up the band into two groups: one who would create a sequence of sounds and another who would hammer it all into something more full-bodied. Even if it didn't result in any kind of finished product, it at least made everyone in Radiohead appreciate a newer, more improvised approach. By April 2000, the band had enough material for two whole albums. Now it was a matter of whittling it down.

The most remarkable thing about the final version of *Kid A* is that, fragmented approach aside, it's the most cohesive of Radiohead's albums—best listened to all the way through in one sitting. That's not because it has some kind of linear narrative, but because the band establishes a consistent temperature right off the bat. Cold wouldn't necessarily be the right word; the atmosphere of *Kid A* is more techno-organic than just plain technological.

The Songs

"Everything in Its Right Place"

Similar to "Lucky" on *OK Computer*, "Everything in Its Right Place" has been characterized by Radiohead as a lynchpin moment for *Kid A*. Yorke wrote it during his piano-playing phase in Cornwall, and more classically trained composers such as Steve Reich believe that Yorke's inexperience with the instrument is exactly what led to the song's unconventional tone.

"It's three-chord rock, but it's not," Reich told *The Guardian* in March 2013, shortly before releasing his own interpretation of Radiohead's work, *Radio Rewrite*. "It was originally in F minor, and it never comes down to the one chord. The F minor chord is never stated. So there's never a tonic, there's never a cadence in the normal sense, whereas in most pop tunes it will appear, even if it's only in passing."

All of that is a fancy way of describing a song whose success comes from its sense of simplicity and escalation. While "Everything in Its Right Place" consists of little more than a synthesizer (only when Godrich moved the song from piano to something more mechanized did it truly take off), blips from a drum machine, and Yorke's modified voice, these stripped-down elements keep multiplying and building on one another, like cells rapidly dividing. It's the perfect opener and a natural catalyst for Radiohead figuring out the aesthetic of *Kid A*—software updating itself by way of adding flesh and blood.

Like most of *Kid A*, the lyrics to "Everything in Its Right Place" are singular yet cryptic—simple phrases repeated until they can take on many meanings. This is a result of Yorke's fragmented writing approach on the album. For most of the songs, he would write down evocative phrases on little slips of paper, pull them out of a top hat at random, then refine the mess of words into a song from there. That's why some of the original lyrics for "Everything in Its Right Place" (first posted on Radiohead's website during the *Kid A* sessions) ended up being used for the *Amnesiac* B-side "Cuttooth."

Many of Radiohead's other lyrics from *OK Computer* onward would be culled from different times and places in the band's career. While Yorke hasn't written the words for every Radiohead album with the same cut-and-paste method as *Kid A*, the advent of the internet and the band's increasingly dense website has allowed him to document a furiously paced output. For instance, some of the lyrics for *In Rainbows'* final version of "Weird Fishes/Arpeggi" scrolled across the bottom of radiohead.com as early as 2004, despite the album not being released until late 2007.

Likewise, a number of lines (but not all of them) from *Hail to the Thief*'s "Myxomatosis" appeared as a link on the site in 1999, four years before the song was finalized. Portions of *In Rainbows* closer "Videotape" also appeared online in the *Kid A* era, *In Rainbows* B-side "Four Minute Warning" was mentioned under three different titles in O'Brien's internet diary during this time, etc.

The constant repurposing of words makes it difficult to suss out any kind of deliberate narrative arc for *Kid A*, although anyone is welcome to try by venturing into the website Citizen Insane. It's here that every single Radiohead song has its own page, with all of the disparate lyrical sources documented in exhausting detail. These might include screenshots from radiohead.com over the years, excerpts from O'Brien's diaries, interviews with the music press, and even images of physical artwork from Yorke and Stanley Donwood that contain song fragments. The site is invaluable yet dizzying, and there's a good chance one might come out of it even more confused about the meaning of the song in question. There's an even better chance that Radiohead prefers it that way, likely welcoming any interpretation from any listener.

Still, band members have occasionally commented on the meaning of individual lines from *Kid A* songs, if not the entire track. Yorke confirmed to *Rolling Stone* in a August 2, 2001 interview that the line "Yesterday I woke up sucking a lemon" in "Everything in Its Right Place" comes from how others described his facial expression following the *OK Computer* tour—frustrated and unsure of how to deal with success.

This suggests that the song's title is meant in jest, that everything's *not* in its right place. Ironically, though, once Godrich, Yorke, and Selway figured out the song's final form after almost a year of tinkering, the rest of *Kid A* soon followed. It's the piece of music that helped them figure out everything else.

"Kid A"

Of all the songs on *Kid A*, Yorke's unconventional approach to the lyrics is most evident on the title track. Reading the words on paper, they sound unflinchingly brutal, a red whirlpool of heads on stakes and a Pied Piper figure luring all of the children and rats out of a small town. In fact, the words were so nightmarish that Yorke had a hard time performing it live. Despite a well-received July 4, 2000 performance of "Kid A" in Berlin, Radiohead dropped the song after one more performance and didn't revive it again until 2003 for the *Hail to the Thief* tour.

To soften the lyrics and disconnect Yorke from their violence, Jonny Greenwood filtered them through a vocoder connected to his ondes Martenot. This made Yorke's voice a more friendly version of the SimpleText application from "Fitter Happier" and "Paranoid Android," as if Fred Cooper had transformed into a real boy.

Then again, there's a case to be made for this arrangement actually making "Kid A" *more* creepy. But if one can ignore the words (which is hard), the gentle bass, keyboards, and Roland TR-505 drum sequencer form a strange aural comfort. It's music that could be played on a baby's mobile in a space station, from a nursery looking out into the stars.

Although Yorke hasn't confirmed any specific interpretation about "Kid A"'s lyrics, he has debunked one theory that became widespread among fans and critics before the album was even released. Due to the song and record's title—as well as a demented Yorke/Stanley Donwood cartoon about genetic mutation—many people believed *Kid A* to be a concept album about the first human clone. As Yorke told *Rolling Stone* in their 2000 People of the Year profile, none of this was correct, and the title actually came from a nickname for one of the band's sequencers.

"The National Anthem"

If "The National Anthem" sounds the most direct of all the songs on *Kid A*, that's probably because Thom Yorke wrote its central riff while the band were still teenagers at Abingdon School, practicing under their original name, On a Friday.

As Colin Greenwood recalled on KCRW's *Morning Becomes Eclectic* on October 12, 2000, Yorke demoed the song on a four-track tape recorder, most likely with a Boss Doctor Rhythm drum machine accompanied by a "guitar fuzz bass line." The band would eventually release the demo on the boxed version of *OKNOTOK*. While it's mildly fascinating to hear such an early form of one of Radiohead's most iconic melodies, this early version barely stands on its own as a complete song.

When isolated, the repetitive bass sequence is more akin to punk—raw, driving, and instantly memorable. But by the time "The National Anthem" was in its final form for *Kid A*, Yorke's bass line—while still the engine—would be surrounded by radio transmissions, banshee wails from Jonny's ondes Marte-not, and an eight-piece brass section.

But just as most of *Kid A* isn't true electronica as much as Radiohead's slightly off-kilter take on electronica, "The National Anthem" isn't true jazz. Rather, it's the band figuring out how to use the most basic elements of jazz as a tool to build something completely different. Let's call it caveman jazz—jazz overseen by a frontman who has no formal jazz training; jazz where the eight horn players are merely instructed to "Just blow, just blow, just blow!" by Yorke. Along with Jonny as co-conductor, he would hop up and down whenever he wanted them to be louder, then calm down his movements when he wanted them to get softer. Other instructions included for the musicians to play as if they were stuck in traffic.

If that sounds chaotic, there was a modicum of control, as each player still had to perform within a scalar sequence more akin to blues. Jonny's genius was realizing that eight different people could play without having any idea what the others were doing, and when all of the sequences were laid overtop each other, it would still sound harmonious.

Mark Beaumont of *The Guardian* was right to call "The National Anthem" "Mingus-in-a-tumble-dryer racket" in his initial assessment of *Kid A*. Although he meant it as an insult, I—and so many other Radiohead fans who don't hap-pen to be jazz aficionados—view it as a compliment. If one wants to listen to jazz in the purest sense, they can easily throw on a Charles Mingus record. But where else can one find horn blaring through a science-fiction landscape?

Live, "The National Anthem" remains one of Radiohead's most electrifying songs, but none of the performances are likely to top their October 14, 2000 appearance on *Saturday Night Live*. In a rare treat for fans, Radiohead got to use the house band's horn section—a luxury not usually afforded to them on tour. On the show, the extra brass moves Yorke to dance like a man possessed, all while Colin Greenwood adds a dangerous speed to the bass line and Jonny hops between the ondes Martenot and running radio transmissions through his effects pedals. As the perfect tie-off, Yorke leaps in the air to silence all of the musicians—the inverse of his traffic-jam signal in the studio.

"How To Disappear Completely"

In the documentary *Meeting People is Easy*, Yorke devolves into a kind of dumb panic as the pressure of Radiohead's fame continues to mount. Michael Stipe, Yorke's friend and mentor from R.E.M., would eventually give him advice on how to cope with it all: Be still, close your eyes, focus, and repeat the words "I'm not here. This isn't really happening" in order to calm down.

This mantra became the recurring theme of "How to Disappear Completely," so much that its words are sprinkled throughout the song. That makes it the most lyrically decipherable track on *Kid A*, with a somewhat conventional arrangement to match. Unlike all of the other compositions, honeycombed with synthesized vocals, transmissions, and electronic effects, "How to Disappear Completely" is more in the vein of "Exit (Music For a Film)"—mostly acoustic strumming and a string arrangement composed by Jonny Greenwood on the ondes Martenot, but played by the Orchestra of St. John's. In another echo of its *OK Computer* predecessor (whose vocals were recorded in a cavernous 16th-century stairwell), the strings for "How to Disappear Completely" were laid down in Dorchester Abbey, a 12th-century church near Radiohead's recently built studio.

But the naturalism sticks out on *Kid A*, tonally off in its lack of morphing technology. And because it relies on the most unlikable parts of Yorke's interviews from *Meeting People Is Easy*—his sulkiness and alienation—it's a somber affair to sit through, devoid of the wonder found on the rest of the album.

At the same time, it's important to note that such an opinion is grounds for crucifixion in certain circles of Radiohead fans, many of whom view "How to Disappear Completely" as a high-water mark for the band. Radiohead themselves have expressed an equal amount of love for the song. In a June 1, 2006 interview with *Rolling Stone*, Yorke declared that "How to Disappear Completely" was his favorite of the *Kid A* era, which means it's likely one of his favorites from any era.

"Treefingers"

It's amusing that, despite O'Brien's initial resistance to a Radiohead album with significantly fewer guitars, he ended up being responsible for the most experimental track, the ambient instrumental, "Treefingers." In yet another twist, it's the only song played solely on guitar, even though the arrangement sounds completely electronic. O'Brien elaborated on the recording process to *MC* in January 2001:

"'Treefingers' is an ethereal, spacey song built from guitar loops. I'm not taking any credit for it, because Thom arranged it. He recorded me playing the guitar for 10 minutes, then loaded parts into his sampler, played bits on his keyboard, and made sense of it. It doesn't sound like a guitar, which is great."

Described as Eno-esque, "Treefingers" functions as a palate cleanser after "How to Disappear Completely," a reminder that this is an album rooted in the abstract; an album that values texture and chilly landscapes over solipsistic moaning. It forms an ice bridge to the second half of *Kid A*.

"Optimistic"

On "Optimistic," O'Brien ventures back into more traditional territory by playing his guitar and making it *sound* like a guitar. This stronger bent toward classicism and Selway's jungle-scouting floor toms made the song a natural contender for being *Kid A*'s lead single—almost. Although never officially released as such, promotional copies of "Optimistic" were sent to radio stations in the United States.

Naturally, many stations put it on regular rotation. I remember the Tampa Bay area's 97X playing "Optimistic" almost hourly. And because DJ Michael Sharkey's nickname on the air was "Shark" and he introduced himself before the song without saying its actual title, I thought for quite some time that "Optimistic" was actually called "I Am Shark."

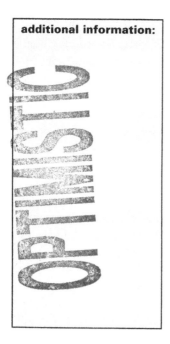

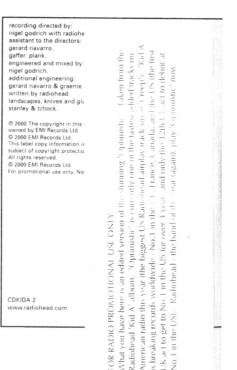

additional information:

recording directed by:
nigel godrich with radiohe
assistant to the directors:
gerard navarro.
gaffer: plank.
engineered and mixed by:
nigel godrich.
additional engineering:
gerard navarro & graeme
written by radiohead.
landscapes, knives and glu
stanley & tchock.

℗ 2000 The copyright in this
owned by EMI Records Ltd.
© 2000 EMI Records Ltd.
This label copy information is
subject of copyright protectio
All rights reserved.
© 2000 EMI Records Ltd.
For promotional use only. No

CDKIDA 2
www.radiohead.com

FOR RADIO PROMOTIONAL USE ONLY
What you have here is an edited version of the stunning "Optimistic." Taken from the Radiohead 'Kid A' album. "Optimistic" is currently one of the tastest added tracks on American radio this year (the biggest US Radiohead airplay track since "Creep"). 'Kid A' is breaking records worldwide - No.1 in the US, France, Canada, and the US (the first UK act to get to No.1 in the US for over 3 years, and only the 12th US act to debut at No.1 in the US). Radiohead - the band of the year (again), play "Optimistic" now.

2000 Radio promo for "Optimistic."   *Author's collection*

To be fair to my idiotic 16-year-old self, "I Am Shark" would have been an apt title. With its prehistoric imagery of little fish being swallowed up by bigger ones, "Optimistic" hones in on a food-chain mentality that could apply to the stone age, a prison system, or corporate America.

But a slightly more uplifting key change in the chorus takes us to a place that honors the song's title with sincerity, with Yorke encouraging himself to try the best he can, and that that alone will be good enough. He revealed to Q magazine in October of 2000 that those words came during a mini pep talk from his partner at the time, Rachel Owen, when he didn't think anything the band had recorded for *Kid A* was releasable. At one point in his online diary for the *Kid A* sessions, O'Brien even referred to "Optimistic" as "Rachel's Song." And where many of the other songs for *Kid A* were recorded in fits and starts, he praised "Optimistic" several times as being fully formed.

"In Limbo"

A song that also lives up to its name, "In Limbo" could be a companion piece to "Treefingers." Though not exactly ambient, its meandering nature explains the title, as well as the original one, "Lost at Sea." As Yorke describes drifting about in a fantasy world and a body of water in Ireland, the band's cross rhythms become more chaotic—the jazz-like hiss of Selway's cymbals getting interrupted by static from Jonny's guitars. By the end, everything is distorted through a software plug-in until the song concludes with what sounds like waves crashing on a shore, then settling back into calmer waters.

"It's a nightmare to play live," Yorke admitted to *Rolling Stone* in 2004. "The cross rhythm is very hard to get right. And the fact that the guitars on the record are impossible to reproduce live. You can only hear two, but Jonny did loads of them. The mix is very subtle. Jonny hasn't built a machine yet [to reproduce it]."

The title of the song and some of the lyrical content must once again be partially credited to Owen, who at the time, was getting her PhD at the University of London. Her degree focused on the works of Dante, specifically the illustrations in the *Divine Comedy*. During long road trips, she and Yorke would listen to audio tapes of Dante's *Inferno*, where the first circle of Hell is, indeed, Limbo.

Appropriately, "In Limbo" comes off as a minor track that feels like purgatory in the grander scheme of *Kid A*, caught between the traditionalism of "Optimistic" and the most danceable track on the album.

"Idioteque"

In his online diary, O'Brien referred to "Idioteque" several times as "Thom and Jonny's Drum Thing." After hearing the first 12 seconds, it's easy to see why. Despite a four-note melody sampled from *Mild und Leise*—an 18-minute piece of early computer music from Paul Lansky—"Idioteque" is that rare song where the hook lies in the percussion.

In a 2001 interview with *The Wire*, Yorke described wanting to capture the sort of beat "where you're at the club and the PA's so loud, you know it's going to do damage."

The final product of "Idioteque" isn't quite that. Rather, the programmed drums have the ability to sound both explosive *and* tinny at the same time. Jonny elaborated on this on KCRW's *Morning Becomes Eclectic* on October 12, 2000.

"The starting point for that was trying to build a drum machine out of very old style synthesizers," he said. "[Kind] of using the same things that I suppose the Roland technicians would have had in 1978 or whatever, to decide how to make something sound like a snare drum out of white noise and how to create the sound of a bass drum, a kick drum out of filters. We basically built a drum machine, and I played a record on top, at random, and had a radio playing, and was just trying to generate all this chaos over this drum pattern."

The "chaos" he's referring to is *First Recordings—Electronic Music Winners*, a compilation of early electronic music. Yorke listened to Jonny's 50-minute sprawl, and his ear caught a small 40-second section that contained the Lansky sample, as well as some well-timed spacecraft blips from another composition called "Short Piece" by Arthur Kreiger. Yorke's ear must have been especially keen that day, as the portion of *Mild und Leise* that makes up the melody of "Idioteque" only appears once in the original song for a 10-second stretch.

Because "Idioteque" borrows so much from the past, there's a crudeness to its beat—techno for cretins, maybe?—that matches the lyrics. When Yorke frets about the ice age, he does it with little finesse. Beyond squeezing into a bunker, there's no complex planning to cope with the apocalypse. Instead, everyone sounds panicked and, most likely, doomed.

And that's how it would be, isn't it? For all the science surrounding potential doomsday scenarios, would we, as a civilization—even the wealthiest of us—be truly prepared for something cataclysmic? No. We'd all revert to our most animalistic states. Our brains wouldn't be equipped to handle something as big and scary as climate change or nuclear holocaust. That's what "Idioteque" manages to capture—feeling so helpless that you can't do anything but throw your hands in the air and flail around. Call it dancing if it makes you feel better.

Jonny eventually tracked down Paul Lansky and discovered he was—and still is—a professor of music composition at Princeton University, having composed *Mild und Leise* in 1973 when he was 29, the same age as Greenwood during the *Kid A* sessions. Lansky was such an admirer of "Idioteque" that he wrote an essay on it for the 2005 book *The Music and Art of Radiohead*. Although he appreciated being credited, he pointed out that he, too, was sampling someone else's music: the progression found in "Idioteque" is merely using the Tristan chord from the opening phrase of Richard Wagner's opera *Tristan und Isolde*. The phrase "Mild und Leise" even comes from the opening lines of the opera's finale.

"Morning Bell"

It's become common practice for Radiohead to record multiple versions of their songs before they land on one that sticks. That practice was even more frequent with *Kid A*, due to its throw-it-all-against-the-wall approach, which resulted in two very different versions of "Morning Bell."

The original ended up appearing in 4/4 time on 2001's *Amnesiac*, slow and haunting with its clanging chains and bicycle bells. It's a tone that matches the macabre nature of the lyrics, seemingly about a divorce where the couple is forced to "cut the kids in half" and succumb to other violent behavior during their separation.

Save for an extra verse, the lyrics on the *Kid A* version are almost the same, but set to an off-kilter 5/4 time signature, upbeat dance fills from Selway, and a liqueur bass line from Colin, all of which work to make Yorke sound elated and free. Even though he has insisted to *Morning Becomes Eclectic* that "Morning Bell" isn't about a divorce, it's still intriguing to look at the two versions as different outlooks on the same breakup.

"Motion Picture Soundtrack"

Like "Morning Bell," there are two drastically different versions of "Motion Picture Soundtrack" available. But they were recorded several years apart. The first was cut live for the Dutch radio station VPRO on April 21, 1995, its stripped-down arrangement (just Yorke and a guitar) allowing the words to ring crystal clear. The straightforward imagery of longing for a past lover would have made it a natural fit for *Pablo Honey*, which it actually predates as a song.

As with many tracks from the *Pablo Honey* era, the earnestness of the early version of "Motion Picture Soundtrack" doesn't work as well as the final incarnation. When Yorke describes taking wine and sleeping pills to numb his pain, it's too whiny, too on the nose, too adolescent. The band tried to make the song a bit more avant garde during the *OK Computer* sessions by setting it to the pulse of a life support system, but it still didn't click.

Radiohead finally found success with "Motion Picture Soundtrack" on *Kid A*, primarily by owning up to the implied artifice of the title. Once again drawing inspiration from Tom Waits (specifically songs from the *swordfishtrombones*/*Rain Dogs* era such as "Anywhere I Lay My Head"), the guitar becomes a harmonium pedal organ from the 19th century, and the song ends—and ends and ends and ends—with an extra-thick sample of choirs and harps. There's even a false fadeout before the music reenters as if the orchestra is warming up to start all over again.

It *has* to end this way. It wouldn't make sense for *Kid A* to conclude in such a raw, sincere, and organically vulnerable fashion, which would have been the case with the original version of "Motion Picture Soundtrack." For the past 50 minutes, we've heard the sounds of machines trying—and perhaps succeeding—to become human. But even with a humanized machine, there still needs to be a trace of metal, of circuitry, of awkwardness. That's what Radiohead achieves with the overly sappy strings and choirs, an idea introduced by Jonny Greenwood, who drew inspiration from old Alice Coltrane records. With those final touches, "Motion Picture Soundtrack" borders on satire, drawing attention to the melodrama of Yorke's lyrics by wrapping them in an aesthetic usually reserved for Golden Age Disney songs and Busby Berkeley films.

Amusingly, the song also contains another strong connection to *Pablo Honey* with the harmonium pedal organ. Originally from West Virginia circa 1850 (approximately), it's the exact same instrument that Jonny played on *Pablo Honey*'s "Thinking About You." Only instead of lulling in the background, it's brought to the forefront to close out *Kid A* in sepia-tinted, cinematic glory.

Conclusion

Unlike its predecessor, *Kid A* was not met with immediately ubiquitous adoration. While it earned raves from *Pitchfork*, *Rolling Stone*, *The Village Voice* (from consistent Radiohead detractor Robert Christgau, no less), and elsewhere, many critics were turned off by what they perceived as the most stereotypical kind of art-for-art's-sake indulgence.

In the most vicious review of the *Kid A* press cycle, *Melody Maker*'s Mark Beaumont (the same Mark Beaumont who trashed "The National Anthem" in *The Guardian*) called *Kid A* "the sound of Thom Yorke ramming his head firmly up his own arse, hearing the rumblings of his intestinal wind and deciding to share it with the world."

Predictably, *Kid A* did achieve more unanimously positive status sooner rather than later. Whether because of sales (it was certified Platinum in Australia, Canada, France, Japan, the United Kingdom, and the United States), Grammy nods (a nomination for Album of the Year and another win for Best Alternative Album), or the simple fact that it's an album that takes time to grow on the listener, it would go on to receive universal acclaim as soon as 2001. *Q*, the *Los Angeles Times*, and numerous others all put it on their year-end lists. Even *Melody Maker* had a quick change of heart, citing it as one of the best albums of 2000. In just about every retrospective Best Albums Ever/of the Decade/of the 2000s list, *Kid A* ranks near the top. Today, it's safe to call it a classic.

More notable than *Kid A*'s critical reception was its method of release. Radiohead wasn't quite in *In Rainbows* territory yet in terms of agency, but they explicitly put out the album with little marketing and no singles, beyond promos sent to radio stations at cable music channels like MTV2. There were few interviews and no press junkets—none of the feeding frenzy that surrounded *OK Computer*.

In an admittedly savvy move for a major label, Capitol accepted Radiohead's hands-off marketing approach as a welcome challenge, coming up with innovative solutions such as "blips," which were essentially short films set to portions of *Kid A*'s music. Capitol distributed them online, in addition to offering up a Java applet called the iBlip that allowed listeners to embed a stream of the album onto a website and play it in full before *Kid A*'s release. Naturally, the stream also led consumers to a pre-order link for the album on Amazon. Over 1,000 different sites took advantage of the iBlip, resulting in over 400,000 streams leading up to *Kid A*'s October 2, 2000 release date. Capitol itself released more visible streams through Amazon, Heavy.com, and MTV.com.

All of this probably sounds unremarkable in a present-day context, but in 2000, streaming wasn't the primary vehicle for audio and visual consumption like it is today. Releasing an album without the traditional press wave of singles, music videos, and interviews was unheard of. Even more radical was a major-label record company letting fans hear such a highly anticipated album *before* it hit stores. To Capitol's great surprise, their gamble paid off, and *Kid A* debuted at number-one in the United States, with roughly 210,000 units already sold.

But Capitol doesn't deserve all of the credit for *Kid A*'s financial success. Another key element has to do with a technological groundswell that no one— not even Radiohead, with their frequent predictions about technology—saw coming. Because the band premiered almost all of their *Kid A* songs on a lengthy European tour, fans were able to assemble various live bootleg recordings of the album, many of which appeared on the brand-new file-sharing service Napster three months before *Kid A*'s release date.

Although the band was slightly dismayed and baffled at first—wondering how everyone at their shows already knew the words to songs that wouldn't be released for another three months—they eventually accepted it. And they were smart to. Without Napster, who knows if *Kid A* would have ever hit the Top 20 in the United States, let alone given the band their first number-one debut overseas?

5

"I Had Never Seen a Shooting Star Before."

Reviewing *Pitchfork*'s Review of *Kid A*

By the time *Kid A* came out, Radiohead was no stranger to critical acclaim. But even with the near-unanimous praise of *OK Computer* in the band's rearview mirror, the reception for their fourth album felt more seismic.

While the praise wasn't as immediately universal as it was for *OK Computer*, the reviews were more extreme in their opinions and writing style. And why not? The sonic evolution from *OK Computer* to *Kid A* was more drastic than the jump from *The Bends* to *OK Computer* or *Pablo Honey* to *The Bends*. It's only natural that there would be a shift in the in the way critics began writing about Radiohead as well, whether they were praising the album or trashing it.

And no 2000 review of *Kid A* is as memorable (or, depending on who's being asked, infamous), than the one that appeared on *Pitchfork* (then *Pitchfork Media*) on October 2. Written by Brent DiCrescenzo, it captures the *Pitchfork* house style of the time: unapologetic about its high concept, strong in it opinion, and by turns maddening and intriguing—all reasons people cite for both loving and hating the publication in its early days.

Although the publication's tone has mellowed considerably since then, back in 2000, the site leveraged its polarization into tastemaker status. To receive the highly coveted "Best New Music" rating was a near-guarantee of critical and commercial success for indie acts. But there's a dirtier, scratched-up side to that coin. An abysmal rating often meant a severe roadblock in an artist's career. Travis Morrison—once a critical darling of *Pitchfork* as the frontman for the Dismemberment Plan—saw his solo career all but squashed when his 2004 debut, *Travistan*, was slapped with a damning 0.0. Australian AC/DC disciples Jet got it even worse when 2006's *Shine On* didn't get an actual review, but a looped video clip of a chimpanzee pissing in its own mouth.

The *Kid A* review has the same amount of notoriety, but for its stream-of-consciousness praise rather than its cruelty. Beginning with the line "I had never seen a shooting star before," DiCrescenzo goes on to describe a transcendent Radiohead concert he attended at Piazza Santa Croce in Florence on June 22,

2000. He begins by painting the experience of seeing *Kid A*'s songs live as a sort of come-to-Jesus-moment for the reader, then uses that as a gateway to discuss the greater context of the album. The writing is, at times, hyperbolic and unintentionally funny. Take this paragraph:

> "The butterscotch lamps along the walls of the tight city square bled upward into the cobalt sky, which seemed as strikingly artificial and perfect as a wizard's cap. The staccato piano chords ascended repeatedly. 'Black eyed angels swam at me,' Yorke sang like his dying words. 'There was nothing to fear, nothing to hide.' The trained critical part of me marked the similarity to Coltrane's 'Olé.' The human part of me wept in awe."

At other times, though, DiCrescenzo accurately captures what it's like to listen to the album and hits the nail on the head regarding why *Kid A* seemed so immediately important as it came out:

> "For months, I feared playing the song about car crashes in my car, just as I'd feared passing 18-wheelers after nearly being crushed by one in 1990. With good reason, I suspect Radiohead to possess incomprehensible powers. The evidence is only compounded with *Kid A*—the rubber match in the band's legacy—an album which completely obliterates how albums, and Radiohead themselves, will be considered."

Regardless of one's feelings about the review, there's no arguing with that second graf. *Kid A* remains a watershed moment in Radiohead's career and the rock album as a long-form body of work. DiCrescenzo isn't writing in a dark shade of purple for nothing—he's trying to describe an album with no precedent. And at times, he really does succeed.

I remember reading DiCrescenzo's review when it was first published, and at the time, it didn't seem ridiculous our overwrought. This was before I even liked Radiohead as a band, and it still seemed to capture exactly what made the album so unique. It wasn't until years later that the review started getting mocked online, particularly on Reddit. There are several Radiohead subreddits devoted solely to discussing the article, with titles like "The last paragraph of *Pitchfork*'s 'Kid A' review is a bit…Over the top."

But even within the bowels of Reddit hate, there are users who acknowledge that DiCrescenzo was onto something: "I don't know, sounds pretty much spot-on to me…" (Beetso); "This surmises my feelings and thoughts towards the album, I just think I could never put it into words." (black-eyed_angel); and "a bit over the top…yet pretty damn right." (internetflex)

But what does the writer himself think after all these years? When speaking over the phone, DiCrescenzo is quick to acknowledge that the review is a bit bonkers, even by the *Pitchfork* standards of the day. But he also makes no apologies for it. And why should he? Are there better-written reviews of *Kid A* from that time period? Probably. But no one's talking about them, and we're definitely not devoting an entire chapter to them in this book. If nothing else, DiCrescenzo's review was a protomartyr for the ride-or-die attitude that so many fans, haters, and critics adopt when talking about Radiohead.

When you first heard *Kid A*, did you immediately know it was going to be something special?

I knew it was definitely a strange, important album on a couple fronts. It was the first album I can really recall illegally downloading on Napster. You'd have to download each song one at a time. I like the traditional album experience where you drop the needle or hit "play" and sit back. But this was like, "Okay, I have to sit here for 30 or 40 minutes to download four megabytes?" You waited however long it took.

But then it's a song like "Treefingers," and you're like "Shit, I waited all this time for an ambient track?" It puts a strange weight on each track. I felt like that showed up in the criticism.

The band had already played most of the songs on *Kid A* live before the album was released. Did you hear any of them in that setting?

In 1998, I went to the Tibetan Freedom Concert with my best friend from college who's from D.C. Radiohead was headlining, but a kid got struck by lightning during Herbie Hancock's set. This was in RFK Stadium, and they evacuated and canceled the rest of the show. We were all fucking bummed. We got in our car and were like, "Oh, the Dismemberment Plan's playing in Baltimore. We'll drive up to Baltimore and do that instead."

As we were driving, we had the radio on, and this announcement came on: "If anyone has their Tibetan Freedom Concert tickets, hold onto them and go to the 9:30 Club for a very special secret show." So we raced over there and were pretty early. We found out it was going to be Radiohead and were like "Oh shit!" It was the tiniest show, and it was Radiohead, Pulp, and Michael Stipe, who came out to sing "Lucky." It was weird. Brad Pitt was there with Jennifer Aniston.

We were pressed up against the stage, and it was the one of the first times they played "How to Disappear Completely." I recall it being 8 or 10 minutes long, and it had this really long, looping arpeggio keyboard part that Jonny Greenwood played. It was completely different from what ended up on the

Ticket stub for the 1998 Tibetan Freedom Concert.

Courtesy of Quentin Werrie

record. That was the first taste of where they were going. So I kind of knew that they were going in a trancier, artsier direction. They had played those shows in Europe before the record came out.

Long story short, I had heard a lot. I had probably heard "How to Disappear Completely" in a couple forms. I think they may have played "Optimistic." It all kind of runs together. So I wasn't thrown for a complete loop.

Back then, I'd read *NME* and *Melody Maker* when it existed, *Select*—all these British trade mags. In the runup to any major British album, there would be like 10 cover stories, and they would talk about it and break it down track by track. So you knew something sort of strange and different was coming.

What was your own gut reaction to the album?

I immediately loved it. But I just tend to be that way with bands I love. I have a deep, personal, almost pseudo-familial relationship with them. The reason I like them is because I like their personalities. I like their aesthetics. I like their interviews. So I'm kind of all in to begin with. I knew I wasn't going to hate it or be confused.

I was also working at a record store and was going through that phase where you're expanding from your high-school and college tastes. You're getting into weird Brazilian and African records. So I was listening to a lot more world music—dub, ambient, stuff like that. *Kid A* was what I was ready for. I was probably changing just as Radiohead was.

You were already known for your high-concept record reviews at *Pitchfork*. At what point did you figure out how you were going to write about *Kid A*?

I tend to not like music criticism. I know that's weird to say because I used to write it and I worked as a writer for a long time. It plays into the stereotype of critics being self-loathing people, I guess. I take it really personally. I don't want to hear what other people say about things. I totally get why people hate, hate, hate what I've written.

So the sort of standard "The drums sound like this and the guitars do this …" I didn't care about that at all. And I didn't like any academic style of writing. It has its place, but for the most part, I think there are more important things to be academic about than pop music.

So I think I was trying to amuse myself. If you have an outlet on the internet to do whatever the hell you want, why not just do whatever the hell you want? Be weird. Let's make this strange. My approach was always to listen to the records as I was writing and just go with whatever came in my head. I tried to write pieces that captured the feeling of listening to the record. If you couldn't hear the record for whatever reason, and you read my review, I was hoping in its style and tone, you would get a sense of what the record was trying to convey. It was a sort of impressionist, turning what musicians are doing into words and prose.

If something was really personal, I'd try to make the review personal. If the record was a goofy lark, I'd make the review a goofy lark. If it was really terse and minimalist, I'd try to write in that style. If it was kind of pretentious, I'd try to be pretentious. Just capturing the basic vibe of the record.

In the review, you tie the record to a time you saw the band play in Italy.

With music, even to this day, I have a very strong association of place. I know exactly what record I was listening to when driving from Toronto to college after having my heart broken. When I play *The Bends* now, I picture driving through the mountains in Tennessee, because I used to always listen to that record when I was driving to school. At some point, I must have been blasting it on that stretch of highway. It's like a synesthesia sort of thing.

Seeing that music in Italy, which I had not been to too many times . . . It meant so much to me because I had been there and seen that. I thought that the record, too, captured that same sort of mysterious feeling and awe.

At *Pitchfork*, I was like "Well, we want people to read this." If I was to write a standard record review, no one would pay attention to it. No one would care. It was definitely trying to get attention and just trying to fulfill my own creative itch. Nobody who writes record reviews truly wants to be a record reviewer, right? We all want to write a book or something. So I was like "Why wait? I can write my weird short stories here instead of a standard record review." Even when I listen to albums today, I think "How would I have written a record review of this in the old *Pitchfork* style?"

How do you feel about some of the backlash toward the review?

Even today, I'll get an email from a young Tool fan who finds my review for *Lateralus* the first time and just hates on me. Or even Radiohead. You can go on Reddit and find a thread making fun of the *Kid A* record review. And it's like "Man, how many record reviews from the year 2000 are being talked about?" I don't care. I feel like I achieved what I was trying to achieve by doing that.

6

"The Wise Man Said I Don't Want to Hear Your Voice"

Thom Yorke

Unlike so many of their contemporaries, Radiohead has had the same five-man lineup for its entire existence. This isn't lost on the band members, who have always viewed themselves as a democracy, no matter how exhausting a tour or how tense a recording process. In keeping with this equilateral mindset, it seems only fair that each of them—in addition to long-term band producer Nigel Godrich and visual artist Stanley Donwood—gets a chapter or so dedicated to their life and work.

There's only one member of Radiohead whose chapter could go first—not because he views himself as more important than the others, but because fans tend to see him, for better or for worse, as their messiah, their prophet, their avatar for their own emotions and experiences. We're of course speaking of Thom Yorke.

In the band's early days, Yorke was often viewed by Radiohead's detractors as the British poster boy for the sad-bastardisms of '90s rock music: a serious, moody person who sang serious, moody music in a serious, moody falsetto. They weren't exactly wrong.

But Yorke is also a human being, and like any human being, he's complex. While his interviews, outlooks, and music have, at times, been grim, they're paired with an acidic sense of humor and playfulness that's become more apparent as Radiohead's career has progressed and he's mellowed out as a person. He's also long transcended the delicacy of his voice. His vocals have always been gorgeous and heartbreakingly resonant, but from *Kid A* (maybe even *OK Computer*) onward, he's pushed its limits by viewing it as another instrument—one capable of coldness, viciousness, detachment, and every other color of the emotional rainbow.

Childhood

Born on October 7, 1968 in the market town Wellingborough of Northampton-shire—a county in the East Midlands of England—Thomas Edward Yorke has always claimed to have a middle-of-the-road childhood, filled with building Legos, drawing cars, and working on his bike.

He was constantly keeping himself busy, a trait that was perhaps caused by his family moving several times during the first 10 years of his life. His father Graham was a nuclear physicist who sold equipment to chemical engineering companies, a venture that brought the family to Scotland shortly after Yorke was born. While there, the Yorkes lived near an abandoned defense fortress from World War II. One can't help but wonder if his father's occupation and living so close to a former war site inspired some of Yorke's songwriting about nuclear fallout and other apocalyptic scenarios.

While Yorke has never confirmed this one way or another, and has said he's always had a hard time writing music about his childhood, he has frequently commented on the significance of another early event in his life. When he was born, his left eye was fixed completely shut, leading to a series of five operations before he was six years old to correct it. After doctors botched the final one, he had to wear an eyepatch for a whole year. To this day, he has a drooping left eyelid that was the cause of much ridicule when he was a boy. His father—a prize-winning pugilist in college—gave him boxing lessons so Yorke could learn to defend himself. While he never became a prizefighter, he at least developed a saltiness and strength that would come in handy as a professional musician.

After returning to England and moving several more times, the Yorkes had settled in Oxfordshire, where Thom and his brother Andy attended the Stand-lake Church of England Primary School in Whitney (their mother Barbara also taught there). By this point, Yorke had begun dabbling in music and idolizing Queen's guitarist, Brian May. Hoping to stoke his passion and confidence, his parents bought him a Spanish guitar for his eighth birthday.

Yorke had attempted to learn the steel guitar four years earlier, but the experiment ended with hurt fingers and an instrument smashed to bits. The second go-around was much more successful, with Yorke soon taking lessons and, by the time he was ten, forming his first band with a fellow student at Standlake.

Even this early experiment hinted at what was to come. For instance, Yorke was more interested in his friend rewiring television sets so that they would explode rather than hearing him play an actual instrument—an omen of the avant garde ways Radiohead would eventually treat their recording processes. Even more telling, Yorke's first composition was titled "Mushroom Cloud," a ditty whose lyrics described what a nuclear blast might look like.

Of course, the most important musical partnership of Yorke's young life would occur not at Standlake, but the Abingdon School, which he began attending in the early eighties. It was here that he met Ed O'Brien, Phil Selway, and Jonny and Colin Greenwood to form On a Friday, the rock outfit that would eventually morph into Radiohead.

College Years

Toward the end of 1988, Thom Yorke left his home to study English and Fine Arts at the University of Exeter in Devon, South West England. Although that meant On a Friday had to take a break from gigging regularly (they still made time to rehearse), he bonded with two people that would become integral to the band's future after they had changed their name.

The first was artist Stanley Donwood, who wouldn't start working with Yorke right away, but would stay in touch with him leading up to their first band collaboration, 1994's *My Iron Lung*. As Yorke revealed in a Reddit Ask Me Anything on February 18, 2013, "I met him first day at art college and he had a better hat and suit on than me. That pissed me off. So I figured I'd either end up really not liking this person at all, or working with him for the rest of my life."

The second crucial figure from Yorke's Exeter days was Rachel Owen, a Welsh printmaker, photographer, and eventual Dante scholar and lecturer who would become his romantic partner from 1992 until 2015. Owen and Yorke would secretly marry in 2003 amidst having two children together, Noah (born in 2001) and Agnes (born in 2004), both of whom would pop up occasionally in

Thom Yorke attended college at the University of Exeter in Devon.

Photo by Benjamin Evans/Wikimedia Commons

Radiohead's work. Owen tragically lost a battle with cancer on December 18, 2016, a little over a year after she and Yorke had announced their separation as a couple.

In addition to meeting these two crucial collaborators, Yorke's time at Exeter allowed him to write at least one future Radiohead song, even if he didn't know it at the time. With his Pixies-influenced punk band, Headless Chickens (eventually changed to just Headless), he played 30 or so gigs around Exeter. Among his fellow Chickens were bassist Simon Shackleton, who would go on to become a DJ and electronic musician with compositions in *The Matrix* and *Charlie's Angels*, and John Matthias, who would go on to play violin and viola on *The Bends*.

One of the band's gigs was at the student venue the Lemon Grove, where someone recorded them playing an early, laughably fast version of "High and Dry." The band would break up after a year, but they got to open for De La Soul and Eat and, most importantly, road-test what would become one of Radiohead's most successful songs.

Another college gig that was indicative of where Yorke would eventually go with Radiohead was a taped performance with a contemporary classic ensemble. In the video, which was unearthed on Reddit in 2015, a 22-minute improvisational recital finds Yorke playing various percussive instruments and letting out an impressive, vibrato-soaked wail over live string music. At one point, several Exeter students take the stage in silence and count down as they throw cardboard boxes around the space.

On one hand, the performance stinks of the most stereotypical art-school pretension. On the other, it shows Yorke's early interest in combining various artistic mediums and genres. Also of interest: the composition is titled Flicker Noise, the name of Shackleton's electronic project that would form out of the Headless Chickens after Yorke went back to Oxford to rededicate himself to On a Friday.

When asked about his college years, Yorke has looked back with a mixture of gratitude and distaste. He's admitted he was probably drinking too much, and his malcontent attitude got him into at least one physical altercation. And while he found most of his coursework to be a slog, he got to expand his love of dance music and learn the basics of graphic design, thanks to the university's laboratory of Apple computers.

"It was a really buzzing environment, and it was the first time I'd seen anything like that," Yorke told Rockview Records for a 1995 interview CD of his time at Exeter. "But I came out the end of it thinking, 'Why do you have to artificially set up an environment in which to work like that?'"

Solo Work

As they've gotten older, it's become standard for Radiohead to take extended breaks between their albums. But that doesn't mean Yorke has been content to rest on his laurels. In between every record since *Hail to the Thief*, he's used the downtime to carve out a solo career, putting out a new LP (under both his name and a supergroup's) during the gaps leading up to *In Rainbows*, *The King of Limbs*, and *A Moon Shaped Pool*.

At the time of this writing, Radiohead has just wrapped up their most recent tour of 2018 and Yorke has just announced a solo tour. With no new Radiohead album on the horizon, it's not unreasonable to expect a new Yorke solo project—and that's in addition to an already forthcoming soundtrack.

The Eraser

As fortunate as Radiohead has been to find success at such a young age, it also meant the band members didn't have many opportunities to branch out at first. Thom Yorke changed that for himself during the band's hiatus following 2004's *Hail to the Thief* tour. Challenging himself to make a solo record, he announced *The Eraser* in May 2006 and released it just two months later on July 10.

Album art for Thom Yorke's 2006 solo debut, *The Eraser*.   *Author's collection*

With Godrich back at the production helm, the nine songs aren't dissimilar to *Kid A*, once again created via a collage-like approach that found Yorke randomly copying and pasting different samples he had recorded over the years. He would then sift through the abundance of material and, at the urging of Godrich, select the ones that sounded like actual songs. While much of the final product consists of the original samples, Yorke still combined them with a significant amount of music played by Godrich and himself at Radiohead's Oxfordshire studio, Godrich's studio in Covent Garden, and Yorke's own home (many listeners falsely believe *The Eraser* was composed *and* performed using nothing more than a laptop).

For instance, Yorke added twitchy guitar notes among the stalking bass line and deep-space synths of "Black Swan," a single whose genesis came from the *Kid A* sessions. Similarly, "The Clock" contains added riffs and hummed, almost chanted vocals inspired by Yorke listening to Arabian music, as he told *The Globe and Mail* on June 14, 2006.

It's a fitting genre to draw from given *The Eraser*'s subject matter. Yorke made no bones about writing lyrics that criticized, lamented, and simply observed global events at the time. The lead single, "Harrowdown Hill," remembers David Kelly, the biological warfare expert and whistleblower who told the BBC that the British government was incorrect in identifying weapons of mass destruction in Iraq. Kelly killed himself on July 17, 2003, although many people are skeptical that it was a suicide.

The Eraser's artwork, a linocut created by Stanley Donwood, reflects these themes of governmental ignorance, as it uses the anecdote of King Canute trying to control the ocean as a metaphor for inaction toward climate change. Titled *London Views*, the sprawling image reveals the city being overrun by the swirling water—proof that the figure attempting to play God is failing. With his dark cloak and wide-brimmed hat, he almost looks like a medieval plague doctor—a harbinger of death. That the water is swirling and rather whimsical-looking adds to the chilling effect. Even as the ocean overruns our buildings, we still view it as something friendly and controllable.

That's not to say every last track on *The Eraser* is political. Despite its title, "Atoms For Peace" was written in the vein of "Optimistic;" inspired by another tough-love talk from Yorke's then-partner Rachel Owen.

"It was my missus telling me to get it together basically," he told the *Observer* on June 18, 2006. Likewise, Yorke wrote "Analyse" after seeing a blackout in Oxford and marveling at how beautiful and primitive the darkened buildings looked.

Most of this isn't immediately clear from the lyrics, even if Yorke's vocals are intentionally clearer and less filtered than on Radiohead's more recent releases at the time. Like most of the band members' later work (solo projects or otherwise), *The Eraser* is steeped in crypticism and metaphor. And isn't that part of the fun? Considering its content and recording methods, the album could have easily been an overly glitchy and cold affair.

But because Yorke and Godrich managed to land on samples with actual melody—the opening title track, for example, is built around chopped and shuffled piano chords played by Jonny Greenwood years before—then infuse the digitization with human playing, *The Eraser* has accessibility and charisma to spare. The same can't quite be said for its B-sides EP, *Spitting Feathers* (released a few months later on November 22, 2006), and a 2008 remix compilation, *The Eraser Rmxs*. The songs on both works lean too heavily on static-laden disruptions and grooves. Unlike their parent album, there's not a lot too grab onto.

Some critics felt the same way about *The Eraser* as well. Despite it having a 76 "generally favorable" rating on Metacritic, constant Radiohead champion *Pitchfork* bestowed a modest 6.6 rating, with critic and site founder Ryan Schreiber feeling that Yorke's continued foray into electronica was beginning to run its course. The album still landed on the year-end lists of *Rolling Stone*, *NME*, and other notable publications, with Gold certification in Canada, Japan, and the United Kingdom.

Atoms For Peace

Although *The Eraser* came out in 2006, Thom Yorke didn't embark on a proper tour for the album until 2009, during the gap between Radiohead's *In Rainbows* and *The King of Limbs*. This came after forming a supergroup comprised of himself, Godrich, Flea of Red Hot Chili Peppers on bass, session musician and producer Joey Waronker on drums (R.E.M., Beck), and percussionist Mauro Refosco (who had also recorded and toured with the Peppers).

They would originally go by the name Thom Yorke and ???, but soon dubbed themselves Atoms For Peace after one of *The Eraser*'s best tracks—itself named after a 1953 speech by President Eisenhower. The band played 13 dates across 2009 and 2010, with Flying Lotus opening at select shows (he would go on to open for Radiohead in 2018).

But their partnership didn't end there. Once the tour concluded, Atoms For Peace spent three days in Los Angeles jamming and recording. On paper, the process should have resulted in mind-blowingly adventurous material: Yorke would show the band an electronic composition so they could recreate it and add to it with live instruments, with digital programming still playing a large role in the songs.

"One of the things we were most excited about was ending up with a record where you weren't quite sure where the human starts and the machine ends," Yorke told *Rolling Stone* on November 5, 2012.

And yet that's precisely the problem with *Amok*, Atoms For Peace's only studio album to date. Most of it sounds mechanized to the point where one wonders why Yorke used a band at all. It never feels as if the virtuosic musicians are elaborating on or humanizing the material—so much that it's impossible to identify their contributions. With someone whose style is as distinct as Flea, that's saying something. Only when the nine tracks fully lean into their cited afrobeat influences (the band members all shareda love of Fela Kuti) does *Amok* come alive and distinguish itself from *The Eraser*.

Tomorrow's Modern Boxes

Brought into the world on September 26, 2014, and announced just a week prior, Thom Yorke's second solo album, *Tomorrow's Modern Boxes*, was initially released for sale as a BitTorrent bundle. Because the distribution model was another attempt to give financial control back to the artist, the music itself often gets overshadowed when discussing the album.

The compositions are admittedly amorphous, created with electronic sketches paired with Yorke's piano playing. Whenever he and Godrich bring the instrument to the forefront, such as on the "Pyramid Song" nod "Guess Again!" (supplemented with beat programming from Colin Greenwood), the album becomes memorable and alive.

But many of the other seven tracks ultimately succumb to their hasty production methods and the fact that they were created in service of a distribution model and not the other way around. The repetitive, indecipherable mumblings of "There is No Ice (For My Drink)" never get a proper anchor, and closer "Nose Grows Some" amounts to little more than pulsing.

The most refreshing element of *Tomorrow's Modern Boxes* ends up being Yorke's lyrics, which are more direct than usual. They aren't exactly narratives, but connect to each other line by line in a way that makes it easy to track what's going on, even if it's someone's nasal bone becoming longer and mutating into metal. But for the most part, *Tomorrow's Modern Boxes* is forgettable, even if its method of release isn't.

Film Work

Thom Yorke's occasional forays into film have usually sprung from a political cause that was important to him. He granted use of a staggering amount of Radiohead music to the climate change-centric documentary *The Island President*, in addition to composing minimal electronic music with Massive Attack's Robert Del Naja (a.k.a. 3D) for *UK Gold*, a documentary that focuses on the HSBC's tax avoidances.

On top of those, there have been a handful one-off projects such as Yorke's chilly yet propulsive score for fashion label Rag & Bone's short dance piece "Why Can't We Get Along" and his duet with Björk on "I've Seen It All" from Lars Von Trier's tragic musical, *Dancer in the Dark*. While actor Peter Stormare sings

Thom Yorke's 2018 tour featured songs from his soundtrack for Luca Guadagnino's Suspiria remake. Here, he's performing with Nigel Godrich (left) at Brooklyn's Kings Theatre.   *Sachyn Mital*

with Björk in the movie, Yorke sings with her on the soundtrack in a version nominated for Best Original Song at the 73rd Academy Awards.

But Yorke's most anticipated cinematic venture has yet to arrive at the time of this writing. He's been tapped to compose all of the music for Luca Guadagnino's upcoming 2018 remake of Dario Argento's art-horror masterpiece *Suspiria*—the first time Yorke has written a feature-length soundtrack. Judging from the music in the two trailers released so far, he's concocted an unsettling potion of slow-burn orchestral crescendos, apocalyptic rumblings, and jarring synth blasts reminiscent of *Blade Runner*.

As of late, Yorke has also dipped a toe into the world of theatre. In 2015, he was tapped to provide original music for Roundabout Theatre Company's revival of Harold Pinter's creepy early play *Old Times*. In a bold stylistic move, director Douglas Hodge spackled the playwright's trademark pauses with electronic ambience from Yorke.

Collaborations

More so than any of his bandmates, Thom Yorke has lent his talents to a wide array of musicians outside of Radiohead.

Early on in the band's career, he tended to be recruited simply for being a good rock singer, contributing straightforward vocals to covers of iconic songs such as Sparklehorse's 1997 take on Pink Floyd's "Wish You Were Here" (his almost inaudible backing vocals mark his first guest spot) and a handful of Roxy Music covers for the 1998 *Velvet Goldmine* soundtrack: "Bitter-Sweet," "2HB," and "Ladytron." All three were recorded under the name the Venus In Furs, a band made up of Yorke, Jonny Greenwood, Suede's Bernard Butler, and Roxy Music's Andy Mackay.

Yorke's other non-Radiohead work around this time ranges from serviceable (a duet on Drugstore's 1998 single "El President") to mighty (three songs with PJ Harvey on her 2000 album *Stories From the City, Stories From the Sea*), but it's widely accepted that his first landmark guest vocal arrived with UNKLE on 1998's "Rabbit in Your Headlights." It was here that his vocals were at last being used as ethereal, ghostly, and otherworldly, which seems natural given that Radiohead was on the cusp of recording *Kid A*.

From there, Yorke's guest spots veer more toward electronica and hip-hop, his voice manipulated and bent so that it's part of evocative sonic landscapes rather than just pretty-sounding window dressing: three songs with Modselektor (2007's "The White Flash," 2011's "Shipwreck" and "This"), another Björk collaboration (2008's "Nattura"), two Flying Lotus team-ups (2010's "… And the World Laughs With You" and 2012's "Electric Candyman"), and two with Burial & Four Tet (2011's "Mirror" and "Ego").

Most recently, Yorke contributed to Mark Pritchard's 2016 song "Beautiful People" after Pritchard contributed two different remixes of "Bloom" (one under his own name and one under his Harmonic 313 alias) to 2011's *TKOL RMX 1234567*. While electronic textures permeate "Beautiful People," the song also has more sylvan touches peppered throughout, with sounds resembling pan flutes and wooden percussion. It's not quite a throwback to Yorke's early days as hired crooner, but its vibe is far more human and of the earth than his other recent collaborations.

7

"Come On and Let It Out"

In Rainbows

Almost all of Radiohead's albums revolve around some kind of Big Idea—our relationship with technology on *OK Computer*; the breakdown of language on *Kid A*; its inverse on *Amnesiac*; the sociopolitical apocalypse on *Hail to the Thief*.

But for all of their unifying themes, each of these works grew out of a spontaneous writing and recording process. With *OK Computer*, Radiohead didn't set out to write songs about alienation and the dangers of human progress—they simply set out to write songs. The Big Idea came later.

The band's seventh studio album, *In Rainbows*, was no different. In fact, Radiohead had an even greater sense of freedom than usual, having fulfilled their contract with EMI/Parlophone and parted ways with longtime producer Nigel Godrich in hopes of getting out of their comfort zone. They began trying out a variety of songs live and in the studio, beginning in February 2005 at Canned Applause. But by December, the band was starting to feel rudderless. Despite having upwards of 21 new songs—the titles scrawled out on a blackboard like complex math equations—the band members were constantly second-guessing how to arrange them and often found themselves preoccupied with their personal lives (at this point, all five members had become fathers).

Historically, this would be where Godrich would swoop in and give Radiohead some direction. But in 2005, he was busy with a variety of high-profile gigs, including the production of new albums from Paul McCartney and Beck. So for the first time since 1997's *OK Computer*, the band hired someone new in the form of producer Mark "Spike" Stent.

Hearing the final product of *In Rainbows*, it's easy to see why Stent seemed like such a natural fit at the time. Similar to the album, there's a warmth to many of the landmark records he's produced for artists such as Madonna, U2, and Björk, despite the music's reliance on sampling and drum machines. But for reasons unknown, his collaboration with Radiohead didn't work out. The wider public hasn't heard what the sessions yielded—if anything.

So it was Radiohead's old standby Godrich who ended up seeing *In Rainbows* to completion after all. When the band reconvened with him in October

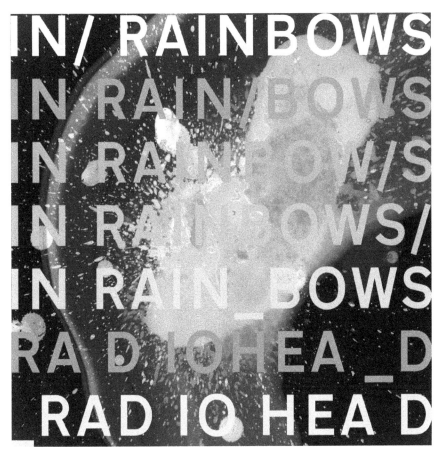

Album art for *In Rainbows*.   *Author's collection*

2006, he once again gave them tough love, forcing them to start giving their nebulous batch of songs a shape.

It's here that *In Rainbows* departs from everything that came before it. It's here that, for once, Radiohead's product also started reflecting the process. That is, the Big Ideas of the album ultimately proved to be flexible—contradictory, even. In an interview with *NME* on December 8, 2007, Yorke called the compositions "seduction songs." Earlier, on April 3, 2006, he used the word "terrifying" when speaking with the publication, while also remarking on the music's complete lack of anger or political agenda. Ed O'Brien has pointed out the universality of the music, which Yorke undercut (or supported) by telling *The Guardian* on December 9, 2007 that the album is "about the fucking panic of realising you're going to die!"

It's not that *In Rainbows* is aimless in its theme; theme just isn't the most crucial element. It's more about a feeling; a vibrance; a band figuring out how to enjoy themselves again without intellectualizing everything into a weighty hypothesis. It's content to just be. It's content to just exist. It's content to just glow.

The Songs

"15 Step"

At first, it sounds like *In Rainbows* will have the subarctic temperature of *Kid A*, the electronic drum loop on "15 Step" reminiscent of "Idioteque." It lasts for about 42 seconds until Jonny Greenwood melts the ice with a bossa nova guitar riff on his Telecaster.

From then on, the song becomes a battle between the cold and the warmth; the synthesized and the human. Every time a detached effect such as a cemetery moan or a space-battle blast enters, it gets pushed back by Colin Greenwood's boiling bassline or a choir of children from the Matrix Music School & Arts Centre screaming "Yeah!" Fun fact: the exclamation was the result of their inability to clap along with the song's complicated 5/4 time signature. As an alternative, Colin and Godrich asked them to shout the song's crucial syllable.

By the time "15 Step" ends, it seems that the organic has become the dominating force for the rest of *In Rainbows*. Raspy breathing permeates the space and the most prominent percussion now comes from Phil Selway's standard drum kit rather than a loop.

Radiohead took the human element to the extreme at the 51st Annual Grammy Awards, where they performed "15 Step" with Spirit of Troy, the marching band for the University of Southern California. The only members of the band visible onscreen are Yorke and Jonny, with the rhythm section completely replaced by a battalion of drummers and brass players. Yorke may be referencing an execution by hanging or a failed relationship in the lyrics, but the atmosphere of "15 Step"—especially in this performance—is ultimately one of pure joy.

"Bodysnatchers"

Radiohead transform the triumph of humanity into complete rawness on "Bodysnatchers," a burst of straightforward rock where Yorke's vocals were recorded in one take, with no obvious effects added. Instead, the dynamics and textures arrive when the singer slides from yelping to mid-range, falsetto, and back. Yorke has credited the unhinged take to a 120-hour bout of hypermania that he experiences every time before he gets sick. The guitars match the viscera of his voice, even though he had to re-record his own part to clean up some sloppy playing.

Like *OK Computer's* relationship to the 16th-century manor house St Catherine's Court, the band believes the eerie yet rushed atmosphere of "Bodysnatchers" was also influenced by its recording space. This time around, the locale was a spooky Grade-I listed building called the Tottenham House in Wiltshire, England. It came at the suggestion of Godrich once the band reunited with him.

Fittingly, Yorke has said this song was inspired not by Jack Finney's namesake novel, but Victorian ghost stories, *The Stepford Wives*, and the feeling of physical disembodiment. Perhaps one of Radiohead's most human-sounding songs could be about the sensation of not feeling human at all. Released as a single in 2008, it would peak at number eight on *Billboard*'s Hot Modern Rock Tracks chart, the band's highest-charting song since "Creep" back in 1993.

"Nude"

As with most of Radiohead's albums, several of the tracks on *In Rainbows* had been floating around for years. In the case of "Nude," the band had actually recorded an earlier version of it for *OK Computer*, the first album where Godrich served as producer. It only feels right that he—not Spike Stent—would shepherd "Nude" to its final draft.

According to Godrich, Radiohead was satisfied with the song's original incarnation, but soured on it as time went on. Watching old live footage of "Nude" from before it even had a title, it's hard to see why. While it's certainly Radiohead at their most straightforward, the song follows up on the band's intent to pay homage to Al Green. Like so many of Green's best ballads, it's driven by the Fender Rhodes piano (played by Thom Yorke) and organ (played by Jonny Greenwood). This version would eventually surface on Cassette B of the special edition of *OK Computer OKNOTOK 1997 2017*.

The *In Rainbows* version isn't radically different, but its color comes more from Colin Greenwood's modified bass line. In the old version, he often stuck to root notes, playing along with the guitar and piano chords. For *In Rainbows*, he diverted from the song's throughline, going higher on the neck for something slinkier. Yorke also credits the song's newfound success to altered lyrics and being comfortable with a more feminine vocal line—something he felt odd about back in 1997.

The definitive version of "Nude" doesn't just pay tribute to Green—it subverts his vulnerability with Radiohead's distinct brand of weirdness. As the second single from *In Rainbows*, it outperformed "Jigsaw Falling Into Place" by placing at #37 on the US *Billboard* Hot 100, also the band's strongest performance on that chart since "Creep."

"Weird Fishes/Arpeggi"

"Weird Fishes/Arpeggi" is one of a handful of tracks on *In Rainbows* that could be filed under Yorke's label of "seduction songs." But the seduction has dire

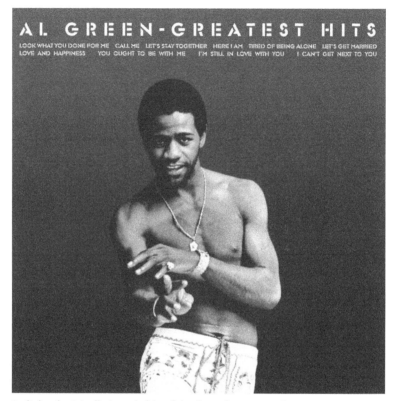

Radiohead originally intended "Nude" to be an homage to Al Green.

Author's collection

consequences. Here, it seems the narrator has followed their loved one to the bottom of the sea. Their partner turns on them, and they find themselves lost in the ocean's depths, feasted upon by worms and the fish of the title.

Such lyrical content could quickly turn gruesome, but the words remain secondary to the gorgeous arrangement. That's why the two-handed title is so important—the "Weird Fishes" represent the primal lyrics and the "Arpeggi" represent the steadfast arpeggios that twinkle throughout, ensuring that the composition retains its majesty even in an aquatic nightmare.

"Weird Fishes/Arpeggi" had even more splendor in its live debut at the Ether Festival on March 27, 2005, over two-and-a-half years before *In Rainbows* was released. Conducted by Martyn Brabbins, the arrangement featured the Arab Orchestra of Nazareth and a total of seven ondes Martenots, including one played by Jonny Greenwood. While lacking the momentum of the more rock-oriented studio version, it has an elegance unrivaled by anything else on *In Rainbows*. The brutal lyrics are nothing more than an afterthought.

"All I Need"

"All I Need" ends side one of *In Rainbows*, bookending the first half with two songs that pit the mechanical against the human.

Like "15 Step," the song is one of Radiohead's warmest, but the space-heater glow of the central chord progression—a combination of Colin's bass and Jonny's Fender Rhodes—dies out by the end. Jonny wanted to replicate the white noise that fills the air whenever the band plays loudly in a small room, and achieved the effect by having a string section, the Millennia Ensemble, play every note of the scale.

This blanketed the audio frequencies, giving the second half of "All I Need" a blurry live feel. It's still pristine, but it's a dingy-club kind of pristine, as if the listener is being blown away by the force of a Radiohead concert in their own basement. The false white noise interlocks with the core melody, the cacophony aided by several violas added by Jonny himself. The sonic tug of war rings out until the song fades.

For Yorke's part, the lyrics err on the organic side. Similar to "Weird Fishes/ Arpeggi," he once again gets into animal mode, comparing his infatuation with a lover to a moth who needs light. But an earlier comparison of being trapped in a hot car adds toxicity to the relationship.

"Faust Arp"

At 2:10, "Faust Arp" is the shortest *In Rainbows* song by almost two minutes. But it's also the wordiest, which means it's inspired many heated debates on Radiohead message boards. Fans have theorized that the title and lyrics refer to everything from German krautrock act Faust to the actual Faust legend. One fan theory even believes that all of *In Rainbows* revolves around Johann Wolfgang von Goethe's adaptation of the story.

Yorke, in typical Thom Yorke fashion, has neither confirmed nor denied any of this, only going on to say that "Faust Arp" is the result of too much over-thinking; of not living in the moment and sifting through pages and pages of writing to come up with something musically substantial. That makes the song's flippance—with nothing more than acoustic guitar, vocals, and strings, it almost feels like a jingle—all the more fascinating. The band's obsessive nature doesn't always result in epics.

"Reckoner"

"You listen to something like 'Reckoner' and think, maybe this is just a bad break beat," Jonny Greenwood told *Mojo* in January 2008. "Now I can hear what's good about it."

Many bands go through a period when they begin to doubt their material on a new album, especially when they spend as much time as Radiohead did on *In Rainbows*. But Jonny's initial feelings about "Reckoner" shouldn't just be chalked up to spending too much time with the music. It points to a stylistic trait—whether by choice or coincidence—in the second half of *In Rainbows* where the beauty tends to be quieter and more nuanced.

In the case of "Reckoner," the first thing we hear is a clang of percussion that never goes away, the most prominent drum piece being Selway's tambourine. The tiny builds throughout—a string section toward the end, a shimmering guitar line influenced by Red Hot Chili Peppers' John Frusciante, and even the moaned title of the album—all take a backseat.

The song is all the better for it. Every listen seems to unveil something new, its nooks and crannies making "Reckoner" a popular remixed track with other artists, from Flying Lotus to James Holden and Diplo (as with "Nude," Radiohead released the music's original stems to the general public). The song's commercial performance is further testament to its subtlety. Though released as a single, it only charted at #74 on the UK singles chart. To be a wildly popular earworm, it would seem that the hook needs to be more explicit.

Fun fact: "Reckoner" was actually the original title of a more aggressive composition that went on to be called "Feeling Pulled Apart By Horses." Radiohead recorded a coda for the song, then deemed it the only portion worth keeping. This soon became what we now know as "Reckoner," and Yorke reworked the scrapped material while recording his first solo album, *The Eraser*, released a little over a year before *In Rainbows*. "Feeling Pulled Apart By Horses" didn't make it onto *The Eraser*, either, but got released as a double A-side single with another Yorke solo composition, "The Hollow Earth."

"House of Cards"

Of all the songs on *In Rainbows*, "House of Cards" most embodies the album's artwork, an explosion of color chemically created by Stanley Donwood. Thom Yorke described it as "mellow and summery" to *Mojo* in July 2006, comparing it to "Albatross" by Fleetwood Mac.

Indeed, both songs have an illuminated guitar riff at the center, backed by a bass drum that sounds emitted not from an amplifier, but a wave gently lapping a shore. But "House of Cards" also has destruction at its edges, thanks to the ghostly reverb that came from recording at Halswell House. Like St Catherine's Court, Halswell is a stately country home in Somerset, occupied by the band in December 2006 for the final recording sessions for *In Rainbows*. Godrich actually recorded the ambiance on his computer, then layered it on top of the song later.

The mixture of beauty and deterioration perfectly reflects the lyrics. Yorke sings to a partner who, like him, is trapped by another relationship. He begs them both to forget about the other people and structures that confine them—to bring their respective houses of cards crashing down so they can be together as lovers. There's beauty in the destruction and destruction in the beauty; as Yorke points out, it likely won't be a long-term relationship and both of their lives will be shattered by the affair.

The lyrical complexity deeply resonated with audiences—as a single, "House of Cards" charted at #24 on *Billboard*'s US Adult Alternative Songs and was nominated for Best Rock Performance by a Duo or Group with Vocal, Best Rock Song, and Best Music Video at the 51st Annual Grammy Awards.

"Jigsaw Falling Into Place"

Ever since Radiohead released "Jigsaw Falling Into Place" as the lead single from *In Rainbows*, Yorke has been uncharacteristically consistent in his explanation of the lyrics.

"'Jigsaw Falling Into Place' says much about the fact I used to live in the center of Oxford and used to go out occasionally and witness the chaos of a weekend around here," Yorke told *NME* on December 8, 2007. "The lyrics are quite caustic—the idea of before you're comatose or whatever, drinking yourself and getting fucked-up to forget."

This realization can only be heard in Yorke's vocal performance, not the instrumentation, which remains upbeat throughout. As the liquor drenches the lyrics in abstraction and the narrator inches closer to a hookup that both parties will surely regret, Yorke grows more panicky—his pitch higher, his breath shorter, his inflection less steady. It's all going too fast—too fast for him to stop dancing; too fast for him to start drinking water; too fast for him to call a cab and go home alone.

Because "Jigsaw Falling Into Place" stays dancy, it retains an accessibility, despite the *NME* interview being a morning-after killjoy. Had the music matched the self-hatred of the lyrics, it may not have peaked at #14 on *Billboard*'s Hot 100. The chart performance spiritually links it with "Paranoid Android," another track that sprung from observations about debaucherous nightlife and became one of the band's most popular songs.

"Videotape"

Like many Radiohead songs, "Videotape" began with a full-bodied arrangement that was eventually reduced to something more sparse. As Yorke describes dying and leaving recorded farewell to a lover, he's accompanied by little more than his own piano. A performance at Bonnaroo 2006 started off in a similar way, but he was soon joined by the rest of the band, ending the final track on *In Rainbows* in a raucous style more akin to "Jigsaw Falling Into Place."

But "Videotape" stands out from other less-is-more Radiohead songs for its off-kilter rhythm. As pointed out by host Estelle Caswell and music teacher Warren Lain in *Vox*'s video series *Earworm*, "Videotape" actually has a hidden syncopation. That is, Yorke is plays the four repeating piano plunks of "Video-tape" outside the notes, on the "ands." However, it's difficult for the casual ear to identify the syncopation without a constant stream of bass and percussion.

Had Radiohead gone with their original arrangement, that wouldn't be the case. The full-band attack of the Bonnaroo performance makes it easy to count one-and-two-and-three-and-four. But on the album version, the band gives several false starts without ever fully joining Yorke. The energy of the Bonnaroo performance is promised, yet never arrives.

Radiohead has never given much of a reason for the shift other than Godrich playing the stripped-down version for Yorke, and Yorke falling in love with it. But if we can put on our music-geek hats for a moment, the album version more accurately captures the spirit of death. The act of a soul—if one believes in such a thing—leaving the body is invisible, at least to the human eye, just like the syncopation in "Videotape" is unidentifiable to the human ear. Godrich didn't simply make "Videotape" more haunting—he infused it with an actual ghost.

B-sides

"I Want None of This"

Alright, we're admittedly cheating by including this song here. Although Thom Yorke recorded it by himself while the band was in the middle of working on *In Rainbows*, it was never going to be included on that album. Instead, it was custom-written for *Help!: A Day In the Life*, another compilation album produced by War Child (the same organization behind 1995's *The Help Album*, where "Lucky" first appeared). But since it's at least of the same period as the *In Rainbows* sessions, this chapter seems as good a place as any.

A predecessor to "Harry Patch (In Memory Of)," "I Want None of This" finds Yorke experimenting with a more straightforward aesthetic. Since it's just him and a piano, the arrangement highlights the anti-war lyrics, which sarcastically beg a militarized government to strip war-torn nations of everything that's good. The somber nature makes it hard to return to on a regular basis, but "I Want None of This" shows that, when Yorke wants to get his point across, he knows the best approach is to sometimes get quieter.

Conclusion

It's impossible to talk about the release, reception, and overall legacy of *In Rainbows* without talking about how it was distributed. There were the usual glowing reviews (an 88 "universal acclaim" score on Metacritic), certifications (Gold in Belgium and the United States; Platinum in Canada and the United Kingdom), and accolades (a Mercury Prize shortlist; Grammy wins for Best Alternative Music Album and Best Boxed Set Limited Edition Package; nominations for Best Rock Performance by a Duo or Group with Vocal, Best Rock Song and Best Music Video), but 11 years later, it's the unconventional rollout that remains most groundbreaking.

In May 2007, EMI—which had been acquired by the venture capital firm Terra Firma—approached Radiohead about re-signing to the label, now that the band's contract had been filled. There was tension almost immediately.

EMI's new chairman, Guy Hands, claimed Radiohead wanted a bigger advance to the tune of £10 million. Band co-manager Bryce Edge denied this, insisting that Radiohead were more interested in gaining control of their back catalog. The label and artist parted ways for good, and by 2009, EMI went on to release two-disc "Collector's Editions" of all of Radiohead's albums through *Hail to the Thief* without the band's approval. In their eyes, it was final proof that they had made the right move by walking away.

Regardless of whether Radiohead or EMI was telling the truth (it was probably somewhere in the middle), the band suddenly found themselves as the most sought-after unsigned musical act in the world. Rather than seek out a new home, they pulled off a release plan that was, in late 2007, wildly unconventional. On October 1, Jonny Greenwood posted a short statement on the band's new website, Dead Air Space: "Hello everyone. Well, the new album is finished, and it's coming out in 10 days. We've called it *In Rainbows*. Love from us all."

The post included a link that clarified *In Rainbows* would first be released as a pay-what-you-want digital download, long before that phrase had taken its place in the cultural lexicon. The download was delivered via the network provider PacketExchange, which was able to bypass public internet servers and offer a ZIP file of the entire album. Each of the 10 tracks was encoded as a 160kbit/s, DRM-free mp3—an audio quality that many detractors would unfavorably compare to being on par with a Myspace stream.

As for physical editions, any hardcore fan could purchase a special "Discbox" for £40, but most consumers opted to pay anywhere between zero dollars and £99.99 for a digital download of the album's 10 songs.

In somewhat of a repeat of the *Kid A* release and press cycle (or lack thereof), Radiohead's then unheard-of move paid off, not only gaining the band £3 million in presales and getting their product to their fans at an affordable cost, but changing the face of music distribution forever, even if that wasn't the intent. What's more is that the band's publisher, Warner/Chappell Music, arranged a physical vinyl and CD release around the world throughout December 2007 and

January 2008, this time through British independent record label XL recordings (the same label that released Yorke's 2006 solo debut, *The Eraser*).

That meant Radiohead still retained ownership of *In Rainbows*, all while turning a further profit on a standard physical release. Although there was some backlash from both fans and other musicians over the audio quality of the digital files, problems with the website, and the unconventional release schedule (more on all of that in chapter 30), for the most part, Radiohead got to have their cake and eat it, too.

That was certainly the case sales-wise. By October 2008, Warner/Chappell revealed that *In Rainbows* had been bought a total of 3 million times across all formats. Of that number, 1.75 million were from CDs and 100,000 were from the Discboxes, both of which were sold for actual cash. The Discboxes alone raked in £4 million.

Yorke summed it up most succinctly to Talking Heads singer David Byrne in a December 2007 interview with *Wired*.

"In terms of digital income, we've made more money out of this record than out of all the other Radiohead albums put together, forever—in terms of anything on the net. And that's nuts."

8

"Light Another Candle and Release Me"

In Rainbows Disk 2 and In Rainbows: Live from the Basement

Radiohead has never had a shortage of B-sides and non-album tracks. But in the first half of their career, much of the material that got left on the cutting-room floor more than deserved the dismissal. Whenever a song felt flimsy, the band's go-to approach seemed to be adding more volume (see "Faithless, the Wonder Boy" and "Inside My Head"), resulting in odds and ends powered by little more than hot air.

By the time Radiohead got to *In Rainbows*, the collage-like writing approach they had developed during *Kid A* was leading to a wealth of bonus material that wasn't getting dumped in the land of compilation EPs and singles. Anyone who purchased the physical Discbox version of the album in 2007 also received a whole disc's worth of other songs, all unified by a title that strongly tethered the tracks to their parent album. It wasn't called *In Rainbows B-sides* or *In Rainbows Bonus Disk*, but the more declarative *In Rainbows Disk 2*. By June 9, 2009, it became available for download on Radiohead's online w.a.s.t.e. store, in addition to a physical version without the original box.

Rather than function as a hodgepodge of leftovers, *Disk 2* serves as a proper second half to *In Rainbows*, as indicated from the title and the music within. Colin Greenwood even confirmed to *Mojo* that the band had at one point sequenced the album as a 16-track LP until manager Chris Hufford stressed that it was way too long, prompting the band to pare it down to 10 songs.

At the same time, it's easy to see how *In Rainbows* could have functioned as a longer work. When pressing play immediately after "Videotape," it becomes clear that *Disk 2* is an extension of the first disc's closer, adopting its funereal mood and pace. It's a coda; an epilogue; an appendix. Perhaps we've joined "Videotape"'s narrator in their afterlife. The red, blue, and green of the VHS recording has faded out, leaving us to explore the stony darkness—a realm with more surprises than we realize.

The Songs

"MK1"

Supporting the idea that we're now sucked into the recording of "Videotape" and the world beyond, the opening ambient track of *Disk 2* replays the piano motif from *In Rainbows'* closer. It begins with a repetitive flutter of the final note, backed by labored breathing and Yorke's lower register. As the breathing picks up speed, crawling closer to death, the full four notes of "Videotape" ring out, taking us through a tomb and to the other side of the veil.

"Down is the New Up"

In a mixed review for *Pitchfork*, Chris Dalen derided *In Rainbows Disk 2* for its "incessant horror film piano."

Agree to disagree. For me, the use of piano as a melodic driver rather than an accent becomes a necessary unifier. And if we truly are in the afterlife, the horror film descriptor feels apt, so much that it makes sense to link some of *Disk 2*'s remaining songs with an assortment of scary movies.

If "Down is the New Up" was a horror movie, it would be the original *Nosferatu*—its piano a creeping and antiquated soundtrack to a silent movie. Yorke's ringmaster proclamations only add to the old-timey nature of it all. The swell of strings at the end—a sound we typically associate with age and classicism—actually modernize the song, transporting it to the 1960s work of Alfred Hitchcock. As yet another nod to "Videotape," Yorke tells the listener they're on *Candid Camera*, perhaps a more frightening horror film than *Psycho* ever was.

"Go Slowly"

As revealed by Radiohead's blackboard used during the *In Rainbows* sessions, the original title of "Go Slowly" was "Can Stylee," and fittingly so—the song bears a striking resemblance to Can's 1970 waltz "The Thief."

It might be a full-on ripoff if not for an added scale that sounds played from a music box. In keeping with Dalen's horror film description, this addition leans into the kids-are-creepy thesis perpetuated by likes of *The Bad Seed*, *The Omen*, and countless others.

"MK2"

Played on an analogue synthesizer, *Disk 2*'s second instrumental serves as a brief intermission. Audiences should see their way to the lobby or stay in the theater and listen to the organist.

Originally, the song was intended as the intro to *Disk 2*'s final track, "4 Minute Warning," which ended up with an introductory crackle of white noise instead. It works better here as an eerie stopping point.

"Last Flowers"

The horror elements of "Last Flowers" conjure two vastly different subgenres. The piano at the song's core is downright gothic, suitable for Dracula, the Phantom of the Opera, or some other regal yet tortured ghoul moaning at the moon.

The lyrics, on the other hand, come from somewhere trashier and more aggressive—a litany of inanimate objects coming to life a la the Stephen King schlock-fest *Maximum Overdrive*.

Radiohead had dabbled in this kind of musical-lyrical disparity many times over, but because the instrumentation remains so sparse throughout "Last Flowers," the weirdness breaks through the beauty, rendering the song both mournful and comedic.

The somewhat jarring formula apparently divided the band. When they initially recorded it for the *OK Computer* sessions, Colin Greenwood remained its sole staunch defender. Unfortunately for him, his belief in the song wasn't enough to keep it on the album, as Radiohead had established a democracy where everyone must be in agreement about the final track listing. Greenwood eventually got his wish when "Last Flowers" appeared on *Disk 2* with few changes from its earliest performance at a 1997 soundcheck.

"Up On the Ladder"

In the opening line of "Up On the Ladder," Yorke references not a horror movie, but a sci-fi TV show with "I'm stuck in the TARDIS." What follows embraces the existential dread rather than the playfulness of *Doctor Who*. It's a composition more interested in someone displaced by time than someone who has control over it.

It's another potent—if somewhat by-the-numbers—slice of Radiohead paranoia. The percussion stays singular and primitive (consisting of little more than a kick drum and what sounds like a range of pots and pans) while more futuristic synthesizers and white noise creep in and out. According to O'Brien's online diary during the *Kid A* sessions, the band kept futzing with "Up On the Ladder" throughout 1999 and 2000. The final, simple recording was apparently another case of less is more.

"Bangers + Mash"

The perfect rebuttal for anyone who insists that Radiohead only know how to be downtrodden and morose, "Bangers + Mash" bursts forward with Colin's dirtiest bass line to date. Not to mention Selway *and* Yorke on drums.

If little else has been said about the song, that's because it really is as simple as it sounds, its extra oomph coming from Radiohead taking a rare view of the oppressor rather than the oppressed. It's hard to tell exactly what kind of debauchery is taking place inside this freakshow version of Parliament, but the people in charge are clearly enjoying it. Puke on the walls some more and dig on "Sabotage" by way of Radiohead.

"4 Minute Warning"

During the *Kid A* sessions, O'Brien gave "4 Minute Warning" the working title of "Neil Young *9," most likely due to its shambling pace and juxtaposition. Like Uncle Neil did with "Cortez the Killer," Radiohead builds a gentle lull while describing something horrific.

Here, it's the inevitable onslaught of a nuclear attack, an event that, in England between 1953 and 1992, would be preceded by a four-minute warning via air raid siren. The warning was obviously absurd—how does one truly

RADIOHEAD
KARMA POLICE CD1

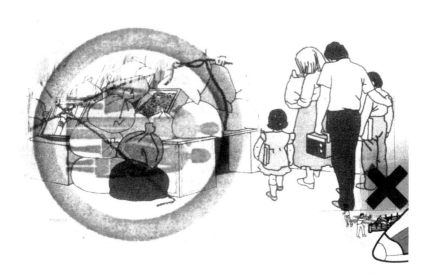

The imagery in "4 Minute Warning" dates back to the artwork of 1997's "Karma Police" single.   *Author's collection*

protect themselves during a Soviet missile strike, unless they have a bomb shelter? The safety measure belongs in a novel by Joseph Heller, George Orwell, or, as long as we're in Horrorland, *I Am Legend* scribe Richard Matheson, whose novel was the source material for the 2007 film of the same name, as well as 1964's *The Last Man on Earth* and 1971's *The Omega Man*.

The genesis of "4 Minute Warning" dates all the way back to August 25, 1997, when Radiohead released the single for "Karma Police." Donwood's artwork featured a father hanging his head while leading his family to a nuclear fallout shelter.

While the actual music of "4 Minute Warning"—Colin's brook-babbling bass, a gentle piano, some salt-shaker percussion—wouldn't be written until later, the artwork signaled a career-long obsession with nuclear war and the apocalypse. Had Donwood not used that image, who knows if "4 Minute Warning" (at one point titled "Bombers") or sister songs such as "I will" off of 2003's *Hail to the Thief* would have ever been created. Then again, Yorke's father *did* have a background as a nuclear physicist.

As a final trick on *In Rainbows Disk 2*, Radiohead made the actual music on "4 Minute Warning"—what else?—exactly four minutes long (four seconds of silence follow at the end). The song is a four-minute warning in and of itself, softly playing as everyone runs for their lives. The contrast of the calm and the chaotic only makes it more unsettling. Whatever afterlife that "Videotape" transported us to has been blown to bits.

In Rainbows—From the Basement

The release of *In Rainbows* was all about giving a band total control of how their music gets distributed. Nigel Godrich's *From the Basement* series had a similar ethos. Filmed at London in Covent Garden's Hospital Club and in the lower level of Maida Vale Studios, the series has allowed musicians to perform their music in a casual setting with no formalized host or audience.

From the Basement premiered on December 18, 2006, with sporadic performances through January 2009. Because it was solely released online, there was no pressure to appease a network or uphold any promotional deals. Godrich—who handled sound duties for the show—would record a performance whenever he wanted and whenever the artists were ready, with none of the decisions driven by revenue. In that regard, he has consistently put his money where his mouth is—a podcast version of the show is currently free on iTunes, the video performances come in at $1.49 per song, and many of the performances (including Radiohead's) are easily found on YouTube.

Despite (or perhaps because of) the casual attitude toward the series, Godrich has been able to feature a heavyweight roster of modern rock acts, from Queens of the Stone Age to Feist, Sonic Youth, and Gnarls Barkley.

Radiohead's first performance on *From the Basement* focused heavily on *In Rainbows*, making it another essential extension of the band's seventh album. Of all Radiohead's work, *In Rainbows* seems best suited to the series' format, and not just because it was their most recent LP at the time. Since *In Rainbows* was recorded over several periods of touring, stopping, recording, and repeating the cycle, it's a work that feels lived-in yet polished.

In Rainbows—From the Basement is one of the few pieces of footage that accurately depicts that balance. It bottles the spirit of Radiohead's concerts from 2004–2009, but because it's not in front of an audience, the band is still able to concentrate and give a meticulous treatment to the arrangements. It also helps that the producer and show creator is one of their closest allies. Rarely does Radiohead seem so comfortable on camera.

The band stands in a circle, as if they're at a rehearsal, seeing each other the entire time in all their quirks, embellishments, and mistakes. The in-the-round formation is also more inclusive for the viewer at home, who gets access to personal moments such as O'Brien grinning widely at Yorke getting lost in the garage frenzy of "Bodysnatchers." Elsewhere, Colin Greenwood smiles in nervous anticipation as he waits for "Myxomatosis" to begin. Band members shamble around between songs, as if they're back at Canned Applause, or maybe even a rehearsal room at the Abingdon School. They sip coffee. They laugh. They crack their backs. This isn't the type of stage business that would happen at just any Radiohead show.

From The Basement's most riveting moment arrives when Yorke takes a seat behind the drum kit on "Bangers + Mash," accompanying Selway as second drummer while still singing. Although Yorke had already done this several times in concert throughout 2008, *From The Basement* marks the only professional live recording of him doing so. Yorke and Selway both nail their drumlines, but we also get humorous banter before the performance. "Goosey-loosey!" shouts Yorke before someone asks if he's got his "flying goggles" that he typically wears for the "Bangers + Mash" performance (he doesn't).

In addition to being broadcast/available for purchase online, *In Rainbows—From the Basement* premiered on VH1 on May 3, 2008, at midnight. The subsequent iTunes version left off the four non-*In Rainbows* tracks ("Optimistic," "Myxomatosis," "Where I End and You Begin," and "The Gloaming"). Not only did this transform the recording into an altered version of *In Rainbows* ("Faust Arp" and "Jigsaw Falling Into Place" are left off, with *Disk 2* cuts "Go Slowly" and "Bangers + Mash" in their place)—it further transformed what could have been a run-of-the-mill live record into another appendage of the album. Only when paired with *Disk 2* and *From the Basement* does *In Rainbows* give a full picture of what Radiohead was like at the time.

9

"Music for a Film"

Radiohead in Popular Culture

I f one wanted to chart Radiohead's growth—their evolution from post-grunge torchbearers to art-rock icons—they wouldn't have to read this book. They could just as easily watch the various movies and television shows to feature the band's work over the years. The pop-culture usage of Radiohead's songs has been as wide-ranging as the music itself.

But even with such diversity, there are patterns that emerge when examining Radiohead's relationship with pop culture. More often than not, a specific instance can fit into one of a handful of categories in regards to genre, format, and mood. While this list is by no means complete, it at least catalogs the most notable uses of their songs in other artistic mediums throughout the years.

Stories About Teen and 20-Something Angst

The first feature film to use a Radiohead song was 1994's *S.F.W.*, an acronym for "so fucking what." The title says it all. In the movie, an angsty teenager, Cliff Spab, gets taken hostage by terrorists at a convenience store. Rather than display fear, he responds to their threat with Gen X indifference, which gives him a celebrity status that follows him after the ordeal is over. His piss-off mantra throughout the film remains—surprise, surprise—"so fucking what."

"Creep" plays over a scene that marks the height of Cliff's callousness. Clad in dark shades and smoking a cigarette in slow motion, he strides to a book signing, quietly loathing (but totally loving) his newfound fame. Although Cliff will come to realize the diminishing returns of his own nihilism by the end of the film, "Creep" is used unironically here, further conveying the angst of a character who's as self-hating and stubborn as the song's narrator.

Other early pop-culture usage of Radiohead is similarly downtrodden. "Fake Plastic Trees" was used in the 1996 film *For Hope*, whose IMDb summary reads "The life and death of a young woman who suffered from scleroderma, and how she and her family coped." Likewise, 1997's *Nowhere* (which featured the "Fake Plastic Trees" B-side "How Can You Be Sure?") is described as "A group of teenagers try to sort out their lives and emotions." Other films and TV shows such as

1994's *S.F.W.* was the first feature-length film to use a Radiohead song.   *Author's collection*

1994's *Dead at 21*—which featured "Creep," but at least boasted a science-fiction angle—and 1996's *This Life* ("Street Spirit (Fade Out)") are as moody and self-serious as their titles suggest.

And why not? As embarrassingly dark and tied to the 1990s as some of these stories are, Radiohead wouldn't be recognized as a truly groundbreaking band until the release of *OK Computer* in 1997. And even today, the band's most pointed critics consistently attack what they perceive to be an abundance of gloominess and pretension. It makes sense that early uses of Radiohead in TV and film wouldn't exactly be subversive or even all that creative.

Parodies of Stories About Teen and 20-Something Angst

Of course, whenever someone is being overly serious, there's always someone else to make fun of it, and that's what a handful of TV shows did early on in Radiohead's career. On April 11, 1994 (predating the release of *S.F.W.* by five months), Mike Judge's *Beavis and Butt-Head*—perhaps the Holy Grail of Gen X satire—skewered Radiohead during one of the show's trademark music video segments.

At one or several points in almost every episode, the numbskull title characters would break the narrative by making fun of an actual music video from the era. The video in season four's "Blackout!" was "Creep," the very song that would be used more sincerely by MTV on *Dead at 21* that June.

"It better start rocking or I'll really give them something to cry about," Butt-Head says during the song's lulling intro. Beavis assures him that the music will get better in just a minute, and sure enough, once Jonny Greenwood heralds the chorus with his distorted chords, the teens are fully onboard—at least until the gentler verses start again.

The much softer "Fake Plastic Trees" would get no such praise from Beavis and Butt-Head when they watched its music video in the 1995 episode "Whiplash." "Sometimes if I have a boner that won't go down, I listen to this kind of music," quips Beavis. The show's spinoff, *Daria*, would go on to feature two *OK Computer* songs, "No Surprises" and "Paranoid Android" to less comic effect. As the intellectual foil to Beavis and Butt-Head, their classmate Daria Morgendorffer was exactly the type of high-schooler who would have listened to Radiohead at the time.

Other shows have gotten even more specific in their ribbing of Radiohead. In the 1998 series finale of the British Channel 4 sitcom *Father Ted*, the title character stops a younger priest, Father Kevin, from committing suicide. He then cheers him up by playing Isaac Hayes's "Theme From *Shaft*." But Hayes' feel-good funk is soon defeated when Father Kevin hears "Exit Music (For A Film)" on a bus, which immediately sends him back into a depressive state.

Another British television show, 2013's *My Mad Fat Diary*, also uses "Exit Music (For a Film)" to reflect a character's suicidal tendencies. The series' overweight, mentally troubled 16-year-old protagonist almost takes an overdose of pills in a bathtub while the song plays, but decides at the last minute to deal with her problems. Right as it seems she's about to slip away, the words "FUCK THAT" blare across the screen in all caps, the music shuts off, and she emerges from the water. The show manages to simultaneously find a sympathetic voice in Yorke's lyrics, then silences that voice by forcing the character to take charge of their life.

But the most complex satirical use of a Radiohead song comes with 1995's *Clueless*, Amy Heckerling's teen update of Jane Austen's novel *Emma*. Toward the beginning of the film while she's getting ready to go out, valley girl protagonist Cher hears the acoustic version of "Fake Plastic Trees" being played on the radio by her stepbrother, Josh, a socially conscious college student with a penchant for Nietzsche, environmental law, and, yes, Radiohead.

"The maudlin music of the university station?" says Cher in disgust. In the same scene, a metafictional joke lands when she switches their mansion's TV to an episode of *Beavis and Butt-Head*, which would make fun of the video for "Fake Plastic Trees" just a couple months later.

"Amy [Heckerling] had thought that Radiohead was just this whiny, whiny band," *Clueless*' music supervisor Karyn Rachtman told *Idolator* in 2013. In the same interview, Rachtman reveals that Radiohead actually bucked their serious reputation by saying yes to the song's use in *Clueless*. Although the band's sense of humor hadn't been well-documented by the media at that point, maybe they found the scene to be funny.

For her part, Heckerling actually subverts her own distaste of Radiohead's music in a later scene where Cher is down in the dumps, reflecting on all of the mistakes she's made throughout the film. Jewel's cover of Eric Carmen's "All By Myself" fittingly plays over the sequence, which culminates with Cher realizing she's actually in love with Josh. Right beforehand, though, we hear the opening guitar line of "My Iron Lung," seamlessly blending with the sequence's main song.

This second use of Radiohead obviously connects to Josh and Cher's feelings for him, but it also unveils the diverse appeal of the band's music. The character who, just an hour ago was trashing Radiohead, suddenly finds them on her internal soundtrack during her own moment of self-pity. It's natural to make fun of Radiohead. But you can also be moved by them, too.

Procedurals

Several crime and medical procedurals have also featured the music of Radiohead, albeit in a much more sober fashion than the comedies we've already discussed. This is in line with the genre's utilitarian nature. Shows such as BBC's *Doctors* and *Silent Witness* (both of which have featured "Creep") are *serious* shows and Radiohead is *serious* music. It isn't so much about the lyrics as the vibe, making it a logical—if boring—audiovisual pairing.

"Devil's Backbone," a 2016 episode of the CBS crime drama *Criminal Minds*, made equally stone-faced use of "Creep" by playing it over a suicide scene, but at least mixed up the formula by featuring an even slower, sadder, and softer cover performed by the Belgian girls' choir Scala & Kolacny Brothers, who have since released reinterpretations of several other of the band's songs, including "Exit Music (For a Film)" and "Everything In Its Right Place."

The sequence is definitely melodramatic and on-the-nose, but what procedural isn't? When mixing the genre with Radiohead's music, it's best to go big or go home and own up to the high emotionality of it all. 2009's sixth-season premiere of *House* takes this philosophy to heart by playing a two-minute chunk of "No Surprises" over the opening scene and credits, where the title character undergoes severe Vicodin withdrawal in a psychiatric hospital.

While *CSI* gets bonus points for being the only procedural audacious enough to feature a whopping five Radiohead songs ("Little By Little," "A Punchup at a Wedding," "There there," and the UNKLE remix of "Everything in Its Right Place"), CBS' *Cold Case* is the procedural that does the most justice to the band's work. Throughout its seven seasons, every episode would end with a musical epilogue, a montage where we'd see the aftermath of the show's events play out over a specific song. It's similar to *The Wire*, only with every installment of the show rather than just the season finale.

Cold Case scored two of these sequences to Radiohead songs. Season four's "Stand Up and Holler" concludes with "High and Dry," and season seven's "Forensics" concludes with "Karma Police." With so many storylines getting tied up for so many characters, each episode's finale functions as an unofficial Radiohead music video.

Sitcoms

Sitcoms have tended to fare better when using Radiohead, as the genre is already at odds with the music. While humor certainly hides within some of the band's lyrics, Radiohead songs rarely come off as funny upon first listen. So if a series rooted in comedy features such an overtly serious composition, chances are it's designed to divert from the usual tone, whether to land a rare and significant moment of drama or to make fun of that very thing.

In a 2014 episode of Dan Harmon's *Community*, for instance, a sandwich shop owner has her two children perform an a cappella version of "Creep" in honor of her eatery's reopening. Since *Community* was a series steeped in hyper-specific pop-culture parody, the two boys sing in a style almost identical to the Vega Choir, whose rendition of "Creep" had recently scored the trailer for *The Social Network*.

Their performance syncs up with an attack from an on-campus prankster dubbed the Ass Crack Bandit, who makes their return on the episode. While the boys sing "Creep," the assailant drops a quarter down the pants of an unsuspecting victim.

The entire sequence has an ominous feel to it, heightened by the use of such a stereotypically eerie song. When the opening credits roll in the dark and gloomy style of any number of crime procedurals, *Community* is suddenly making fun of a genre that has already featured so much of Radiohead's music.

Elsewhere on NBC, the action-comedy spy series *Chuck* featured "Codex" in a pivotal sequence on May 2, 2011. Since *The King of Limbs* had only been released not even three months earlier, *Chuck* earned the distinction of being the first TV show or movie to feature one of the album's songs.

Where *Community* used a Radiohead song to heighten the seriousness for laughs, *Chuck* plays "Codex" over a moment that's more earnest. Up until that point, the series' primary antagonist is the unseen Agent X, a ruthless arms dealer. But a will and series of photographs reveals that his true personality is that of a pacifistic scientist. Due to a botched intersect upload (it makes sense if you watch the show), he unwittingly has taken on a new, more villainous identity.

Don't get lost in the intrigue and spy jargon. The point is, over two-and-a-half minutes, the show's heroes discover that the menace they've been fighting is more a victim than a cartoon villain. It pivots the series into something more complicated and tender, and the contemplative piano of "Codex" amplifies the vulnerability.

A Radiohead song precedes a similar watershed moment in *How I Met Your Mother*. In the pre-credits sequence of the third-season episode "Miracles," protagonist Ted Mosby recalls a cab ride that changed his life. "(Nice Dream)" plays as he gets into a taxi, which soon gets T-boned and prompts his friends to all drop what they're doing and run to the hospital.

The sequence plays in slow motion, and Ted's friends begin receiving the phone calls in tandem with the lyric "I call up my friend," giving the entire sequence a reflective, dreamlike quality. It plays nicely to the show's themes of looking back on one's life, and how small choices can have big consequences for the future. Even when the show undercuts the sequence's lucid tone by cutting off the music and revealing that Ted's injuries are only minor, the whole ordeal does lead to him proposing to his girlfriend, who recently broke up with him.

HBO Series

We've talked about many shows on network television, with NBC most inclined toward using Radiohead in its programming. But cable giant HBO deserves a section all to itself. Beginning with a 2002 episode of the prison drama *Oz*, which plays "I Might Be Wrong" over a flashback where a prisoner accidentally shoots someone, HBO has consistently turned to the band's music.

Most interesting of all, the songs have almost always been used during the final scenes of episodes. The notable exceptions are *Oz*; *Girls*, which, in its final season, played Skeye's straightforward cover of "Karma Police" on a car radio; and *Westworld*, which has included four Radiohead songs on its soundtrack so far.

After "I Might Be Wrong" on *Oz*, *The Sopranos* featured Radiohead a few months later in September for its fourth-season episode "No Show." In the final scene, Tony and Carmela Soprano discuss the troubles of their daughter, Meadow. She has gradually started to resent her father's criminal activity, as her boyfriend got entangled with the mob and ended up getting killed.

The camera cuts to black while Tony and Carmela fret silently in their bathroom. After a few moments of silence, "Kid A" kicks in. Some fans have speculated that the song was chosen for its title—a large part of the episode centers around Tony and Carmela's oldest child or "kid." Or it could just be that the music supervisor or even series creator David Chase, who played a huge role in the soundtrack choices throughout the series, found the song's ponderous vibe to fit in with the episode's final scene, a moment where Tony and Carmela are left without resolution regarding someone they love.

Six Feet Under continued the HBO Radiohead trend in 2004 with the fourth-season episode "Parallel Play." This time, the song in question ("Lucky") starts before the credits, played in real time on a stereo by Claire Fisher as her family starts a bonfire to burn items from their past. Once the credits roll, the volume rises, taking "Lucky" from the background to the forefront and upping the level of catharsis. Netflix's *Ozark* would adopt HBO's pattern of playing Radiohead over the credits with its first episode, which ended with spooky usage of "Decks Dark."

Entourage's use of "Fake Plastic Trees" in the final scene of season five's "Gotta Look Up to Get Down" is meant to be just as emotionally hefty as *Six Feet Under*, but comes off as goofy. Some of the cheese can be attributed to the overall nature of the show—the "bromance" between actor Vincent Chase, his cutthroat manager Ari Gold, and his sleazy group of friends has never been all that likable, as much as the series wants it to be.

But the scene's laughability also comes from the song selection ("Fake Plastic Trees" remains the most uninspired choice of Radiohead song when aiming to tug at the heartstrings) and the episode's storyline. The big emotional dilemma comes at the airport, when Ari reveals to Vincent that he's been offered a job as head of Warner Bros. That means he won't be individually repping Vincent's career anymore, a decision that leaves both of them emotionally conflicted.

The problem is, Ari's dilemma isn't in line with the shark-like persona of his character. Even if he and Vincent are in a bromance, Ari could help him even more as the head of a powerful studio (something he points out in the scene), and it's hard to believe that he would even consider passing up such a great opportunity when Vincent's career is in as bad a place as it was in *Entourage*'s fifth season. Still, both men depart on a bittersweet note, even as Vincent's private jet is filled with booze, his best friends, and a cadre of models. That brings the softer side of the episode and the use of "Fake Plastic Trees" to the edge of parody.

The next HBO show to use a Radiohead song was *The Newsroom*, and its results are equally as mixed as *Entourage*. In the series' second episode, another heart-on-its-sleeve hit from *The Bends*, "High and Dry," plays as series protagonist Will McAvoy gazes out over the Statue of Liberty. Not only has he just been asked to be the "moral center" of the newsroom at a once politically moderate cable news network—he also donated to the cause of an illegal immigrant whose livelihood is under attack. When the writer of his blog asks him on the phone if he should publish Will's good deed online, Will tells him no, as it would be vain and put the attention on him. With the idealistic chords of "High and Dry" playing over the scene, it becomes even more of a humblebrag, fulfilling the accusations of self-congratulation that dogged *The Newsroom* throughout its three-season run.

Prestige Films

By the time the early 2000s rolled around, filmmakers had gotten more creative in their use of Radiohead songs, partly thanks to the band's rise in stature. If a director in the mid-'90s wanted to feature "Creep" as background music or to reflect a character's angst, it wasn't all that noteworthy. At that point, Radiohead was just another post-grunge imitator whose music would get the job done.

But by 2001, the first year since the release of *OK Computer* that one of Radiohead's songs would be used in a feature film, filmmakers often recognized that including a Radiohead song in a movie was a big deal and should be treated as such. If a director or music supervisor was lucky enough to get the rights to one of the band's compositions, they better use it well, or at least dramatically. Not all of the following films are all that imaginative or subtle in their use of Radiohead's music, but they at least go for broke.

The first feature film to use a Radiohead song in the post-*OK Computer* era was 2001's *Life as a House*. The script centers on George Monroe, an architectural model fabricator who wants to reconnect with his rebellious teenage son, Sam, after getting diagnosed with terminal cancer. All goes well until, about three-quarters of the way through the film, George reveals his illness. Sam flips out, accuses his father of being selfish, and runs to the home of his eventual love interest, Alyssa, falling into her arms and bursting into tears.

The film is as over the top and weepy as it sounds, so it's understandable why the entire sequence is scored by "How to Disappear Completely." Though heralded as a masterpiece by many Radiohead fans and music critics, it's still the most obvious, self-pitying, and uninteresting song on *Kid A*—perfect for *Life as a House*'s construction-site level of bluntness. *The Bang Bang Club* and *And They Lived Happily Ever After* were equally as literal when including Radiohead on their soundtracks, using the crescendo of "Just" to intensify a sex scene in a radio DJ's booth and "Creep" at a CD listening station, respectively.

Vanilla Sky used a *Kid A* track in a much more abstract, impressionistic fashion. "Everything In Its Right Place" plays in the opening few minutes of the film, before we even know what its emotional palette is going to be. After a few soaring shots of Manhattan from above, interrupted by frames of blackness, the camera takes us into an apartment at the Dakota, where we meet David Aames. He's about to embark on a strange journey that blurs the line between constructed dreams and brutal reality; between romance and murder; love and hate.

He doesn't know yet that his life will soon spiral into a weird and unpredictable mix of science fiction and romantic drama. If "Everything In Its Right Place" is announcing anything in *Vanilla Sky*, it's a sense of mystery. Director Cameron Crowe would also use an *Amnesiac* track later on in the film in a more straightforward manner, playing "You Might Be Wrong" in the background during a bar scene to convey tension.

The little-seen 2009 film *Veronika Decides to Die* also features "Everything In Its Right Place" early on to score an attempted suicide. But in a smart twist, it's actually a live version from *I Might Be Wrong: Live Recordings*. There's cheering at the beginning, followed by an enthusiastic audience clapping along to the opening organ line, as if egging on Veronika to go through with it. Like "Exit Music (For a Film)" in *My Mad Fat Diary*, it turns the usual suicide scene on its head. Veronika's journey only gets further disrupted when the pills she takes don't end up killing her right away, but leaving her susceptible to a brain aneurysm that could kill her in a few weeks. It's hard to know whether to laugh or cry, and the crowd going apeshit over the music certainly doesn't help.

Choke's use of "Reckoner" traffics in a similar emotional ambiguity, Sure, it plays over the final scene and credits, where protagonist Victor Mancini and would-be love interest Paige finally share an elongated, passionate kiss. The problem is, Victor's a sex addict and Paige is a mental patient—they met because she posed as a doctor for Victor's dying mother. Their kiss could be redemptive for both of them, or it could be damning, rapidly sending them both down a tragic, codependent path. Since "Reckoner" doesn't clearly broadcast its emotions, it offers no easy answers. It only reinforces the characters' uncertain future together.

Of all the filmmakers in this subchapter, Dennis Villeneuve has been the most thoughtful and inventive in his use of Radiohead. He establishes *Incendies'* entire narrative lens by playing "You and Whose Army?" over a scene of Arab boys getting their heads shaved and becoming militarized. Even though the sequence centers around an unnamed civil war in the Middle East, Villeneuve told *SBS* that he used a British band to establish that this story would be from a westerner's point of view; it would be fiction. Because the lyrics themselves are still military-oriented, it almost fetishizes a conflict taking thousands and thousands miles away.

Villeneuve intentionally clashes the two cultures again later on when the opening drone of "Like Spinning Plates" takes us into a wartorn environment. Perhaps as a nod to *Incendies* (or maybe because he just really likes Radiohead), he used "Codex" in his later 2013 film *Prisoners*—not to begin the movie as in *Incendies*, but to end it. Right before the final scene, it briefly plays on a radio.

Science Fiction

After *OK Computer*, Radiohead became a band forever tied to the science-fiction genre. It was only a matter of time before their music would be included in sci-fi TV shows and films.

2005's made-for-TV adaptation of Warren Ellis's comic book *Global Frequency* was the first bona fide work of sci-fi to feature a Radiohead song ("There there"), but *A Scanner Darkly* was the first to get any kind of significant attention. Richard Linklater's film was based on the novel of the same name by Philip K. Dick, a writer whose work already shared similar themes with *OK Computer*. In the future of *A Scanner Darkly*, the United States is facing a crippling drug epidemic, which has led the government to monitor citizens via an intrusive surveillance system and a shadow network of undercover police.

Outside of "Reckoner" Linklater pulls from fairly obscure Radiohead songs, several of which rely on ambience more than an overt meaning from the lyrics. "The Amazing Sounds of Orgy," "Pulk/Pull Revolving Doors," and Four Tet's remix of "Scatterbrain" are more about contributing to the atmosphere than tying directly to the meaning of the film (although the songs' themes are certainly in its wheelhouse). Linklater also uses "Fog" and and even plays Yorke's solo composition "Black Swan" over the credits.

Together, the considerable number of Radiohead songs form a sort of mini-suite for *A Scanner Darkly*, weaving in and out of the trippy narrative to highlight its mood and rotoscoped world-building. Apparently, an early test screening featured only Radiohead songs—further proof that Linklater, like Cameron Crowe before him, viewed the band's music more as a score than a soundtrack.

Composer Ramin Djawadi took this conceit even further in 2016 for HBO's update of Michael Crichton's 1973 film *Westworld*. In the first season alone, Djawadi created one new version each for "Fake Plastic Trees" and "Exit Music (For a Film)," and two new versions of "No Surprises." And that's in addition to featuring Vitamin String Quartet's tear-jerking cover of "Motion Picture Soundtrack."

Most of the covers created specifically for *Westworld* are performed on player piano to keep with the show's setting. In the series, guests enter an old-West theme park, where they interact with automatons that allow them to indulge in the sex and violence of the frontier days, apparently without consequence. Of course, everything goes wrong.

On the surface, Djawadi's Radiohead covers are fascinating because of the arrangements. The band's music begs to be tinkered with in the most futuristic sense, meaning that many of the covers rely on modern technology or elaborating on what's already there. *Westworld*, on the other hand, is all about simplification. If a viewer isn't already familiar with the band's music, they might not realize they're hearing Radiohead at all. The player-piano covers are right at home in an old-timey saloon, underscoring the archetypal card-playing cowboys and swinging doors.

But as Djawadi pointed out in a November 8, 2016 interview with *Pitchfork*, the Radiohead covers *do* reveal an eerie future when considering how they're used in the show.

"You see the settings and the way people are dressed and even though you know it's robots and it's all made to be modern entertainment, you would think the people in control would make everything authentic, including whatever is played on that player piano," he said. "It would be from that time period. And when it's not, it's that subtle reminder that, 'Wait, there is something not right. This is not real.'"

One of *Westworld*'s contemporaries, the historical crime drama *Peaky Blinders*, uses Radiohead's music to similar juxtapositional effect. In its third series, three songs from *Amnesiac*—"You and Whose Army?", "I Might Be Wrong," and "Life In a Glasshouse"—score theft, murder, and general mayhem in London in the early 20th century. By using a contemporary soundtrack in a period piece, the show highlights how prevalent crime still is today.

Not every work of sci-fi to use Radiohead has been as comprehensive as *A Scanner Darkly* and *Westworld*. Several films and television shows have used just one of the band's songs to equally memorable effect. The *Black Mirror* episode "Shut Up and Dance" shows a man returning home after completing several horrible tasks to avoid being blackmailed, all to the tune of "Exit Music (For a Film)." *Children of Men* softly plays "Life In a Glasshouse" in the background during a scene that precedes an act of government violence, its soft-loud structure mimicking what's about to happen on-screen.

Elsewhere, "Paranoid Android" plays over the end credits of the anime *Ergo Proxy*, "I Might Be Wrong" scores a brief shootout in a season-three episode of CBS' sci-fi crime drama *Person of Interest*, and *Nip/Tuck*, while not a science-fiction show in the traditional sense, uses Radiohead in what feels like a sequence straight from a sci-fi film. The title of "Everything In Its Right Place" takes a gruesome meeting as two surgeons perform an autopsy on a dead woman stitched together with parts from other women.

"The Daily Mail" soundtracked a pivotal scene in FX's science-fiction series *Legion*.   *Author's collection*

Most recently, FX's *Legion*—equal parts X-Universe yarn and psychological thriller—used almost all of "The Daily Mail" to soundtrack one of the show's most chilling sequences. Everything moves in gentle slow motion for the song's first half as a psychiatric therapist drives to a government facility for studying mutants. The song's explosive shift happens when she and several others reach the facility to discover that the mutant of the title has incinerated everyone there.

It feels appropriate to end this subchapter with talking about 2014's *I Origins*, as it was the first feature film to include the aptly titled "Motion Picture Soundtrack" on its motion picture soundtrack. The song gets used twice in two different ways. First, the acoustic version syncs up with a pivotal death. In the film's final sequence, as the protagonist walks toward a moment of likely resurrection of a loved one, the full song—complete with choir and Busby Berkeley strings and Yorke's "little tweety angels"—takes us into the credits. The whole affair of course comes with a dose of irony, as "Motion Picture Soundtrack" seems to be about someone dying, not coming back to life.

Horror/Thriller

The darkness of much of Radiohead's music seems prime for use in the horror genre. But only a handful of horror movies and television shows have featured their songs. And even those have been slight. A&E's contemporary *Psycho* prequel, *Bates Motel*, has used two Radiohead songs, but only as background music. In the first episode, "The Tourist" plays faintly at a teenage party scene, and "Bodysnatchers" plays on a truck radio as a character gets pulled over in season two.

But both of those instances at least trump Radiohead's appearance in the film adaptation of *Twilight*, the most famous example of a horror movie to use the band's music. Then again, to call it a horror movie is being generous. Stephenie Meyer's YA series is more steeped in a hoky, antiquated outlook on romance where most of its characters happen to be vampires.

The series' first film ends with romantic leads Bella and Edward dancing at the school prom. Bella wants Edward to make him a vampire like him, a request that he refuses. Deciding to accept their human-vampire romance as is, they continue to dance blissfully, unaware that their enemy, the vampire Victoria, is watching from afar. As she descends a staircase, silently plotting her revenge on them, "15 Step" takes us into the credits.

Despite the timeliness of the song (*Twilight* hit theaters on November 21, 2008, a little over a year after the release of *In Rainbows*), there's nothing menacing about "15 Step." It's one of the warmest and dance-inducing songs in Radiohead's discography, which might work if *Twilight* was aiming for ambiguity or disorientation, as many of the other films in this chapter have.

But the *Twilight* series only knows tonal straightforwardness. It flat-out tells the audience when it's supposed to be funny, when it's supposed to be touching, when it's supposed to be sad. And when we're told the final moment of the film is meant to foreshadow the danger to come, playing a groove-laden track like "15 Step" only adds confusion. A menacing Radiohead song such as "I Might Be Wrong" or "Climbing Up the Walls" would have worked better.

Documentaries

It's unclear what exact considerations the members of Radiohead take when allowing a filmmaker to use one of their songs. After all, they denied Cameron Crowe use of "True Love Waits" (then just a live recording) for *Vanilla Sky* while still allowing him to use two other tracks. Who knows why?

But let's say the band has thoroughly discussed every single project where someone wanted to feature their music. That's probably not the case, but let's just pretend it is. If so, then it's no surprise that they granted unprecedented use of their songs to *The Island President*. Released in 2011, the documentary follows Mohamed Nasheed, then-President of the Republic of Maldives, a South Asian island country whose entire existence is threatened by climate change. The film follows his efforts to be heard in the climate change debate, in hopes of preventing his country from being overtaken by the ocean.

Thom Yorke—a prominent voice in the fight against climate change—announced on Radiohead's Dead Air Space blog that the band would be granting a staggering number of songs from their back catalog to the film. In the end, 14 tracks were used. Unsurprisingly, most of the songs came from *Kid A*, the album of Radiohead's that most often gets associated with an uncertain future.

Radiohead continued their environmental licensing in 2017 with the release of BBC's nature documentary *Planet Earth: Blue Planet II*. For both the teaser and the opening of the show, the band collaborated with composer Hans Zimmer to record a new, orchestral version of "Bloom," retitled "(Ocean) Bloom." In the reworked song, Yorke's voice has more room to breathe when backed by elated strings rather than a frenetic dance beat. And whether because of age or an increased worry over the planet, his vocals are infused with more wear and anxiety.

The teaser alone functions as a new Radiohead video, the lyrics about sea turtles and jellyfish seemingly custom-made for a documentary about the ocean. With these visuals, the word "bloom" has a double meaning that may not be immediately apparent on record—not just applicable to plant life, but the aliveness of creatures big and small. Whether it's a killer whale lunging at the camera or a sea anemone stretching out its venomous tendrils, the ocean, as seen by the creators of *Blue Planet*, seems to be in constant bloom.

Original Songs

"Spectre"

While more and more filmmakers seem to feature Radiohead's music in their work every year, the band has only written original music for a film together twice. And neither time resulted in the typical soundtrack experience.

First, Baz Luhrmann commissioned Radiohead to write something for his film version of *Romeo + Juliet*. After watching the final half hour of the movie, Radiohead came away with "Exit Music (For a Film)." Although they permitted Luhrmann to play it over the credits, they requested that it not be included on the actual soundtrack album, as *OK Computer* wouldn't come out until the following year. In its place on the soundtrack (and featured on a lonely beach scene in the movie) was "Talk Show Host," a B-side from "Street Spirit (Fade Out)."

"Spectre" had an even more unpredictable arc, although this time, it was the filmmakers who ended up not wanting to include the song on the soundtrack—not the band. In 2015, Radiohead was commissioned to write the theme song for the new James Bond film. The band already had a long-running relationship with the series, having covered Carly Simon's "Nobody Does It Better," which served as the theme for 1977's *The Spy Who Loved Me*, then writing their own Bond-theme homage, "Man of War," during the *OK Computer* sessions. Later on, Colin Greenwood even compared "Sail to the Moon" (from 2003's *Hail to the Thief*) to the theme from *Moonraker*.

For the new film, titled *Spectre*, the band first submitted the then-unreleased "Man of War," but the producers rejected it on the grounds that it wasn't written specifically for the movie. So Radiohead came back with a whole new composition.

With strings that perpetually swoop like seabirds diving for fish, it's easy to see how "Spectre" could have fit in over the opening of the 25th James Bond film. Over three minutes, we get a kaleidoscopic credits sequence with all the Bond staples—slow-motion flames, silhouettes of curvaceous women, and even some trippier additions such as octopus tentacles reaching out toward Daniel Craig making out with the latest Bond girl.

But the film's production team deemed the song too melancholy, which is strange since they ended up going with a Sam Smith composition that embodied all the loneliness of "Spectre," but with more obvious lyrics and orchestration that bordered on treacly.

10

"I've Got 99 Anthems"

Radiohead in Hip-Hop

When shattering the "music to cut your wrists to" stereotype surrounding Radiohead, it's important to talk about the band's relationship with hip-hop, a genre that's the often seen as the opposite of sad bastardism. Since 1996, rappers, producers, and DJs have reinvented the band's music, sometimes sampling the already existing songs and occasionally collaborating with the band members themselves for new, original compositions.

Jaydiohead

Scour any Radiohead subreddit and *Jaydiohead* often gets praised as the high-water mark of the intersection of Radiohead and hip-hop.

Released on January 1, 2009—with a second *Encore* disc on July 12 of that year—the mashup was the brainchild of Max Tannone (alias Minty Fresh Beats), who blended the music of Radiohead and Jay-Z. In the vein of Danger Mouse's *The Grey Album*—which combined the Beatles' "White Album" with Jay-Z's lyrics from *The Black Album* Tannone pulled from Jay-Z's a cappella tracks for *The Black Album* and *American Gangster* for the vocals (plus one song from *The Blueprint*) and various Radiohead songs from throughout their career for the instrumentation.

But *Jaydiohead* stands apart from *The Grey Album* for its deliberate simplicity. Where Danger Mouse would pull from up to three Beatles songs per track, then break down their most minute elements and repeat them—sometimes to the point of being unrecognizable—Tannone stuck to a strict one-song-per-artist regiment.

"When I was listening to *The Grey Album*, the beats were super chopped up," Tannone tells me over the phone. "I really enjoyed it, but it was so dissected. When I made my album, I knew that people were going to compare the two, so I thought about making it more like a DJ mix, but with additional production. It's also a lot different than a Girl Talk type of remix that draws from dozens and dozens of different samples."

In the continued interest of staying true to the source material, even when adding his own embellishments, Tannone gave himself the parameter of never altering the beats per minute (BPM) for either artist's music. So when

Album art for Max Tannone's Radiohead/Jay-Z mashup *Jaydiohead*.   *Max Tannone*

starting with a particular a cappella Jay-Z song, he would comb through Radiohead's catalog (which, in 2009, included everything through *In Rainbows*) to find something that would match the tempo. Naturally, the band's later, more groove-oriented work proved to be the best fit. Of the two discs' 15 songs, only one, "Song and Cry," contains a sample from before *OK Computer*, combining *The Bends'* "High and Dry" with Jay-Z's "Song Cry."

Tannone affirms that the band's later work tends to be a better fit for hip-hop mashups.

"You're at the mercy of which a cappellas are available for the lyrical side, the spoken-word voice side," he says. "There's only a certain range of BPMs that you can use on either end, plus or minus of what the original vocal BPM is. So already, you've pruned a lot of the catalog. It's about which songs have open musical sections that can be looped. Do you want one with acoustic guitar or do you want one with these crazy drums and weird synthesizer sounds?"

When I ask him if there were any Radiohead songs that he wanted to make work, but couldn't, Tannone laughs and replies "Idioteque," which is a surprise since it's Radiohead's danciest song.

"It's just so fast," Tannone says. "It's like 150 BPMs, somewhere around there. So you would need a rap song that's at that speed. I chopped that song up so many ways and tried to make it sound cool, but it just wasn't working."

The songs that did make the cut burst with carefully controlled kinetic energy. Jay-Z's verses from "99 Problems" add further defiance and scuzz to "The National Anthem" in "99 Anthems" (every song has a title that cleverly combines the names of its two source songs); in "Dirt off Your Android," the acoustic intro to "Paranoid Android" gets funkified with a wah-wah effect before Hova adds extra muscle to the chorus with his own refrain from "Dirt off Your Shoulder"; and on "Optimistic Moment," the dinosaurs on "Optimistic" stomp even louder thanks to an amplified snare drum and Jay's verses from "Moment of Clarity."

It's not just Radiohead's hits that get their due, either. Ever the studious fan, Tannone combines the *Hail to the Thief* B-side "Gagging Order" with Jay-Z's "Never Change" on "Change Order," and even closes the first disc with a mashup of a Thom Yorke solo song ("Black Swan") with Jay's "Ignorant Shit" on "Ignorant Swan."

In addition to garnering praise from various music publications and attention from pop-culture sites such as *The Daily Beast*, Tannone's project got the seal approval from Jay-Z himself, who tweeted "There are 3 or 4 REAL gems on jaydiohead…" on April 29, 2009.

"It was early on in the days of Twitter," Tannone says. "Someone told me had tweeted about it. I didn't even know he had Twitter. He literally had maybe two-dozen tweets or less, and there it was. I was like 'Whaaat?'"

Not long after that, Tannone serendipitously bumped into Jay-Z while walking through Soho.

"I introduced myself and was like, 'I'm the guy who made the *Jaydiohead* thing' and he totally knew what it was," he continues. "It was crazy. I told him I was a producer and he asked if I had a business card. I'm like 'Oh no, I don't carry business cards.' It was cool, though. Nothing ever happened after that, but in the 30 seconds I spoke with him, he was a nice guy."

Radiohead, on the other hand, have been more elusive. When I ask Tannone if they've heard *Jaydiohead*, he says he has no clue.

While *Jaydiohead* remains the longest and most substantial teamup of Radiohead and hip-hop music, there are plenty other briefer, more isolated instances. Here are some of the most notable in chronological order.

Chino XL—"Kreep"—1996

Bronx rapper Chino XL was the first hip-hop artist to sample Radiohead by a long shot, releasing "Kreep" as a single from his debut album, *Here to Save You All*, on July 22, 1996.

As the title suggests, Chino XL riffs on the song's mantra, combining elements from "Creep"'s verses and choruses for his own chorus. "I'm a kreep / I'm a loser / You're so very special / I wish I was special." According to the rapper, Yorke was a fan of the song and cleared his interpolation of the lyrics in just two days.

Outside of the borrowed lyrics, "Kreep" actually bears little resemblance to "Creep." The chord progression is completely different, and the backbone of the song doesn't come from a '90s alt-rock band, but a jazz duo and two heavier psychedelic-rock acts from the 1960s. The Brecker Brothers' "Levitate," Procul Harum's "Repent Walpurgis," and Iron Butterfly's epic "In-A-Gadda-Da-Vida" are all listed as being sampled by producer Eric Romero for the song's soap-opera arrangement. "Kreep" even contains another lyrical interpolation from the Stylistics.

Such a strange mashup of genres could get messy, but "Kreep" remains defiant and charismatically self-pitying throughout, much like the original song. Chino XL's work might hit even harder, thanks to its specificity. Where Yorke tends to remain vague about his problems, Chino XL describes all the ugly ins and outs of a broken relationship. It's admittedly misogynistic at times, although that unfortunately remains par for the course for hip-hop.

The Roots featuring Jack Davey—"Atonement"—2006

Many of the songs in this chapter make no attempt to hide that their Radiohead samples are samples. After all, sampling is a fundamental building block of hip-hop, and part of the fun is spotting when another recognizable song gets used.

The Roots are different. While they've occasionally turned to samples in their 30-plus years together as a group, they're also a full band that's eight members strong. That means that when they sample another song, it needs to fit in seamlessly with their live show. It needs to sound like just another instrument.

That's certainly the case with "Atonement," which samples the quiet guitar line of "You and Whose Army?" without ever turning to the song's distinct orchestral crescendo. The sample could have just as easily been played by Roots guitarist "Captain" Kirk Douglas. It almost lives in the background, overshadowed by Jack Davey's chorus and and Black Thought's verses about rising above the tragic fates that have fallen upon so many successful Black men before him. Only at the tail end when Yorke's echo-chamber wail plays separately from the other voices do we suspect that "Atonement" might be using a Radiohead sample.

And to think that the sample almost didn't get cleared by Radiohead at all.

"We toured with them in Europe when *Kid A* came out, and I felt my relationship was cool enough with Thom to ask if the Roots could have liberal use of 'You and Whose Army,'" drummer Questlove told *Spin* on November 9, 2011. "Of course, the label said no. The lawyers said no."

It was actually another iconic rapper—and one who would go on to have his own work merged with Radiohead on *Jaydiohead*—that stepped in on the Roots' behalf. "Jay-Z was still president of the label then," Questlove continued. "I was like, 'Can you get me on the phone with those guys in five minutes?' . . . Sure enough, in five minutes I was jogging on the treadmill talking to the Radiohead guys. Lawyers can't make it work, but Jay-Z can."

Blu—"Untitled(LovedU)2"—2006

Los Angeles rapper Blu's take on "You and Whose Army?" is the opposite of the Roots', the sample purposely left crackled and tinny enough to sound like Blu's listening to it on a boombox. He even sings along with Yorke on the opening "drive my crazy." He's not trying to seamlessly blend Radiohead with his own music—he's using it as a jumping-off point for his rhymes. It's a reminder that so many Radiohead fans grow to love the band by poring over the lyrics and singing along at home.

Plan B—"Missing Links"—2007

Plan B's mixtape *Paint It Blacker: The Bootleg Rapper* finds the London MC paying tribute to his musical heroes by listing them as collaborators. No, Leonard Cohen, Coldplay, and Rick Ross didn't actually contribute as guest artists—they're all just heavily sampled on their corresponding tracks.

That goes double for Thom Yorke, whose solo composition "Analyse" gets used on "Couldn't Get Along," in addition to "Pyramid Song"'s piano motif providing the main beat for "Missing Links." While Plan B's regretful lyrics about friends who have succumbed to drug addiction are a little on the nose, the Mingus-inspired chords add a sense of palpable grief, as if his dead mates are floating down the time-bending river Yorke sings about in the original.

Unfortunately, Plan B was denied clearance for the sample when he re-released "Missing Links" on his debut studio album, *Who Needs Actions When You Got Words*. Although the band hasn't given any specific reasons, it may have had something to do with the song choice. While Radiohead has granted fairly liberal use of many of their songs to hip-hop artists, they've always held "Pyramid Song" in particularly high regard. Much like Radiohead granted Cameron Crowe permission to use "Everything In Its Right Place" and "I Might Be Wrong" for *Vanilla Sky*, but not "True Love Waits," maybe "Pyramid Song" was too close to Radiohead's collective heart to give out freely.

There were no hard feelings on Plan B's part. He used an eerie original instrumental for the studio version of "Missing Links" and wished Radiohead well in a 2006 interview with *Gigwise*. "They don't owe me anything and I still think they're a great band."

Jak Progresso—"Bad Eden"—2008

It takes an astute hear to pinpoint the sample of Radiohead's "Lucky" in Jak Progresso's aggressive "Bad Eden." He didn't crib the central melody or any other immediately noticeable element, but the hi-hat and spacey, high-pitched whir that underscores the song. This makes it a slightly fascinating, if minor entry in the saga of Radiohead and hip-hop.

dan le sac vs Scroobius Pip—"Letter From God to Man"—2008

When sampling or reinterpreting a Radiohead song, many hip-hop artists depart from the original subject matter, repurposing it for lyrics that may be more personal for them. Literate British hip-hop duo dan le sac vs Scroobius Pip took the opposite approach with "Letter From God to Man," taking the big-picture themes of "Planet Telex" and blowing them wide open.

In the original, Yorke muses on general chaos—on the impossibility of controlling one's own life amidst cosmic and spiritual forces. The organ line, spaced-out effects, and Selway's constant swell of drums keep it from being morbid, and to be honest, Yorke's lyrics never got specific enough to drag the listener completely down in the dumps.

Beatmaker dan le sac ratchets up the playfulness, adding more space sounds and constantly interrupting the main riff with machine-gun bursts of sound. All the while, lyricist Scroobius Pip does away with Yorke's crypticism and writes a letter to the human race from God's point of view. By the end, the Creator has expressed how proud He is of humankind, while also insisting that it was never His intent for things to get so out of hand. It was never His intent for human beings' flaws to take over to the point where Mother Nature gets destroyed.

After hearing "Letter From God to Man," one can't help but apply its deeper meaning to "Planet Telex." It's that rare hip-hop sample that actually elevates the source material.

King Krule—"Flailing Out of Place"—2009

London's King Krule (birth name Archy Ivan Marshall) was only 15 when he recorded a monotone rap over Radiohead's "Jigsaw Falling Into Place." It's not that he does little to alter the original song (Blu did the same with more successful results)—he just doesn't have much to say and hasn't yet perfected his abilities. The mixing is off, the rapping is subpar in its clunky A-B-pause rhyme scheme, and he sounds hesitant in his deadpan demeanor. Maybe he'll take a stab at Radiohead again, now that he's older, wiser, and more confident.

Joe Budden—"Never Again"—2009

The most interesting thing "Never Again" has going for it is an added guitar solo to "Street Spirit (Fade Out)." Outside of that, Joe Budden's rhymes never get past his mid-level bark and usual braggadocio style.

People Under the Stairs—"All Good Things"—2009

"Reckoner" remains one of the most emotionally complicated songs of Radiohead's canon, impossible to peg as a moment of romantic despair or undying love. Maybe it's this flexibility that has made it such a heavily sampled song among hip-hop and electronic artists. The fact that Radiohead released the stem tracks for remix purposes doesn't hurt, either.

Keeping with their frequent throwbacks to Golden Age hip hop, Los Angeles duo People Under the Stairs transforms the song into something that's unquestionably uplifting. Selway's clattering percussion remains, but the Frusciante-inspired guitar riff gets scrapped, replaced with a more hopeful, major-scale progression. It syncs up perfectly with the string sequence at the end of the song, actually making the Millenia Ensemble sound optimistic as well, despite no alterations to their notes. The tonal shift also suits the People's lyrics, which center on enduring hardship to find a successful career in music.

Lupe Fiasco—"National Anthem"—2009

If a rapper's going to borrow from a band as iconic as Radiohead, it's usually best for them to make some alterations. Unless they're Lupe Fiasco.

The politically radical Chicago MC is acrobatic enough to play an unchanged version of "The National Anthem" and give it a brand-new identity. He doesn't have to slow down the toothy bass line. He doesn't have to lower the volume of the horns. He doesn't have to drown out the ondes Martenot. Instead, he defiantly spits fire through it all, skirting around jaw-dropping metaphors and reclaiming the battle rap as a bona fide art form.

Rather than stay on any one subject in particular, he tears up everything from lesser MCs to the commercialization of rap, a failing education system, the AIDS epidemic, and more. And for his beat, all he had to do was press play on track three of *Kid A*.

Frank Ocean—"Bitches Talkin' (Metal Gear Solid)"—2011

Frank Ocean has always bucked the conventions of hip-hop. He started out as a member of Odd Future Wolf Gang Kill Them All, the rap collective who garnered controversy for lyrics often criticized for being violent, misogynistic, and homophobic. Ocean usually took on a more sensitive R&B role within the group, but still participated in some of the more unsavory lyrical content with songs such as Tyler, The Creator's "Fish."

In 2012, Ocean turned the rap world on its head when he revealed that he was in love with a man when he was 19. Although he refuses to label his sexuality, he put accusations that he was anything but sexually progressive to bed.

Even before then, Ocean seemed aware of being somewhat of an anomaly in the hip-hop and R&B world, as indicated by the "Bitches Talkin' (Metal Gear Solid)" sketch on his debut mixtape, *Nostalgia, Ultra*. Its 22 seconds mostly consist of Ocean playing "Optimistic" in the background, all while two women he's hanging out with complain about the music.

"What is a Radiohead anyway?" one of them whines, prompting Ocean to complain that all the women ever want to listen to is R&B quartet Jodeci. Slight and humorous, the skit once again confirms Ocean as an artist who goes against what's usually expected of him. It also foreshadowed his heartbreaking cover of "Fake Plastic Trees," which he performed at New York's Cedar Lake Contemporary Ballet during a Spotify press conference on December 6, 2012. And in 2016, Ocean's love of Radiohead came full circle when Jonny Greenwood contributed strings to his visual album *Endless* and "Seigfried" off of his studio album *Blonde*.

Cevlade—"Fade Out"—2011

Cevlade is one of the few—and maybe the only—rappers to take on a Radiohead song in a language other than the band's own. The Chilean rapper spits in Spanish over a beefed-up sample of "Street Spirit (Fade Out)," his calm, voiceover tone racing to keep up with the amplified drums and sped-up guitar. Cevlade deserves further props for sticking with older—and thus more difficult—Radiohead material.

Lloyd Banks—"Cold Corner 2 (Eyes Wide)"—2011

Maryland-born, Queens-raised rapper Lloyd Banks has built his career on a love-hate relationship with New York City. This extends to his lyrics as well as his album titles and artwork. For instance, the cover of his second record depicts him overlooking the skyline through a glass window. It's a nod to the movie poster for *King of New York* and fictional crime lord Frank White, played by Christopher Walken.

But the album is called *Rotten Apple*, an affirmation that powerful men in the city—White, Banks, whoever—achieve their control through dangerous means. Just look at the bullet scars in Banks' back and abdomen—received the night before 9/11, no less—for proof.

The second installment of Banks' *Cold Corner* mixtape series once again flips NYC's iconography on its head. Over 17 tracks, Banks growls and gets short of breath as he spits hardened tales of street life. He more than earns the rather blunt album cover—an image of the Statue of Liberty crying in the middle of a snowy winter.

On the title track, Banks and producer Nick Speed draw urban menace from the chord progression of Radiohead's "Climbing Up the Walls." The sampling itself is fairly straightforward, the familiar Bm, G, Em sequence repeating over and over. But Speed raises the volume on Selway's snare until the tightened pitch becomes almost grating, and that's the point. The listener can feel Banks's struggle. They can feel his shortness of breath.

DOOM and Thom Yorke with Jonny Greenwood— "RETARDED FREN"—2011

Radiohead's relationship with hip-hop goes both ways. Rappers and producers don't just sample the band's music; sometimes, the band members themselves become their collaborators.

Since 2009 (and possibly before) Thom Yorke has had a working relationship with the late idiosyncratic rapper Daniel Dumile, a.k.a. DOOM (formerly MF DOOM). Their music may seem vastly different on the surface, but when one considers DOOM's love of cryptic non-sequiturs, science fiction, and multiple aliases, it seems that he and Radiohead have similar interests.

In 2009, Yorke remixed DOOM's "Gazillion Ear" and would release yet another remix of the same song in 2016. But the pair's most fascinating collaboration occurred in 2011, when they enlisted Jonny Greenwood for a brand-new song. It would appear as the seventh track on *Complex Vol. 1*, a tenth-anniversary compilation for DOOM's label, Lex Records. It hasn't been confirmed who did what on the song, but it's likely that Yorke handled the muted synths, surges of white noise, and clattering percussion (the arrangement could have easily been a *King of Limbs* outtake) and Greenwood took care of the cinematic strings, which infiltrate the song shortly before the two-minute mark.

DOOM, of course, penned the lyrics, which he would also use for a track of the same name (but with a different beat) on his 2012 collaboration with JJ Doom, *Keys to the Kuffs*. "No question / an ounce of prevention / is more than a pound raw, cure, pure intention / Attention! / No throwing stones at the homeless"

Sounds like a Radiohead song.

Quakers—"Fitta Happier"—2012

Portishead and Radiohead have a lot in common. Both bands are English, have an interest in trip hop music, have featured Clive Deamer on drums, and have the word "head" in their name. To benefit the Mary Hare School for the deaf, Portishead's multi-instrumentalist Geoff Barrow and Phil Selway even played on the same charity soccer team in 2016, the cheekily named United Heads.

So when Barrow formed the hip-hop supergroup Quakers in 2012 with fellow producers 7-Stu-7 and Katalyst, it was only natural to sample Radiohead on their debut album. At 41 tracks spread out over nearly 70 minutes, there was plenty of room.

They actually ended up referencing two Radiohead songs in one track, "Fitta Happier." In the intro, a crowd chants the slogan "Fitter, happier, more productive," before a full brass band blasts out an explosive version of "The National Anthem." At that point, it doesn't really matter what guest MCs Guilty Simpson and MED are rapping about—the power is already there.

Roman GianArthur—*OK Lady* (2015)

Though not as epic in scope as *Jaydiohead*, Roman GianArthur's six-track mashup of D'Angelo and Radiohead is just as innovative.

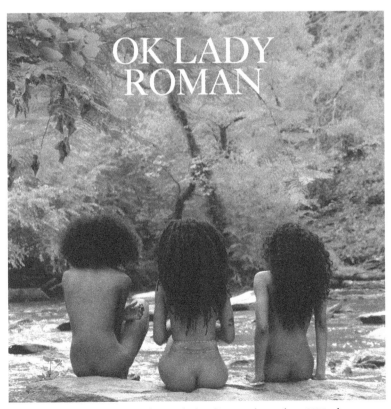

Album art for Roman GianArtuhr's Radiohead/D'Angelo mashup *OK Lady*.
Photo by Spencer Charles, art direction by Joshua R. Dean

Because the R&B wunderkind handles most of the vocals himself and doesn't put any restrictions on what material to draw from, he keeps the musicality seductively fluid. On opener "ALL:NEED," GianArthur amplifies the instrumental of "All I Need" with a deeper drum beat, mixes in some funk guitar from D'Angelo, then sings the lyrics of his hit "Lady" for the verses before going to "All I Need"'s lyrics for the chorus. "NO SURPR:SES" flips the formula with a pristine guest vocal from Janelle Monáe that adheres to a neo-soul cover of "No Surprises." Halfway through, the song eases into a riff on D'Angelo's easy-going "Greatdayndarmornin' / Booty."

Monae would go on to sample the first five seconds of "Climbing Up the Walls" as a loop for one of her own songs, 2018's "Don't Judge Me." It appeared on her third album *Dirty Computer*, which obviously shares half a title with Radiohead's third album. On top of that, Monae has a career-long fascination with science fiction and androids, showing that, despite having vastly different sounds, she and Radiohead have a lot in common.

D.R.A.M.—"Everything In Its Right Place"—2016

On July 29, 2016, Radiohead continued their tour for *A Moon Shaped Pool* with a stop at Chicago's Lollapalooza festival. The band's fans weren't just in the audience.

When teddy-bear rapper and R&B crooner Shelley (then D.R.A.M.) took the smaller Pepsi Stage two days later, he expressed regret at not being able to catch Radiohead's set.

"I wish I could've seen those motherfuckers!" he exclaimed, then launched into a minimalist cover of "Everything In Its Right Place." Although brief, he laced the song with a number of vocal improvisations, moving up and down the scale and adding a bit of soul to what's usually a chilly track, even by Radiohead standards.

Shelley hasn't recorded a proper version of "Everything In Its Right Place" (yet), but his impromptu live performance further supported how beloved Radiohead's music is in the hip-hop community.

11

"I'll Laugh Until My Head Comes Off"

The Comedy of Radiohead

We should never forget that Radiohead named their first album after a Jerky Boys skit.

On the opening track of the prank-callers' second album, *Jerky Boys 2*, Kamal Ahmed calls up an unsuspecting victim named Pablo. "Pablo, honey?" he asks, drawing from his family's heritage and putting on his thickest, most stereotypical Bangladeshi accent. Pretending to be the mother of the man on the other end, he asks the poor guy to come to Florida before checking if he's been washing his ass regularly. It goes on for about 40 seconds before Pablo hangs up.

"Pablo Honey" isn't highbrow comedy. It isn't even the best Jerky Boys sketch. But for one reason or another, it resonated with the members of Radiohead, who liked the phrasing and the skit's title enough to use it for their own full-length debut. Yes, Radiohead have been self-serious at times. But to say that's all there is to them and their music is flat-out incorrect.

Since *Pablo Honey*, the band has dabbled in comedy themselves from time to time (most notably during their webcasts), and for all the seriousness of their music, it's inspired some humorous material from other artists both amateur and professional.

Richard Cheese—"Creep" (2001/2006) and "Airbag" (2010)

For almost 20 years, Richard Cheese has followed the path of a more niche "Weird Al" Yankovic, dressing up popular songs in a retro-lounge style.

It's not just a matter of adding standup bass and horns. In fact, his 2001 debut, *Lounge Against the Machine* was made on the cheap, with all of the big-band arrangements synthesized instead of played by numerous musicians. To make up for the lack of grandeur, Cheese leaned hard into his martini-swiveling persona on "Creep," alternating between crooning "you're so fucking special" and "you're so freakin'" special while peppering in some inside jokes for Radiohead fans. "I was talking with my honey the other day—my Pablo Honey," he says in the beginning. A command of "OK, computer" kicks off the barreling piano, and the song ends with him belting a verse from "Fitter Happier."

"Creep" would get a more fully realized big-band version on 2006's *The Sunny Side of the Moon: The Best of Richard Cheese*, although it lacks some of the puckish quirks of the original. Cheese dabbled in Radiohead again with the title and artwork of 2010's *OK Bartender*, which opened with an equally swinging cover of "Airbag." Its definitive version? The live take that appeared earlier on 2009's *Viva la Vodka: Richard Cheese Live*—complete with lengthy banter and an actual audience, many of whom appreciate Radiohead as much as Cheese does.

South Park—"Scott Tenorman Must Die" (2001)

To date, Radiohead have played themselves on a fictional television show just once: an episode of *South Park* from 20 years ago. Their role is actually quite small and insubstantial for musicians of their stature, which only adds to the comedy; a big and serious rock band who could just as easily have been edited out with no one noticing.

In the fourth-season episode "Scott Tenorman Must Die," Eric Cartman gets tormented by an older bully named Scott Tenorman, who convinces him to buy his pubic hair. Cartman's plans for revenge become increasingly elaborate and more effective, culminating in a move borrowed from *Titus Andronicus* where he gets Scott's parents killed by a gun-happy farmer, cooks them into chili, and tricks Scott into eating them.

Radiohead functions as the cherry on top in Cartman's "li'ol scheme" of revenge. Since they're Scott's favorite band, Cartman convinces them to fly to the States by lying that Scott has cancer. Radiohead arrive to grant the supposed victim his dying wish of meeting them in person, only to see him sobbing over his dead parents. In just a few lines, the band chastises Scott for crying. Thom Yorke's line, "You know, everyone has problems. It doesn't mean you have to be a little cry-baby about it," is especially rich, as he's received so many similar criticisms himself. The dialogue works as a self-aware wink at the audience.

In an April 12, 2010 interview with *Pitchfork*, *South Park* co-creator Matt Stone revealed that he couldn't remember exactly how he and his partner Trey Parker got Radiohead to agree to be on the show, considering they rarely make those kinds of cameos or do anything they don't want to.

But it happened, and the production was almost as funny as the episode. While Yorke was recording his lines, Stone had to get him to exaggerate more, as is the norm with cartoons.

"I'm like, 'OK, say this line,' and he starts to talk," remembered Stone. "And I kind of had to say, 'No, man, you need to, like, really *emote*.' It's such a funny line to give some guy who's such a brilliant singer and who's so brilliant at emoting perfectly, exactly, in such a complex and beautiful way. I'm just trying to get him to do this dumb line, and I have to say, 'Hey man, you've got to put some *feeling* into it!'"

Hard 'n Phirm—"Rodeohead" (2005)

Long before *The Nerdist Podcast* and *Talking Dead*, host Chris Hardwick was exploring the realm of pop culture in his comedy with Hard 'n Phirm, a musical duo with fellow UCLA alum Mike Phirman. They only released one album together, 2005's *Horses and Grasses*, which was anchored by a bluegrass medley of Radiohead songs called "Rodeohead."

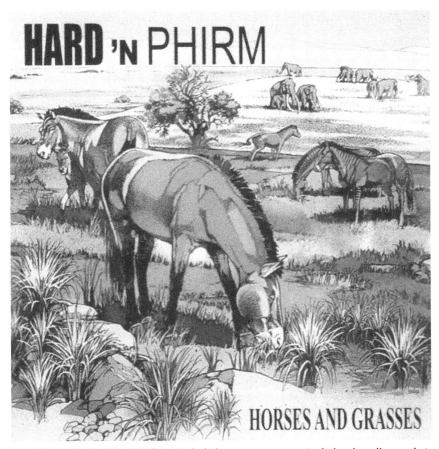

Musical comedy duo Hard 'n Phirm included a country-western Radiohead medley on their debut album.   *Author's collection*

Similar to "Weird Al" Yankovic's polka medleys—but with the accordion switched out for banjo, fiddle, and standup bass—the song moves through snippets of 16 different Radiohead songs, touching on every album from *Pablo Honey* through *Hail to the Thief*.

"Rodeohead" isn't as funny as it is impressive in its fluidity and genre transformation. The transitions between songs are seamless, despite many of them being in different keys. Foley effects such as whip cracks and train whistles add to the fun, and many of the lyrics actually work well as unironic country music. "We rise tonight, we ride tonight" from "You and Whose Army?" conjures the image of a posse galloping on horseback across the desert, ready to take down an evil sheriff. Maybe Radiohead's songs should be used in more Western movies.

Thom Yorke "photobombing" (2007)

Thom Yorke has come a long way since *Meeting People Is Easy*. In Grant Gee's alienating cinéma vérité documentary, the Radiohead frontman went out of his way to avoid crowds, often hopping on subway cars and hiding so he could be alone.

Thom Yorke's 2007 "photobombing" at the Louvre.
Photo by Taylor Holland

By 2007, he had sorted out some of the more crippling aspects of his agoraphobia—not only did he peruse the Louvre with the rest of the museum's attendees; he even photobombed one of them. Taylor Holland was posing for a picture of his wife in front of Paolo Veronese's *The Wedding Feast at Cana*, the painting directly across from the *Mona Lisa*. Little did he know that Yorke was behind Elli, seemingly flexing his arms and putting on a snooty face, as if some kind of military leader in the middle of a self portrait. He's also holding a leather jacket at his side, which, at first glance, makes it look like he's wearing a kilt.

The photobomb didn't end up going viral until three years later, and quickly inspired photoshoppers to pull some pranks of their own. They began madly altering the photo, with one fan inserting several Thom Yorkes into the image.

When asked about the photobomb during a Reddit AMA on February 18, 2013, Yorke kept the joke going. "That is not me," he insisted. "This is madam Tussauds. misspelt probably." But there's more to the story. Over email, Holland tells me that Yorke's photobomb wasn't actually a photobomb at all.

"In October 2007, I intentionally took a photo of my wife with him in the background because we're huge Radiohead fans, and this was literally right after *In Rainbows* came out," Holland writes. "While I was shooting rapid frames, [Yorke] happened to turn around, making it appear as if he were looking in the camera. So, in the most literal sense, he didn't actually photobomb anyone. It was just a manifestation of internet insanity. I love that he knows about it."

In Rainbows Webcasts (2007)

Some of Radiohead's most brilliant bits of comedy can be found in their 2004 "TV series" (later compiled into a single DVD) *The Most Gigantic Lying Mouth of All Time*. But its aesthetic of nonstop chaos isn't always easy to sit through, causing many of the jokes to get lost in disruption and information overload.

It turns out, Radiohead's comedy is best paired with high-quality performances, as indicated by *Entangled* and *Thumbs Down*—two webcasts released in the month following *In Rainbows*. Where *Lying Mouth* had only a handful of full songs, *Entangled* and *Thumbs Down* overflow with laid-back rehearsal-room renditions of most of the tracks from *In Rainbows*, as well as a pitch-perfect cover of the Smiths' "The Headmaster Ritual." The performances serve as the anchor for both webcasts, balanced out by the moments of humor. Just when you're ready for another song or another joke, one always seems to come along.

The most memorable moment comes in *Thumbs Down* when, out of nowhere, we're in the disturbing climax of the film *Seven*. Morgan Freeman approaches a cardboard box, which, in the movie, contains Gwyneth Paltrow's severed head. Only when he opens it, he finds the head of Thom Yorke, singing

"15 Step" with his most deadpan expression. The webcasts also premiered the first music video from *In Rainbows*, "Jigsaw Falling Into Place"—a slice of audio-visual comedy in its own right.

On New Year's Eve, Radiohead released a more structured webcast titled *Scotch Mist—A Film With Radiohead In It*. Although there are a handful of humorous moments (most notably the premiere of the amusing slow-motion video for "Nude"), the focus has a noticeable shift toward the performances, which cover every single song from *In Rainbows*. Some of the takes are absolutely gorgeous, such as an "All I Need" where Jonny Greenwood pulls double duty on glockenspiel and Fender Rhodes piano, and an outdoor performance of "Faust Arp" where Yorke and Jonny run up a hill at sunset, then launch into the song.

Scotch Mist was also released with a jabbing statement at their former label, where Yorke insulted EMI chairman Guy Hands and professed a sardonic kind of joy at finally being able to do whatever the hell he and his bandmates wanted. The *In Rainbows* webcasts were clearly products of that freedom.

Conan O'Brien—"Creep" (2010)

Surprisingly, "Weird Al" Yankovic has yet to churn out any humorous covers or parodies of Radiohead songs. And even if he did, it would be hard to top Conan O'Brien's take on "Creep" during his Legally Prohibited From Being Funny On Television Tour.

At a soundcheck in Eugene Oregon on April 12, 2010, a fan captured footage of the late-night host singing the Radiohead hit with an over-the-top Cockney accent. He even added his own lyrics about chimbley sweeps.

O'Brien eventually cut a high-quality version of "Creep," along with several other comedic covers, while performing live at Jack White's Third Man Records on June 10. Radiohead themselves stopped by White's studio in 2012, but Ed O'Brien has insisted to *BBC Radio Music 6* that, despite getting along well with White, the sessions wouldn't be released anytime soon and aren't worth waiting for. Maybe he's just upset that another O'Brien recorded a Radiohead song at Third Man before the band did.

"Dancing Thom Yorke" (2011)

Call it the music video that launched a thousand gifs. One of Radiohead's simpler cinematic experiments, "Lotus Flower" features Thom Yorke executing his most spastic, improvised dance moves for the camera.

Some of them are funny enough on their own, such as when he makes a disco karate stance or puts his hands in his pockets, then walks around and grimaces like Charlie Chaplin's Little Tramp, black fedora and all. As Yorke told the audience during Radiohead's gig at New York City's Roseland Ballroom on September 28, 2011, he relished getting to show his "embarrassing dad" side.

But the comedy really took off when, soon after the video's release on February 16, 2011, fans all over the internet started messing with it. Some would put another song over the choreography, such as Beyoncé's "Single Ladies" or Ginuwine's "Pony." Since Yorke isn't following any kind of strict rhythm, it works with just about any piece of music. Other amateur editors would insert outside objects or people into the video. For instance, one YouTube user placed a dancing Spider-Man alongside Yorke, while another added digitized guns to his hands.

But the most popular riff to come out of the "Lotus Flower" video was the Dancing Thom Yorke gif. When taken out of context, a few seconds of Yorke busting his moves can be used for any number of gif-related purposes. Want to express excitement? Just send a gif of the 90-second mark, where Yorke rises up from the ground and flails his arms.

BBC Comedy—"Radiohead Fan Speaks Out" (2011)

Some Radiohead fans are serious to the point where they can't even get along with other people who love Radiohead, heatedly arguing over the best live performance of a song or whether *Kid A* or *OK Computer* is the superior album. BBC Comedy effectively skewered this infighting on March 11, 2011 in an online sketch.

The King of Limbs hadn't even been out a month, and fans were already polarized by its seeming lack of structure and traditional melody. In the BBC sketch, their inner crisis manifests itself in a Radiohead support group. Modeled after Alcoholics Anonymous, it centers on a man who's ashamed to admit he doesn't like *The King of Limbs* all that much. The rest of the group agrees with him, but their enthusiasm begins to taper off as he reveals his negative feelings toward everything from *Kid A* onward.

Their support turns to full-on disgust when he describes *OK Computer* as overrated when compared to *The Bends*. "Get out," growls someone in the circle. The man exits to the lonely tune of "Creep."

In just two-and-a-half minutes, BBC Comedy captures the warring factions of the Radiohead fanbase. Tellingly, the comments section of the sketch's YouTube link is a battleground of fans arguing over their own personal album rankings. Even when presented with their own combativeness, it seems some fans just can't control themselves.

Consequence of Sound—Radioheadz (2016)

The BBC Comedy sketch should have told us that Radiohead fans can't always take a joke. But that didn't stop myself and three other writers at *Consequence of Sound*—Editor-In-Chief Michael Roffman, Senior Writer Randall Colburn, and Senior Writer Justin Gerber (with the occasional appearance from Justin's brother McKenzie)—from starting our own humorous Radiohead podcast in 2016.

The gimmick was simple: Since *CoS* was always getting flak for fawning over Radiohead, we would present the world with "The No. 1 Radiohead Podcast" that, in actuality, was packed with false facts, shoddy recording quality, and us badly impersonating celebrities talking about their experiences with the band. In our minds, the key to its brilliance was marketing it as a serious podcast. Choice bits included *The Bends* being inspired by the band's love of scuba-diving in the Caribbean and Roffman impersonating KISS' Gene Simmons, who,

Consequence of Sound's Radioheadz podcast was a joke that backfired.

Image by Michael Roffman

in our mythology, had developed a grudge against Radiohead after meeting them backstage at a festival.

The problem is, as a legitimate music site, most listeners didn't get that we were joking, and immediately went off on us in the comments section of the first episode, pointing out that no, Clive Deamer wasn't Radiohead's full-time drummer, and criticizing us for going on an especially long tangent about *The Godfather* series.

In what was admittedly a troll move on our parts, we only leaned further into the absurdity in the following episodes, including a "live" broadcast from Lollapalooza where we recorded parts of M83's set and passed it off as Radiohead's. After that fourth episode, we realized that we were alienating *CoS*' readership more than entertaining them, and decided to call it a day.

As fun as it was, we now recognize that *Radioheadz* was more of an inside joke than a universally appealing bit of comedy. And it probably would have been smarter to market it as humorous from the start (better audio quality wouldn't have hurt, either).

At the same time, we stand by the fact that the podcast reflected a huge flaw in many Radiohead fans: They're so serious about their love of the band's music, they can't fathom that someone would even *think* to make fun of it or their fandom.

"Meet the Real World Coming Out of Your Shell"

Hail to the Thief

In 2003, the distorted rising action of *Hail to the Thief*'s opener, "2 + 2 = 5," was enough to convince any Radiohead fan that the band had made a triumphant return to straightforward rock music. But it was only a half-truth.

It's true that Radiohead wished to return to the more live sound of *OK Computer* and *The Bends*—a departure from the tinker-and-smash collage approach to *Kid A* and *Amnesiac*. The idea came from Ed O'Brien, who suggested that, at the end of a six-month, post-*Amnesiac* break for the band (following an October 4, 2001 show in Yokohama, Japan, they didn't regroup until April 2002), Thom Yorke would present whatever song ideas he had been working on to everyone else. As a unit, they would painstakingly rehearse his demos at the Courtyard Studio complex in Sutton Courtenay before road-testing the songs that showed the most potential on a short summer tour.

True to his word, Yorke emerged from hibernation with three CDs of demos. Titled *The Gloaming*, *Episcoval*, and *Hold Your Prize*, they were a throwback to the *OK Computer* days, when he would present his bandmates with demos on various cassette tapes. After rehearsing his latest batch of material, Radiohead embarked on a five-city tour of Portugal and Spain, playing 12 dates on the Iberian Peninsula from July 22 to July 31, 2002. During this stretch, they performed 11 of the 14 songs that would go on to appear on *Hail to the Thief*'s final track listing (the only omissions being "Backdrifts" and "The Gloaming").

Another indicator of a more live direction for *Hail to the Thief* was the liner notes. As fans saw when the album came out on June 9, 2003, Radiohead had finally returned to listing who played what. Not that it meant Radiohead had completely abandoned the electronic elements they had been exploring over the past three or so years. In fact, much of *Hail to the Thief*'s fun comes from its thumping backbeat. "Backdrifts," "The Gloaming," and "Where I End and You Begin" all fall into the dance-like-it's-the-apocalypse subgenre.

Yorke described the compromise rock-meets-electronica (not to mention a few curious curveballs) as such to MTV in June 2003, shortly after *Hail to the*

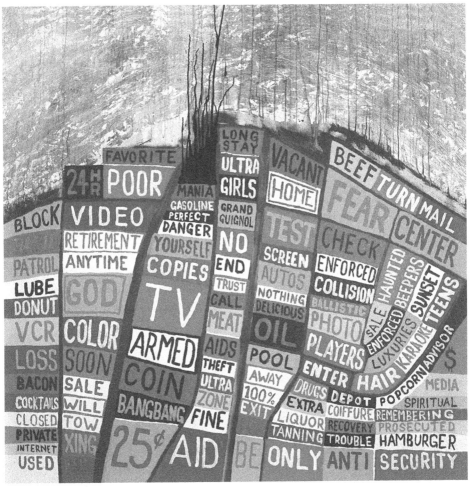

Album art for Hail to the Thief.   *Author's collection*

Thief's release: "This time, we used computers, but they had to actually be in the room with all the gear. So everything was about performance, like staging a play."

More specifically, a children's play. Radiohead began recording *Hail to the Thief* the year after Yorke's son, Noah, was born. Despite not setting out to write anything with any specific political agenda (isn't that always the case with Radiohead albums?), Yorke found himself troubled by raising his son amidst the administration of George W. Bush, the War on Terror, and his own sense of existential dread. Although Yorke is British, he still felt the sting of Bush's ascent to power overseas, the fact that, in his eyes, "the most powerful country on earth is run by somebody who stole an election," as he told *Fast Forward* on July 10, 2003.

God knows what the album would have sounded like if written during the Trump administration.

The birth of Noah didn't just influence *Hail to the Thief*'s subject matter, but the often crass way in which it was presented. Despite the complex—if often visceral—musicality, the lyrics owe a lot to children's literature and television. Well-known phrases repeat; each track contains a sing-songy, sometimes nonsensical subtitle reminiscent of a fairytale (a device lifted from music-hall programs in Victorian England); and images of wolves, rabbits, and other animals populate the song titles and lyrics.

When *Hail to the Thief* was released, it was easy to see this approach to politics as sophomoric. From the title to the direct lyrics to Stanley Donwood's congested grid on the album's cover that practically screams words like "TV," "Oil," and "Fear," there's nothing subtle or even complicated about the LP's themes and stance. The band even recorded in Los Angeles for the first time, the Hollywood setting of Ocean Way Recording surrounding them on all sides with American consumerism and greed.

Granted, producer Nigel Godrich enforced a change of place mainly as a means of efficiency, prompting Radiohead to record the bulk of *Hail to the Thief* over just two weeks in September 2002 before they finalized the album back at Canned Applause that winter. But there's no denying the creative osmosis

Radiohead recorded most of *Hail to the Thief* in Studio B of Ocean Way Recording.

Photo by Allen Sides, courtesy of Ocean Way Recording

that came into play when working in Tinseltown. On one hand, the breezy L.A. weather and strolls through the hills surrounding the Griffith Observatory made for a relaxed and productive recording process. On the other hand, celebrity culture and parties attended by the band no doubt reflected the anxiety of the lyrics.

Radiohead leaned into their proximity to showbiz for the album's release by plastering "talent management" posters all over Los Angeles and London in April 2003. The posters used lyrics from "We suck Young Blood" and encouraged people to call a phone number that led them to the *Hail to the Thief* customer care hotline," which, in the tradition of "Fitter Happier," spat nonsense: "Hungry? Press 2." "For information about sucking young blood, press 4 now." The right combination of buttons could bring listeners to snippets of songs from the album.

Blunt as *Hail to the Thief* may be, isn't that how most of us consume show business and politics? Isn't that how most of us form our political opinions? While the album may not be the cleanest, insightful, or most complicated Radiohead work in terms of ethos, it's the most accurate in how it portrays the fear of the average person. And yet it still manages to land on the more energized side of the Radiohead spectrum thanks to its partial return to the live-sounding record. Having fun in the face of dread is part of being a responsible citizen, too.

The Songs

"2 + 2 = 5" (The Lukewarm.)

The phrase "2 + 2 = 5" was of course popularized in George Orwell's *1984*. While glaringly incorrect as an equation, it represents total control of the totalitarian "Party" in the novel. Once someone believes that 2 + 2 does indeed equal 5 and not 4, they have thrown logic out the window. They have given themselves to the Party and no longer have to accept fact—just whatever ideology the Party wants them to believe.

If the lyrics matched the music, the narrator would lash out against this belief once the guitars kick in with full distortion and "2 + 2 = 5" goes from a nervous experiment to a full-on rock song. But in a cruel twist of fate, this is when the narrator gives in. In the previous verse, he laments how there's "no way out" from the totalitarian regime, then begins chastising anyone opposing today's rulers for not "paying attention." By the end, he's dogmatically screaming the album's title over and over, showing that he's fully submitted. Yorke also cites—and subverts—his first nursery rhyme with the Chicken Little nod "Go and tell the king that the sky is falling in."

The subtitle "(The Lukewarm.)" also comes from another piece of apocalyptic literature, Dante's *Inferno*. Yorke had become increasingly familiar with the poet's work due to his partner, Rachel Owen, studying his *Divine Comedy* for her PhD.

As stated by Yorke, "The Lukewarm" is a reference to "the people who don't give a fuck … The lukewarm are on the edge of the Inferno, cruising around near the gates but they can't actually get out." This could easily apply to "2 + 2 = 5"'s protagonist, who knows they should fight for their freedom, but doesn't have the bravery to actually do it.

And yet, it's easy for none of that to matter to an old-school Radiohead fan who prefers *Pablo Honey* and *The Bends* to the band's later work. Literary references aside, "2 + 2 = 5" is easily the album's biggest rocker, going as far to start with the sound of Jonny Greenwood plugging in his guitar and Yorke telling him "That's a nice way to start" (the song was the very first thing recorded at Ocean Way).

Fans who could do without the more experimental side of Radiohead probably thought the same thing in the opening minutes of *Hail to the Thief* (this likely helped propel "2 + 2 = 5" to #15 on the UK singles chart as the album's third single), even though the album would buck against the straightforward rock aesthetic just one track later.

"Sit down. Stand up." (Snakes & Ladders.)

"Sit down. Stand up" is notable for predating Thom Yorke's writing period of *Hail to the Thief*. While the song was by no means fully formed on Radiohead's 1998 tour, Yorke can be heard plunking out the melody of the title phrase on a QY70 sequencer in the documentary *Meeting People is Easy*.

Initially influenced by the Rwandan genocide of 1994, the lyrics could just have easily applied to the Iraq War in 2003, or any military conflict, really. Most of the song consists of the title phrase, mixed with the further command of "Walk into the jaws of Hell" (yet another shade of Dante). The other repeated standout phrase is "The rain drops," which Yorke has confessed to having no significant meaning that he's aware of. So maybe it came from his subconscious, as it could easily apply to missiles falling out of the sky on unsuspecting civilians.

Like "2 + 2 = 5," "Sit down. Stand up" relies on the device of crescendo, its Mingus-inspired piano riff gradually getting interrupted by blips and Jonny Greenwood's bass synthesizer until everything explodes into a flurry of space-battle effects.

"Sit down. Stand up" also shares "2 + 2 = 5"'s conceit of a character resigned to their role in an Orwellian government. They know they're marching into the gates of Hell. They know they're eroding their own morality by being asked to kill. And yet they never question it. It's a reversal of Bob Marley and the Wailers' similarly titled "Get Up, Stand Up"—protest music in which the main character never actually protests.

The subtitle "Snakes & Ladders." didn't start out as loaded as "The Lukewarm." or some of the other parentheticals on the album, but took on a deeper meaning as the Iraq conflict progressed.

"That was one of the titles for the record that kept running around, but didn't make it," Yorke told XFM in spring 2003. "When I sing it, though, I always think of the 'We can wipe you out anytime' line. And they've developed that missile now that they can just launch, and target it on the strength of your mobile signal. Then they wipe someone out on that."

"Sail to the Moon." (Brush the Cobwebs out of the Sky.)

"Sail to the Moon" began as a lullaby for Yorke's infant son, Noah. Of course, this being Radiohead's most politically bleak and direct album, it was impossible from some doom and gloom not to creep into the lyrics.

Over a gentle piano that gradually reduces by two beats with each phrase, a duo of brief verses recount Yorke's ambitions getting too big, causing him to fall from the night sky. He holds out more hope for Noah, though—perhaps he'll be a morally just and kind president or live up to his Biblical namesake by building an ark to save humankind. The words are both soothing in their optimism and unnerving in their dread. Both feelings are unavoidable when becoming a parent, even in the best of worldly circumstances. In keeping with this paradox, Yorke has called the song both fatalistic and optimistic in interviews.

As for the subtitle, Yorke has claimed he can't remember exactly where the rather lovely phrase "Brush the Cobwebs out of the Sky" came from, although he told XFM it may have been from BBC's 1974's children's series, *Bagpuss*.

On *Bagpuss*, the old cat of the title would come alive inside a little girl's shop and tell various stories. Similar to the fairytale element of *Hail to the Thief*, the series' 13 episodes were a huge inspiration on the album, their colorful and dreamlike storytelling contributing phrases and tonal color to the music and lyrics. *Bagpuss* was also a favorite of children in Britain, meaning Yorke has most likely showed it to his own child. Naturally, Radiohead made sure to thank Oliver Postgate, the show's co-creator, composer, narrator, and voice of Bagpuss himself, in *Hail to the Thief*'s liner notes.

For the record, Yorke was right about "Sail to the Moon"'s subtitle coming directly from the show. In the 12th episode, "Flying," the mice in the shop sing about an old woman who lives "17 times as high as the moon," where she brushes the cobwebs out of the sky.

"Backdrifts." (Honeymoon Is Over.)

A cousin to "The Gloaming," "Backdrifts" is all chilly electronica, its earliest skeleton sketched out by Yorke on QY70 sequencer in 1998. The Greenwood brothers then expanded it as a rhythm track in early 2000, a time that Colin described as successfully figuring out "how to make all the boxes and machines talk to each other."

Although "Backdrifts" was instrumental in figuring out the aesthetic for *Kid A* and *Amnesiac*, it wouldn't be completed until the early part of *Hail to the Thief* sessions. By that time, Yorke had dreamed up some panicked lyrics inspired by the band getting caught in a snowdrift while on a bullet train in Japan.

"The snow was piled high on the branches, and then a bullet train would go past, and the snow would drop off the branch," he recalled to *NME* on May 10, 2003. "The whole world was utterly blanketed except for these straggly bits of black and white." He had earlier referred to "Backdrifts" as being "the slide backwards that's happening everywhere you look."

Once the song made its way onto *Hail to the Thief*, that feeling had taken on greater meaning, not just being about snow, but being caught in a world that's becoming more destructive and chaotic. That vagueness makes "Backdrifts" far from an essential track on *Hail to the Thief*, as other songs capture this sentiment more interestingly and effectively. The same goes for the musicality. Phil Selway's spliced-up drums and Jonny's reverse-recorded guitars are neat tricks that complement the song's themes, and yet at the same time, "Backdrifts" never really goes anywhere. It just lives in the same spaced-out zone, coasting by on vibe alone. Yorke himself even omitted it from the alternate track listing for *Hail to the Thief* that he posted on Radiohead's w.a.s.t.e. site in 2008.

The band hasn't made any official comments on the subtitle, but it's easy to imagine "Honeymoon is Over." being a direct reference to the return of right-wing politics in the White House, once Bill Clinton's two terms had ended with the election of George W. Bush. Or maybe there's a couple on their honeymoon somewhere in Japan, only to have their good time ruined by an oncoming snowstorm . . .

"Go to Sleep." (Little Man being Erased.)

Both Godrich and the members of Radiohead have admitted to putting together the tracklist of *Hail to the Thief* in somewhat of a hurry, causing the final product to suffer from bloat. So it's unlikely that there's any bigger game or theme at play with the sequencing.

That being said, there is a strange—and entirely subjective—coincidence within the tracklist. After "2 + 2 = 5," every fourth song falls into what one might call "traditional Radiohead." That is, Radiohead the Rock Band. In other words,

"2 + 2 = 5" (track 1), "Go to Sleep" (track 5), "There there" (track 9), and "Scatter-brain" (track 13), would have all fit in on a pre-*Kid A* album.

Of all those, "Go to Sleep" embodies the loud/soft dynamics heard primarily on *Pablo Honey* and *The Bends*. The first half embodies what Colin has referred to as an "early Garfunkel" kind of shuffle. The groove builds at the minute-and-a-half mark before Jonny pulls a "Creep"/"My Iron Lung" with a sequence of serrated guitar notes. Although it initially started out as him improvising—somewhat clumsily, by the band's own admission—he eventually played it through a digital Max/MSP, computer software typically used by electronic artists. On record, it still has a live feel, but has been carefully rearranged and manipulated to match up with the focused acoustic strumming.

Lyrically, Yorke scribbled down some nonsense words in a hurry, then ended up changing some of them each time the band performed the song live before recording the final version. Although he initially hated the randomness of imagery that includes monsters and pretty horses, he grew to appreciate the lack of agenda.

"They're involuntary, there was no mandate, no trying to make a statement, but obviously somewhere in the back of my head, it was happening," Yorke revealed to *NME* on May 3, 2003.

This ties back to *Hail to the Thief*'s central idea of viewing dread and political malaise through the eyes of layman; the eyes of children; the eyes of anyone who's not a politician; the eyes of most people on the planet. "Go to Sleep" isn't about capturing a specific ideology, but how it feels to be caught up in the madness. This, along with the return-to-rock approach, had a similar effect as "2 + 2 = 5" in regards to its commercial performance, helping it reach #2 on the UK singles chart and #32 on the US *Billboard* Modern Rock Tracks chart as *Hail to the Thief*'s second single.

As for the "little man" of the title, Yorke confirmed to XFM in spring 2003 that it was a callback to an animation sequence by Donwood. The full phrase, "Little Man Being Erased," was also considered as a possible album title. With all that in mind, it's easy to imagine which "little man" in American politics Yorke was fantasizing about scrubbing from the history books.

"Where I End and You Begin." (The Sky Is Falling in.)

Whenever Thom Yorke mentions a *Hail to the Thief* song written years earlier on his QY70 sequencer, he regards it with disposability. Take "Where I End and You Begin."

"I wrote the initial idea for it on that in this desert, and then just finished it in the studio, in my very rough and ready studio," he recalled on *Hail to the Thief*'s promotional interview CD. "And then we had it kicking around and didn't know what to do with it for ages."

He goes on to describe how Selway's drums made it worth recording. Shortly after, Colin remembers how the song's slippery bass line was Yorke's, not his, and compares it to New Order.

And that's about all there is to say about "Where I End and You Begin." Catchy, but far from essential, it consists of recycled parts, even in the lyrics. Yorke has copped to using the "dinosaurs roamed the Earth" imagery before, as well as the song's preoccupation with cannibals. It's hard to get excited about a song the band can barely get excited about themselves. And yes, the subtitle once again comes from Chicken Little, a fable already referenced in *Hail to the Thief*'s opening track (more recycling).

"We suck Young Blood." (Your Time Is up.)

Vampirism is an apt and oft-used metaphor for show business, but Radiohead take it somewhere different by dressing it up in a New Orleans funeral on "We suck young Blood." A successor to "Life in a Glasshouse" by way of Anne Rice, the band was inspired to write it after film director Paul Thomas Anderson visited the studio with a camera from the 1920s.

"It was exactly the same camera model, that they shot the original *Nosferatu* on," Yorke said on the *Hail to the Thief* interview CD. "This camera is basically just a box and you wind it. And you have to have a sort of tempo to wind it to. And if you wind it fast or slow, you get this extraordinary movement. And we wanted to shoot this sort of really over the top, vaudeville sort of b-movie thing with it."

The band's cinematic aspirations influenced the woozy pacing of "We suck Young Blood." Drunken clapping drives the majority of its runtime, then gets overtaken by a clatter of sped-up piano halfway through before the sluggish pacing returns, as if the bloodsuckers of the title have massacred a roomful of debutantes and are now the trodding back to their tombs before sunrise.

Although "We suck Young Blood" is by far the most gimmicky of *Hail to the Thief*'s songs, it's also the most unique—a Halloween trick that's enjoyable, if only for the novelty. Anyone who thinks the song is deeper than its obvious metaphor and joke-shop spookiness should read Yorke's explanation of the subtitle: "I think it's called 'Your Time Is Up.' simply to take the piss out of the fact that we're basically old gits now and that we need to suck young blood to keep young!"

Clearly getting a kick out of the ridiculousness of the song, the band sold t-shirts with some of "We suck Young Blood"'s lyrics written in antiquated font on their online w.a.s.t.e. store. Posed as questions, the phrases read like old-timey sales pitches: "Hungry? Sick? Begging for a break?"

"The Gloaming." (Softly Open our Mouths in the Cold.)

"The Gloaming" is purely a victim of sequencing. It comes right after "We suck Young Blood," another song built from a relatively slow pace and surface-level spookiness. This time around, the atmosphere is more electronic, rising from mechanized white noise and spellotape. A low bass hum from Colin rattles throughout, keeping the sonics at the bottom of a swamp. And like "We suck Young Blood," the title metaphor is obvious—an outdated word for "twilight" that represents, in Yorke's words to XFM in spring 2003, "the rise of fascism." Maybe the subtitle represents the change in temperature after the new regime has taken over.

It's worth noting that, in Yorke's alternate track listing for *Hail to the Thief*, "The Gloaming" serves as the second track, sandwiched between the muscular krautrock of "There there" and the nocturnal majesty of "Sail to the Moon." Each of these songs has a completely different tone, making for an opening triptych that thrives on variation.

But in the original track listing, the back-to-back placement of "We suck Young Blood" and "The Gloaming" cause the middle of *Hail to the Thief* to sag. "We suck Young Blood" is the easier listen only because it comes first.

"There there." (The Boney King of Nowhere.)

Given the tone of most of *Hail to the Thief*, it would make sense for the title "There there" to be meant sarcastically. But as Radiohead have noted in interviews, the song is a consistent source of comfort.

Even if Colin's low-high bass notes tingle with unease, Selway's bottom-heavy drumbeat locks into a trance-like groove that gets tripled when O'Brien and Jonny each hop on their own set of toms when playing the song live. There's no proper chorus, the distortion keeps rising, and the song runs five minutes. But it's hard to stop listening.

It took Radiohead a few tries to nail the seamless momentum of "There there." A February 10, 2000 webcast finds Colin out of sync with Selway as they try to fit the song into a throwback arrangement that sounds more akin to *Pablo Honey* or *The Bends*—heavy on volume and with a straighter drumbeat that relies more on the snare. Yorke would cut the more offbeat, spacious arrangement as a demo, but an attempted recording in Los Angeles fell short as the band tried to capture a live-sounding version of the song, which they had been playing for months. It took going back to England in winter 2002 to get it right.

As is often the case with Radiohead's best songs, they've had a hard time pinpointing why.

"What I discovered, I think, in making this record is that along the way, things form themselves," Yorke explained on *Hail to the Thief*'s interview CD. He then recalls how he cried when Godrich played him the final mix. It would go on to be *Hail to the Thief*'s lead single and chart at #14 on the US *Billboard* Hot Modern Rock Tracks.

"There there"'s subtitle, "The Boney King of Nowhere," sounds like it comes from some nightmare realm. But it's another sincere homage to *Bagpuss* creator Oliver Postgate. In an animation sequence on the show, the titular monarch is so frail, he can't find a comfortable place to sit. His throne makes him cold, his bed gives him allergies, he can't keep himself in a hammock. Given the comforting tone of "There there," Radiohead likely sympathizes with him. For once on *Hail to the Thief*, they seem to have compassion for a hapless ruler.

"I will." (No man's Land.)

"I will" comes from the *OK Computer* era, its clean and gentle guitar tone reminiscent of "Lucky." The stripped-down allows the lyrics to shine, with Yorke matter-of-factly taking on the role of a man who brings his family into a bomb shelter. It's implied that he's going to mercy-kill them all, as to keep them from experiencing an atrocious war outside and the eventual desolate environment of the song's subtitle.

Yorke reportedly wrote the song as a response to the United States' obliteration of the Amiriyah bomb shelter in the Gulf War. 408 women and children had sought refuge in the shelter, and the damage was so horrific, hand imprints of the dead were visible on the wall.

Radiohead had experimented with several full-band arrangements during the *Kid A* sessions, many of which were described by O'Brien on his blog. They ultimately went with a quiet take mostly driven by guitar and two vocal lines—one tenor and one falsetto—on the final version, putting the words front and center for a direct and haunting message. Yorke has described "I will" as the angriest he's song he's ever written. And he barely had to raise his voice.

"A Punchup at a Wedding." (No no no no no no no no.)

Fascinating as it is musically, "A Punchup at a Wedding" loses some of its power after one discovers its somewhat petty origins. Yorke revealed on the *Hail to the Thief* interview CD that he wrote the song as a response to a bad review Radiohead got for their widely praised hometown show at Oxford on July 7, 2001. Ironically, the concert took place at South Park, a venue that shares its name with the show the band had guest starred on just four days earlier.

Yorke admitted that he doesn't deal well with negative press, and, in "A Punchup at a Wedding," he used the title as a metaphor for how he saw the review—the idea of a critic shitting on everyone's good time. He's never confirmed what exact review he's talking about, but fans have speculated it's either a lukewarm account from *The Telegraph*, or a *Guardian* article that unfavorably described Yorke as trying to imitate Freddie Mercury during a flamboyant performance of "Pyramid Song."

Now, as a critic, I'm somewhat predisposed to scoff at "Punchup"'s subject matter. At the end of the day, Yorke has led an amazing life, and part of being a musician in the public eye is having people review your work. And despite what so many Radiohead fans believe, no band is beyond a healthy dose of criticism.

Then again, Yorke's not saying that critics *shouldn't* write about him and his bandmates; just that he has a hard time digesting the concept and the content. Maybe if the rest of *Hail to the Thief* wasn't so steeped in politics, "Punchup" wouldn't feel so out of place. It's a song where the lyrics *could* easily be about political discontent or the rise of a fascist. Maybe it would be more likable if Yorke had never revealed the meaning at all—and if the press wasn't already being framed as the enemy by so many people in power today.

Musically, though, it's hard to argue with the swinging rhythm piano—a first for Radiohead—charismatic sway, and the so-simple-it's-brilliant subtitle consisting of nothing but eight "no"s (42 get uttered in total during the song's intro).

"Myxomatosis." (Judge, Jury & Executioner.)

Outside of a handful of music dropouts—for a split second, everything goes away except for Yorke's vocals and Selway's drums—"Myxomatosis" stays stubbornly static throughout. Face it, the only thing anyone really remembers from the song are Jonny's keyboards, cranked up to the point where they take on the sound of Tubeway Army, or, as Yorke put it to *NME* on May 10, 2003, the "evil worm keyboard."

Luckily, that sonic touch is so immediately gripping that the lack of variety doesn't matter. This is Radiohead in full-force pummel mode, rattling the eardrums and never letting up.

The aural invasion is directly in line with the song's meaning and the absolute power conveyed by the subtitle. Though the word "myxomatosis" comes from a horrifying disease that afflicts rabbits, Yorke has repeatedly said the song is about "mind control," specifically as it relates to the global politics during *Hail to the Thief*'s recording. Because it's so hard to forget the aggressive keyboard riff, it feels like the song, like an oversaturated news cycle, is invading one's brain and altering the way it thinks.

Although no one from Radiohead has mentioned it in interviews, myxomatosis plays a significant role in Richard Adams' anthropomorphic rabbit odyssey, *Watership Down* (rather than refer to the ailment by its scientific name, the rabbits refer to it as "white blindness"). Given *Hail to the Thief*'s preoccupation with fairytales and children's entertainment (if the ultraviolent *Watership Down* can even be called a children's book at all), it's very possible that Adams' work could have been on Yorke's mind when piecing together the song's phrases over the years.

As for the subtitle, "Judge, Jury & Executioner" seems to fit with the theme of mind control, and would also be the name of the third single from Thom Yorke's supergroup, Atoms For Peace.

"Scatterbrain." (As Dead as Leaves.)

The members of Radiohead have spoken fondly about "Scatterbrain." But their reasons for loving it are the same reason others find it to be weak; minor, at best, when compared to much of the rest of *Hail to the Thief*.

O'Brien has praised the "warmth" of the instrumentation on the *Hail to the Thief* interview CD, how it sounds like *Talking Book*-era Stevie Wonder or "Sunday morning music." In the same segment, Jonny uses the adjective "floaty" and marvels at the song's inability to resolve. They're both right. The absence of synths does indeed give "Scatterbrain" a soulful warmth, and the lack of resolution creates a melody that's constantly in search of itself. And there's some tension to be had between the calmness of the arrangement and the furious weather hiding inside the lyrics and swirling dead leaves of the subtitle.

But where one listener sees all of that as a virtue, another sees it as the reason it's hard to remember what "Scatterbrain" actually sounds like. Among all the thunderstorms and alarming news headlines, some of us would prefer to stay inside and listen to *Talking Book*.

"Wolf at the Door." (It Girl. Rag Doll.)

How many great Radiohead songs can Yorke write from observing people he despises in social settings? According to an April 2004 *Rolling Stone* interview, he came up with "Wolf at the Door" while trying to find some peace and quiet on a train.

"But what I got was a bunch of rowdy, posh city boys, obviously rich as hell, who were going to some fucking stag party," Yorke said. "These guys had two crates of Stella, a ghettoblaster, and the guy who was getting married was dressed as Elvis. And for three hours, I sat there while they 'enjoyed' themselves. They were awful, aaaaaaahhhhh! And the whole lyric is just about my revenge on them."

It's a story similar to the genesis of "Paranoid Android," and like its predecessor, places grotesque, violent lyrics over music that's rather lovely in a macabre sort of way—driven by a synth line that would be at home in the Phantom of the Opera's pipe organ.

When taken in the greater context of *Hail to the Thief* as an album, however, "Wolf at the Door" becomes chilling. As much as Yorke fights against the slobs on the train—the entitled jerkoffs who will someday be running his town, his country, his continent, the world—he's forced to succumb to their every will. He's forced to watch him objectify others and himself until they're nothing more than the ragdolls of the subtitle. Because that's the way the world works. He's forced to cook. He's forced to clean. He's forced to get the flan in the face.

That last lyric is a reference to an act of real-life political protest on March 5, 2001, when a friend of Yorke's lobbed a custard pie at British Cabinet Minister, Clare Short, while she was promoting globalization in a lecture at Wales' Bangor University.

Yorke has obviously had a more fortunate life than the working-class people he sympathizes with in the song. But the point remains: the big eat the little and the worst people often take control. If all of *Hail to the Thief*'s earlier dark moments still had the surreal bent of a fairytale, "A Wolf at the Door" is a stark reminder that this isn't a storybook. The fairytale was just a device. The wolf was real, and he looks a lot like the asshole sitting next to you. And with the way Yorke breathlessly froths the lyrics—a technique inspired by a CD of ragga freestyling, as he told Q magazine in July 2003—one wonders if he's becoming an animal as well. A different wolf, but a wolf all the same. Wired to eat. Wired to kill. Wired to destroy.

Conclusion

Yet again, *Hail to the Thief* received all of the usual Radiohead anticipation and accolades: a leak of the unmastered tracks 10 weeks before the official release date; a "Best New Music" designation from *Pitchfork*; a Grammy nomination for Best Alternative Music Album (the fifth in a row for the band); a win for Godrich and engineer David Thorp for Best Engineered Non-Classical Album; Platinum certifications in the UK and Canada; Gold in Australia, France, and the United States.

The reviews were slightly higher than *Amnesiac*, with several critics indifferent toward the length and fairytale lens of the band's politics, if only slightly. Even the Dean of American Rock Critics and eternal Radiohead detractor, Robert Christgau, praised the band more so than usual, while still criticizing their pessimism in a column titled "No Hope Radio."

The criticisms of *Hail to the Thief*'s bleakness and bluntness seem moot these days. Though easier to parse out and more obvious than the ideologies flaunted on *OK Computer*, the fairytale/children's-literature lens could be switched out with a science-fiction one, and the album would still have more or less the same viewpoint. And considering who occupied the White House these last four years, that viewpoint isn't exactly irrelevant.

If there's one criticism that does hold up, however, it's the album's length. As early as 2006, Yorke admitted to the band having somewhat of a "meltdown" when putting together the final tracklist. Godrich echoed the sentiment on June 7, 2013 when he criticized the album to *NME* as having "too many songs."

As a mea culpa—or maybe just for shits and gigs—Yorke posted the following alternate 10-song tracklist for *Hail to the Thief* on Radiohead's w.a.s.t.e. site in 2008.

1. "There there"
2. "The Gloaming"
3. "Sail to the Moon"
4. "Sit down. Stand up"
5. "Go to Sleep"
6. "Where I End and You Begin"
7. "Scatterbrain"
8. "2 + 2 = 5"
9. "Myxomatosis"
10. "A Wolf at the Door"

At a lean 40 minutes, it's certainly more digestible than what was originally released, but the absence of weirdo genre experiments such as "We suck Young Blood" and "A Punchup at a Wedding" leave the reordering feeling a bit defanged. Personally, I would have omitted "Scatterbrain" in favor of one of these or, if Yorke preferred to keep a softer middle, swapped it out with the more effective "I will."

But that's splitting hairs. All of this goes to show that there's something for everyone on *Hail to the Thief*, even if they might have to dig a little bit to find it. It's as strange, enchanting, imperfect, and confounding as a fairytale.

13

"A Couple More for Breakfast"

Com Lag (2plus2isfive)

By 2004, Radiohead had already fulfilled their six-album deal with EMI after releasing *Hail to the Thief*. But they still stuck around for one more release—*Com Lag (2plus2isfive)*, a compilation EP of remixes, rarities, and B-sides that, unlike the record that came before it, feels like a true contractual obligation, even though it's not.

So why dedicate a whole chapter to a work that's viewed by many as being a throwaway? It's not like it stacks up against any of Radiohead's proper albums or even some of their other shorter projects. But there's a certain freedom in its disposability. For all their strengths, Radiohead will always be a band who overthinks their track listings. That's why the studio version for a song as perfect as "Lift" sat in a vault for so long. That's why *Hail to the Thief* has its fair share of filler.

But when saddled with a project where they have little creative or personal investment, Radiohead seems more willing to curate a track listing that lets their freak flag fly. At a brisk 36 minutes, the collection of preexisting material explores the nooks and crannies of the band's eccentricities, flirting with electronica, acoustic ballads, cold ambience, and robot funk. While this didn't impress critics at the time (*Pitchfork* slammed it with a 4.0—their lowest rating to date for any Radiohead release), it fits nicely into their discography; a fun and free-spirited respite from the monster scope of *Hail to the Thief* before the band reinvented themselves yet again with *In Rainbows*.

Even the most redundant material has its merits. A live version of "2 + 2 = 5" is similar to the one on record, but packs extra combustion thanks to the presence of a screaming audience at Earls Court. On the quieter end of the spectrum, the live rendition of "Fog" solely features Thom Yorke on piano—an arrangement many fans argue as being the definitive version of the song. The Los Angeles version of "I will" rounds out the already-existing album tracks, and is essentially the *Hail to the Thief* recording with drums. None of these alternate

Album art for *Com Lag (2plus2isfive)*.   *Author's collection*

takes reinvent the wheel, but there's a case to be made for them possessing more energy than their studio counterparts.

The Songs

"Remyxomatosis" (Cristian Vogel RMX)

As the first remix to by collected on a proper Radiohead EP or LP, "Remyxoma-tosis" laid the groundwork for 2011's *TKOL RMX 1234567*. Most of those tracks wouldn't just involve added bass or modified vocals; they functioned more as radically different interpretations of Radiohead songs.

   Cristian Vogel takes that same approach seven years earlier, not just delay-ing "Myxomatosis"' immediate explosion of deep keyboards, but doing away with them altogether. For the majority of the song, Yorke's voice is only scored by a rattle of intentionally puny drums and interruptions of space-junk synths. While not as propulsive as it source material, it's nonetheless atmospheric and a fine example of a musician putting a compelling tension between another artist's vision and their own.

"Paperbag Writer"

The title has little in common with the Beatles song of (almost) the same name, its bass line more rooted in dystopian funk than Britpop. The groove provides a fun distraction from the lyrics, which once again find Thom Yorke coping with anxiety. His neuroses go to an animalistic place here, forcing him to fend off paranoid thoughts of bees and rats by blowing into a paper bag.

While the song's sparse arrangement and a drum sound that would be more fully realized in "Reckoner" give "Paperbag Writer" a slightness, it still earns its place in the Hall of Minor Radiohead Curiosities.

"I Am a Wicked Child"

A supposed outtake from the *Kid A* sessions, it's hard to imagine "I Am a Wicked Child"'s post-grunge shuffle and boxcar harmonica fitting in with that album's frosty soundscapes.

But it's refreshing to see Radiohead at their most straightforward, the arrangement more prototypically "alternative" than anything on *Pablo Honey*; the low-fi production and conflicted religious imagery would have fit in on Nirvana's *In Utero*.

As for the trainyard harp-playing, the liner notes don't list who the musician is, but it sounds awfully similar to Jonny Greenwood's harmonica cameos on two Pavement songs ("Platform Blues" and "Billie") from their fifth and final album, *Terror Twilight*. Curiously, when Radiohead played an instrumental version of "I Am a Wicked Child" at a 2006 soundcheck in San Diego, Greenwood played the banjo.

"I Am Citizen Insane"

"I Am Citizen Insane," meanwhile, would have fit in perfectly on *Kid A*, although it's unknown when exactly the song was recorded (the phrase first reared its troubled head on the artwork for *Amnesiac*). A sort of mutated "Treefingers," the electronic textures get boosted by a jovial beat reminiscent of Dntel, as well as a subtle clanging similar to the bell at a railroad crossing.

There's enough melody to keep the effect from ever becoming abrasive, and if nothing else, the song became the namesake to one of the most informative Radiohead fan sites out there.

"Skttrbrain" (Four Tet Remix)

Another reinterpretation, and the rare case where the remix actually improves upon the original. Four Tet's cavalcade of bells add more levels to and resolution to *Hail to the Thief*'s most directionless song. Suddenly, the sonic warmth Radiohead has always used to describe "Scatterbrain" becomes more apparent.

Unfortunately, "Skttrbrain"'s beauty was quickly overshadowed by a mastering error at the time of *Com Lag*'s release. In the original Japanese pressings (the EP was initially released as an exclusive in Japan and Australia on March 24, 2004), abrasive static crackled four times in the left channel, effectively ruining the song.

The error had no effect on Four Tet and Radiohead's musical partnership—Kieran Hebden would contribute a remix of "Separator" under the Four Tet name to *TKOL RMX 1234567* in 2011. And by the time the EP received wider distribution in Canada on April 13, 2004; the United Kingdom on April 16, 2007; and the United States on May 8, 2007, the glitch had been corrected.

"Gagging Order"

One of Thom Yorke's greatest tricks is making the sinister sound sweet, and there may be no finer example of this than "Gagging Order" (originally titled "Move Along"). Is it about drugs? Censorship? An actual dead body? When the strumming and singing are so delicate, it doesn't matter.

The only insight Yorke has given to the lyrics comes from an interview with XFM in 2003, when he claimed to be the subject of an actual gagging order: "I had a gagging order served on me. Indirectly, at one point. Over something, which I obviously can't tell you about."

The British two-CD version of "Go to Sleep" single placed "Gagging Order" alongside "Fog (Again)" (Live) and "I Am a Wicked Child," rendering it one of the band's strongest singles and a miniature EP in its own right.

"Where Bluebirds Fly"

On record, "When Bluebirds Fly" serves as a template, a piecing together of jittery electronica that wouldn't be out of place on Yorke's solo debut, *The Eraser*. It's competent, though not all that memorable.

But at the Ether Festival in 2005, London Sinfonietta's orchestral arrangement of the song revealed its hidden layers and strengths. With the synths replaced by fleshy strings, the central melody played on a xylophone (think the ribcage of a skeleton), and the electronic drums switched out for tympanies, "Where Bluebirds Fly" finally lived up to the otherworldly aspirations of its title—is it a dream or a nightmare?

The vocals of Lubna Salame and Yorke himself (who performed the wordless verses with dance moves and all) didn't make it any easier to tell. Nor did the presence of six different ondes Martenots.

14

"So I Give In
to the Rhythm"

Colin Greenwood and Phil Selway

I f Thom Yorke has been (sometimes unfairly) criticized for being the brooding frontman of Radiohead, the band's rhythm section make up his mirror image. Always polite, affable, and just plain happy to be there, Colin Greenwood and Phil Selway are responsible for a great deal of joy found in both the band's collective personality and the music.

Granted, the same could be said for most rock bands' rhythm sections—at least musically. The word "rhythm" implies a sense of movement; kinetic energy; vibrations that mobilize crowds to turn affected shuffling into actual dancing. The rhythm section tends to aim for the pleasure zones. It gets the endorphins going.

That's especially true of Radiohead, a band with many songs that would melt into dourness without a sturdy groove behind them. Where would "Bones" be without Colin's bubbly, up-and-down bassline? Where would "Weird Fishes/Arpeggi" be without Selway's punchy drum rolls and relaxing cymbal ride? Precision and unconventionality have been hallmarks of Radiohead's rhythm section, but so have beats that appeal to every listener's lizard brain.

Likewise, their interviews tend to be good-natured. Colin seems to be the only band member actively trying to be friendly in *Meeting People is Easy*, his apologies constant and his permanently surprised eyes retaining their wonder even as a lack of sleep tugs at their lids.

Selway hardly talks at all in the film, but has been much chattier in band and solo interviews, not to mention unflinchingly friendly and humorous. When asked by the *Financial Times* on February 6, 2015 what his biggest disappointment was, he responded "Losing my hair just as Radiohead was taking off. When I dreamt of being a rock star, it was always with a sharp haircut." Ironically, his completely bald head has given him one of the most distinct appearances among rock drummers.

When examining their careers outside of the band, their amount of solo work isn't as staggering as Yorke's or Colin's brother, Jonny. But Radiohead's bassist and drummer have clearly filled their lives with a number of passions, from film work to solo albums and even photography.

Childhood

Unlike Thom Yorke, Colin Charles Greenwood was born in Oxford on June 26, 1969, and has lived there for the majority of his life. The only exception in his childhood was when the work of his father Raymond, a major in the Royal Army Ordnance Corps, brought the Greenwood family to Germany. Raymond died when Colin was only seven, leaving him and his younger brother Jonny to be raised by their mother Brenda.

When examining Colin's early musical influences, his bass playing in Radiohead makes complete sense. Thanks to the record collection of his older sister Susan, he started out getting into post-punk music, and one can hear the echo of Joy Division/New Order's Peter Hook in more aggressive, primitive Radiohead rockers such as "Bangers + Mash" and "Bodysnatchers." He later developed an interest in the bassists of Motown and Stax Records, forming a direct connection to the more soulful, complicated bass lines of songs like "Airbag" and "Talk Show Host."

As the oldest person in Radiohead, Philip James Selway came into the world on May 23, 1967 in Hemingford Grey, Cambridgeshire, which also makes him the only band member other than Yorke to be born outside of Oxford. His parents Dorothea and Michael eventually found their way there (Hemingford Grey and Oxford are about two hours apart), where Selway began attending the Abingdon School.

While at Abingdon, Selway studied classical percussion, including the tympani, but stopped after two years. Considering that his parents gave him a drumset for his third Christmas and became mildly annoyed by the constant racket, it seems he was destined to become a rock drummer. And that's exactly what happened when, along with Yorke, Ed O'Brien, and the Greenwoods, he formed the band On a Friday.

College Years

Since he has a year or four on everyone else in Radiohead, Selway had the time to get the most schooling. Despite being an admittedly poor student at Abingdon, he went on to study English and history at Liverpool Polytechnic, followed by postgraduate studies in publishing at Oxford Brookes University.

Shortly after arriving in Liverpool, Selway began volunteering for a suicide prevention organization called Samaritans. He remained a volunteer for 17 years, starting off by talking to suicidal and depressed callers over the phone and eventually shifting his duties to campaigning for the the group at schools and elsewhere once his personal and professional life became too busy. He left in 2008 when he realized he no longer had the time needed to dedicate himself to the Samaritans in a beneficial way.

Of all the members of Radiohead, Selway also has the most experience working a dayjob outside of music. He taught English as a foreign language, worked at a sub-editor at a medical publishing house, and even left On a Friday for a time to be with the woman he was dating in Ireland. He returned to Oxford when the relationship didn't work out, and would eventually marry his long-time girlfriend Cait while recording *The Bends*. They have three sons together: Leo, Jamie, and Patrick.

While Colin didn't have quite as much schooling as Selway, he has kept ties throughout the years to Peterhouse, Cambridge—a constituent college of the University of Cambridge where he studied English Literature from 1987 to 1990 and was actively involved in campus life. While there, he served as Head Entertainments Officer, allowing him to organize parties and other events that required him to book musical acts. An added bonus was that he got to book several of his own bands.

Colin has professed his love of academia in interviews, even saying that he could picture himself as a college professor. In 1997, he participated in a Cambridge marketing campaign for the school aimed at diversifying its applicants, and in band interviews, he's known for showing his academic roots by frequently recommending books to fans. That's not a huge surprise for a man whose undergraduate thesis examined the works of Raymond Carver.

In December, 1998, Colin married American novelist, poet, and literary critic, Molly McGrann, with whom he has three sons, Jesse, Asa, and Henry. As a couple, Colin and Molly often attend literary readings, with poet Robin Robertson dedicating his poem "The Oven Man" to them in 2002. Robertson would go on to be named one of the Next Generation Poets, a contest on which Colin served as a juror. This came in addition to being a panel judge for the Forward Prizes for Poetry and the inaugural BRITDOC film festival.

Colin's other outside passion is amateur photography—an interest he's used to give fans an insider's look at Radiohead. He's frequently posted both posed and candid images of his bandmates, their travels, and recording sessions on Dead Air Space, so much that they've jokingly referred to Colin as their David Bailey, in reference to the famed English fashion photographer. Colin has been known to use both a Canon PowerShot 70 and a Panasonic DMC-LX1 for his photos, and in May 2003, he was asked to discuss his favorite works from other photographers at the Victoria and Albert Museum's V&A Photography Gallery in London.

Solo Work

To date, Colin and O'Brien are the two members of Radiohead to have never released a solo album. Colin has, however, lent his bass skills to a handful of other artists' compositions, including James Lavino's score for the 2008 small-town docufiction film *Woodpecker*. Alongside twin brothers Lee and Tyler Sargent of Clap Your Hands Say Yeah, Colin works his way through music that's distinctly Americana—hypnotizing in a more laid-back and rustic way than Radiohead. A few years earlier, he got to collaborate with his own brother on "24 Hour Charleston," a low-lurking number from Jonny's soundtrack for the 2003 documentary *Bodysong*.

Selway also teamed up with Jonny for a film, although not in the way one would expect. In the fourth *Harry Potter* movie, *Harry Potter and the Goblet of Fire*, a rock band called the Weird Sisters plays the end-of-semester Yule Ball. The rather goth-looking band members were portrayed by a sextet of well-known British rockers, including Selway, Jonny, Steven Claydon of Add N to (X), Jason Buckle of All Seeing I, and Steve Mackey and Jarvis Cocker of Pulp. But Selway's most notable musical work outside of Radiohead is a trio of solo albums.

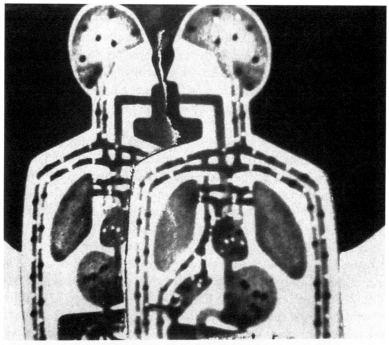

Bodysong. Jonny Greenwood.
Music from the film.

Colin Greenwood played bass on his brother Jonny's soundtrack for the 2003 documentary *Bodysong*.   *Author's collection*

Familial

In a reversal of Yorke's work with Atoms For Peace, Selway's solo career didn't arrive until after he had played with a supergroup.

In 2001, he took on drum duties for 7 Worlds Collide, a charity project spearheaded by New Zealand singer-songwriter and Crowded House frontman Neil Finn, where an all-star band performed songs by himself and others for five nights, then released a live album. O'Brien, Eddie Vedder, and Johnny Marr were all among the other players.

It was around this time that Selway started thinking about the possibility of a solo career, and by the time the 7 Worlds Collide reconvened in 2008 for a studio album, *The Sun Came Out*, Selway had two of his own songs, "The Ties That Bind Us" and "The Witching Hour," to contribute. They would also appear on his 2010 solo debut, *Familial* (recorded using his full first name) alongside eight other tracks.

For *Familial*, Selway preferred to be the frontman rather than a drummer, meaning he had to—in his words—teach himself how to sing, and hand drum duties to Glenn Kotche of Wilco, the band that has so often been labeled the "American Radiohead." Kotche had performed on *The Sun Came Out* with his multi-instrumentalist bandmate Pat Sansone, who ended up playing on *Familial* as well, resulting in a hushed and shuffling record in the vein of Nick Drake. Even as Selway breaks through the often repressive attitude we take towards our own relatives to sing about loyalty and loss (his mother's 2006 death inspired many of the words on the album), his voice clings to a calming tone.

While that doesn't help most of *Familial*'s songs stand on their own, there's nothing the least bit objectionable about the record. With bass work and additional playing from Soul Coughing's Sebastian Steinberg and session player Lisa Germano (both of whom also contributed to 7 Worlds Collide), *Familial* manages to be soothing even as it dives into heavy personal subject matter. Selway's subsequent EP of scrapped material, *Running Blind*, works in the same pristine and quiet medium: the drums crackle, the voice relaxes, and the creak of every guitar note can be heard.

Weatherhouse

With one straightforward solo effort under his belt, Selway got more adventurous with 2014's *Weatherhouse*. More electronic textures such as programming and drum machines tastefully blend with cavernous vocals and an orchestra pit's worth of instruments played by bassist Adem Ilhan (Fridge, Silver Columns) and renowned London multi-instrumentalist Quinta. Contemporary classical string help comes from the Elysian Quartet.

Philip Selway
Weatherhouse

Album art for Phil Selway's second solo album, *Weatherhouse*.   *Author's collection*

As for Selway, he returned to drum duties in addition to playing guitar on *Weatherhouse*, which makes for an overall more emboldened approach than *Familial*. "Miles Away" embraces the mechanized, deceptively simple drum style found in his later work with Radiohead, and opener "Coming Up For Air" relies on an otherworldly synth pulse for its hook. Most striking of all is "It Will End In Tears," a yearning piano ballad that Selway performed on *The Tonight Show* with soul revivalists the Dap Kings.

That's not to say any of the songs on *Weatherhouse* will be radio hits or celebrated in rock-critic circles anytime soon. The music is too modest for that, even with the expanded palette on the second record. But there's enough growth between Selway's first two albums to instill interest in his still-burgeoning solo career. Like his primary band, he seems to have a natural passion for evolving.

Let Me Go soundtrack

Selway's most dramatic solo work hasn't been on a proper studio album, but a movie soundtrack. Then again, the movie's subject matter was always going to call for a spike in emotional range.

Based on Helga Schneider's memoir of the same name, *Let Me Go* (directed by Polly Steele) follows Schneider as both an adult and a little girl circa 1941, when her mother abandoned her to pursue a career as an extermination guard at the Auschwitz death camp. Reflecting the wide array of themes and moods in the film, Selway's soundtrack is fittingly mournful and, at times, redemptive. "Helga's Theme" sinks the listener with strings from the Elysian Quartet while "Days and Nights" twinkles with a pastoral landscape of bells, vibraphone, and a singing saw.

All of this points to Selway having a potential film-scoring career in his future, similar to Jonny Greenwood. It would also be exciting to see him apply the higher stakes of the *Let Me Go* soundtrack to his own solo albums.

15

"Children First"

At Abingdon

Welcome to the most boring part of this book.

Unlike most famous rock bands, Radiohead doesn't have a salacious origin story. There are no sordid tales of post-show orgies, no urban legends about fish being used for sexual purposes, no overdoses, plane crashes. Anyone looking for something more hedonistic should read Mötley Crüe's seminal autobiography with Neil Strauss, *The Dirt*.

Granted, it isn't out of the ordinary for a band to form while at school together, as Radiohead did. What makes them unique is that they've all stayed close to their home county of Oxfordshire, England, and have maintained a relatively low-key profile in the press. And even if they hadn't, there probably isn't all that much there for the tabloids. They're all parents who, outside of their musical career, live fairly quiet lives. They seem to have valued that kind of normalcy from the very beginning.

Thom and Colin Meet

The genesis of Radiohead took place at the Abingdon School, an all-boys public institution in the small Oxford suburb of the same name. Founded in 1256, Abingdon is tucked away across 37 acres, its pastoral setting somewhat ironic given the colder, more disturbing aspects of some of Radiohead's later work. Among its considerable number of notable alumni are actor Toby Jones, musician and technology entrepreneur Thomas Dolby, and of course, all five members of Radiohead.

The first two to connect (outside of the Greenwood brothers, who have obviously known each other their whole lives) were Thom Yorke and Colin, who, as 11-year-olds, both joined a student body of approximately 750 boys in the fall of 1980. It wasn't long before they were drawn to each other's musical tastes and abilities, and a rather loud fashion sense. As Yorke told *Select* in April 1995, "We always ended up at the same parties. He'd be wearing a beret and a catsuit, or something pretty fucking weird, and I'd be in a frilly blouse and crushed velvet dinner suit and we'd pass 'round the Joy Division records."

They were clearly a long way from becoming the rock outfit that would make them famous. But everyone has to start somewhere, and for Yorke and Colin, that meant playing in a punk band called TNT when they were both roughly 14 years old. Yorke says that he had to take on the role of lead singer when no one else was willing to, prompting him to attach a mic to a broomstick with little success. The gesture was indicative of the overall sound of TNT, who lived up to their name by doing little more than bash around. The act was short-lived, and Yorke and Colin sought out the next step in their informal musical education.

Theatre Days

Yorke and Colin didn't meet Ed O'Brien in music class, but through the school's theatre program. O'Brien was something of a regular actor during his Abingdon days, performing alongside Colin in the Gilbert and Sullivan operetta *Trial By Jury* and in an experimental production of *A Midsummer Night's Dream* where Yorke was composing background music. All three students appear in the December 1986 edition of the school paper of *The Abingdonian*—with Yorke contributing artwork (it's unclear which drawings are his) and Colin and O'Brien getting called out for their acting chops.

Yorke ended up asking O'Brien to play music with him and Colin not because of any evident skill, but for his laid-back personality and passing resemblance to Morrissey of the Smiths. O'Brien happily obliged and later admitted that he learned to play the guitar while in this earliest incarnation of the band. Colin, on the other hand, was already proficient on bass and trained in classical guitar. Meanwhile, Yorke continued to improve his craft by taking guitar and voice lessons.

A Band Without a Drummer

Yorke, Colin, and O'Brien found the solitude they needed within the music department, a section of Abingdon where they discovered no one would bother them. Even though music was heavily woven into the school's curriculum, it tended to be of the classical variety—something the newly formed trio had little interest in playing collectively on their own, at least in the early days.

The only problem was, a bassist and two guitarists (one who could barely play) wasn't exactly enough for a whole band, so the three musicians had to rely on a handful of additional players, some of who stuck around for a while. Most notable was a trio of saxophonists—Rasmus "Raz" Peterson and sisters Liz and Charlotte Cotton—who appeared on some of the early band's demos.

Another thing the group was lacking was a suitable name. Dearest, Gravitate, and—most amusing of all—Shindig were all used at one point or another. Needless to say, none of these titles point to any kind of concrete sound, and it's safe to say that, at such an early stage in Radiohead's career, they probably didn't have one.

Still, Dearest/Gravitate/Shindig made due for a while, even without a human drummer. Instead, they relied on a Boss Dr. Rhythm drum machine, which may have been used in the earliest known recording of "The National Anthem." However, when it broke down at the beginning of a birthday performance, it was clear that the band needed a timekeeper made of actual flesh and blood.

Phil Selway Joins

While Dearest/Gravitate/Shindig was searching for a drummer, Phil Selway was in a band with the equally embarrassing name of Jungle Telegraph. Being a slightly older Abingdon student than the rest of the future bandmates, he actually once ran with a crowd that had beaten up Yorke on a few occasions. Undeterred, Yorke still approached him at a pub and asked to hear his drumming.

Despite playing too slow for Yorke's liking (at least at first), Selway was asked to join. As an in-joke, the rest of the band dubbed him "Mad Dog," a nickname that implied a supposedly vicious temper. Of course, Selway is known for being unfailingly kind and polite, which only made the joke funnier whenever the band introduced him to others.

Faculty Adoration (and Resentment)

Whenever Radiohead talks about Abingdon, it's likely that two faculty members will come up.

The first is Terence Gilmore-James, the school's music teacher who spotted the band members' talent early on. Although he admits that he didn't always understand their musical direction, he encouraged them to keep following their own path.

He helped out more than he probably realized at the time by introducing them to music outside their sphere. His selections ranged from jazz to film scores, classical music, and avant-garde compositions that arose out of World War II. While none of these genres are apparent in the group's early compositions, who knows if Radiohead would have ever written something like "Pyramid Song" or the final version of "Motion Picture Soundtrack" had they not expanded their musical tastes early on.

If Yorke was to designate a bizarro version of the kindly and informative Gilmore-James—the supervillain to his superhero—it would be Abingdon's then-headmaster Michael St. John Parker. In early Radiohead interviews, Yorke's distaste for the headmaster borders on comical—straight out of a slobs-versus-snobs comedy from the '80s.

"He was a power-crazy, lunatic, evil, petty little man with ridiculous side-burns who used to flick his hair across his head to hide his bald patch," he said in Mick St. Michael's 1997 book simply titled *Radiohead*.

But beyond this description, Yorke has offered little insight into why he despised Parker so much. He's alluded to hating the fact that the headmaster delivered morning chapel services twice a week despite not being an officially ordained minister, plus Parker eventually didn't allow rock bands to practice on campus. But this was toward the end of Yorke's time at Abingdon, and he and his mates simply found another space at a nearby church (they just had to tell the vicar that they were a jazz band).

Only Yorke and the rest of Radiohead know the whole truth, but if we're going off of interviews, his resentment of Parker seems to have stemmed from his general distrust of authority. If anything, it probably provided fuel for later song material, although the one composition that's generally accepted to be about Parker, "Bishop's Robes," isn't all that spectacular.

While Yorke's attitude toward Parker is indicative of how he and the rest of the band have often spoken about their time at Abingdon in interviews, it's hard to determine the accuracy of their statements. On August 20, 2001, Yorke told *The New Yorker* that he was "sort of a leper" during his school years. To be fair, it has been documented that he got teased about his drooping eyelid, and his pugilistic attitude probably didn't help. But he was also clearly involved in a great deal of extracurriculars, and there have been many quotes from his non-Radiohead peers that insist most of the student body recognized how talented the band was, even back then.

There's also the matter of Yorke and the rest of Radiohead having stayed so close to their old stomping ground well into their adult lives. Even if they've rarely commented on how their childhoods in Oxfordshire and at Abingdon have influenced their music, there has to be something other than resentment that's kept them so close to home.

The Final Piece

With the core of Yorke, Colin, O'Brien, and Selway in place, an important order of business was coming up with a proper name. They chose On a Friday for the simple fact that Friday was the day when they rehearsed. It wasn't all that clever (then again, neither is the name Radiohead), but it would do. And it was still leagues above Gravitate. Maybe not Shindig, though.

Radiohead originally formed as On a Friday at Abingdon School in Oxfordshire, England.
Photo by Reading Tom/Wikimedia Commons

Although On a Friday wouldn't quite nail down a distinctive sound until they had become Radiohead (and even then, it would take a couple albums for them to really start cooking), the final member to join, Colin's little brother Jonny, would at least nudge them in the right direction.

Five years younger than Colin, Jonny was prone to quietly hanging out at On a Friday's rehearsals. Even though he was by far the most musically skilled member of the five—having already learned guitar, piano, harmonica, viola, and an assortment of other instruments—the band wasn't keen on letting one of their little brothers join.

After roughly a year of coming around with a portable keyboard, the 13-year-old was invited to play harmonica, of all things, in a guest-spot capacity at rehearsals and house parties, usually in front of an audience of Abingdon schoolmates.

Sometime in 1986, before Greenwood was an official member of On a Friday (or at least before the others allowed him to play on record), the band cut a demo tape at the school. Depending on the source, the tape is said to have been five, six, or eleven tracks. For instance, a 2016 YouTube upload lists out the first five songs with timestamps, but the visual contains a handwritten tracklist that indicates an additional song, plus an entire second side with one other song and a handful of slightly tweaked dub remixes where the vocals and instruments cut in and out at certain moments.

Album art for On a Friday's 1986 demo tape.   *Author's collection*

It's impossible to verify the authenticity of the physical tracklist (who knows if it was written by a band member back in 1986 or a fan today), but a YouTube link from 2011 does indeed include the extra songs and second side. The upload came from the username Klootme, who claims that her husband used to party with On a Friday back at Abingdon, and that they both went to university with Selway.

While there's no reason to distrust Klootme's explanation—the songs are definitely all from the actual tape—it confirms that it's hard to piece together a definitive narrative for the music recorded by On a Friday. Who knows if the band members themselves at this point would even remember what was recorded when and which physical release each song appeared on. Perhaps knowing that it's difficult to verify any one story, one savvy eBay user posted what they claim to be original physical copies of On a Friday's assorted demo tapes for a whopping $50,000. This was back in 2012, so it's unclear whether anyone took the bait, especially since the seller offered no proof of authenticity.

Conflicting accounts aside, the songs on both versions of the first demo tape calls for some brief examination. Despite being all over the place in terms of sound, the musicianship already shows a locked-in competency that's kind of mindblowing considering it was hammered out by a bunch of high-schoolers. Most importantly, the tape is catchy as hell in an '80s kind of way, even through the hissing DIY production quality.

The 1986 Demo Tape

"Fragile Friend"

O'Brien has said on more than one occasion that he learned to play guitar by ripping off the Smiths, and this upbeat opener about a sensitive young lad has shades of Johnny Marr all over it.

But the most notable musical flourish is a burst of saxophone notes from Raz Peterson that syncs up with Selway's cymbal ride and eventually escalates to the band yowling like chimpanzees. It's hard to imagine the Radiohead we know today pulling such a goofy move.

"Girl (In a Purple Dress)"

At an early age, Yorke was already exploring the incessant *Pablo Honey* theme of crumbling to bits in front of a woman.

"I'll do whatever you want me to and stay for jasmine tea," he croons, somewhat laughably, on "Girl (In a Purple Dress)." One can tell he's still finding the right singing voice. While his vibrato is impressive, he's aping the full-bodied melodrama of both Morrissey and Robert Smith of the Cure. The song gets even more overblown with a sax solo from Peterson that's straight out of the "Baker Street" handbook.

"Everybody Knows"

The first time the musicianship starts to show some cracks, Colin's bass notes never quite sync up with the guitar and synthesized strings on "Everybody Knows." Still, the contrast of skeletal plucking and bombast actually connects to some of the material on *The Bends*. And yes, there's another sultry sax solo from Peterson.

"Mountains (On the Move)"

On a Friday verges on psychedelia with "Mountains (On the Move)," although the wooziness gives way to a jauntiness that prevents it from ever going full-on Pink Floyd. Nice echo effect on the guitar, though.

"Fat Girl"

"Fat Girl" isn't as ugly as the song name suggests—Yorke actually writes about the title character from a sympathetic point of view. But the sugary rhythm makes the song feel a little exploitative.

"Lemming Trail"

It's amusing that Yorke asked Selway if he could play any faster when they first met, as the tempo stays fairly brisk throughout most of On a Friday's first demo. He starts off "Lemming Trail" with a surf-rock drum roll that, with double-tracked horns, soon becomes—wait for it—a ska song, or at least a high-schooler's approximation of a ska song. Thankfully, the band never went down that route again once they became Radiohead, although they did a couple more times as On a Friday.

"Lock the Door"

"Lock the Door" features the tape's best use of Peterson's saxophone, employed for primal bursts rather than a howl-at-the-moon solo. The song also includes several latter-day Radiohead hallmarks, including four sharp left turns in dynamic and at least one lyric—"Soon, when the sun dies, we'll lose control"—that would have been right at home on any album from *The Bends* onward.

"In the Breeze"

This closer demo tape's closer is curious for its two distinct halves. For much of the song, "In the Breeze" is unknowing '80s cheese, drenched in a new-wave bass line from Colin and more sax wailing. But after every verse, it's as if the band gives the listener a glimpse into their future as Radiohead for just a moment: the group's voices form a caterwaul and everything cuts out except the static of the drums and several bent guitar lines. It's On a Friday's first toe-dip into the avantgarde.

The First (Real) Gigs

By 1987, On a Friday's first demo tape had begun to circulate around the school and the Oxford scene at large, even leading to a positive review in a new, short-lived college publication called the *Oxford Enquirer*. The writer and head of the paper, Dave Newton, praised the band in the *Enquirer*'s first issue on February 24 for steering away from the goth-influenced music that was so popular at the time.

But just as it seemed like On a Friday was beginning to get some local attention, the end of most of the band members' time at Abingdon loomed over their heads. That spring marked the final semester for Yorke, Colin, and O'Brien, and by the fall semester, the latter two would be off at college, along with Selway, who was already at Liverpool Polytechnic. Of the future members of Radiohead, only Yorke, who decided to take a year off, and Jonny, who still had three more years to go at Abingdon, would remain in town by the fall.

The timing was unfortunate, as On a Friday would get to play their first club gig in Oxford at Jericho Tavern during the summer of 1987. It seemed they would have to end right as they were just getting started.

Or not.

Unlike so many other high-school bands before and after them, the members all made a commitment to rehearsing and playing shows on weekends and when everyone was home for holiday breaks. What could have been a death-sentence year for the band ended up resulting in several notable gigs around Oxford. In February 1988, On a Friday played the Old Fire Station with Illiterate Hands, which included both Jonny and Yorke's little brother Andy. Andy would go on to have his own success in the band Unbelievable Truth.

By the time the fall rolled around, On a Friday finally inducted Jonny as an official member. Unfortunately for him, their gigs were put on hold when Yorke decided to follow his bandmates' lead and take the collegiate leap. And yet they still made time to rehearse for the next three years, unknowingly preparing for the huge career shift that would take place once most of the musicians in On a Friday were finished with university.

16

"I Feel My Life Could Change"

On a Friday's Ascent

When Thom Yorke graduated from Exeter in the spring of 1991, the lineup of the band that would soon become Radiohead was complete. Jonny Greenwood was officially guitarist and eventual pianist/organist, and Phil Selway was back as full-time drummer after a brief period in Ireland.

But before we veer down the road to Radiohead's *Drill* EP and beyond, let's take some time to discuss the rest of On a Friday's discography. For being a high-school band, they released demos at a fairly regular clip of every two years. Following the first 1986 demo, the group recorded an additional three-song demo at Woodworm Studios in Barford St. Michael, Oxfordshire. This marks Jonny's first appearance on one of the band's releases as keyboardist, as well as the first recorded appearance of sisters Liz and Charlotte Cotton on saxophone (saxophonist Raz Peterson makes his return as well).

More significant is a demo tape of songs recorded at various times and locations during the summer of 1990 when most of the band members were home from university. The one exception was Selway, who was in Ireland at the time and only appears on one track: "What Is That You See," which was recorded at Nuneham Courtenay Village Hall. While he was gone, percussive duties were filled out by a drum machine and schoolmate Nigel Powell, who had played in Illiterate Hands with Jonny and Yorke's brother Andy, and would go on to collaborate with the latter in Unbelievable Truth. His tracks were recorded at Clifton Hampden Village Hall, with the drum-machine tracks recorded in various of the band members' bedrooms.

Depending on the source, the 1990 tape contained 13, 14, or 15 songs, and may have been released under the name Shindig. It's unclear whether this was the first time that band name was used or whether On a Friday was reverting back to one of their old monikers. Whatever the case, they'd abandon it (perhaps for the second time) shortly afterward as they continued to hone in on their sound, which was still all over the place from 1988 to 1990, as heard in the increasingly whacky genre experiments on these tapes.

1988 Tape

"Happy Song"

Unlike the 1986 tape, the 1988 tape received actual engineering and mixing from Dave Pegg, resulting in a vastly improved production quality.

In the case of "Happy Song," that means On a Friday's sunnier tendencies shine that much brighter. An odd yacht-rock/ska hybrid, the guitars are all upstroke, the horns are more expertly blended than before, and something that sounds like a marimba ups the goo factor.

But it's hard to criticize the tape's opener for being cloying, as Yorke actually describes violent acts and darker internal feelings. As annoying as it is to listen to, "Happy Song" continues his exploration of lyrical-musical juxtaposition.

"To Be a Brilliant Light"

The most Radiohead-sounding On a Friday song up to this point, "To Be a Brilliant Light" plays like a mini-suite in the vein of "Paranoid Android." Even the sax solo kind of makes sense due to the constant shifting.

However, it's not devoid of cheesiness. For some reason, Jonny keeps his keyboard permanently locked in organ mode, which works when he's underscoring the central melody, but sounds cartoonish whenever he slides his fingers down the keys.

"Sinking Ship"

Radiohead would eventually have a connection to a Neil Finn through his 7 Worlds Collide project, but it's natural to think the members of On a Friday were already fans of an earlier supergroup from the New Zealand singer-songwriter. "Sinking Ship" sounds like their answer to Split Enz's "Six Months In a Leaky Boat"—maritime imagery and all.

1990 Tape

"Climbing Up a Bloody Great Hill"

The summery weirdness from the 1988's opener continues with yet another oddity. This time around, Jonny's keyboard resembles the klutzy organ heard in a baseball stadium. It's a ballsy move on his part (pun very much intended)—Steve Nieve of Elvis Costello and the Attractions may be the only rock musician who can make this particular sound work.

"Somebody"

Yorke puts on a fake snarl and unknowingly prepares for some of the lesser tracks on *Pablo Honey*. Surprisingly, the drum machine fits in seamlessly with the rest of the jangly arrangement.

"Mr. B"

This personification of death has its moments, especially when Yorke describes the reaper's clothing and purposely stutters his vocal delivery. It seems like somewhat of an important early cut given the creepy subject matter of later Radiohead songs.

"What Is That You See?"

The only track from the 1990 cassette that Selway plays drums on, "What Is That You See?" is also the tape's song that sounds the most like Radiohead. This could also be because it's the first time Jonny was permitted to play guitar. It sizzles under everything else—not exactly a solo, but a lead that's steeped in atmospherics, as if he's trying to make it sound like an ondes Martenot.

The band may have felt the song was something different compared to the rest of their material. Of all the songs from the early demo tapes, "What Is That You See?" was the only one to stay in On a Friday's live setlist until they signed their record deal.

"Everyone Needs Someone to Hate / Dance Sucka"

Thom Yorke's faux evil persona isn't any more effective here than it is on "Somebody," but there's something bizarrely fascinating about the drums. The band actually took the beats from a Public Enemy song, which Yorke had to play from his walkman into a Portastudio four-track. It's a crude yet effective solution from the days before the members of Radiohead had a proper looper or editing software.

"Upside Down"

Yorke's fake growl and the machine's fake drums actually work better here, when they're paired with a warm guitar strum—almost a primitive riff on some long-lost XTC B-side. It goes without saying that Jonny could still stand to get rid of that ballpark organ tone.

Thom Yorke sampled the beat of a Public Enemy song for the early *On a Friday* track "Everyone Needs Someone to Hate / Dance Sucka." *Photo by Mika Väisänen/Wikimedia Commons*

"The Greatest Shindig (Of the World)"

As a B-side of "High and Dry" / "Planet Telex" during *The Bends* era, "The Greatest Shindig (Of the World)"—at that point retitled "Maquiladora"—has a compelling roughness, even in its final version. The version on the demo tape is even more lo-fi, but not distractingly so, thanks to a meaty chord progression that was intact from the very beginning.

"Give It Up"

With the absence of both Selway and Powell, On a Friday recorded the drums for "Give It Up" in a similar fashion as "Everyone Needs Someone to Hate / Dance Sucka," this time stealing the beat from Soul to Soul. The result isn't quite as successful, partly due to Jonny's keyboards, which sound customized for a '90s fashion show.

"How Can You Be Sure?"

As close as On a Friday/Radiohead would ever get to a campfire sing-along, this marks one of the 1990 tape's strongest and most melodic tracks. A more polished take appeared as a US B-side to "High and Dry" during the *Bends* era. That rendition is far superior to the one heard here, but the demo has some crackling background noise and chatter that's almost always welcome in Radiohead songs.

"Life With the Big F"

Considering where the band ended up going as Radiohead, it's amusing to hear how jaunty so many of On a Friday's songs are. "Life With the Big F" even has a series of unironic "la-la-la"s breaking through its cowpunk arrangement.

"Keep Strong"

Rising seamlessly out of "Life With the Big F," "Keep Strong" once again finds On a Friday flirting with surf rock, proving once again that On a Friday should never flirt with surf rock.

"Rattlesnake"

"Rattlesnake" is one of the few early On a Friday songs that Radiohead has actually elaborated upon in interviews.

"[It] just had a drum loop that Thom did himself at home on a tape recorder with bad scratching over the top and kind of Prince vocals," Jonny told *Q* magazine in June 1997. The description is spot-on and shows why "Rattlesnake" is one of the 1990 tape's more fascinating—if strange—songs. Even if the track doesn't quite hold up on its own, the homemade drums have more agency than a machine or sample. They also hint at where Radiohead would go with *Kid A* and where Yorke's interests would lie with his first two solo albums.

"Burning Bush"

One of the biggest weaknesses of On a Friday's music is that Yorke hadn't yet figured out his voice as a frontman. One of the few exceptions is "Burning Bush," where he finds the emotional confidence that would arrive with *Pablo Honey* and get fleshed out with everything that came after. Coupled with some evocative keyboard drones (one of the few times on the tape when Jonny Greenwood would get away from "Take Me Out to the Ball Game"), it's enough to make one forget the clunky political lyrics (the "Bush" of the title refers to then-American president George H.W. Bush).

"Tell Me Bitch"

Thom Yorke's most misogynistic lyrics of the On a Friday era doesn't work any better as a ska song. Most things don't.

"New Generation"

Another goof, "New Generation" has a leg up on all of the other dismissable songs from the On a Friday era for having a lead vocal from none other than Colin Greenwood. Over a drum machine and a bass line programmed by Jonny on his Roland U20, the elder sibling fully throws himself into a nonsensical and rather frightening rant, as if he's standing on a street corner, yelling at passersby. Yorke, who handles the chorus, can be heard laughing at his bandmate toward the end.

The Dungeon Demo

Despite a large amount of the material on the 1988 and 1990 demos coming off as silly by today's standards, On a Friday decided to re-record two of its tracks—"Give It Up" and "What Is That You See?"—at the Dungeon studio. By this time, the horn section was gone and they had access to a 16-track console, making for a more polished product than ever before.

Dungeon owner and engineer Richard Haines found the two already existing songs to be unremarkable, but was impressed by the new third track, an anthemic cut called "Stop Whispering."

The group also decided to take the leap and move in together—an arrangement that lasted less than a year. Even though Selway, Colin, and O'Brien had already been renting a detached house together, all five members staying in one place proved to be too much. The various factors included conflicting musical tastes, the fact that no one knew how to cook, and the band unwittingly trashing the home from constant rehearsals. Only Yorke and Colin—the two original members of On a Friday—rode out the entire lease.

Fortunately, the botched living situation didn't affect the band as a unit. In the summer of 1991, they started gigging regularly around Oxford, from the Jericho Tavern, where they played their first club show, to the Zodiac, known today as the O2 Academy Oxford. On a Friday's increased presence was aided by the circulation of their new demo tape—simply titled On a Friday—with O'Brien taking on an unofficial managerial role in the band and passing it around to record stores, music fans, and local publications such as Curfew. Apparently, some of the larger shoegaze acts in Oxford such as Ride were fans, which helped create more good buzz around a live act that was, by this point, highly energized.

Chris Hufford and Bryce Edge

Chris Hufford and Bryce Edge had been out of the professional music game for a while.

After achieving little success in a band called Aerial FX, the two friends started exploring the world of real estate. In 1987, they partnered with a developer named George Taylor for a mixed residential and business complex called Georgetown. Within Georgetown was a 24-track recording studio that wasn't as much of a business venture as it was a pastime for the two former bandmates—a place where they could keep their expensive musical hobbies afloat.

But when Georgetown tanked financially, Hufford and Edge were forced to sell their shares in the complex, although Taylor allowed them to still run the studio—albeit with the caveat that they now had to pay rent. They soon found themselves on the production/engineering side of things as a way to bring in some money.

The three-song *On a Friday* demo eventually made its way into their hands, although the identity of the messenger is debatable. While Hufford remembers it being a friend of the band named Jim Butcher, Mac Randall notes in his book *Exit Music: The Radiohead Story* that, in all of his extensive research around Oxford, none of the band's or the studios's associates could recall anyone by that name.

However Hufford and Edge got the tape, it was promising enough for them to want to catch On a Friday live. Hufford attended a Jericho Tavern show on August 8, 1991, and was so impressed that he approached them backstage afterwards. They agreed to collaborating with Hufford, and by October, they were recording a new five-song tape at Courtyard. Three of the songs, "I Can't," "Thinking About You," and "You," would appear on Radiohead's full-length debut, *Pablo Honey*, and the other two would be tossed to the land of forgotten rarities.

"Phillipa Chicken"

An antiwar raveup that raves all the harder via a guitar solo from Jonny that's so high it flies, even if the same can't be said for the lyrics (mostly a pigheaded soldier listing their artillery). In the early days, so much of On a Friday/Radiohead's success relied on a stronger musical element drowning out a weaker one. Luckily, that's exactly what happens here.

It still wasn't enough for Radiohead—so often their own worst critics—to keep "Phillipa Chicken" around very long. While celebrating their eventual record dea with Parlophone over champagne, EMI executive Rupert Perry expressed his enjoyment of the song to Jonny, who told him it had fallen out of favor with the band. They ended up dropping "Phillipa Chicken" from their live show and any future release.

"Nothing Touches Me"

In a rare instance of full disclosure, Thom Yorke told *Curfew* in December 1991 exactly what "Nothing Touches Me" is about.

"'Nothing Touches Me' is based on an artist who was imprisoned for abusing children and spent the rest of his life in a cell painting, but the song is about isolating yourself so much that one day you realise you haven't got any friends anymore and no one talks to you."

When the writer points out that the song's frenetic beat and instrumentation—including what sounds like a real car horn of a harmonica, possibly played by Jonny—offsets the rather miserable subject matter, Yorke backpedals. A mere 20 minutes later, he says that he doesn't actually know what any of his songs are about.

This would happen in countless interviews throughout the years—Yorke growing cagey when someone seems poised to break through a lyrical truth or tie a Radiohead song to any one thing. Maybe that's why the band decided to never release "Nothing Touches Me" on a proper album, EP, or single.

It works quite well on the Hufford/Edge tape, though. As condescending as it sounds, the casette's biggest strength was that, for once, all of On a Friday's songs sounded like they were being written and played by the same band.

Manic Hedgehog

Hufford and Edge—now finding themselves as de facto managers of On a Friday—got a local independent record store, Manic Hedgehog, to sell the new tape for £3. The spine read *ON A FRIDAY first tapes*, but it's become colloquially known as *Manic Hedgehog*.

Album art for On a Friday's 1991 "Manic Hedgehog" demo tape.   *Author's collection*

By this point, On a Friday were hungry to take their career to the next level. In a stranger-than-fiction twist, the chance would soon fall into their lap.

Enter Keith Wozencroft, a sales rep for EMI that was about to get transferred to the A&R department of one of EMI's record labels, Parlophone. Before the transition, he was making stops at various record stores to thank them for their business. One of them was Our Price, where an employee named Colin Greenwood was working a shift. And wouldn't you know, he just happened to be in a band. Wozencroft left with a tape of On a Friday's various demos in his hands.

Like Richard Haines at Dungeon before him, Wozencroft wasn't wowed by every last track, but was drawn to "Stop Whispering"—so much that he decided to go catch the band live at Oxford Park. Of course, it wasn't a completely selfless act. As a new A&R rep, Wozencroft was on the lookout for fresh talent that could get him some attention from the rest of Parlophone. While he talked up the personnel at the label, Hufford and Edge started reaching out to the people they knew at EMI—they very place they were signed to back when in their Aerial FX days.

The teamwork paid off, and within months, there was intense interest not just from Parlophone, but numerous other major labels who all converged on a show-stopping November gig at the Jericho Tavern. Lucky for Wozencroft, On a Friday decided to go with Parlophone, inking a deal on December 21, 1991.

17

"I'm Going Out for a Little Drive"

Drill EP

Calling *Drill* an EP feels like a stretch. Considering its 10:33 runtime and that most of its songs would be reworked for the more substantial *Pablo Honey*, it plays more like a demo. It's not quite as raw as *Manic Hedgehog* (despite it containing the same version of "Thinking About You"), but nowhere near the finished product and production of Radiohead's first proper album. Still, EMI wanted some music to sell under the Parlophone label, and they wanted it quick.

The band recorded most of *Drill* with Chris Hufford at Courtyard Studio, not too far from their old stomping ground of the Abingdon School. Still in operation today (though now under the ownership of Ian Davenport), Court-yard bills itself as "a residential studio out in the wilds of Oxfordshire." Whether intentional or not, that down-home spirit comes across in *Drill*'s music. Slightly clumsy and naive (a result of growing pains and Hufford now pulling double duty as producer and band co-manager), the arrangements are nothing if not in the moment—the sounds of a young band still figuring out how to get the best sound on tape and solidify other aspects of their identity. Part of that identity was having Hufford, along with his partner Bryce Edge, stick solely to manage-rial duties from there on out.

Drill's transitory nature also extends to the more external aspects of the EP, such as the splatter-collage artwork (better-suited for a Trapper Keeper than a Radiohead album) to the band name. While cutting the majority of *Drill* in February 1992 (the band opted to use the *Manic Hedgehog* version of "Thinking About You," which was recorded that previous October), Radiohead still went by On a Friday. A live review from *Melody Maker* that praised the band's performance, but relentlessly criticized the generic name, prompted them to change that.

A month after they finished recording, On a Friday casually drew inspiration from a forgettable Talking Heads song called "Radio Head" and changed their name to its current moniker. Ironically, George Orwell is buried nearby Courtyard

Album art for the *Drill* EP.   *Author's collection*

at All Saints' Church in Sutton Courtenay. Perhaps his spectral presence was daring the band to get more serious and complex in their subject matter.

Despite its rough-and-tumble nature, *Drill* still deserves some attention for being the first official Radiohead release, even if it failed to make any kind of widespread impression when it was hit stores on May 5, 1992. It's telling that, when its songs were included on the two-disc Collector's Edition of *Pablo Honey* in 2009, EMI merely listed them as demos, rather than originally being part of a separate work.

The Songs

"Prove Yourself"

Of all the songs on *Drill*, "Prove Yourself" sounds the closest to the more polished studio version that would appear on *Pablo Honey*. For the most part, the latter version remains superior, with Ed O'Brien's backing vocals ringing loud and clear. Only then does the title phrase become a mantra bellowed from the sky. Here, it sounds meek and gets smothered by guitars.

The compressed loudness does have one added benefit. While the power of O'Brien's vocals is sorely missed on the demo, the increased indecipherability of Thom Yorke's lyrics remains a boon. The words to "Prove Yourself" have always been somewhat cringeworthy—symptomatic of the confessional, heart-on-the-sleeve diary Yorke clung to in Radiohead's earlier work; a self-imposed challenge to claim his own life. The less understandable, the better.

For all its faults, the demo version of "Prove Yourself" did receive some airplay from disc jockey and *Top of the Pops* presented Gary Davies over at BBC Radio 1. That makes it the first Radiohead song heard by a national audience. It was a small audience, but a national audience nonetheless.

"Stupid Car"

"Stupid Car" stands out for being the only song on *Drill* to not appear on *Pablo Honey*, or any other Radiohead album for that matter. It also marks the first proper recording where Yorke explores his deep-rooted fear of automobiles.

It doesn't have the obsessive paranoia of "Killer Cars" or the subversive rebirth metaphor of "Airbag." Instead, Yorke simply talks about how it's difficult to drive his girlfriend's car, then ties it to some tension in their relationship. He elaborated on the origins of the song (and all the car-themed songs that came after it) to the now defunct magazine *Addicted to Noise* in 1996:

"I used to have this one car, and I very nearly killed myself in it one morning, and gave my girlfriend at the time really bad whiplash in an accident. I was 17 … Anyway, eventually, my dad bought me another car, a Morris Minor, you know, and when you drove around corners in it, the driver door used to fly open … It was like standing in the middle of the road with no protection at all. So I just gradually became emotionally tied up in this whole thing."

Maybe it's because there's no later studio version to compare it to, but of all the songs on *Drill*, "Stupid Car" feels the most complete. Like a British counterpart to Bruce Springsteen's "Stolen Car," it relies little more than a handful of sustained bass notes, a repetition of clean, ethereal guitar chords, and Yorke's voice. It cycles through a retracted crescendo with every other chord sequence, only fully rising in the final stretch with the lyric "I cannot see the road."

A slightly altered "Tinnitus Mix" of "Stupid Car" popped up on the the *Volume* series, Total Record Company's compilation of demos, alternate versions, and non-album singles from a variety of alternative bands in the '90s. "Stupid Car (Tinnitus Mix)" had the distinction of appearing on both *Volume 7* and *Volume*'s best-of disc, *Sharks Patrol These Waters*.

The alternate mix isn't all that remarkable—it's just the *Drill* version of the song with an ambient wind effect thrown over it. Still listenable, but not essential.

"You"

Similar to "Prove Yourself," "You" sticks close to the studio version on *Pablo Honey*. The only difference is that the demo is a touch sloppier, while the later rendition stays heavier, consistent, and more precise.

"Thinking About You"

"Thinking About You," on the other hand, stands apart from its *Pablo Honey* counterpart by going full-on cowpunk. The mournful strumming gets replaced by an off-kilter drumbeat, as well as yelping and guitar work straight from a ranch somewhere in the American West.

While nowhere near as pristine as the melancholic *Pablo Honey* rendition, its stubbornly slash-and-burn nature suits the song much better. As far as love songs go, "Thinking About You" is lethargic and, as we'll see in the *Pablo Honey* chapter, more than a little gross in its lyrics. The demo version injects it with an energy that distracts from the words. It's as close to a barnburner as early Radiohead would ever get.

18

"Anyone Can Play Guitar and They Won't Be a Nothing Anymore"

Pablo Honey

Radiohead's first proper full-length, *Pablo Honey*, is the sound of a rock band embracing that they are in fact a rock band. A departure from the '80s jangle and failed genre experiments of On a Friday, the guitars are bigger, the choruses are more anthemic, and the lyrics are moodier.

In order to put a brighter coat of polish on their sound, the band pivoted from manager Chris Hufford (who was probably never suited to produce the band in the first place) to Paul Q. Kolderie and Sean Slade. Based out of Boston, the producers had worked on records from fellow New Englanders Dinosaur Jr. and Buffalo Tom at their own recording studio, Fort Apache, and were in London trying to make some business connections. When they tried to sell one of EMI's A&R men, Nick Gatfield, on their work with Nashville-based jazz-metal act Clockhammer, he thought the multilayered guitar work might make them a good fit for Radiohead. Ironically, Clockhammer drummer Ken Coomer would go on to serve seven years in Wilco, a band that often gets hailed as Radiohead's American counterpart.

Kolderie and Slade were onboard after hearing "Prove Yourself," "I Can't," and the early demo of "Stop Whispering." For the band's part, they were excited at the prospect of working with a new production team, especially since one of the members (Kolderie) had engineered the Pixies' debut EP, *Come on Pilgrim*. They also looked forward to having pre-production sessions at their own rehearsal space. Stationed in a shed on an apple farm in the Oxfordshire countryside, the makeshift headquarters would come to be known as Canned Applause.

While Hufford would continue to co-manage the band with Bryce Edge and still get to helm "I Can't" and "Lurgee" at their Courtyard Studio, Kolderie and Slade set up shop at nearby Chipping Norton Recording Studios, taking over production duties for the remaining 10 songs and a handful of B-sides and unused tracks. According to Ed O'Brien, Slade in particular wanted a gnarled

Album art for *Pablo Honey*.   *Author's collection*

wall of sound, directing the band to heap on the guitar tracks and overdubs. They happily obliged.

The final result ended up being the most straightforward rock album of Radiohead's career, and arguably the only time the band cherry-picked from the musical trends of the past and the present, rather than forging their own path. Even the equally digestible *The Bends* would go on to subvert the cliches of grunge, alternative, and classic rock, rather than just aping them.

The Songs

"You"

Packing a heavier punch than the demo version from *Drill*, *Pablo Honey*'s "You" also contains an extra verse that references Yorke and whoever the title refers to getting trapped in a fire.

The added verse is an example of an oft-used Radiohead pivot, where Yorke transforms what could be a love song into an exercise in misery. While the muscular guitar workouts don't sound too different from most other alt-rock bands in the early '90s, the shift gives some insight into Yorke's self-destructive tendencies with his lyrics—namely his difficulty at writing an honest love song without crashing the whole mess into the sea.

Yorke and Jonny Greenwood went on to perform a stripped-down version of "You" on *MTV's Most Wanted* in October of 1994. Besides better suiting the song's 3/4 waltz time, the rejiggered arrangement of just Yorke's acoustic guitar and Greenwood's electric adds a moroseness that actually ends up being more surprising.

"Creep"

As far as subject matter goes, "Creep" isn't all that different from "You" or most of the other songs on *Pablo Honey*—another first-person account of a guy who's obsessed with a woman he'll never have. Yorke supposedly wrote it about someone he worshipped from afar—but never actually interacted with—while studying at the University of Exeter. As Jonny Greenwood recounted to the *Chicago Sun-Times* on June 7, 1993, the woman in question actually showed up at a Radiohead concert in Yorke's former college town.

"Thom was mortified, because he's never spoken to her or anything," Greenwood said. "He just followed her for a couple of days or a week or whatever about two or three years ago. And here she was. He was very shaken up after that."

If we're being honest, that story—not to mention the self-loathing and woe-is-me navel-gazing—comes off as rather toxic when viewed through a contemporary lens. On a good deal of *Pablo Honey* and especially "Creep," Yorke comes off as someone who knows that what he's doing and singing about is, well, creepy. Unlike Radiohead's later work, the whole schtick feels miserable and starved for attention.

But to write off "Creep" would be to write off Radiohead's entire legacy. For one, it granted the band much deserved popularity. After they played the song for Slade and Kolderie at a 1992 rehearsal for *Pablo Honey*, the producers insisted on pitching it to EMI as the album's first single, rather than "Lurgee" or the B-sides "Inside My Head" and "Million Dollar Question," all of which were then under consideration.

Released on September 21, 1992—a full five months before the album came out—"Creep" went on to chart around the world, although its success wasn't exactly immediate, especially in Radiohead's homeland. It only reached #78 on the British charts, the blow worsened by a lukewarm review in the *Evening Standard*. Surprisingly, Israel was the first country to give the single any kind of significant attention.

This was thanks to Uzi Preuss, who had recently begun working as a promotions man for EMI's international division. He excitedly passed along "Creep" to Yoav Kutner, a DJ often heralded as the Israeli equivalent to BBC's John Peel. Kutner's repeated airplay of the song helped it reach the upper echelon of the country's pop charts, with word of mouth soon leading to further international success in New Zealand, Spain, Scandinavia, and the US, where "Creep" reached #34 on the US *Billboard* Hot 100 and #2 on the US *Billboard* Modern Rock Tracks.

Radiohead eventually found love in England, with "Creep" reaching #7 on the UK Singles chart and receiving Platinum certification, in addition to going Platinum in Italy, and Gold in Australia and Canada. And to think that the band initially wrote it off as their "Scott Walker song" (at first, the producers thought it actually *was* a cover of Walker).

"Creep"'s significance isn't solely about its financial success, either. At the end of each of Yorke's rather quiet verses, Jonny disrupts the G-B-C-Cm chord progression with a series of jarring "dead notes." Each sequence only lasts three notes, but launches the song into an orbit of garbled noise as Yorke taunts "You're so fucking special."

Jonny reportedly hit the notes out of frustration over how quiet and repetitive the verses were, as if unable to control the creativity inside himself. *Pablo Honey* may not be as adventurous as all of Radiohead's other albums, but the distorted sections of "Creep"—however brief—show a band itching to burst out of the grunge/alternative box. Without the dead notes, Yorke has wondered if the song would have even been successful in the first place.

Not that everyone was all that taken by "Creep." Although Scott Walker never accused Radiohead of plagiarism, Albert Hammond and Mike Hazlewood noticed a striking similarity to their 1972 ballad "The Air That I Breathe," which was first recorded by Hammond, then popularized by the Hollies. When the songwriting team sued Radiohead for co-writing credits on "Creep" and a percentage of the song's royalties, the band obliged, more or less admitting that they had committed an act of love and theft.

Jonny told *Fender Frontline* that, while writing "Creep" in fall of 1993, "Ed stopped [us] and said, 'This is the same chord sequence as that Hollies song,' and then sang it. So Thom copied it. It was funny to us in a way, sort of feeding something like that into [it]."

Hammond and Hazlewood appreciated Radiohead's honesty and ended up taking just a small, undisclosed percentage of "Creep"'s royalties, in addition to receiving co-writing credit. The members of Radiohead were lucky to get a much happier ending to their plagiarism scandal than their contemporaries the Verve, who ended up relinquishing *all* of their royalties to Mick Jagger and Keith Richards for "Bittersweet Symphony" (an "homage" to the Rolling Stones' "The Last Time").

In a strange twist of fate, pop iconoclast Lana Del Rey claimed in January 2018 that Radiohead was suing her for 100 percent of the royalties of her song "Get

Free," which they claimed was a ripoff of "Creep." In a somewhat ugly dispute that played out on Del Rey's Twitter account and through the mouths of Radiohead's lawyers, it was revealed that publisher Warner/Chappell Music was indeed suing Del Rey on behalf of all of "Creep"'s songwriters (including Hammond and Hazlewood), but not for the entire percentage, as Del Rey originally claimed.

While no one has confirmed the specifics of the legal arrangement, on March 25, 2018, Del Rey told her crowd at Lollapalooza Brazil that the lawsuit had been settled, and she was now permitted to once again perform "Get Free." Which she immediately did.

"How Do You?"

Lyrically, "How Do You?" leaves a lot to be desired, finding Yorke leveling vague accusations of bigotry and stupidity at an even vaguer enemy. But at 2:12, it's by far the breeziest on *Pablo Honey*, given an extra bit of bombast from Jonny's collapsible piano and a chord progression that borders on pop punk.

Even at their lightest, Radiohead would never again sound so spritely and full of joy. It makes perfect sense that this is the song where they included a sample from the album's namesake *Jerky Boys* prank call toward the end.

Pablo Honey's title came from a *Jerky Boys* prank call of the same name.

Author's collection

"Stop Whispering"

To their credit, Radiohead have always been open about their tendency to crib from other artists on *Pablo Honey*. They included a sample of the Jerky Boys on "How Do You?", happily cooperated with the Hollies' lawsuit over "Creep," and on "Stop Whispering," embraced the influence of the Pixies to the point where they damn near replicated the cover of *Surfer Rosa* for the single's artwork.

The band recorded an early version of "Stop Whispering" during their On a Friday days in April 1991, two years after the Pixies released *Doolittle* and not even a year after they released *Bossanova*. However, Radiohead admitted that the final result sounded more akin to Bono than Black Francis and co. That the lyrics call for some kind of generic political uprising didn't help.

Perhaps the U2 similarities are what inspired EMI and Parlophone to release "Stop Whispering" as the fourth single from the *Pablo Honey* era. The song's stratospheric vibe certainly is catchy. In hindsight, though, Radiohead has admitted to wishing they had taken some of their own advice in the song—to speak up and ask their record labels to choose something else. "I was for releasing 'Blow Out,'" Jonny told *B-side* magazine in summer of 1995.

The band's instincts were on point. "Stop Whispering" failed to even touch "Creep"'s success as a single, peaking at #23 on the US *Billboard* Modern Rock Tracks and a meager #131 on the Australian ARIA charts with no certifications.

"Thinking About You"

Propelled by inward acoustic strumming, "Thinking About You" would actually be a romantic ballad if it weren't soured by the band's true intent.

"[It] was about wanking," Jonny bluntly told *Select* in 1995.

"I feel tremendous guilt for any sexual feelings I have, so I end up spending my entire life feeling sorry for fancying somebody," Yorke told *Rolling Stone* that same year. "Even in school, I thought girls were so wonderful that I was scared to death of them. I masturbate a lot."

To be fair, the song does contain the line "I'm playing with myself," which should have made its true meaning clear from the get-go. But there are more clever ways to write about masturbation (see Jackson Browne's "Rosie"), and any deeper meaning about unrequited love gets undermined by a dick joke, further worsening *Pablo Honey*'s overall feeling-sorry-for-one's-self ickiness.

"Anyone Can Play Guitar"

Of all of *Pablo Honey*'s songs, "Anyone Can Play Guitar" achieves the greatest sense of subversiveness by taking down the myth of the rock 'n' roll messiah—an archetype Yorke himself would one day embody in the eyes of his most ardent fans.

He even goes as far to growl the name Jim Morrison, another musician who wound up developing a cult of personality (and embracing it), only to end up, in Yorke's words during an MTV performance in 1993, "Fat! Ugly! Dead!"

"It's really just a series of thoughts about getting up onstage, making a brat of yourself and making a career out of it," Yorke told *Melody Maker* that same year.

As a sort of in-joke and nod to the title, all of Radiohead's members—along with producers Kolderie and Slade—played guitar for the song's collage-like intro. Jonny even took his experimental spirit one step further by strumming his Telecaster Plus with a paintbrush.

Judging from the opening's atonal nature, it becomes clear that no, not just anyone can play guitar. Before we can figure out who's playing what, the sound collage gels into something coherent, with Colin Greenwood's woozy bass line eventually spinning into a punky, slightly sped-up chorus. Even if the song didn't achieve the success of "Creep" as *Pablo Honey*'s second single, it remains a bright spot on the album for its humor, subversion, and force.

"Ripcord"

Over a quiet-loud-quiet chord progression that, at its best, is by the numbers, Yorke bemoans the tyranny of modern politicians. He doesn't have much to say here beyond the metaphor of the title, and the band would go on to examine The Futility of It All much more interestingly on later albums.

"Vegetable"

The lazy metaphors continue in a mid-tempo ditty that O'Brien once explained was about people not being controlled. Along with "Ripcord," "Vegetable" puts a big mid-album slump in *Pablo Honey*—a record that's already fairly slumpy to begin with.

"Prove Yourself"

Around the time of *Drill* and *Pablo Honey*, Yorke would sometimes say that Oxford was was so bad, it had the potential to induce suicidal urges.

While that's not the most insightful or likable message (and probably didn't reflect Yorke's true feelings), at least the mid-20s angst gets offset by Radiohead's musicianship. Simply put, "Prove Yourself" soars, especially in the chorus, when O'Brien's anthemic backing vocals dare the listener to go through with their most dangerous idea. There are many later Radiohead songs that make better use of musical-lyrical juxtaposition, but "Prove Yourself" somewhat picks up *Pablo Honey*'s lumpy middle by trying something different.

"I Can't"

The viewpoint in "I Can't" amounts to the usual *Pablo Honey* misery, but stands out from most of the other tracks for a handful of reasons. First, it's one of just two songs to be produced by Hufford at Courtyard Studio. Second, Jonny somehow makes his guitar sound like a singing saw in the outro.

Finally, there's a concert performance of "I Can't" circulating online from an unknown gig in 1990, making it the earliest known live video recording of the band's final lineup. It may have even predated the song's appearance on the *Manic Hedgehog* demo. Although Radiohead would play it a handful of times in their early days, they dropped "I Can't" from their set by 1993 and haven't played it since.

"Lurgee"

The second Hufford-produced track, in which Radiohead once again prove they do soft better than loud on *Pablo Honey*. Without ever fully exploding, the dueling guitars build around Colin's bass line, which provides the central progression of the song. By the end, Yorke isn't singing as much as wailing in the background, emitting a looseness that breaks up *Pablo Honey*'s overreliance on loud/soft dynamics. It's the most gorgeous cut on the record.

"Lurgee" also stands out for being an early example of Radiohead borrowing from British pop culture for lyrical content. The strange word of the title is a riff on "lurgy," the name of an imaginary disease popularized by writers Spike Milligan and Eric Sykes for a 1954 episode of *The Goon Show*. On the November 9 edition of the iconic BBC comedy program, the characters face a deadly outbreak of the "Dreaded Lurgi." Of course, the sickness turns out to be nonexistent.

It's unclear where the word "lurgy" originated, and just as *The Goon Show* tweaked the spelling for their own comedic purposes, Radiohead replaced the "y" with a double "e." In the lyrics, Yorke uses the epidemic as a metaphor for a toxic relationship. It's not the most inventive device, but the gossamer of the music makes up for it.

"Blow Out"

Unlike most of the electric songs on *Pablo Honey*, "Blow Out" leans on a clean guitar sound. Outside of being sonically different from the rest of the album, it ends the proceedings with a warmth that, along with the jazz-like hiss of Phil Selway's drums, wouldn't be out of place on *In Rainbows*.

Even when the distortion comes in full force at the minute-and-a-half mark, there's enough atmosphere throughout to make "Blow Out" a true anomaly—guitars squelch and the palm-muted chords on the outro sound straight out of a hair-metal song. While that dates the track somewhat, it displays a sense of experimentation that would come to define Radiohead as a band.

It's also one of the few times on *Pablo Honey* that Yorke's imagery holds its own against his later lyrics. Sure, the words are once again examining his own self-obsessed fragility, but the metaphors—Yorke wrapped in cotton, coated in sugar, and held together by glue—have a repulsive body-horror quality that ties to Stanley Donwood's visuals, despite him having not collaborated with the band at that point.

B-sides

The *Pablo Honey* era contained a handful of B-sides that weren't on the album or any of its corresponding EPs. Most of them are even more derivative than the tracks on Radiohead's full-length debut, leaning into the grunge and alternative trends that Radiohead would avoid like the Dreaded Lurgi plague later on.

"Inside My Head"

"Inside My Head" almost has a "Creep" moment, when Colin's finger-walking bass line gets interrupted by an off-tone squeal from his brother's guitar. But just when it seems that the band is going to lock into full disruption mode, the note draws out and everything congeals into just another '90s guitar workout.

The lyrics are equally angsty, with Yorke reaching into his lower register to, according to him, rail against his old workplace. After making it as a musician, he apparently fantasized "about getting in a car and ramming the shop where I used to work. I just wanted to do that so badly." This makes "Inside My Head" little more than a grunge tantrum, with the live version on the "Creep" reissue pushing the pissiness to the point of parody. Today, it seems shocking that EMI initially wanted to release it as Radiohead's debut single.

"Million Dollar Question"

Also released on the first issue of the "Creep" single, "Million Dollar Question" finds Yorke yet again longing for the destruction of his old workplace. "Was always waiting for the crush / the car to drive right through the shops," he confesses in the opening line. He eventually descends into more grumpiness about being on a major label (yawn).

What "Million Dollar Question" does have going for it is a sense of fun—at least sonically. As strange as it sounds when looking at the weight of

Radiohead's later material, the pop punk of some of their earlier cuts was usually a welcome genre experiment, injecting the malaise with a shot of caffeine. It's exhilarating to hear the band go from frenetic pogoing to a psychedelic breakdown and back in the short space of just under three-and-a-half minutes.

"Yes I Am"

Appearing on the reissue of "Creep," "Yes I Am" is the third "Creep" tie-in to once again mention cars. It's also the umpteenth Radiohead song from the *Pablo Honey* era to present Yorke as the underdog resenting an undefined enemy. Despite the redundancy of the subject matter, the song has some nice stop/start moments at its core and a face-melting guitar freakout at the end.

"Pop is Dead"

On the other hand, jauntiness wasn't always a recipe for success in early Radiohead songs. This standalone single got rightfully crucified by the press for containing some of the band's most uninspired satire. Over what might be the poppiest chord progression in a Radiohead song (Get it? They're being *ironic*), Yorke criticizes the most obvious bastions of music-industry fakeness, including plastic surgery, cocaine, and sexual favors.

To the band's credit, they recognized "Pop is Dead" as a failed experiment a few years after its release.

"We don't do irony," O'Brien told *Melody Maker* on May 24, 1997. "The only times we've tried were when we were in America, where it just goes over everyone's heads, and on 'Pop Is Dead,' which was rubbish. Surprisingly, those Saturday morning TV show offers didn't come pouring in."

To add insult to injury, O'Brien's own father would constantly make fun of it, ribbing him about the pretentiousness of the music video when his friends were over for beers.

"Coke Babies"

The snottiness of the title aside, "Coke Babies" doesn't have any of the embarrassing angst of the other *Pablo Honey* B-sides. It almost functions as a soundscape, the guitars weaving and bending through grunge and psychedelia as Yorke mumbles some thrown-together lyrics about "teething" and "easy living." Colin hums to himself at the end (he didn't know the tape was rolling), adding to the low-key surrealism that feels like a prototype for some of the stranger cuts on *Amnesiac*.

Conclusion

It would be hard to find a Radiohead fan, critic, or band member who believes *Pablo Honey* to be the group's best album. But it was far from lambasted in the press upon its release. In typical British hype-machine fashion, *NME* praised the band as being "one of rock's brightest hopes," and *Q* classified it as a solid, if somewhat forgettable, work. Even the more negative reviews, such as the write-up from go-to Radiohead hatchet man Robert Christgau, recognized the greatness of "Creep."

Ironically, Radiohead's later work continues to render *Pablo Honey* more distinct—and more inferior. Radiohead has never written another album like it and probably never will again. Its lack of character gives it all the character in the world, ultimately making it a true curiosity in the band's catalog. And if nothing else, the record more than put them on the map, going Gold in Argentina and Australia, Platinum in the United States and Belgium, and Double Platinum in Canada and the United Kingdom. Without *Pablo Honey*, no one would have cared about the superior work that came later.

19

"One by One"

Itch EP

Of Radiohead's six EPs, no fewer than three of them were originally released as exclusives in Japan, with *Com Lag (2plus2isfive)* also getting distribution in Australia. All three mini-albums have been criticized for being somewhat piecemeal.

That's most true of *Itch*, a placeholder in between *Pablo Honey* and the much fuller *My Iron Lung* EP that plays more like a compilation of live recordings, a smattering of unreleased material, and alternate versions of *Pablo Honey* songs.

While that latter category might make the EP seem inessential, it begins a trend that Radiohead would continue to embrace (and perfect) throughout their career—unveiling various incarnations of their songs, some of which would prove to be improvements over the final studio versions.

Album art for *Itch* EP.
Author's collection

The Songs

"Stop Whispering" (US version)

With *Pablo Honey* songs, it's usually a good policy to smother the lyrics. Here, they play second banana to added strings and a slightly faster piece. The emphasis is suddenly on the exhilarating mood rather than the dour words.

"Thinking About You" (*Drill* version)

Although it's merely an encore of the demo of "Thinking About You" from *Drill*, we'll take cowpunk energy over a spotlit dick joke any day.

"Faithless, the Wonder Boy"

Thom Yorke wouldn't perfect the art of the revenge-fantasy song until later in his career, which means "Faithless, the Wonder Boy" succumbs to the same fate as "Inside My Head." That is, he paints his rivals in broad strokes (skate rats or grunge musicians or drug addicts or something). The one saving grace is a spacy guitar squelch that ignites the chorus.

"Banana Co."

It's hard to tell what's going on lyrically in "Banana Co.," and for once, that's a good thing. Gone is the romantic despair and angst of most of the other *Pablo Honey*-era material, replaced by something vaguely political or perhaps even anarchic. The title conjures images of an uprising in a banana republic nation, but then again, who knows?

The big takeaway from "Banana Co."—outside of its refreshing crypticism—is that there's little volume. Jonny Greenwood and Ed O'Brien trade what sound like nylon guitar lines without ever exploding into distortion.

The song's overall weirdness made it a natural contender for *The Bends*, but Yorke opted to include it on the *Criminal Justice: Axe the Act* benefit compilation instead. This version has a full-band arrangement, unlike the quieter one on *Itch*, which was taken from an acoustic performance at Signal Radio on February 11, 1993.

"Killer Cars" (live version)

Radiohead's finest song about vehicular paranoia becomes extra nightmarish on *Itch*, thanks to enthusiastic cheering from the crowd at Chicago's Metro. Given the quiet nature of the arrangement (just Yorke and an acoustic guitar) and the darkness found in the lyrics, it's hard to square a bunch of drunk Chicagoans clapping off-rhythm and enthusiastically screaming like they're at a Poison concert.

Then again, that's also what makes this version so twisted and great. Despite being a B-side, Radiohead would go on to obsess over a definitive version of the track, prompting them to record two alternate takes during the sessions for *The Bends*.

Ironically, when Radiohead was recording *Pablo Honey*, Phil Selway would give his bandmates and producers rides in his brand-new Morris Minor—the same automobile Yorke crashed as a teenager and the vehicle that went on to inspire all of the band's car songs.

"Vegetable" (live version)

The live guitar work on one of *Pablo Honey*'s biggest duds recalls Radiohead's heroes R.E.M., and the boneheaded lyrics get buried by Thom Yorke's unhinged delivery and yet another apeshit crowd. It's all kinds of hysterical, which makes it all kinds of wonderful.

"You" (live version)

Mostly the same as the studio version, this has less gloss and not as many guitar atmospherics during the verses. It almost functions as yet another demo, similar to the one that appeared on *Drill*.

"Creep" (acoustic version)

Exactly what it sounds like: "Creep" without the very thing that makes "Creep" great. Yorke tries to make up for the absence of Jonny's groundbreaking dead chords by delivering a raspier vocal performance, but it's just not the same.

Despite its defanged nature, the acoustic version of "Creep" has appeared on numerous Radiohead releases, from its own UK single to the *My Iron Lung* EP and the Collector's Edition of *Pablo Honey*.

20

"All My Past and Futures"

Amnesiac

Since both albums' respective songs came out of the same recording sessions, detractors of *Amnesiac* tend to write it off as a collection of B-sides for *Kid A*. But according to the members of Radiohead, the band was very aware of the differences between the tracks while they were writing them.

For lack of a better term, *Amnesiac* could be described as more "organic" than its immediate predecessor. When speaking to *Rolling Stone* on May 24, 2001, just 12 days before the record's June 5 release date, Ed O'Brien remembered Stanley Donwood using an apt analogy: "He said, '*Kid A* is like you pick up the phone, you call somebody, and there's an answering machine on the other end. With *Amnesiac,* you get through to that person. And you're engaged in the conversation.'"

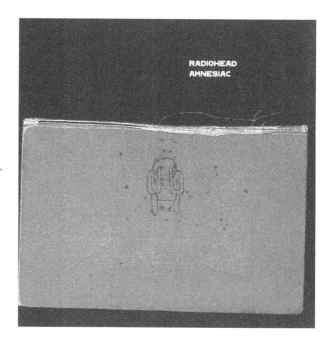

Album art for *Amnesiac.*
Author's collection

"But there are two frames of mind in there," Phil Selway elaborated. "[A] tension between our old approach of all being in a room playing together and the other extreme of manufacturing music in the studio. I think *Amnesiac* comes out stronger in the band-arrangement way."

That's not to say *Amnesiac* is without samples and electronic elements. But for every loop and intentionally glitched typo, there's a live jazz arrangement or snapshot of a New Orleans funeral. If both albums are concerned with time, *Amnesiac* is more expansive in its history. It looks to the past, present, and more naturalistic future, where *Kid A* stays stubbornly preoccupied with an ice age so cold and distant that it can barely be described in human speech. In that way, *Amnesiac* should never be viewed as *Kid A*'s leftovers album, but as its sister album.

The Songs

"Packt Like Sardines in a Crushd Tin Box"

One of the most electronically minded songs on *Amnesiac*, the album's opener still has an overt warmth. Yorke turns to his mid-range and uses vocal distortion sparingly, allowing the lyrics of claustrophobia and a futile quest to ring clear.

The tones also come from a more homey and domestic place than anything on *Kid A*. The central synth melody could just as easily be a group of kids playing Simon in someone's basement. And as hollow as the opening percussion sounds, it also resembles pots and pans—objects found in just about any kitchen. From the get-go, Radiohead is already exploring a more accessible (or at least more immediate) environment than their last album.

Kid A sister song:

"Idioteque"

"Pyramid Song"

Like "The National Anthem" before it, "Pyramid Song" borrows heavily from Charles Mingus, paying homage to the plodding pace and chord progression of his composition "Freedom," then leaning further into jazz at the two-minute mark. It's here that Selway rides his cymbals into a swing beat with a time signature that still gets debated by fans.

But "Pyramid Song"'s most fascinating characteristic is how it kicks off *Amnesiac*'s view of time as a flexible, unifying force. Not only does Radiohead move from the singular digitization of "Packt Like Sardines In a Crushd Tin

Box" to the older art form of jazz—Thom Yorke's lyrics draw inspiration from even further back with ancient Egyptian art and the *Tibetan Book of the Dead*. But he's mentioned more modern thinkers such as Stephen Hawking as also having an influence on his words. The variety of inspirations from different time periods comes out in the lyrics, with Yorke observing ex-lovers, futuristic vehicles, and black-eyed angels all congregating in the same cosmic soup.

Yorke elaborated on this theme to *NME* on January 30, 2001: "I read that the gnostics believe when we are born, we are forced to forget where we have come from in order to deal with the trauma of arriving in this life. I thought this was really fascinating. It's like the river of forgetfulness. [*Amnesiac*] may have been recorded at the same time [as *Kid A*] . . . but it comes from a different place, I think. It sounds like finding an old chest in someone's attic with all these notes and maps and drawings and descriptions of going to a place you cannot remember."

In the case of "Pyramid Song," there are many places: the Jazz Age, ancient Egyptian tombs, and even the 12th-century church of Dorchester Abbey, where Jonny Greenwood recorded the song's haunting string section with the Orchestra of St John's.

Kid A sister song:

"The National Anthem"

"Pulk/Pull Revolving Doors"

Nonsensical by design, "Pulk/Pull Revolving Doors" stays anchored by a drum sequence and several loops created by Yorke on a Roland MC-505 groovebox. Elsewhere, it's gibberish—the cryptic phrases run through an Autotuner.

Although the device was already used on "Packt Like Sardines In a Crushd Tin Box" for slight tonal variations, here, it's meant to completely distort what Yorke is saying. This marks an early departure from the Autotoner's original purpose of pitch-correcting vocals, instead using it to add more evocative textures to songs. This practice would be widely adopted by hip-hop artists after Kanye West's 2008 album *808s & Heartbreak*.

Like so many of the other songs on *Amnesiac*, "Pulk/Pull" is also a mashup of different time periods, with some of the loops pulled from the *OK Computer* sessions at St Catherine's Court and snippets of an early version of "True Love Waits," the live fan favorite that would later be recorded for 2016's *A Moon Shaped Pool*. This makes "Pulk/Pull Revolving Doors," trivial as it is, an amalgamation of Radiohead's past, present, and future.

Kid A sister song:

"Kid A"

"You and Whose Army?"

The throwbacks continue with "You and Whose Army?", where Radiohead dabbles in archaic technology. To replicate the warm timbre of the 1940s harmony vocal group the Ink Spots, the band recorded everything live through an egg box, then bolstered the muffled delivery with a Palm Speaker. Described by Greenwood as "a bit like a harp with a speaker in the middle of it," it was also invented by Maurice Martenot, creator of Radiohead's oft-used instrument, the ondes Martenot.

As is the case with any of Radiohead's genre experiments, the final result isn't quite an homage, but a new and warped version of something old, especially when the tinniness gets overtaken by an orchestral crescendo. Also, it's unlikely that the Ink Spots ever sang defiant lyrics against the Blair administration.

Kid A sister song:

The hidden portion of "Motion Picture Soundtrack"

"I Might Be Wrong"

Though it would eventually receive a more amplified, electronically textured treatment on record, "I Might Be Wrong" premiered as a solo acoustic composition at a Radiohead concert on June 19, 2000, in Monza Italy. When Yorke couldn't remember the lyrics to "Killer Cars," he spontaneously launched into a new song.

Despite the stripped-down arrangement, the original "I Might Be Wrong" still has the same key and drop D tuning of its future counterpart. Built around a bass line designed by Colin Greenwood to invoke Bernard Edwards of Chic, it plays like a dark, minor-key take on disco as Yorke criticizes his own pessimism. When answering fan theories in an online "Lyrics Lounge," Yorke coyly alluded to the song addressing everything from Buddhism (which he was exploring in in the late '90s) to a bad relationship to "the merging of life and death" and alcoholism.

Other fans have pointed out that the song contains river and waterfall imagery perhaps drawn from a *Siddhartha* quote that appeared on Radiohead's website in spring of 2001, right around the time of *Amnesiac*'s release. This imagery links it to "Pyramid Song" and "Like Spinning Plates," perhaps suggesting some kind of loose beginning, middle, and end to the album.

But Yorke's most direct quote about "I Might Be Wrong" relates to yet another bit of advice from his long-term partner Rachel Owen. In June 2001, he told *Mojo* "Rachel was saying to me, like she does all the time, 'Be proud of what you've done. Don't look back and just carry on like nothing's happened. Just let the bad stuff go.' When someone's constantly trying to help you out and you're trying to express something really awful, you're desperately trying to sort yourself out and you can't—you just can't. And then one day you finally hear them—you finally understand, after months and months of utter fucking torment: that's what that song is about."

So "I Might Be Wrong" becomes a natural companion to *Kid A*'s "Optimistic"— another more rock-oriented composition whose title and lyrics grew out of a pep talk from Owen.

Kid A sister song:

"Optimistic"

"Knives Out"

According to Radiohead, "Knives Out"'s simplicity is why it took the band such a long time—a whopping 373 days—to finish it.

"We couldn't possibly do anything that straight until we'd gone and been completely arse about face with everything else, in order to feel good about doing something straight like that," Yorke told *NME* in May 2001.

He's right about the aesthetic: Jonny's Smiths-cribbing guitar lines would not have been out of place on *The Bends*, and the lyrics, while applicable to a variety of topics, are straightforward in their violent imagery. However, Yorke has insisted that it's not an intentionally cruel song, despite mentions of human cannibalism and eating mice.

Kid A sister song

"How to Disappear Completely"

"Morning Bell/Amnesiac"

The *Kid A/Amnesiac* sessions resulted in two separate versions of "Morning Bell" (the second also paired together with the album title). This alone seems to be proof that *Amnesiac* was always meant to be a twinner counterpart to *Kid A* rather than a dumping ground for supplemental material.

The *Amnesiac* take of "Morning Bell" was actually recorded first, and in keeping in line with the rest of the album, has a more grounded and dirge-like musicality. Free of *Kid A*'s cooler electronic tones, the acoustic strumming, xylophones, and bicycle bells place the song more firmly in suburbia—the everyday quality of the music making the couple's divorce or separation that much more relatable and disturbing.

Kid A sister song

"Morning Bell"

"Dollars and Cents"

Radiohead may have designed "Dollars and Cents" to be an homage to krautrock legends Can, but its mashup of jazz and strings render it a less urgent relative of "Pyramid Song."

The recipe is familiar: Charles Mingus gets switched out for Alice Coltrane (Colin originally played one of her records over the recording) and Jonny once again turns to the Orchestra of St John's for the string parts. Whether it's the repetitive formula, subdued dynamics (it lacks "Pyramid Song"'s build), or less interesting lyrics (Yorke rails against our blind allegiance to capitalism), "Dollars and Cents" is one of the few times that *Amnesiac* truly does feel like a collection of B-sides and not a proper album.

Kid A sister song

"In Limbo"

"Hunting Bears"

The sole instrumental track from *Amnesiac*, "Hunting Bears" could be seen as having the same function as "Treefingers" on *Kid A*. But where the latter has shifts that rely on nuance, the former goes down a laundry list of changes and calls it a day.

It begins with some ominous guitar noodling reminiscent of Neil Young & Crazy Horse, backed by a canned wind effect. At 32 seconds, a simplistic, almost primitive progression on what sounds like an organ creeps in. This goes on for another minute-and-a-half or so, and we're done.

Disposable? Yes. But the title of the song does tie it to an important aspect of the Radiohead mythos. During the *Kid A*/*Amnesiac* era, Yorke admits to being obsessed with genetic engineering and how it could lead to the creation of monsters. This manifested itself in a cartoon created by Yorke and Donwood, where terrifying, crudely drawn, mutated bears wreak havoc.

Then there's the band's bear logo, which Yorke has dubbed the "Test Specimen"—the world's first mutant who promptly starts eating children. It's worth noting that Donwood has also claimed that the Radiohead bear came from a story he drew for his daughter, where old, dusty toys come alive to attack their owners.

While none of this gives any additional musical depth to "Hunting Bears," it hints that maybe the band intended it to be something bigger than it was. Or maybe the band just *really* likes mutant bears.

Kid A sister song:

"Treefingers"

"Like Spinning Plates"

Easily the most disorienting track on *Amnesiac*, "Like Spinning Plates" was born from the frustration over an unused song, "I will," which Thom Yorke referred to as "dodgy Kraftwerk."

The band would later re-record "I will" in a more straightforward ballad arrangement for *Hail to the Thief*, but it still got some use on *Amnesiac* when Yorke decided to play the track backwards, sing a new set of lyrics in reverse, then reverse those words so they were in the correct order.

But because they were recorded in such an intentionally convoluted fashion, everything about "Like Spinning Plates" sounds slightly off—the old Radiohead image of a synthetic being trying to act human. Maybe the spinning plates of the title are meant to be similes for the delicateness of living in a chaotic world. Personally, the image recalls a sky full of flying saucers; of staring at them and feeling hypnotized—and more than a little sick.

Kid A sister song:

"Everything In Its Right Place"

"Life In a Glasshouse"

Album closer "Life In a Glasshouse" had been kicked around for years by the band, both during the recording of *OK Computer* and during several sound-checks on the subsequent tour (as heard in the documentary *Meeting People is Easy*).

But like "The National Anthem" and "Pyramid Song," it didn't fully click until being blended with jazz music. When Jonny Greenwood realized that an aesthetic shift could be the key to unlocking the song's success, he wrote English jazz trumpeter Humphrey Lyttelton about contributing. Lyttelton eventually agreed at the behest of his daughter, a Radiohead fan, with he and his band ending *Amnesiac* in the fashion of a New Orleans funeral. Clarinetist Jimmy Hastings actually overpowers Lyttelton until the whole band crashes in, turning the funeral into a march.

The lyrics have nothing to do with New Orleans, but the sound of death in the Crescent City turned out to be the perfect soundtrack to Yorke's elegy for the wife of a famous actor who gets hounded by the tabloids. Unlike other songs where he's offered several conflicting explanations, he's always been clear about the meaning here, and perhaps that's why it needs the aesthetic of that most human of rituals: the funeral. All the band had to do was turn to an older kind of music so they could mourn properly, just as Tom Waits did for the closing of *Rain Dogs* with "Anywhere I Lay My Head."

Kid A sister song:

"Motion Picture Soundtrack"

B-sides

Due to the heavy experimentation of the *Kid A/Amnesiac* sessions, the leftovers from that era tend to be more obtuse than the usual Radiohead B-sides. While that makes them endlessly fascinating, they can also be somewhat difficult to penetrate. There isn't anything as infectious or complete as "Killer Cars" or "A Reminder" here. The tracks are perfect for musical academia; bad for hitmaking.

It's telling that Radiohead distributed all of these songs as B-sides to *Amnesiac* rather than *Kid A*—an album that saw no singles introduced to the music-buying public. This reinforces the case for *Kid A* being more of a complete and perhaps less human work than its successor, meant to be digested in one sitting rather than isolated chunks.

"The Amazing Sounds of Orgy"
Appears on: "Pyramid Song" single

Although its arrangement feels stilted compared to the rest of *Amnesiac* (even some of the B-sides) the junk percussion and a spectral moan do earn those overused music-critic adjectives of "haunted" and eerie." This makes "The Amazing Sounds of Orgy" a minor curiosity.

As Yorke pointed out to *Rolling Stone* in April 2004, the word "orgy" could refer to any number of things that aren't necessarily sexual—"an orgy of sound, an orgy of light. An orgy of violence. An orgy of gluttony."

"Trans-Atlantic Drawl"

Appears on: "Pyramid Song" single

Despite being a somewhat forgotten B-side, "Trans-Atlantic Drawl" has what might be the most specific political context of any of the songs from the *Kid A/Amnesiac* era. Three months after Saddam Hussein severed Iraq's ties with the UN special commission, UNSCOM, in August 1998, Iraqi Deputy Prime Minister, Tariq Aziz, conducted a press conference to discuss the country's development of weapons of mass destruction.

When a CNN correspondent pressed him about why Iraq abandoned UNSCOM and the possibility of peace, Aziz said "We don't see any light at the end of the tunnel ... there is a tunnel after the tunnel."

The quote appeared as being attributed to Aziz on Radiohead's website, and popped up several times again in portions of unused lyrics.

While Yorke hasn't commented on its use in "Trans-Atlantic Drawl," the phrase becomes somewhat of a mantra for the aggressive first half of the song. All fuzz pedals and grimy bass, it's possible that Aziz's quote is meant in sarcasm or was simply used because Yorke liked the sound of the words. Unfortunately, it falls into the Radiohead trap of never transcending its own fury; of just repeating a phrase over and over until the band runs out of steam.

"Fast-Track"

Appears on: "Pyramid Song" single

Another instrumental from the *Kid A/Amnesiac* era, "Fast-Track's" depth makes a good case for being included on *Amnesiac* over "Hunting Bears." Selway clatters away on an old jazz kit that belonged to the great uncle of Radiohead's guitar technician, Peter "Plank" Clements. The aged percussion adds an extra coat of grease to the subterranean lounge jazz, with Yorke bursting forth with indecipherable yips. The general playfulness could also be attributed to O'Brien and producer Nigel Godrich experimenting with the GR-500, Roland's earliest guitar synth.

"Cuttooth"

Appears on: "Knives Out" single

In which Radiohead finally get krautrock right. Considering that the band reworked "Dollars and Cents" when they couldn't successfully tackle the genre, it's a wonder why "Cuttooth"—a song that actually *does* work as krautrock—didn't make the cut.

In his online diary, O'Brien confessed that the song could easily become a product of over-tinkering; several mentions are made of Godrich feeling "side-tracked" by it and unable to get it right. Then again, the band must have felt that it was good enough at some point, as it made its way onto a French promotional copy of *Amnesiac* as track 9. Strangely, it wasn't listed on the album sleeve, leading the DJ to mistakenly introduce it as "Hunting Bears."

All of this points to "Cuttooth" being a back-and-forth affair for the band, and that's a shame. Because regardless of their feelings toward it, it's the strongest of the *Amnesiac* B-sides, beefing up the krautrock recipe written by Neu! by adding hopeful piano and effects. Maybe it was just too happy-sounding for *Amnesiac*.

"Kinetic"

Appears on: "Pyramid Song" single

Formless and constantly mutating, "Kinetic" is the B-side that best represents Radiohead's approach to music throughout the *Kid A/Amnesiac* sessions. Fan site Citizen Insane points out that its phrase "I waited for you, but you never came" appeared as far back as 1998 as part of a questionnaire in the *Airbag / How Am I Driving?* EP.

But this shouldn't be considered proof that "Kinetic" was germinating a full three years before the band recorded it. It's more a testament to Radiohead's eventual approach of splicing apart their music and lyrics, then putting them back together in any number of combinations. For instance, we get Selway's hissing jazz drums mixed in with electronic kit textures similar to the ones employed on "Idioteque." Jonny couples his gorgeous organ tones with guitar squelches, and Yorke blends clear lyrics about constant movement with unintelligible murmuring.

"Worrywort"

Appears on: "Knives Out" single

Like "Kinetic," lyrical fragments of "Worrywort" appeared in the *Airbag / How Am I Driving?* questionnaire, but Radiohead has said little about the song's inspiration, recording, or arrangement.

What's clear is that it's one of the warmer tracks from the *Kid A/Amnesiac* era, driven by a twinkling arpeggio as Yorke implores a friend or a lover to forget about the cruelty of the world and simply enjoy their surroundings. Unlike so many descriptions of happiness on *OK Computer*, there doesn't seem to be anything false or ironic about his words, making it a rarity in the canon of Radiohead's "happier" songs.

"Fog"

Appears on: "Knives Out" single

Another gentle Radiohead B-side in the vein of "Worrywort," but with far more nightmarish lyrics. Yorke's description of glowing fog rising up from the sewers recalls Marc Caro and Jean-Pierre Jeunet's spindly sci-fi masterpiece, *The City of Lost Children*, with mentions of baby alligators only adding to the surreal dreamscape.

In its live incarnation, Yorke plays "Fog" by himself on a piano, but the melancholia all but disappears when the song gets tackled by all five members Radiohead. In particular, Colin's constant tambourine adds some light to the shadows, making "Fog" a complex fairytale—one where we're unsure whether to be appalled or magnetized by the imagery.

Conclusion

No matter how good it was, *Amnesiac* was always destined to get overshadowed by *Kid A* due to the closeness of their release dates and the fact that the albums were spawned from the same recording sessions. Not only did *Amnesiac* come out just eight months after *Kid A*—by June, the latter had long secured its place on most critics' year-end lists, been nominated for Album of the Year at the 43rd Annual Grammy Awards, and won the Grammy for Best Alternative Album.

To be fair to *Amnesiac*'s detractors, it's definitely no *Kid A*—at least song for song. There's a bit more filler; a bit more meandering. But its themes and sonic palette are equally as cohesive, with its sense of sonic time travel separating it from every other Radiohead release. Its current status as a minor masterpiece as opposed to just a flat-out masterpiece seems apt.

Outside of critical consensus, *Amnesiac* trailed slightly behind *Kid A* in sales and certifications. It reached Gold in Argentina, Australia, France, Japan, and the United States, and Platinum in the United Kingdom and Canada. For the Grammys, it was nominated for Best Alternative Music Album (just like every Radiohead from *OK Computer* onward) and the more minor category of Best Recording Package (the only time the band would receive that nomination).

21

"I Just Snapped and Lost Control"

Assorted Live Recordings

As of this writing, there has yet to be a definitive document of the Radiohead live experience—at least in the traditional sense. Most of the live recordings officially released by the band have been closed off to the general public (the *Live From the Basement* performances), recorded and edited by fans (*Live In Praha* and *Radiohead For Haiti*), or captured so long ago, the setlist isn't the least bit comprehensive (*Live at the Astoria*).

In fact, Radiohead has only released exactly one conventional live album—that is, an actual album unattached to a niche web series, consumer-led project, or outdated concert video. Luckily, a seemingly endless number of Radiohead fans has constructed a network of bootlegs over the years. While the quality of these renegade recordings varies, they cover every era of the band and then some, and when listened to alongside *I Might Be Wrong: Live Recordings*, they form a somewhat comprehensive chronicle of Radiohead's career as a live act. Granted, it would be nice to get an officially sanctioned, traditional live recording of one of their most recent concerts—perhaps the audio from the landmark 2017 Glastonbury set—but for now, this will have to do.

Make no mistake; it's a lot to sift through. But as they've proven with the bootleg recordings, Radiohead fans are a dedicated bunch.

I Might Be Wrong: Live Recordings

It's hard to find fault with any of the performances on *I Might Be Wrong*. With songs pulled from four different tour dates in 2001—July 7 at South Park in Oxford, England; May 28 at Vaison-la-Romaine in Provence-Alpes-Côte d'Azur, France; August 8 at Blossom Music Center in Cuyahoga Falls, Ohio; and September 9 at Oslo Spektrum in Oslo, Norway—the album finds songs from *Kid A* and *Amnesiac* performed at their most wiry.

"The National Anthem" almost matches the energy of its historic *SNL* performance sans horns, "Everything In Its Right Place" becomes sped-up and

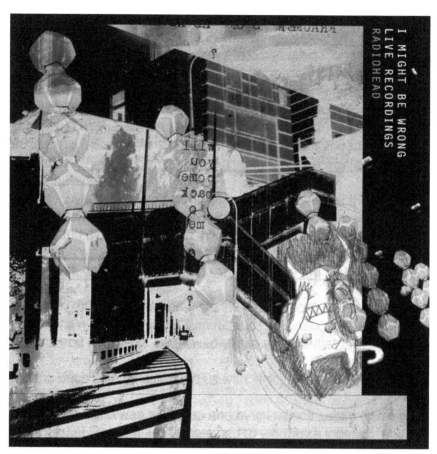

Album art for *I Might Be Wrong: Live Recordings.*   *Author's collection*

angular, and the title track takes on extra menace with a more inward central guitar line and ramshackle percussion (throughout the album, Phil Selway's drum kit sounds on the verge of collapsing). *I Might Be Wrong* also benefits from an audience that truly functions as just another instrument. The Oxford crowd shouts along to every last word of "Idioteque," transforming it into the rave-up it was always meant to be. And with every song, the four separate audiences start screaming the millisecond after the first note rings out—a testament to the astuteness of their fandom.

To *I Might Be Wrong*'s benefit, not every last track gets higher than usual wattage. The low-hum traffic jam of "Like Spinning Plates" becomes an earnest piano ballad, and "True Love Waits" finally gets a proper recording as the album's closer. By 2001, Radiohead's biggest tearjerker had been circulating on bootlegs as somewhat of a live staple, first performed in 1995. The arrangement would vary depending on the night. Sometimes, it was Thom Yorke on solo acoustic guitar. Other times, it was Rhodes electric piano.

On *I Might Be Wrong*, it's the former, leaving plenty of room for his yearning and aching vocal. While lacking the weight of the definitive studio version that would eventually surface on 2016's *A Moon Shaped Pool* (backed by piano, it's worth noting), it still closes out the band's only proper live album with the loudest of whispers. And the fact that it was included at all was a treat for Radiohead fans at the time.

The most common (and often only) criticism of *I Might Be Wrong: Live Recordings* concerns its length. At only eight songs spread across 40:11, it's considered by many to be an EP rather than an LP, clocking in at only about a third of what a Radiohead concert would usually be. And because the band decided to cherry-pick from their *Kid A* and *Amnesiac* sets, it's far from being a suitable live retrospective.

And yet that's what also makes it so distinct, distilling the energy of Radiohead's live show into a fast, toothy little package. While it may not nail the scope of a Radiohead concert, it certainly captures the sweat and passion that comes with being in the crowd.

Bootlegs

Ever since two mystery figures by the names of Ken and Dub released Bob Dylan's *Great White Wonder* in 1969, rock bands of a certain level have had to contend with fan-created bootlegs. Musicians have dealt with it in a variety of ways. Frank Zappa was notoriously anti-bootleg, going as far as to create a hotline where fans could report anyone behind an unauthorized Zappa recording, live or otherwise. The Grateful Dead, on the other hand, often let bootleg recordings slide, as the practice continued to bind their fans together.

As the internet has grown beyond anyone's control and free video streaming has become wildly popular, many artists have taken a similar approach to the Dead, refusing to fight—and sometimes even embracing—the distribution of fan-recorded concerts. It's the most practical stance, given that the profitability of the bootleg market has long been on the decline. If a sly fan secretly records a show, they'll have a hard time making a buck when someone else has likely already uploaded the entire thing to YouTube for free. A quick scroll through any of the Radiohead bootleg threads on Reddit shows that most people despise the mere idea of trying to sell a bootleg in the first place. It's about sharing an experience with fellow fans—not turning a profit.

Still, a few have tried to do just that. Although it's rare to find a Radiohead bootleg circulating in a record store anymore these days, you can still find someone trying to hock a concert recording, homemade collection of rarities, or record promo on eBay. These discs are usually marked by shoddy album art, scratched discs, and ghastly Comic Sans font. Completists are better off exploring one of the many free, fan-led bootleg sites.

The Essential Radiohead Bootlegs' easy-to-use layout was designed by Kaspar Oja.

Kaspar Oja

One of the most notable ones is fittingly titled Radiohead Not For Profit (RNFP). Specializing in lossless live recordings, the homepage of RNFP has a firmly worded warning that reads "Please, do not buy any bootlegs (audio or video) from anyone. Just share FREELY."

Whenever a fan uploads a show on RNFP, they list details specific to their experience. For example, a recording of Radiohead's performance at the Greek Theater in Berkeley, California on April 17, 2017 has the descriptor "Recorded from dead center, 4th step," accompanied by a photo of the uploader's vantage point. After that, they specify their recording equipment and format specs and instructions ("Schoeps MK4/NBox Platinum Tascam DR-2D 24 Bit 48K," "Processed using Soundforge 11, resample, to 16bit 44.1K," "TLH to convert to Flac").

Other users go into the challenges they faced while recording ("The location created a very bass-heavy recording, which required a significant cut in the lower frequencies to remove a build-up of 'mud'") and often list the personnel for each song. All of these details give every bootleg an individuality, complete with extensive liner notes and makeshift album art, thanks to the photographs. And of course, every recording comes proudly slapped with the same bit of text: "NOT FOR PROFIT—NOT FOR SALE" in red block letters. Of all the Radiohead bootleg communities, RNFP places the highest value on high-fidelity audio and sharing freely.

The only downside is that it can be a lot to unpack, even for the most dedicated fan. As wonderful as it is to have so many Radiohead concerts at one's fingertips, the open-market format makes it hard to know where to start.

Radiohead newbies (or anyone who just prefers a more consolidated collection) should head over to the Essential Radiohead Bootlegs Tumblr. The landing page simply reads "These are the essential Radiohead bootlegs." You can click on nine different bars (one for each of the band's albums), which then leads to complete, high-quality recordings of some choice concerts from the corresponding era.

The Essential Radiohead bootlegs began on the dearly departed Radiohead forum Atease. Around the time of *The King of Limbs*, Radiohead superfan/historian Jeff Blehar started a thread that included lossless files of what he deemed to be the band's best concerts. For each one, he wrote accompanying text that explained the merits of each show, as well as any rarities included in the set. For instance, the blurb for a 1993 show at Chicago's Riviera Theater reads:

> "Radiohead is still touring *Pablo Honey*, but once they've returned to Chicago, they bring far more energy to this material than they would either before or later. 'Stop Whispering' is a monstrous performance (the band is egged on by the fact that the audience is singing along with it en masse), 'Yes I Am' is given one of its few read-throughs, and 'Thinking About You' is brought out for one its comparative rare early acoustic performances. It all ends with a unique rarity as Thom duets with the opening act (Tanya Donelly, of the now-forgotten indie-pop band Belly) on 'Untogether.'"

That last sentence has particular resonance post-2018, when Belly has reunited and put out their first album in 23 years.

Once Atease tragically went the way of the buffalo, fellow poster George Dunkley approached Blehar about compiling his text and all of the bootlegs onto a Tumblr account. Blehar agreed on one condition: They would only include lossless versions of the shows.

"Let people make mp3s out of them on their own," he tells me over a direct message on Twitter. "I don't want to propagate lossy material, especially if it's audience tapes we're talking about."

The Essential Radiohead Bootlegs' user-friendly interface, sleek design, and informative text make it a standout in the endless sea of sites about the band. While not as all-encompassing as Radiohead Not For Profit and some of the other bootleg sites, the word "essential" is in the title for a reason. Blehar's curation is meant to pare down the overwhelming number of recordings. It's meant to give fans something canonical; a concrete idea of where to start.

And to Blehar's credit, he has great taste. The shows he's chosen for the site really are something to behold in dynamic, setlist, and audio quality, even if he hasn't included some of the band's most universally hailed concerts. Radiohead's 2007 set from Glastonbury is nowhere to be found, nor is the 2001 South Park performance.

"It's not a particularly interesting show!" Blehar says.

22

"We All Like Stars"

Ed O'Brien

When a band has three guitarists, it doesn't work if they all do the same thing. So if Thom Yorke usually handles rhythm in Radiohead and Jonny Greenwood takes lead, where does that leave Ed O'Brien?

In the early days of the band, it wasn't much of an issue. *Pablo Honey, The Bends*, and to some extent, *OK Computer*, are all big-sounding guitar records with plenty of room for traditional interplay between three of the instruments. Then *Kid A* came along and changed everything.

Up to that point, every Radiohead album had increasingly relied on effects, but with *Kid A*, the group was interested in tearing down the conventions of a rock band. For O'Brien, who admitted to at first being somewhat insecure about the experiment, that meant leaning more into effects. It meant turning to loops and sustain units to create textures and atmospheres rather than just arpeggios and chord progressions. This stylistic shift is now one of the defining traits of the band.

Since *Kid A*, O'Brien has tended to talk about guitar-playing in visual terms when giving interviews: "light and shade," "magnetic field," and "feminine" are all terms he uses to describe sounds in a November 14, 2017 interview with *Music Radar*.

Along with Colin Greenwood, he's also known for having one of the stronger connections to Radiohead's fans. In addition to providing powerful backing vocals underneath Yorke, he started an online diary on Radiohead's website during the recording of *Kid A* and *Amnesiac*. Although it's since been deleted and archived elsewhere (along with most of the other Dead Air Space material from that time), his detailed insights into the recording process forever forged a bond with the band's most rabid listeners.

Childhood

Edward John O'Brien was born on April 15, 1968 in Oxford to John and Eve O'Brien, who divorced sometime in the late '70s. Although he was raised primarily by Eve, he developed good relationships with both sides of the family.

Ed O'Brien performing at the 2008 Catalonia Daydream Festival in Barcelona.
Photo by Alterna2, edited by Billy Brown/Wikimedia Commons

While at Abingdon, he bounced easily between different activities at school, participating in both theatre (where he met Yorke and Colin) and sports. Reaching 6'5" as an adult, his height and lanky frame made him an ideal fit for everything from football to field hockey. But rock 'n' roll would become his ultimate profession, kick-started after he began making music with Yorke and Colin, despite not really knowing how to play guitar. Even as O'Brien has expanded his skills in Radiohead, he's never considered himself a virtuoso.

His early musical heroes weren't virtuosos, either. It's only natural that the guy who would go on to spearhead the spacious effects in Radiohead's songs would worship at the altar of the Police's Andy Summers.

"When you heard 'Walking On The Moon,' it was guitar, but with all the delay and the chorus, it sounded like he was on the moon," O'Brien told *Music Radar*. "And then with people like Edge and Johnny Marr, we were spoiled for choice—

One of Ed O'Brien's favorite guitar lines comes from the Police's "Walking On the Moon."
Author's collection

there were all these amazing guitarists who were trying to do things that didn't sound like the guitar. I've always been drawn to people who put the song first."

College Years/Family Life

Like everyone in the band except Jonny Greenwood, O'Brien headed to college after Abingdon, while still rehearsing with their early band On a Friday during weekends and holiday breaks.

Oddly enough, none of the members of On a Friday earned a degree in music, including O'Brien, who studied economics at the University of Manchester. After graduation, he hightailed it back to Oxford to focus on the band full-time. While he never had to pursue a job in the financial industry (he did clock some hours as a bartender), his time at school did foster a lifelong love for the Manchester United Football Club.

In their personal lives, Radiohead remains one of the most family-oriented bands in rock, and O'Brien is no different. He's married to Susan Kobrin, with whom he has two children—son Salvador (born in 2004) and daughter Oona (born in 2006). In a January 13, 2018 interview with *The Huddersfield Daily Examiner*, he admitted to wanting to spend more and more time at home as his family has expanded. When the children were little, he even began to question if staying in Radiohead was the right thing to do.

"I come from a split family, so the most important thing in my life has always been wanting to have a family and create an environment where the family didn't fall apart," he told the *Examiner*. Fittingly, two other musicians—Johnny Marr and Neil Finn—convinced him to stay in the band.

"Neil said, 'When your kids are 14 or 15, they're not going to thank you if you leave Radiohead to bring them up. They'll say, 'What the fuck are you doing?' I thought that was very good advice and my wife said, 'You don't want to do that, and I don't want you to do that!'"

Collaborations

Alongside Selway, O'Brien has collaborated with both Marr and Finn in Finn's supergroup 7 Worlds Collide. On the outfit's first release, *7 Worlds Collide: Live at the St. James*, he contributed guitar and backing vocals to a series of five shows at the St. James Theatre in Auckland, New Zealand. He came back for the second release as well, a proper studio album called *The Sun Came Out*. This time around, O'Brien even earned two co-songwriting credits for "Learn to Crawl" (written with Finn, Finn's son Liam, and Marr) and "Bodhisattva Blues" (also written with Liam).

But outside of 7 Worlds Collide and lending guitar work to three songs on Asian Dub Foundation's fifth album, *Enemy of the Enemy*, O'Brien has taken his time when it comes to his work outside Radiohead. An announced solo album has yet to materialize, although according to a November 14, 2017 interview with *Esquire*, it could be released in late 2018 or early 2019, which means it might beat the publication of this book.

O'Brien says the album was inspired by the rhythms he heard at Carnival in Rio when he and his family lived briefly in Brazil. So far, he's namechecked drummer Omar Hakim (who has played with Miles Davis, Mariah Carey, and David Bowie), bassist Nathan East (Eric Clapton, Stevie Wonder, Daft Punk), and lead guitarist Dave Okumu of the Invisible as his backing band, with additional contributions from Catherine Marks and producer Flood.

Until O'Brien's solo album drops, his most notable project outside of Radiohead is the EOB Sustainer Stratocaster, a guitar he designed with Fender. As he explained to *Esquire*, during the *Kid A* days, one of the band's technicians put

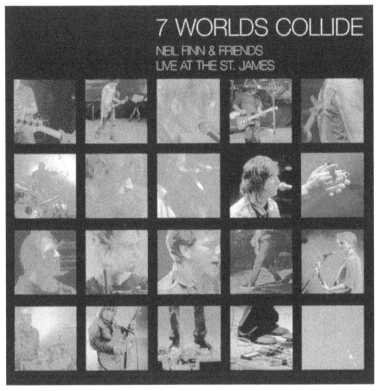

Ed O'Brien and Phil Selway both played on 7 Worlds Collide: Live at the St. James.
Author's collection

a Fernandes Sustainer into O'Brien's Clapton Stratocaster, putting a universe of new sounds and gestures at his fingertips.

"The only problem ... was the clean sound," O'Brien said of the makeshift hybrid. "In rearranging the pickups and gouging out and the work of putting in the sustaining unit, it ceased to function as a normal guitar very well."

O'Brien sought out to change that with the EOB, a versatile guitar outfitted with an arsenal of pickups and a sustainer that can be activated with the flick of a switch. As a final touch, rather than brand the clean white instrument with his engraved signature—as is the tradition with most custom Fender guitars—O'Brien left his mark on the neckplate on the underside.

"It's my tattoo: the flower of life," O'Brien told *Music Radar*. "I didn't want to make a big song and dance about it, but I wanted something on there, and it's not about me: this is a very, very ancient symbol, from all over the world, and I just thought it would be cool. Most people won't even notice it, but it's there."

It's the perfect calling card for a musician who continues to see sounds rather than hear them.

23

"You Paint Yourself White and Fill Up with Noise"

Album Art

N ot every band warrants an entire book chapter dedicated to their album art. *Most* bands don't warrant an entire book chapter dedicated to their album art. But for the majority of their career, Radiohead has crafted a visual identity that's just as important as their musical one.

Since 1994, Radiohead's look has come from artist and writer Stanley Donwood, who, sometimes in collaboration with Thom Yorke, has dreamed up the artwork for everything put out by the band, whether it be a single, EP, full-length album, film, t-shirt, or tour poster. His work has proven to be as versatile as the band themselves, fluctuating between abstraction, crudeness, hypnosis, disorientation, and back.

But if we're going back to the very beginning, we must travel to a time before Donwood—a time when all of the band's artwork came solely from Yorke or a scattershot mixture of designers from various studios. Needless to say, most of it wasn't nearly as effective as what was to come.

Drill (1992)

Perhaps not trusting Yorke's drawing abilities after the crude alien he sketched for the *Manic Hedgehog* demo tape, Radiohead (or maybe their label, Parlophone) contracted the design firm Icon for the artwork of their first officially distributed release.

Although the sloppy neon splatters and obvious image of—wait for it—a *drill* are dated by today's standards, the album art does have a collage effect that was akin—even a predecessor—to other popular acts of the grunge era. It also established a typeset for the band name that would grace all Radiohead releases for the next two years: blurred, almost screen-printed letters with a filled-in circle around the letter "R."

Pablo Honey (1993)

What was it with early-'90s rock bands featuring babies on their album covers? Nirvana's *Nevermind*, Sebadoh's *Bakesale*, Everclear's *Sparkle and Fade*, and the Goo Goo Dolls' *A Boy Named Goo* all had photographs of infants or toddlers (sometimes the band members themselves) as their artwork.

Radiohead got in on the trend with *Pablo Honey*, which places a black and white picture of a baby in the center, circumscribes its head with sprinkled sugar cookies, then rounds the whole thing out with a sunburst of yellow tulips. The band's second use of collage once more came courtesy of Icon, mixed with paintings by Lisa Bunny Jones. Inside lies an artifact of a practice that would cease to exist beginning with the *OK Computer* era: an actual photograph of the band—a very dated photograph, it's worth noting. Yorke is decked out in flannel and shades, Phil Selway sports a beanie, and the entire image is cast in a deep-purple hue.

Pablo Honey's artwork often gets made fun of by Radiohead fans, given that it's so different from the direction put forth by Donwood starting with the *My Iron Lung* EP. But the imagery is just as reflective of the music within as later Radiohead releases—perhaps even more so. No, the album doesn't sound like some kind of demented lullaby. But the aesthetic is indicative of the grunge era and the fact that, in 1993, Radiohead didn't sound all that different from their peers. With a baby on the front cover, they didn't look all that different, either.

Pablo Honey-era Singles (1992–1993)

For the *Pablo Honey* single "Anyone Can Play Guitar," Icon used yet another Lisa Bunny Jones painting mixed with yet another vintage baby photo—this one with googly eyes pasted over its actual peepers.

The various editions of "Creep" also turned to collage, but in a way that's coincidentally more similar to the *OK Computer* era. The muted clashing of automobiles, buildings, and two separate people (one a businessman and the other a more casual pedestrian) signify the collapse of modern life. It lacks the finesse of *OK Computer*, relying on hurried red squiggles over the black and white images. But it's at least in the same ballpark, despite once again being created by a design firm (with help from artist Maurice Jones) rather than Yorke or Donwood.

If "Creep" was an unintentional prototype for *OK Computer*, then the non-album single "Pop is Dead" was a prototype for *Kid A* and *Amnesiac*, its cover a primitive marker drawing of a feline creature standing below what appears to be a spaceship. The album title explodes behind the visual in huge bubble letters straight out of an Robert Crumb cartoon. The similarity to Radiohead's later work is likely a bit more than just happenstance. Although Icon was once

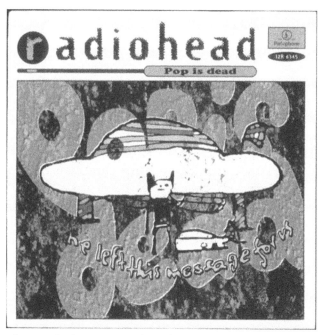

Album art for the "Pop Is Dead" single.   *Author's collection*

again responsible for the design, Rachel Owen was responsible for the actual artwork. Considering she had just started dating Thom Yorke, it's possible that they influenced each other's visual ideas.

"Stop Whispering" goes in a completely different direction than the other *Pablo Honey*-era singles, its cover nothing more than a photograph of a suit hanging in what appears to be a warehouse. If the dull gold border, sepia tone, and slight corner placement of the photo look familiar, that's because the band was trying to mimic the Pixies' *Surfer Rosa* in both sound and visuals. The music turned out more like a syphoning of U2, but the album art remains a decent homage.

Itch (1994)

The circled "R" of Radiohead's band name would become extinct in 1994, so it's only fitting that it gives a triumphant death rattle on the outdated cover of *Itch*. It's all over the place, filled in with various colors. The final effect resembles a bunch of "r"-stamped M&M's strewn across a white tablecloth.

My Iron Lung (1994)

The *My Iron Lung* EP marks the first appearance of Donwood and producer Nigel Godrich on a Radiohead release. But the shift is more noticeable in the production than the visuals.

At first glance, the muted front cover is a far cry from the garish color of Radiohead's previous albums. But the grainy imagery—a group of businessmen captured through a cassette camera—isn't exactly indicative of where Donwood would go with his art. It's a bit too simple; a bit too obvious. The perceived criticism against corporate culture might have worked better had more actual technique been implemented into the artistry. It lacks the weirdness that would rear its head on *The Bends* and everything that came afterward.

The Bends (1995)

As Donwood revealed to *Monster Children* magazine on November 8, 2017, not a whole lot of planning goes into his concepts for Radiohead albums, despite their eventual ambition. With *The Bends*, he and Yorke snuck a clunky cassette camera into a hospital in hopes of capturing a real-life iron lung. When they finally tracked down the device, it wasn't much to look at, so they opted for a CPR dummy with misplaced metal nipples (apparently so emergency personnel could practice on it with a defibrillator).

Once they had their image, Donwood recalls there being some debate over what should be more central—the album title or the band name. Yorke won out, and the word "Radiohead" was scrawled across the front cover in the same bold, blocky letters that graced the *My Iron Lung* EP. The sterility of the typeset (not to mention the creepy uncanny valley of the CPR dummy) is certainly more connected to Radiohead's foray into sci-fi than the sloppier font from the band's early days.

The only element of *The Bends*' artwork that tethers the album to Radiohead 1.0 are the band photos in the booklet. Overly saturated and riddled with more outdated fashion choices, it clashes with the eerie futurism of the front cover. It would be the last time any member of Radiohead would appear in the artwork for a non-compilation release.

The Bends-era Singles (1995–1996)

While all of Radiohead's art direction was now being handled by Donwood and Yorke (then going under the alias "The White Chocolate Farm" before shortening it to "Tchock"), the artwork for *The Bends*' singles was scattershot. When laying them all out next to each other, they come off as a Greatest Hits of Radiohead's various aesthetics up to that point, including the early days with Icon.

"Just," for instance, is made up of another collage—a jumble of letters cut from magazines, then rolled across several photos of locked shed doors. "Fake Plastic Trees" harkens back to the *My Iron Lung* EP with another cassette-camera photo of a partially obscured figure—this time a woman on a beach. Where most of the businessmen on the front of *My Iron Lung* have their heads out of frame, the woman has her eyes blurred out by a white rectangle. The artwork for *The Bends'* title track is a simple graphic of an inhaler—an image that would occasionally recur in Donwood's artwork. The cover of Radiohead's concert video from this era, *Live at the Astoria*, also appears to have been shot on the cassette camera, or at least altered to appear like it was. A blue tint covers Thom Yorke's face and peroxided hair as he emotes into the microphone.

"Street Spirit (Fade Out)" is the most '90s of *The Bends'* singles, its downward-looking shot of an escalator saturated to the point where everything looks chrome. The oversized font and cringeworthy sleekness isn't far off from several post-grunge acts from the early 2000s. It's probably the only time Radiohead and Fuel's *Something Like Human* could be mentioned in the same breath.

Despite being the most straightforward song on *The Bends*, "High and Dry" (coupled with "Planet Telex" as its B-side), has the most forward-thinking artwork of the album's singles. With its melting doodle of a spaceman (pulled from the *Bends'* booklet), it serves as the most natural transition from *The Bends* to *OK Computer*, while also calling back to Yorke's sketch for *Manic Hedgehog*.

OK Computer (1997)

Because Donwood lives in Bath, only an hour bike ride away from where Radiohead was recording *OK Computer* at St Catherine's Court, he was able to become more heavily involved in the album's artwork.

The increased participation shows in *OK Computer's* visuals. So many of the album's topics get illustrated somewhere in the cover or booklet. We see superficially happy families and congested cities. We see constant airplane and spaceship imagery, ranging from detailed cross sections of aircraft to harsh sketches of aerial disasters, all saddled with safety instructions both scrawled and neatly typed. Elsewhere, emotionless stick figures shake hands. One of them holds a briefcase to symbolize, according to Yorke, the exploitation inherent in sales, corporate culture, and the modern world in general.

The best way to describe Yorke and Donwood's aesthetic on *OK Computer* is curated chaos. Because they bound everything together into a computer-generated collage, the visuals never become too busy. Rather, they remain carefully hidden, revealing something new every time someone looks at it.

The other binding factor between the album's cover seemingly disparate elements comes from the icy streaks of white that permeate every image. Donwood was inspired by the trees outside of Yorke's suburban home in Oxford. But since he was going through some personal struggles, he couldn't help but view the vegetation as part of a scorched-earth landscape. He decided to replicate what was in his mind—"sticks and white ash everywhere"—for the somewhat consistent highway landscape of *OK Computer's* cover, cast in colors attempting to replicate the color of bleached bone.

OK Computer-era EPs, Singles, and Videography (1997–1998)

The *OK Computer* era marked the first time that the artwork for Radiohead's singles and accompanying EPs directly (and intentionally) correlated to the visuals of the album. Most tellingly, every single release has the same bold "X" in the bottom-right corner of the cover, the nose of a cartoon airplane partially visible beneath it.

In addition, each mini-collection of songs boasts a clearer depiction of something found in *OK Computer*'s lyrics, as if Donwood and Yorke wiped the frost away from the album cover to reveal what's beneath the glass. "Karma Police" shows a family with their heads hung as they walk to their doom, "Lucky" displays a diagram of an airplane plummeting into the ocean, *No Surprises / Running From Demons* zeroes in on a car outside a suburban home, and *Airbag / How Am I Driving?* further explores the lives of the album's tragic stick figures. Only "Paranoid Android" embraces true abstraction, anchored by a hasty, purple drawing of a shape that could be a tree canopy, UFO, or jellyfish.

Every single one of these album covers once again draws from Donwood and Yorke's brand of curated chaos. The frequent shadows, blood-red bullseyes, and downward arrows spell certain doom, but because the drawings look like they're straight out of a technical manuals, everything has a narcoleptic sterility. It's the visual representation of the absurd "Don't Panic" catchphrase from Douglas Adams' *Hitchhiker's Guide to the Galaxy*.

Airbag / How Am I Driving? deserves special attention for all the sardonic in-jokes found inside its booklet. The digits on the front cover supposedly made up Yorke's phone number at the time, allowing fans to call and leave a

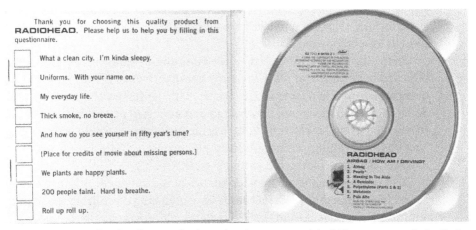

Questionnaire found in the album art for the *Airbag / How Am I Driving?* EP.   *Author's collection*

message if they wished. Inside, a series of surveys embraced the same kind of official-sounding yet ultimately maddening phrases heard on "Fitter Happier." It would have made more sense for the Recording Academy to nominate *Airbag / How Am I Driving?* for Best Recording Package rather than Best Alternative Music Performance.

The *OK Computer* aesthetic even extended to Radiohead's videography at the time, showing that, unlike with *Live in Astoria*, Donwood and Yorke were viewing everything as part of the same project. The smoky silhouettes on the box of the music-video compilation, *7 Television Commercials*, read like a cave drawing of the "Karma Police" single, complete with the "X" and the airplane nose in the lower-right corner.

Meeting People Is Easy doesn't have that signifier, but it does feature the stick figures below a cross section of two cars passing each other. The words "You are a target market" blast out at the viewer, their bluntness a predecessor to the assorted words on the *Hail to the Thief* cover.

Kid A (2000)

Too often, critics overlook the primitive elements of *Kid A*. For all the talk of future landscapes and robotic vocals, so much of the album has to do with pre-history and the evolution of musicians as evolution of humans. The same goes for the album art.

Yorke and Donwood starting brainstorming in an outwardly wild environment: a manor house in the hills and forests of the Cotswolds. When speaking to *Monster Children*, Donwood recalled the locals being somewhat eccentric. In addition to the house being filled with dead insects and stacks of newspapers from the 1950s, the woods were home to many wooden crosses strung with dead birds. The inspiration can be seen in the rough countryside sketches inside the *Kid A* booklet, most explicitly in a row of cross-like structures lit by a bloody red sky.

As for the mountainous structures on the front (drawn from the same bleached-bone palette as *OK Computer*'s trees), they were the result of subsequent art sessions in a rented warehouse in Bath. By Donwood's count, he and Yorke completed anywhere between 20 and 40 different contenders for the cover, often using knives and sticks to achieve the appropriately jagged look. They ended up settling on abstractions of mountains that were these landscapes of power, the idea of tower blocks and pyramids.

Also worth noting is the first appearance of the mutant bear in one of the band's releases (a mob of them can be seen marching down from the mountains inside the booklet) and the "red swimming pool" on the album spine and disc. For the latter, Donwood took inspiration from Alan Moore's graphic novel *Brought to Light*, where the CIA keeps track of mass deaths by filling various

50-gallon swimming pools with blood. Both the bear and the pool (especially the bear) have become de facto logos of Radiohead.

There was even more artwork to unpack for anyone who picked up an initial pressing of *Kid A*. Under the CD tray was a secret second booklet that reads like a nightmarish newspaper, overflowing with more macabre drawings catchphrases and many lyrics that would soon appear on *Amnesiac*.

Amnesiac (2001)

Amnesiac functions as a travelogue through various time periods, spiritualities, and musical genres. Charles Mingus meets the Egyptian underworld on "Pyramid Song," Buddhism gets a wiry guitar line on "I Might Be Wrong," and the whole thing ends in grand fashion with a New Orleans funeral on "Life in a Glasshouse."

Donwood and Yorke haven't commented on whether or not the album art draws from the music's sense of time travel, but Donwood has confirmed that the packaging was meant to look like some kind of dusty artifact. He's likened it to an old library book, and he achieved the desired effect by scanning pages and pages of tomes from second-hand bookshops. For the drawings that would be superimposed upon the pages, he turned to an assortment of typically sad and nightmarish fare—the most prominent image being that of a crying Minotaur.

"I'd been spending lots of time wandering the streets of London and had gotten really obsessed with mazes and the etchings of Piranesi, and also the legend of the Minotaur," he told *Monster Children*. "I'd done some big black and white paintings that were supposed to be the walls of the labyrinth where the Minotaur was imprisoned, so they were marked with 'm's and 'minos' and scratches."

The Minotaur that graces *Amnesiac*'s front cover does indeed look like it was etched into a red library book turned on its side—its dimensions uneven; its silhouette scratchy and purposely sloppy. The strings of binding hanging off the book add to the age. The Minotaurs inside the booklet, however, are cleaner, rounder, and more cartoonish.

Donwood and Yorke took the old library-book aesthetic to a place of maximalism with the special edition of *Amnesiac*, which didn't just have a picture of a book on its cover, but was a book itself. On the inside were stamps of numbers resembling past due dates, which were, in actuality, the birthdays of everyone who worked on the album and their families.

The special edition of *Amnesiac* naturally got nominated for—and won—the Grammy for Best Recording Package, but after receiving their trophy, Donwood and Yorke found themselves right back where Donwood had started—in a labyrinth. Only instead of wandering the streets of London, they were wandering the lower levels of Los Angeles' Staples Center by themselves. The 9/11 attacks had taken place only five months before, and a group of on-edge security guards soon drew their guns on the unsuspecting Englishmen. Someone from the Recording Academy smoothed everything, but it was just that exact kind of global tension that would fuel the artwork for Radiohead's next studio album, 2003's *Hail to the Thief*.

Amnesiac-era singles and *I Might Be Wrong: Live Recordings* (2001)

The artwork for *Amnesiac*'s singles certainly has cohesion, but it's also somewhat pointless to dissect, seeing as the visuals for two of the three songs were merely pulled from *Amnesiac*'s booklet.

"Knives Out" is the sole outlier, its front cover home to another one of Donwood and Yorke's monstrosities. The squiggly white creature looks like it's being stalked by some kind of slave-driving shadow with a whip. Thanks to its muddy palette and decaying environs, it could have easily fit in with the rest of the proper *Amnesiac* illustrations.

I Might Be Wrong: Live Recordings has the same drabness on the cover and in the booklet—perhaps a little too much. Because the muddiness is applied to office buildings and train tracks, nothing really pops out. Even a white sketch of the weeping Minotaur on the front gets lost. No matter. Radiohead would churn out their most colorful album cover yet just one album later.

Hail to the Thief (2003)

Since Stanley Donwood doesn't know how to drive, he spent a lot of time during the recording sessions of *Hail to the Thief* riding around Los Angeles as a passenger. He was struck by the city's endless amount of billboards, their phrases and colors exploding in "this incredibly limited palette of black, white, and five colors [that] looked great," as he described to *NME*. He would write down the words he saw, then use them and a limited palette of his own to build the sloganeering Jenga blocks of *Hail to the Thief*, all of which are laid out in a map pattern inspired by the works of graphic designer Paula Scher.

But the more interesting story comes from Donwood's abandoned initial concept for the album art, which involved inverting photographs he had taken of the sky, then mashing them together with photos of gigantic phalluses he had made from chicken wire and astroturf. Thanks to a new membership in England's National Trust, he was able to cycle around England and place the phalluses in the middle of hedges. The final product would be some sort of bizarre environmental pornography.

"I had this idea that the land and the sky were involved in this kind of congress, so rain is like some sort of arousal, and the way that trees grow is some sort of arousal," he further explained to *Monster Children*.

Although Thom Yorke quickly dismissed the idea, *Hail to the Thief*'s cover does appear to have an inverted sky and extensions coming out of the land. Maybe the billboard-map's spindly black limbs are meant to be sexual? Regardless, they convey the idea of modernity encroaching upon the natural world—an even more horrifying thought than the saturated advertising on the billboards themselves.

Hail to the Thief-era Singles and *The Most Gigantic Lying Mouth of All Time* (2003–2004)

With all three of *Hail to the Thief*'s singles ("There there," "Go to Sleep," and "2 + 2 = 5,") and Radiohead's bizarre short-film collection *The Most Gigantic Lying Mouth of All Time*, Donwood took the *Amnesiac* approach and simply zoomed in on one of the billboard sections. Though somewhat repetitive, it further highlights his mapmaking process with the album.

It may not be immediately apparent, but the outlines of all the various billboard spreads actually resemble several cities involved in the War on Terror at the time, namely Los Angeles, Kabul, and Grozny. The closer view of the *Hail to the Thief* singles allows each city's grid to pop out at the listener. This is most important for Donwood's map of Manhattan, which he used as the cover for the art book *Dead Children Playing*.

Com Lag (2plus2isfive) (2004)

Radiohead's most curious EP was originally released as an exclusive in Australia and Japan, so it's somewhat confounding why Donwood decided to outfit his mutant bears and, in his words, "despotic sperm monsters," in the blue and white shades of Dutch delftware pottery. He told the Radiohead message board Atease that he and the band even packaged the release in a "shiny varnish" similar to a pottery glaze. The end result is a welcome, if slightly puzzling, variation on familiar Radiohead imagery.

In Rainbows (2007)

Donwood originally wanted to keep the artwork for *In Rainbows* in the same vein as the past few Radiohead releases, filling the pages with images of cathedrals, shopping malls, and suburbia to evoke the monotonous decline of human civilization. But once he heard the warmth and sensuality present in the music, he decided the artwork called for a different direction.

In typical Radiohead fashion, everyone got to work at Tottenham House in Southern England's Savernake Forest—a manor house so decrepit that the band had to sleep in caravans outside, with Donwood in a teepee. While working on technical drawings in the library, he accidentally knocked over a candle, spilling wax onto the paper. Once his initial anger had passed, he marveled at the effect that the wax and ink had created together.

"The wax was translucent and where it had gone over the drawing—I don't know what the effect is, like parallax or something—it looked like the line had come up and moved a little," Donwood told *Monster Children*. "It was really interesting. So I scanned it anyway, and that was really how I ended up doing the artwork. I did it with hypodermic needles and ink and wax."

Once Donwood ran his creations through a scanner (which he apparently ruined), then altered the images in Photoshop, he had a collection of homemade rainbows for the standard edition, special Discbox edition, and bonus *Disk 2* of the album—brilliant in their arches, splashes, and luminosity. Donwood described the images as toxic rainbows, and indeed, their glow is reminiscent of plutonium. But that doesn't distract from their calming and hypnotic effect, just as the darker elements of the music don't prevent *In Rainbows* from being one of Radiohead's most uplifting and accessible albums.

In Rainbows-era Singles (2008–2009)

Where the visuals for *In Rainbows* as a complete album are all color, its singles have a monolithic drabness that looks akin to Donwood's description of his original artwork. The etching for "Jigsaw Falling Into Place" features a black and white structure that resembles a cathedral (an image that would get featured in Donwood's subsequent art galleries and book covers), "Nude" is a desolate gray landscape, "House of Cards" / "Bodysnatchers" is a mere beige square with a red tab on the side, and the mounds on "Reckoner" appear to be gravestones outside a factory (the final single, "All I Need," was promotional and just listed the album's seven Grammy nominations).

Most of these singles have the band name and song name scrawled across the cover in the same rainbow-hued, slash- and underscore-populated font seen on the album, thus binding the parts with the sum, despite their differences in color.

On August 5, 2009, Radiohead released a standalone download, "Harry Patch (In Memory Of)," as a tribute to the last-surviving combat veteran of World War I, who died two weeks earlier on July 25. The artwork's smoky field of tree stumps is likely just a reference to war in general, but it also feels tethered to the more colorless affectation of the *In Rainbows* singles.

The King of Limbs (2011)

To date, the last time the visage of anyone in Radiohead appeared on a full-length album was 1995's *The Bends*. Stanley Donwood almost broke that pattern with *The King of Limbs*, setting out to create oil paintings based on photographs

Album art for the "Harry Patch (In Memory Of)" single.

Author's collection

of each member of the band. Citing Gerhard Richter as an influence, he soon realized that he lacked the German artist's skills with oil paints. Depressed over how much he had spent on paint and enormous canvases, he wandered into a field separating his studio from the band's, which was nearby in an old barn.

During his head-clearing walk, Donwood could hear the music Radiohead had been creating and was soon moved by the sonics, as well as the barn's architecture.

"It sounded like being in a cathedral, and these great beams and rafters that come up in the converted barn—they've still got the nature of the tree about them," he told *Monster Children*. "I had this kind of vision that being surrounded by trees is essential to the religious, spiritual idea of our part of the world in our civilisation. Our cathedrals are like forest glades."

Newly inspired by the holiness of nature in the real world and the themes of nature and evolution on the album, Donwood returned to his canvases. With a mixture of oil paints and acrylics, he painted a series of gnarled trees, rendered ghostly by ethereal tentacles and eyes. The sentient plants on the cover of *The King of Limbs* conjure images of octopode or an Elder God from the works of H.P. Lovecraft—mesmerizing yet intimidating.

The trees inside *The King of Limbs'* booklet are much less colorful and more realistic, as if pulled from a field guide. On the back of the album, Donwood gets spikier with his painting, recalling the climax of *Sleeping Beauty* with a thatch of thorns growing up from the band name in sharp-lined, jaggy glory. The album's remix collection, *TKOL: RMX 1234567*, blended the various aesthetics with a colorful starburst of thorns superimposed over the original cover.

The King of Limbs-era Singles (2009–2011)

The only proper single from *The King of Limbs* was a promotional release of "Lotus Flower," which, of all the album's artwork, best captures Donwood's description of the spiritual properties of nature. Surrounded by a regal crest straight out of a J.R.R. Tolkien novel, its identical trees connect in the middle—truly cathedral-like.

All of the other singles from *The King of Limbs* era are non-album tracks, but still borrow artwork from the album. "The Daily Mail" / "Staircase" touts a tighter-cropped image of a black-and-white tree emitting what looks to be sperm-like ghost creatures from its trunk. As for "Supercollider" / "The Butcher," the visuals aren't an exact recreation of the album, but feature the same kind of invasive thorns found on the back of *The King of Limbs*, this time rendered in vivid yellow and burnt orange.

Two years before *The King of Limbs*, Donwood and Yorke previewed their thorn obsession with a single called "These Are My Twisted Words." Presented as a free download, it came with a series of isolated branch and thorn illustrations, along with a note that encouraged fans to print out each image on tracing paper and stack them in whatever order they'd like. The artwork attached to the single was a composite of these images, an example of how fans could rearrange the artwork themselves.

This use of printing an album's visuals on extremely delicate material preceded the special "newspaper edition" of *The King of Limbs*, where the album's booklet was pressed on pulpy paper in the style of a radical 1960s newspaper. Yorke and Donwood brought the newspaper theme further into the real world by donning newsboy caps and passing out a free "tabloid" called *The Universal Sigh*. Stationed outside the Rough Trade East record shop in London, they distributed roughly 3,000 copies, all of which featured lyrics, artwork, and short stories by Donwood, Jay Griffiths, and Robert Macfarlane.

In keeping with a historical trend for the band, the newspaper edition was nominated for Best Boxed or Special Limited Edition Package at the 54th Grammy Awards.

A Moon Shaped Pool (2016)

As Radiohead's career has progressed, the creation of the artwork has mirrored the creation of the music itself: Donwood gets excited about a concept, it turns out horribly, he becomes distraught, gets inspired during his period of despair, then returns to the drawing board to finish—often with a brand-new idea.

A Moon Shaped Pool was no different. When Yorke recommended a documentary about an artist who flung around huge pots of paint at unstretched canvases, Donwood wanted to try a similar approach, though slightly more refined. He began experimenting with painting abstract images, then leaving the canvas in a water tray so that the liquid would "marble" the ink. Wanting to practice the technique on a larger scale, he built a small man-made pond in the south of France, near where Radiohead was recording *A Moon Shaped Pool*. The idea was to leave out the paintings to be affected by the water and weather.

The problem was the Mistral, a nonstop trade wind rumored to drive people mad. According to Donwood, it would destroy anything left on the water. He retreated to the studio and tried to get the desired effect with just a brush, but was once again dissatisfied with the results. After a week-long break, a most miserable Donwood looked at what he had already completed, and spotted one painting he deemed worthy—a simple black and white image.

From that point onward, he scaled back, doing away with his pond idea and only using black and white paints. Since his work was no longer in the water, it was free to get altered by the effects of Mother Nature without becoming completely damaged. He used the same method back in Oxfordshire (the paintings were "more affected by rain and less affected by wind"), with a final count of 13 usable paintings. The image on the front of *A Moon Shaped Pool* comes from the France sessions, forming a cosmic kind of circle slowly being broken apart—a miniature galaxy forming and getting destroyed at the exact same time. This reflects both the elation and grief found in the music.

More colorful swirls populated the inner pages, and for the special edition of the album, Donwood and Yorke scanned tracing-paper prints of the lyrics. Resembling microfilm slides, each image has the final version of the album's words at the forefront, with earlier drafts of the lyrics fading in the background.

A Moon Shaped Pool-era Singles (2015–2016)

Of the *Moon Shaped Pool*-era singles, the only one whose artwork appears to have been created using Donwood's weathering technique is "Daydreaming." The black-and-white visual is runnier than the album cover, which means it likely came from the wetter Oxfordshire sessions.

"Burn the Witch," on the other hand, looks birthed by a separate process altogether. Also black and white, its cover is occupied by a small army of humanoids who obviously had to be drawn and cut out by either Donwood or Yorke. Some of Donwood's weathering technique appears to come back in their coloring, however, which is characterized by more cosmic swirls. Perhaps the artist took a photo of one of his paintings, then simply cut out various figures from its surface. The image also appears within the album booklet.

Though not on the album, Radiohead released their unused James Bond theme, "Spectre," as a free download five months before *A Moon Shaped Pool*'s release. The original Soundcloud artwork was a natural successor to *The King of Limbs*—a green orb emitting dreamlike streaks into the ether. Once the single hit streaming surfaces, its artwork took on an ashier look that doesn't quite fit into *The King of Limbs* or *A Moon Shaped Pool*'s aesthetic. It looks almost charcoal—a cave drawing of a witch with a glowing red eye.

24

"Out of Control on Videotape"

Videography

Music Videos

Since 1994, the artwork for all Radiohead releases has been created by two people, one of whom fronts the band. Not so with their music videos.

Although Thom Yorke and sometimes Stanley Donwood have both been involved with the creative direction of some of Radiohead's videos, the band has worked with many directors over the years—some who have had wildly successful film careers. This has made for a staggering variety of aesthetics, ranging from humorous to animated to tragic (sometimes laughably so).

"Anyone Can Play Guitar" (February 1993)

Directed by Dwight Clarke

Is there a '90s alt-rock trope that Radiohead's first music video doesn't cover? The first image we see is Yorke in a Christ pose—in front of a wall of flames, no less. Elsewhere, the video overflows with figments of half-assed surrealism: random animals, unnecessary shutter speed, and an actual guitar engulfed in flames.

Given the song's sarcastic lyrical content and mock rock-star posturing adopted by the band members, it's clear that none of this is supposed to be taken all that seriously. Still, Radiohead weren't comfortable enough on camera yet to make satire or parody work. But even with a more relaxed band at the forefront, "Anyone Can Play Guitar" would still feel incredibly dated.

"Creep" (April 1993)

Directed by Brett Turnbull

The only crime committed by the visual for Radiohead's career-making song is that it's boring—the type of run-of-the-mill performance video that the band would eventually move away from in later work. Thanks to indigo and amber lighting and moody direction by concert-footage veteran Brett Turnbull, it at least looks pretty.

The venue where "Creep" was filmed over two performances does hold some significance for Radiohead. Back in 1993, it was called the Oxford Venue, before getting refurbished and opening in November 1995 as the Zodiac. The band partially funded the renovations, and the club's owner, Nick Moorbath, was instrumental in arranging a 2001 homecoming gig for them at Oxford's South Park. Today, the Zodiac operates under the name O2 Academy Oxford.

"Pop Is Dead" (May 1993)

Directed by Dwight Clarke

Director Dwight Clarke is responsible for Radiohead's two worst music videos, but unlike "Anyone Can Play Guitar," "Pop is Dead" at least has a clear vision. Whether or not it's a good vision is up for debate.

For the shoot, Clarke and the band ventured to the ancient tombs of Wayland's Smithy in Oxfordshire to stage a mock funeral, where Yorke is the deceased and the rest of Radiohead are the pallbearers. Once Yorke starts singing, he awakens in his glass coffin, revealing himself as both a vampire and an unwatchable metaphor for the music industry. The video for "Pop is Dead" had a chance to redeem the clumsy satire of the song, but it instead just leaned into the lyrics' worst instincts.

Today, the members of Radiohead look back on both the song and the music video as a misguided experiment. Ed O'Brien has remarked multiple times how irony isn't the band's strong suit, and on February 1, 2012, Adam Buxton's music-video showcase, *BUG*, played a recording of the Greenwood brothers shaking their heads in good-natured embarrassment at the videos for both "Anyone Can Play Guitar" and "Pop is Dead."

"Stop Whispering" (October 1993)

Directed by Jeffery Plansker

In some ways, "Stop Whispering" almost sets the standard for later Radiohead videos. Its concept is high and not immediately obvious, with insects crawling over rubble while a man puts on a diving suit to explore an apocalyptic landscape.

The problem is, the eerie imagery gets overrun by footage of Radiohead performing at their most histrionic. By the end of the video, we've seen more of Yorke literally moping in a corner than the mysterious land diver, who only manages to get on his helmet before we fade to black.

"High and Dry" (March 1995, January 1996)

Directed by David Mould (1995) and Paul Cunningham (1996)

Neither of the music videos for "High and Dry" are especially brilliant, but the fact that there are two at all shows that, by the time *The Bends* rolled around, Radiohead were starting to take greater control of their visual identity.

The initial video, released in the UK in March 1995, showed the band playing in the middle of the desert. Director David Mould makes no illusions about being on a set (yet another '90s trope), keeping the cranes, lights, and camera displays in full view. By the end, artificial rain falls on the band—a boneheaded piece of symbolism that answers the song's central plea.

Dissatisfied with the results, Radiohead hired Paul Cunningham to helm a separate US version of the video, which was released almost a year later in January 1996. The visual takes a more cinematic, narrative approach, with the band sitting down at a diner where a series of shadowy events unfold. Two patrons are involved in a vague heist with one of the cooks, who ends up double-crossing them by placing a bomb in their carryout container. Elsewhere, Yorke and a young boy encounter a man in the bathroom who refuses to give up a mysterious briefcase.

The stateside version of "High and Dry" aims to be a tense potboiler, but too much is left unexplained for there to be any kind of real tension. That being said, it's the first Radiohead music video that doesn't look cheesy, and it finds the band figuring out how to be more ambitious. Most importantly, the story actually goes against the romantic sorrow of the song, showing that a band's visuals don't always have to reflect the lyrics. When it came time to compile their music videos for the 7 *Television Commercials* collection, it was clear which version of "High and Dry" would make the cut.

"Fake Plastic Trees" (May 1995)

Directed by Jake Scott

Go figure that Radiohead's first wholly successful music video was directed by Ridley Scott's son, Jake.

As if taking a cue from his father, Scott gave the supermarket in "Fake Plastic Trees" a science-fiction bent—the walls and floors a sterile white; the shelves glowing with strange neon hues. As the band members ride around in shopping carts (looking like overgrown little boys in the process), we meet many of the market's equally strange denizens, from a man who shaves his head in one of the aisles to a gaudily dressed old woman who may be shoplifting. A pre-*Walking Dead* Norman Reedus (then a model) makes a blink-and-you-miss-it appearance as a shopper.

Scott has said that the whole affair is an allegory for death and reincarnation, but that it's also best to not read too far into it. Whatever the case, "Fake Plastic Trees" marks the first time a Radiohead music video was truly entrancing.

"Just" (September 1995)

Directed by Jamie Thraves

In keeping with their newfound agency, Radiohead personally selected Jamie Thraves to helm "Just" after viewing some of his experimental short films.

They certainly got what they bargained for. Depicting a man lying on the pavement for reasons unknown, the music video runs like a Samuel Beckett play in miniature—told exclusively with subtitles and no audible dialogue. As the man refuses to get up, a crowd forms around him (the band is playing above in an apartment). People demand to know why he's lying in the middle of the sidewalk. He agrees to tell them, but warns that there will be terrible consequences. Once he reveals his reasons, the subtitles stop, leaving what he said up to the audience's interpretation. Whatever his words, "Just" concludes with everyone joining the man by lying down on the sidewalk, frozen and despondent.

Radiohead fans have provided their own theories about what the man says at the end of "Just." Of course, it will always be better to not know. The brilliance comes from a sense of cryptic completeness. That is, "Just" still tells a full story with a beginning, middle, and end without beating the audience over the head with answers.

Even without its narrative, it's also the first time Radiohead looks comfortable performing in one of their own music videos. Standing in a circle as if at a rehearsal, they possess the same kind of spastic energy exhibited on the *From the Basement* specials that would air over a decade later.

Mark Ronson ended up making an unofficial sequel to the video after he teamed up with Phantom Planet to cover "Just" for the 2006 tribute album *Exit Music: Songs with Radio Heads*. In the video, Phantom Planet plays in an apartment similar to Radiohead's, while below, a custodial worker begins sweeping up all of the people on the ground at the end of the original. When he hands one man a trumpet, he gets up and starts playing the cover's brass part, with the rest of the group hopping to their feet and dancing. By the end, they're back on the ground, right where they started.

"Street Spirit (Fade Out)" (February 1996)

Directed by Jonathan Glazer

Outside of a handful of otherworldly images (three leaping dancers, a large insect), the music video for "Street Spirit (Fade Out)" largely consists of Radiohead horsing around outside a trailer in the desert.

But director Jonathan Glazer has always specialized in stylizing the mundane until it reaches a level of transcendent beauty. Just look at the opening sequence of his 2000 film debut, *Sexy Beast*. It's little more than Ray Winstone lounging poolside in a Speedo. But the indulgent closeups, gravelly voiceover, and Stranglers soundtrack bring the credits into high-art territory.

The video for "Street Spirit (Fade Out)" is no different. It's a world where Ed O'Brien falling out of a lawn chair is just as poetic as a grasshopper fluttering in the face of a young boy—perhaps even more so.

"Paranoid Android" (May 1997)

Directed by Magnus Carlsson

Though Radiohead was highly pleased with Glazer's work on "Street Spirit (Fade Out)," they wanted something less stylistically heavy for the music video for "Paranoid Android," as to reflect the black comedy of the song.

They turned to Magnus Carlsson, creator of the cult Swedish animated series *Robin*. In addition to relating to the title bachelor's strength and vulnerability, the band thought his chaotic adventures with his friend Benjamin would fit the tone of "Paranoid Android'"s lyrics. But when they sent Carlsson the footage, they intentionally included only the instrumental track, fearing that the lyrics would inspire him to straightforwardly depict the imagery of the song.

Robin and Benjamin's saga may not be a direct translation of "Paranoid Android'"s words, but it does effectively capture their tone. It starts off like a regular day, with Robin taking a shower, then quickly descends into a hellscape filled with mermaids, EU agents, and a man with a parasitic head emerging from his stomach. In the most horrific sequence, an EU agent chases Robin up a lamp post, trying to chop it down like a tree. He ends up dismembering himself and falling into the water below.

Dark as that sounds, the crudeness of the animation prevents the music video from ever losing its sense of comedy. But the cartoon's simplicity also results in its sole flaw. If there's one quibble to be had with "Paranoid Android," it's that Carlsson's primitive colors and squiggly lines feel similar to the "illustrated radio" cartoons of the early 1960s and 1970s (think those vintage Tootsie Pop commercials for reference). Although the imagery matches up with the song's tone, the style never reaches the bigness of the music.

"No Surprises" (1997)

Directed by Grant Gee

Thom Yorke and an astronaut helmet slowly filling up with water. That's all it took to film one of Radiohead's most iconic music videos. That, and some old-school camera trickery.

Shortly after we hear the word "silent," the waterline reaches Yorke's mouth, forcing him to stop singing and hold his breath for what seems like a minute. In reality, director Grant Gee sped up the accompanying audio for Yorke's lip sync, then slowed down the footage in post-production, giving the illusion that the Radiohead singer is underwater for a lot longer than he actually is.

Still, the whole ordeal was exhausting and claustrophobic, as seen in behind-the-scenes footage of Gee's documentary *Meeting People is Easy*. To release the water, Yorke had to yank a rubber seal—something that took multiple takes before he was finally able to come back in with his vocals at the correct time. In an unused take, he screams after releasing the water.

Because the footage gets slowed down for the final product, that tension blends with a sense of calm. While Yorke's frustration is visible when he's underwater, there's a dreamlike quality that couples nicely with the song's depiction of a slow and numb suburban life.

"Karma Police" (August 1997)

Directed by Jonathan Glazer

Like "No Surprises," the music video for "Karma Police" has a simple concept consisting almost entirely of one shot. But achieving such simplicity was a bit complicated.

Glazer, returning to direct again after his success with "Street Spirit (Fade Out)," came up with his idea after watching the opening sequence of David Lynch's *Lost Highway*, which shows nothing more than a two-lane blacktop rapidly passing the camera at night. Glazer added some more Lynchian details, namely a man getting chased down a country road by a car without a driver. Eventually, the car stops and he falls to the ground. The car slowly reverses, revealing a trail of leaked fuel. The man pulls out a pair of matches from behind his back, ignites them, and incinerates the car.

One Glazer had his outline, he pitched the idea to Marilyn Manson for his song "Long Hard Road Out of Hell." Manson passed on the idea, so Glazer brought it to Radiohead, who felt it was a natural fit for the paranoia of "Karma Police." Yorke would be positioned in the back seat of the car—a 1976 Chrysler New Yorker—adding to the eerie feel that the vehicle is running without a driver. To achieve the effect, a stunt driver controlled the Chrysler via an attached sidecar off camera.

Among "Karma Police"'s production troubles were exhaust fumes that kept seeping into the backseat of the car, a pitch-black night sky that had to be color-corrected, and the fatigue of central performer Lajos Kovács. The Hungarian actor burned his thumb on the book of matches while trying to light it, and a severe cramp required an injection so he could run for long stretches at a time during shooting.

Despite its iconic status and praise from the band themselves, Glazer has expressed dissatisfaction with "Karma Police."

"I decided to do a very minimalist, subjective use of camera, and tried to do something hypnotic and dramatic from one perspective, and it was very hard to achieve and I feel that I didn't achieve it," he told *IndieWire* on June 12, 2001. While he's being a bit hard on himself, he is right about the camerawork. "Karma Police"'s least interesting moments are when we cut away from the single tracking shot and get a closeup perspective from Kovács. The music video could have been even more effective had it stayed confined to just one shot.

"Lucky" (October 1997)

Less a proper music video than a PSA for the War Child charity, "Lucky" intersperses shots of Radiohead performing the song with footage of war-torn Bosnia. This ties it more to the song's original appearance on *The Help Album* than *OK Computer* in both name and visual. The message gets delivered by images of injured children and destroyed buildings, which are admittedly hard to watch. And that's the point.

"Pyramid Song" (2001)

Directed by Shynola

When the three-person British art collective Shynola created the promotional "blips" for *Kid A*, the short films were little more than Stanley Donwood's artwork from the album come to life. Many of the blips were eventually strung together for a promotional video set to "Motion Picture Soundtrack."

For "Pyramid Song," Shynola got to flex their creative muscles a bit more, creating a computerized music video that, like so much of the visual identity of Radiohead, seems to take place in a dystopian future. A drab, flattened figure dwells on the roof of what appears to be a derelict building standing in the middle of the sea. The character straps on a SCUBA tank and explores the depths below, stumbling across the remains of a submerged human civilization. Everything from books to streetlights, cars, and other structures populate this strange aquatic world. When the figure reaches a suburban home complete with picket fence and an easy chair, they decide to stay.

While "Pyramid Song" is big on introspection and apocalyptic mood, the digital graphics feel a little primordial and corny by today's standards. Like the main character's findings, the music video is best enjoyed as a relic or artifact.

"Knives Out" (May 2001)

Directed by Michel Gondry

On paper, Radiohead and film visionary Michel Gondry seem like a perfect match, and if we're just going off of the visuals, "Knives Out" is a success. In what appears to be a single shot, the camera circles around a cramped apartment that becomes a nightmarish hospital setting.

In between interludes of watching himself and a former lover enjoy each other's company on TV, Yorke sees the unnamed woman undergo surgery via a life-sized version of the board game *Operation*. The music video becomes increasingly surreal as he opens a trapdoor to a family trying to eat him; witnesses his TV counterpart become violent; and eventually transforms into a mouse. It's a suitably twitchy—though not completely literal—visual for a song that alludes to cannibalism.

Gondry drew inspiration for the "Knives Out" video from a relationship of his own that had recently fallen apart. According to his June 26, 2008 interview with *The Playlist*, Yorke was enthusiastic about the video's concept and storyboards at first, but grew sour on it once he realized the filmmaker was infusing his own personal story into the narrative.

Gondry also said that, while he loves the final product, the shoot ended up being difficult, and that Radiohead wouldn't even let him use the music video for his compilation DVD in Palm Pictures' *Directors Label* series. It's worth noting that Jonathan Glazer was permitted to use his music video for "Street Spirit (Fade Out)" for his own entry in the series.

Gondry eventually was able to include "Knives Out" on his self-released *Michel Gondry 2: More Videos (Before and After DVD 1)*, so perhaps he and Radiohead buried the hatchet. Since none of the band members have ever publicly commented on the experience, it remains a mystery whether Yorke was unnecessarily cold toward the director, or whether the tension was merely a result of two egos clashing. Regardless, it made for a memorable four minutes.

"I Might Be Wrong" (July and October 2001)

Directed by Chris Bran (July) and Sophie Muller (October)

To date, Radiohead has released two different music videos for two of their songs—"High and Dry" and "I Might Be Wrong." In both cases, neither video knocked it completely out of the park.

The more widely circulated version of "I Might Be Wrong" was directed by still-prolific music video veteran Sophie Muller. While not outright horrible, it falls victim to repetition, featuring nothing more than Yorke and Jonny Greenwood performing the song in a dark parking garage. Muller separates it from the typical performance video with grainy camera stock and lighting that comes in sporadic flashes. But she uses up all of her tricks early on, preventing it from ever taking on the dizzying narrative and dazzling ambition of something like "Knives Out." Radiohead still went on to include it on their demented TV series *The Most Gigantic Lying Mouth of All Time.*

Just three months earlier, the band also released an internet version of "I Might Be Wrong," directed by Chris Bran. With animation of the crying minotaur and several burning landscapes, it almost works as the *Amnesiac* artwork come to life. But like Muller's video, nothing ever escalates. Once we see the initial gimmick, it just repeats over and over.

"Push Pulk/Spinning Plates" (2002)

Directed by Johnny Hardstaff

An oddity amongst the *Amnesiac* music videos, "Push Pulk/Spinning Plates" seamlessly blends together "Pulk/Pull Revolving Doors" and "Like Spinning Plates" for a techno-organic nightmare. Via computer graphics, an elaborate machine gets blueprinted and constructed before the audience's eyes.

Once the "Spinning Plates" section starts, a carousel component of the machine begins to revolve, revealing two babies who share limbs and possibly a stomach strapped into its central pod. As the device stops spinning, their stomachs protrude and their ribs are seemingly lifted from their body.

That the babies' ribs resemble holograms or x-rays with no blood or guts makes the whole ordeal that much more disturbing. There's a medical precision to the video, despite no proper explanation as to what's going on. The only downside is that the effects are slightly outdated since the machine is computer-generated and the babies are composites of actual human children. Had director Johnny Hardstaff opted to make the babies CGI or render the entire thing in 2D or 3D animation, the future would look more unified and terrifying in 2018. As with Muller's "I Might Be Wrong," it appeared in *The Most Gigantic Lying Mouth of All Time.*

"There there" (May 2003)

Directed by Chris Hopewell

Oliver Postgate's beloved children's television program *Bagpuss* was a huge influence on *Hail to the Thief*—so much that Radiohead approached him to animate and direct the music video for the album's lead single, "There there."

Postgate, then 78 and retired, respectfully declined, so Radiohead hired artist and stop-motion animator Chris Hopewell to make a video in the style of *Bagpuss*, mixed with a Grimms' fairytale. Hopewell drew further inspiration from someone he's referred to only as "Mr. Potter," a man he knew who kept a museum of stuffed animals in human situations.

The music video for "There there" was inspired by the British children's series *Bagpuss*.
https://commons.wikimedia.org/wiki/File:Bagpuss_in_Canterbury.jpg

That reversal of human and animal comes heavily into play in the music video, which finds Yorke in a feral state as he makes his way through an enchanted forest. To play up his wildness, Hopewell filmed all of Yorke's motions at one-third speed, then sped up the footage, giving the frontman's being a jerky, animalistic feel. As for the wildlife, Yorke witnesses them participating in human activities—various rodents having dinner together; a group of kittens having a wedding, etc.

Throughout the video, there's a separation between Yorke and the critters. He's always placed on the outside looking in—a savage person never invited to partake in the joyous activities. He ends up becoming a more natural part of the environment (though not in the way he wishes) when he steals a pair of magic boots, prompting a murder of crows to viciously attack him before he turns into a gnarled tree.

To achieve the effect of an enchanted world that was nonetheless realistic, Hopewell filmed portions of the video in a small forest in Bristol and the rest of it in a studio filled with logs. According to a November 1, 2017 interview with *Monster Children* (in an issue guest-edited by Stanley Donwood) Hopewell revealed that he actually left one of the miniature trees—complete with a tiny door—intact in the forest. Unfortunately, it's become covered by growth and, to date, no fan has been able to find it.

"Go to Sleep" (2003)

Directed by Alex Rutterford

The benefit to an older style of animation is that, if a director is thinking of using it in the first place, it's most likely withstood the test of time. With "There there," there was no question of whether or not stop-motion animation would look good. It had already been looking good for decades.

"Go to Sleep," on the other hand, uses an outdated polygonal style reminiscent of an early 2000s video game. Bookended by shots of a red rose that blooms, then shuts, the visual shows a creepily animated Yorke wandering about a busy town square. When the song gets heavy, historic buildings around him begin to collapse, only to rebuild themselves into more modern structures. Maybe it's an analogy for the animation.

"Sit down. Stand up" (2003)

Directed by Ed Holdsworth

Radiohead may not have gotten along with Michel Gondry, but the band and director Ed Holdsworth had no problem aping his style for the music video for "Sit down. Stand up." Like Gondry's video for the Chemical Brothers' "Star Guitar," its concept revolves around someone looking out the window of a moving vehicle (likely a bus or train), and watching the passing scenery sync up with the beat of the song.

Whether it's an instance of flat-out plagiarism, well-intended homage, or mere coincidence, "Sit down. Stand up" does have some of its own flourishes. For one, it's at night and stays firmly planted in the city, unlike "Star Guitar," which passes through a variety of landscapes during the day. Also, Holdsworth appears to have used his skills as a digital compositor to overlay different locations on top of each other, creating a kaleidoscopic effect. For all its strengths, however, it's reasonable to expect more originality from a Radiohead music video. It also appeared on *The Most Gigantic Lying Mouth of All Time*.

"Jigsaw Falling into Place" (November 2007)

Directed by Adam Buxton and Garth Jennings

Adam Buxton, who once unveiled Radiohead's reactions to their crappier early-career music videos with his *BUG* showcase, eventually got to capture the band at their greatest with his visual for "Jigsaw Falling Into Place."

Brilliant in its simplicity, the concept (dreamed up by Buxton and co-director Garth Jennings) was to have the band perform the song while wearing bicycle helmets that were spray-painted silver and outfitted with small cameras attached via metal rods. This placed the cameras about a foot-and-a-half in front of each band member's face, giving the illusion that the head is stationary while the rest of the body is moving. The entire shoot lasted for two takes under 20 minutes (Buxton and Jennings ended up going with the second take), and it all cost just £400. That's probably a lot cheaper than the budget for the "Pop is Dead" music video.

"Nude" (December 2007)

Directed by Adam Buxton and Garth Jennings

With "Jigsaw Falling Into Place," Buxton and Jennings filmed the first Radiohead music video to feature all five band members since 1996's "Street Spirit (Fade Out)." They continued the practice with "Nude."

Another less-is-more triumph, the video shows Radiohead (all of them) performing the sensual number in slow motion. It's still impossible to keep some comedy at bay, especially with an elongated shot of Selway ramping up for a single tap on one of his cymbals and an anticlimax where everyone gets covered in feathers.

Fun fact: While Buxton had an earlier Radiohead connection with his *BUG* compilation, Jennings had directed the 2005 film adaptation of *The Hitchhiker's Guide to the Galaxy*, the novel that birthed the phrase "Paranoid Android."

"House of Cards" (June 2008)

Directed by James Frost

As entertaining as the music videos for "Jigsaw Falling Into Place" and "Nude" are, they have a lightness about them. For the third music video for *In Rainbows*, the band got much more ambitious.

Not that one would know from being on set. Unlike every other Radiohead video before it, "House of Cards" used no lights or cameras in its production. Instead, director James Frost turned to light detection and ranging (LIDAR) technology. Developed in the 1960s, LIDAR calculates distance to a specified target by lighting up the target, then measuring the reflected pulses with a sensor. In simpler terms, the video's Director of Technology, Aaron Koblin, described it to a making-of documentary as "analyzing distances, then figuring out how to reconstruct geometry."

He and Frost had become familiar with LIDAR when it was being used at UCLA for research in how to accomplish real-time 3D recording. And if there was any band who would be interested in using such technology for a music video, they suspected it would be Radiohead. They were right. As a guidepost, Yorke gave them two images that the song evoked in his head: vaporization and a party.

With those directions in mind, Frost assembled a team of engineers, with production help from high-school students from G-Star School of the Arts in Palm Springs, Florida. The team used a variety of LIDAR technology to scan Yorke performing the song, people exiting a party, and various suburban landscapes around the Sunshine State (procured during a seven-hour drive). Despite the video's three distinct settings, everything has the same pixelated yet highly concentrated aesthetic: somewhere between the heat vision from *Predator* and one of those pin-point impression toys from the 1990s, where one could put their face in a dense bed of needles and leave behind the outline of their visage.

To achieve the vaporization effect described by Yorke, Frost and his team placed sheets of plexiglass in front of him when he was singing, subtly disrupting the image being generated. For additional flourishes, they dotted the plexiglass with shards of mirror, which made it look like he and the party guests are in a constant cycle of disintegration and regeneration. For the final image of the video, a suburban home in a cul-de-sac seemingly blows away, thus calling back to the fragile structure of the song's title.

If all of that conjures images of destruction and decay, rest assured that, like the overall tone of *In Rainbows*, the music video for "House of Cards" never loses its warmth. There's an entrancing nocturnal glow to the imagery generated by the LIDAR technology, a comforting visual that's akin to Donwood's "toxic rainbows" found in the album art. The Recording Academy was entranced enough to nominate "House of Cards" for Best Music Video at the 51st Annual Grammy Awards. Most exciting of all, Radiohead made the data used to create the video publicly available on Google Code.

"Reckoner" (October 2008)

Directed by Clement Picon

In another Radiohead first, the music for "Reckoner" had zero creative involvement from the band. Instead, they chose the song's official promo video from a fan submission.

Clement Picon was the lucky winner of a contest held in conjunction with animation studio Aniboom. Artists from all over the world submitted incomplete, animated music videos for songs from *In Rainbows*, with the grand-prize winner slated to receive $10,000 so they could finish their project. Radiohead ended up choosing four.

It's easy to see why Picon got the extra award of having an official Radiohead video to his name. Not only does his animation style seem to draw inspiration from Donwood—his video tells a story that dovetails with themes frequently found in Radiohead's music. Plant life grows throughout a drab landscape before the plants get overtaken by industrialization, which eventually leads to the destruction of civilization and the growth of more vegetation.

While it's all a little on the nose, the animation has a thorny impressionism that keeps the music video for "Reckoner" from feeling like an afterschool special. And Picon probably didn't know this at the time, but the power of nature may have already been seeding in Yorke's head, seeing as Radiohead's next album would be *The King of Limbs*.

"All I Need" (May 2008)

Directed by Steve Rogers

Spiritually, the music video for "All I Need" is most similar to "Lucky." Both visuals were tied to a social-justice initiative—"Lucky" with the War Child charity and "All I Need" with MTV's EXIT campaign.

Since EXIT was started to promote awareness and work toward the prevention of human trafficking and modern slavery, the video for "All I Need" presents a split-screen depiction of a day in two boys' lives: one of them from an affluent Western background and one of them from an impoverished Asian background. As they go throughout their days, we discover that the Asian boy made the other boy's dress shoes in a sweatshop. The video ends with the message "Some things cost more than you realise," followed by info on the EXIT campaign.

As with "Lucky," subtlety isn't the point here. Yorke told MTV on April 30, 2008 that if Radiohead can bring even the smallest amount of increased attention to the issue of child labor and make it less taboo to talk about, then he considers it a win. When taking "All I Need"'s frequent airplay and 16 awards into account (including the Asia-Pacific Child Rights Award from UNICEF–CASBAA), it's safe to say that the band landed a victory.

"Lotus Flower" (February 2011)

Directed by Garth Jennings and Wayne McGregor

Subbing out his pal Adam Buxton for acclaimed British choreographer Wayne McGregor of the Royal Ballet and elsewhere, Garth Jennings's recipe for "Lotus Flower" was simple: a bare stage and a business-casual Thom Yorke cutting a rug.

Yorke's hypnotically unpredictable dance moves and bowler hat proved to be polarizing among fans and critics, comedic and confusing enough to launch the famous (or infamous) "Dancing Thom Yorke" meme. McGregor told *Time Out* in May 2011 that he was intrigued by the constant debates about Yorke's supposedly impromptu awkward-Dad moves, seeing as everything was highly choreographed. He went on to call Yorke an incredible dancer and praised him for his authenticity.

Regardless of one's opinion of the "Lotus Flower" video and Yorke's headwear, it's hard to argue with that second assessment. Where so many other performance videos have found Yorke at his most self-serious, "Lotus Flower" feels more sincere. It's hard to hate on someone who's having that much fun. At least the Grammys showed Radiohead some more love by nominating the short for "Best Music Video."

"Burn the Witch" (May 2016)

Directed by Chris Hopewell

Since 2012, Chris Hopewell had retired from making music videos—until Stanley Donwood called up. After hearing Radiohead's newest single, "Burn the Witch," he wanted to know if Hopewell had any ideas for its visual. Hopewell agreed to meet, and after Donwood got him drunk enough on cider, he insisted on doing the video himself. It was probably Donwood's plan all along. With a team of a dozen or so sculptors and animators, they completed the video in 14 days.

Like Hopewell's video for "There there," "Burn the Witch" relies heavily on stop-motion. Once Hopewell, Donwood, and Yorke put their heads together, they decided the animation should be in the style of of another iconic British children's series, Gordon Murray's *Trumptonshire* trilogy. Unlike the more detailed yet muted animation style of *Bagpuss*, everything in *Trumptonshire*'s tiny villages is bright and round (no one has mouths)—a simplicity that only adds to the creepiness of "Burn the Witch."

At first, everything seems fine. Birds chirp and a stuffy man arrives in a small town for some kind of unnamed inspection. Soon, though, it becomes clear that the town has a dark underbelly. A group of men in stag masks prepares to burn a woman at the stake, another woman approaches a gallows to be hanged, and the inspector himself is eventually escorted into a giant wooden figure a la *The Wicker Man*. Strangely, he does nothing to stop any of these violent acts, including his own demise—or so it seems. In the final shot, we discover that he's escaped unscathed. None of the creators have commented on the video's exact meaning, though many of the images from the lyrics (gallows, red crosses on wooden doors) make their way on-screen.

Despite the general acclaim surrounding the music video for "Burn the Witch" (it was released at the exact time as the single), Murray's estate was not as pleased with the final product as *Bagpuss'* Postgate had been with "There there." Murray's son-in-law William Mollett told *The Daily Mail* on May 14, 2016 that he viewed it as a "tarnishing of the brand," so much that he couldn't even bear to show it to Murray himself, who ended up dying just a month-and-a-half later. Mollett ended the interview by hinting at possible legal action. While he's entitled to his opinion, there probably isn't much of a case to be made for plagiarism since so many other TV programs have adopted a similar animation style.

On the more positive side, "Burn the Witch" ended Hopewell's retirement from music videos, and he went on to create visuals for Run the Jewels, Father John Misty, and others. He told *Monster Children* that his dream is to one day work on a video for Queens of the Stone Age. Does he know they also have a song called "Burn the Witch"?

"Daydreaming" (May 2016)

Directed by Paul Thomas Anderson

Paul Thomas Anderson and Radiohead have had similar careers, and not just because they're both indebted to Jonny Greenwood.

Like Radiohead, Anderson gained mainstream recognition in the '90s for work that was kinetic, accessible, and easy to define. But he's relied more on ambiguity and stillness the deeper he's gotten into his filmography—not always explaining his endings, themes, and character motivations in full to his audiences. He's gone beyond being Kubrickian; he's Andersonian.

He applied that aesthetic to his music video for "Daydreaming," where Yorke walks through a series of doors each bringing him to a new location. His bewildered journey is entrancing, if not exactly remarkable, until the climax when he goes full-on Narnia and enters a snowy landscape. He crawls into a cave and falls asleep next to a fire, his breathing synced up with the animalistic cellos that end the song.

As with any Anderson film (or Radiohead music video for that matter), "Daydreaming" has ignited a host of fan theories on Reddit, the most prominent coming from filmmaker and video essayist Rishi Kaneria, who believes the video ties to Yorke's partner Rachel Owen and the end of their relationship—and possibly her fatal illness. Owen separated from Yorke less than a year before the release of *A Moon Shaped Pool* and died of cancer on December 18, 2016, just seven months after the release of the "Daydreaming" video.

Among the supposed clues found by Kaneria are the 23 doors walked through by Yorke—the same number of years he was with Owen. He's also wearing clothes from fashion designer Rick Owens, whose name Kaneria finds too similar to Rachel Owen to be a coincidence.

While it's generally accepted that many of the lyrics on *A Moon Shaped Pool* probably have to do with Owen, it's a stretch that all of the "clues" spotted by Kaneria are indeed clues at all. Then again, that's part of the appeal of Radiohead and Anderson's work. Some people want to analyze it to death; others just want to be moved by the images and emotions: a man walking through many doors, a man crawling into a cave, a man falling asleep in the wilderness.

A Moon Shaped Pool Visual Series (2016)

Directed by Various

Radiohead only released two official music videos for *A Moon Shaped Pool*, a low number compared to previous albums such as *In Rainbows* and *OK Computer*. But in a Beyoncé-in-miniature move, they asked nine different artists to each create short visuals for some of the remaining songs (several were interpreted more than once). From May to July of 2016, Radiohead shared the vignettes on their Instagram account.

First up was an interpretation of "Glass Eyes" on May 13 from Tarik Barri, who set the song's opening piano cascade to a soup of colorful streaks. The final video (set to "The Numbers") was uploaded on July 8, and featured cross dissolves of everyday people walking past flaming smokestacks and oil fields. Directed by Radiohead's old friend Grant Gee, it connected directly to the song's environmentally minded lyrics. Other highlights included a possible "Karma Police" homage from Richard Ayoade for "Tinker Tailor Soldier Sailor Rich Man Poor Man Beggar Man Thief" and Yorgos Lanthimos's "Identikit," which simply features a man eating an imaginary sandwich.

"I Promise" (June 2017)

Directed by Michal Marczak

All of the previously unreleased tracks on Radiohead's 2017 box set, *OK Computer OKNOTOK 1997 2017*, were recorded 20 years ago, so it's only natural that their corresponding music videos would, to some extent, be exercises in nostalgia.

For "I Promise," Michal Marczak (who had directed one of the *Moon Shaped Pool* visuals for "Identikit") follows several people on a contemplative nighttime bus ride through Warsaw. One man appears to be lying down on his seat, but the end of the video reveals that he's actually a severed animatronic head. While the ending is nowhere as evocative or mysterious as the more obtuse "Daydreaming," it's a satisfying bit of science fiction straight from the *Bends* and *OK Computer* eras, as if the CPR dummy on the former's cover learned how to walk out of the hospital, only to have his head fall off.

"Man of War" (June 2017)

Directed by Connor Kammerer and Colin Read

"Man of War"'s waltz-like pacing make it a sister song to "Karma Police," and the music video also orbits around a man on the run.

As he walks around Brooklyn, the environment keeps switching from daytime to nighttime. Initially, the daylight hours find him in a chipper mood, running toward someone who's dropped something. Conversely, the nighttime scenes depict him running away from something in terror. As the video toggles back and forth between the two scenarios, they eventually become one, with a small mob of people chasing him through both settings.

Unlike "Karma Police," however, the man's pursuers prove to be benevolent. Once he falls and they reach him, everyone simply follows him at a calm pace. Maybe it's a sign that Radiohead have gotten more optimistic with age.

"Lift" (September 2017)

Directed by Oscar Hudson

Considering the music video for "Lift" revolves around Yorke encountering different characters from different floors in an elevator (or a "lift" if you're in England), it would have been easy for Oscar Hudson to make the entire visual one big explicit homage to Radiohead's career. Instead, he opted for something more subtle.

Sure, there are obvious references such as a real-life version of Robin from "Paranoid Android" and the disheveled man from "Karma Police." But other visual cues remain more cryptic. Are the trees we see on one floor of the elevator meant to be "Fake Plastic Trees"? Is the upside-down floor a nod to the skewed perspective of the "Daydreaming" video?

Hudson has remained mum on most of the references, telling *Pitchfork* on September 12, 2017 that he's well aware how obsessive Radiohead fans can be, and that he encourages them to conduct their own analysis. He also stressed how he wanted the music video to connect to the present as well as the past. That's why the video starts with Yorke standing with his then-girlfriend/now-wife, Dajana Roncione, and his daughter Agnes, who presses all the lift buttons (much to his annoyance) and sends him on his journey.

For his concept, which involved sliding in a new set every time the elevator doors close, Hudson also drew inspiration from art outside of Radiohead's oeuvre. He referred to a Marc Isaacs documentary (also titled *Lift*) as an essential touchstone.

"[A man] just sits in the back of the same lift in a council estate—which is like what we call the projects in the UK—for a month and silently films as people gets in and out," Hudson told *Pitchfork*. "He builds up relationships with all the characters who come and go."

That's a lighthearted reference for a Radiohead video, but "Lift" is a comparatively lighthearted composition for being from the *OK Computer* era. That's why the band was resistant toward releasing it for so long.

But if time has proven anything, it's that Radiohead has embraced the goodness in life as they've gotten older. The trajectory of their music videos—"Lift" being their most recent video at the time of this writing—is a reflection of that.

The Most Gigantic Lying Mouth of All Time (2004)

Throughout their career, Radiohead have frequently written and performed about dystopian scenarios, but *The Most Gigantic Lying Mouth of All Time* is their piece of art that feels most likely to *exist* in such an environment.

At its core, *Lying Mouth* is a collection of 24 short films that use Radiohead's music or, at the very least, are inspired by it. The creators range from associates of the band to fans that submitted their own homemade visions. Some of the vignettes function as primitive lyric videos ("Myxomatosis" gets scrawled across graph paper); some are official music videos (see "Sit down. Stand up" and "Push Pulk/Spinning Plates"); some are nightmarish original segments, such as Rick Hind and Ajit N. Rao's short films involving dismembered doll parts.

To fill in the space between each listed film, director/editor Chris Bran of the Vapour Brothers includes behind-the-scenes footage of Radiohead, concert footage (including a fan singing along to "The National Anthem" in its entirety), and even some rarities, such as an acoustic ballad called "Morning M'lord" that would go on to become the more electronic "Morning Mr Magpie" on *The King of Limbs*. Elsewhere, snippets of half-formed compositions, such as a bass drone by Jonny Greenwood called "5ths Reversed," would give glimpses into unfinished Radiohead experiments.

All of this makes up the meat of *Lying Mouth*, and like most projects involving over 20 contributors, the results are hit and miss. While the band footage is a surefire point of interest for any Radiohead fan, some of the films embody the shoddiest of art-school cliches. For every bit of artful claymation (see Juan Pablo Etcheverry's "Dog Interface"), there's a barrage of doll parts. For every "Morning M'lord," there's a bland performance music video of *I Might Be Wrong*. Getting through all 110 minutes can be an up-and-down slog.

Which brings us back to dystopia. What makes *Lying Mouth* more than just a curiosity is the structure and format. Although its final form would be all of the footage on a DVD self-released on December 1, 2004, it was originally released in four separate installments on an internet TV channel called *Radiohead Television*, starting on May 26, 2003. Yorke has (perhaps jokingly) said that the band pitched the series to several actual TV stations beforehand, but that they all passed. So instead, fans could watch the show for free using QuickTime, at least for a few months until the DVD came out.

Radiohead truly leaned into the cheap-TV format with *Lying Mouth*, opening the show with 1970s-style introduction music and cutting away to title cards at the end of each segment. Bookending each episode was a host named Chieftain Mews—actually Nigel Godrich, his face digitized and composited to the point where he resembled one of the Coneheads from *Saturday Night Live*. "All

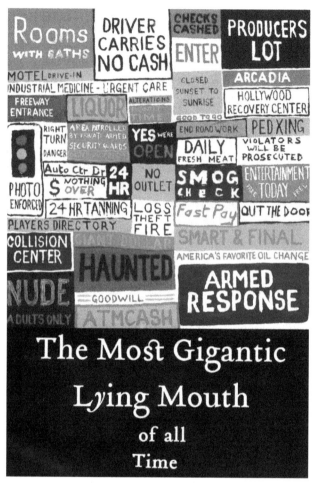

The cover of *The Most Gigantic Lying Mouth of All Time* DVD, featuring Nigel Godrich as Chieftain Mews.   *Author's collection*

of the footage you're about to see has been pre-watched by adults" was just one of many cryptic and creepy nonsense phrases he would utter. Halfway through the show, a voice-modulated Yorke and O'Brien would have to answer similarly ridiculous tabloid-esque questions in a segment titled "My Showbiz Life."

Due to the intentionally wonky editing effects and framing devices, *Lying Mouth* has the same nightmare-television quality of 2000s Comedy Central programs such as *Tim and Eric Awesome Show, Great Job!* Due to its proximity to *Hail to the Thief* (not to mention the almost identical artwork on the DVD cover), it's as if an archaeologist wandered into the album's exaggerated showbiz/political hellscape, recorded an evening's worth of basic-cable TV, and came back out with the tape. It may not be the sturdiest project of Radiohead's career, but it's a worthwhile artifact.

25

"Drawing Bears"

Stanley Donwood

"Reclusive" is a word that often comes up in articles written about Stanley Donwood—the nom de plume of artist and writer Dan Rickwood. The terminology isn't quite accurate. It's true that, beyond the basics, Donwood rarely goes into details about his childhood and personal life. We know that he was born in Essex, England on October 29, 1968, grew up in Colchester, graduated from the University of Exeter (where he met Thom Yorke), and went on to work as a freelance artist in Plymouth until he began his lifelong collaboration with Radiohead, starting with 1994's *My Iron Lung* EP. As of a May 29, 2015 article in *The Sydney Morning Herald*, he was still living in Bath with his girlfriend of 27 years and their two daughters.

But reclusive? He's granted plenty of interviews and always comes off as personable and talkative. He just prefers to talk about the work, which has expanded well beyond the immediate circle of Radiohead. While many of Donwood's exhibitions showcase works either directly from or tied to the eight full-length albums he's visualized for the band, he's also tackled large-scale installations, written books, and even started his own record label.

So no, we don't have enough info for a proper biography. Then again, Donwood would probably say that his staggering amount of work *is* his biography—indicative of his own love, fear, humor, and evolution.

Exhibitions

No Data (1997–1998)

Not a ton of info exists on one of Donwood's earliest post-Radiohead exhibits, which took residence at the F Stop Gallery in Bath in 1997, and the following year at Watershed Media Centre in Bristol. Given that its name ties to an Orwellian-sounding survey on his website, there's reason to think the artwork sprung from his questionnaires from the *OK Computer*, found in the *Airbag / How Am I Driving?* EP.

Dead Children Playing (2006)

Both the *Dead Children Playing* exhibit at Iguapop Gallery in Barcelona and its subsequent 2007 picture book featured Donwood's work with Radiohead up to that point. But it also went beyond the album covers into alternate versions and unused paintings. In addition to expanding the visual universe forged by Donwood and the band, both mediums gave fans and art lovers an epic view of his work. The paintings' textures, imperfections, and overall themes are more visible and evocative when viewed on a giant canvas or in a coffee table book as opposed to a tiny CD case.

London Views (2006)

While Donwood's work tends to be steeped in the downfall of human civilization, the diversity with which he depicts the apocalypse is astounding. Take *London Views*—a series of 14 black and white linocuts that show London getting destroyed. But the flooding water is conveyed by clean swirls that look downright Seussian. Likewise, the smoke curls like vines, almost peaceful and only dangerous if one looks closely.

Donwood drew from portions of *London Views* for the artwork of Yorke's *The Eraser*, a solo debut that's largely concerned with environmental issues and our inability (or complete unwillingness) to do anything about it.

If You Lived Here You'd Be Home by Now (2007)

For his exhibit at London's Lazarides Gallery, Donwood learned a centuries-old engraving technique called photogravure for a series of gloomy etchings, several of which would become the artwork for *In Rainbows*' singles.

I LOVE THE MODERN WORLD (2008)

On October 28, 2013, Donwood summed up the meaning behind a series of paintings that made up *I LOVE THE MODERN WORLD*, first seen at an exhibit at Tokyo Gallery + BTAP.

"It was partly an ironic title because there's loads of things I hate about the modern world, but equally, if it wasn't for the modern world, I'd probably be dead," he told *HuffPost*. "Also, I do actually like the modern world very much." Unlike some of Donwood's more abstract work, the paintings rely on clarity as they depict our everyday existence, such as a closeup of a Ventolin inhaler and a businessman using it for his asthma.

El Chupacabra (2009)

In Donwood's most outwardly horrific collection to date, each of the 13 paintings at Bristol's Weapon of Choice gallery depicted a horned goat-monster in a business suit. Above, glaring shades of red, blue, green, and yellow dripped onto the beasts, as if the maps from *Hail to the Thief* were melting straight into Hell.

As for the name, Donwood (perhaps knowingly) conflated horned gods with the chupacabra, the cryptozoological creature whose Spanish name translates to "goat-sucker."

I've got nothing against goats," Donwood told the gallery's website. "I've simply discovered that if I draw a goat, give it the mouth of a rapacious carnivore, then dress it in the suit and tie of a disgraced banker or politician, it looks fucking evil."

Over Normal (2010)

It's fitting that, for his first US gallery show at San Francisco's FIFTY24SF, Donwood showcased some of the billboard advertisements he created for *Hail to the Thief*, all of which were inspired by his first trip to the States. Despite finding a giddy kind of beauty in the bright colors of Los Angeles advertising, he also recognized the artwork's ominous tone.

"All these colors that I've used are derived from the petrol-chemical industry," he told *Pitchfork* on September 15, 2010. "They're only possible because of the fractioning of hydrocarbons. That's how they get the pigments. None of it is natural. It essentially comes from black sludge. We've created this incredibly vibrant society, but we're going to have to deal with the consequences sooner or later."

For the gallery, he gave his paintings audio accompaniment through something called the Overnormalizer, a vocoder-assisted recording made up of illogical phrases inspired by spam advertisements. Showing that he stays loyal to his collaborators, Donwood created the Overnormalizer with John Matthias, his old Exeter schoolmate who played in Headless Chickens with Yorke and would contribute violin and viola parts to *The Bends*.

Lost Angeles (2012)

The sister work to his *London Views* series, Donwood's first exhibit in Los Angeles featured an 18-foot panorama of Hollywood going up in flames. Like the "Fleet Street Apocalypse" centerpiece of *London Views*, "Hollywood Dooom" was created as a black and white linocut, only the destruction is more immediately chaotic. The Hollywood Hills are on fire, water floods the streets, and meteors hurl from the sky. To accommodate the linocut, the Subliminal Projects gallery hollowed out a concave wall.

Just as portions of *London Views* made up the album art for *The Eraser*, Donwood drew elements from *Lost Angeles* for the Atoms For Peace album *Amok*. To coincide with *Amok*'s release, Los Angeles-based painter INSA covered the outside walls of XL Recordings' L.A. office with murals recreating "Hollywood Dooom." After photographing the murals, INSA and Donwood transformed them into animated gifs, making it look as if the destruction of Los Angeles was playing out in miniature.

Far Away Is Close at Hand in Images of Elsewhere (2013)

The companion gallery to Donwood's artwork for *The King of Limbs*, *Far Away Is Close at Hand In Images of Elsewhere* featured many of his tree drawings from that period. Trunks and branches grow skyward in luminescent colors, their borders often threatened by shadowy monsters and gelatinous ghosts. In some of the more muted paintings, the trees grow in circles to form holloways, as if the vegetation is opening up a tunnel into another world.

Stanley Donwood has designed several posters for the Glastonbury Festival.   *Author's collection*

Many of the holloways in England had been cut down by the time *Far Away* opened at the Outsiders gallery in London. This made Donwood think of an iconic piece of graffiti on one of the walls of the Paddington railway station. "Far away is close at hand" comes from the poem "A Song for Contrariety" by Robert Graves, but the second half of the tagged phrase—"in images of elsewhere"—came straight from the graffiti artist. The public artwork has since been removed, which, for Donwood, connected it to the trees.

"There's nothing left of it now," he told *Juxtapoz* in 2013. "Like the holloway, it's entirely disappeared."

Installations

Minotaur (2011)

When the Lazarides Gallery commissioned multiple artists to construct installations based around the Minotaur myth in London's Old Vic Tunnels, Stanley Donwood could have easily just provided one of his pieces from *Amnesiac*.

But rather than rehash the Crying Minotaur or make any version of a Minotaur at all, he drew inspiration from the labyrinth in the story. Made up of fractured mirrors and blood-red propaganda posters, his maze proved to be a disorienting experience.

The Panic Office (2015)

A retrospective of Donwood's work up to that point, *The Panic Office* was more notable for its new sounds than its new visuals. To accompany the large-scale installation at Carriageworks in Sydney, Australia, Donwood sought help from Thom Yorke. Yorke created the soundscape by manipulating peaceful field recordings from a holloway in Dorset until they sounded menacing, making it a sequel to a similar soundscape he had created for Donwood's *Minotaur* installation.

In a real treat for Radiohead fans, Yorke also brought back Fred Cooper, the deadpan SimpleText narrator from "Fitter Happier."

"[Fred] hasn't taken his own advice," Donwood told *The Sydney Morning Herald*. "He's become cynical and disillusioned."

The Bomb (2016)

The Bomb wasn't a proper installation per se, but a film created by Smitri Keshari and Eric Schlosser. Featuring a relentless series of nuclear tests and mistakes, it premiered at New York City's Gotham Hall, projected onto eight screens surrounding the crowd, all to the tune of disorienting live electronic music from the Acid.

Donwood was asked by the filmmakers to be art director, which involved the instruction to, as he told *Noisey* on April 22, 2016, "Make the horribly beautiful." That meant watching endless amounts of footage, walking away, then coming back with suggestions of how to make everything more hypnotic and arresting, despite its disturbing context. Luckily for Donwood, he had already been doing that for years with Radiohead albums.

Even before that, he had always been in close proximity with the topic of nuclear warfare. In 1983, at the age of 14, he joined a protest against America stationing cruise missiles at Greenham Common and Molesworth. As he became more passionate about the cause, he started a Campaign for Nuclear Disarmament chapter at his school.

"It was around then that I began a series of pictures of my hometown with mushroom clouds above," Donwood told *Huck* on May 8, 2016. "Thinking about my formative years under the ever-present threat of imminent nuclear annihilation might go some way to explaining [my style]."

Optical Glade (2017)

By 2017, Donwood had years of experience painting trees for *The King of Limbs* and his exhibit *Far Away Is Close at Hand In Images of Elsewhere*. He took the practice to a larger-than-life scale with the *Optical Glade* installation.

Created by Donwood and six other painters inside a silo-like dome at the Bonnfantenmuseum in the Netherlands, *Optical Glade* drew inspiration from what the inside of a grove might look like. Donwood described it as such on his blog:

> Optical Glade represents a sacred space, in the form of a stylised ring of upturned trees, the fluted trunks descending from the octagonal light-well at the apex of the Bonnefanten's cupola, and the branches and twigs of the trees wrapping around the walls to create the illusion of a moonlit shadow-cage, a haven—or a trap.

For such a massive undertaking, the painters used pencils and chalk dust to transfer the design to the walls in eight separate panels. After that came the actual painting of the lines. The final effect is like standing inside one of the gnarled trees from *The King of Limbs* artwork—colorful on the outside, black and white on the inside.

Miscellany

Short Story Collections

Even just a quick glance at his blog shows that Donwood has a way with words, whether describing one of his paintings or musing on the apocalypse. From 2001 onward, he's put that talent to good use in the form of the short story through three collections: *Slowly Downward: A Collection of Miserable Stories* (which also gave him the name of his website), 2011's *Household Worms*, and 2014's *Humor*.

Most of the short (and we mean short) stories deal with Donwood's usual themes of apocalypse, corruption, and existential dread, but are a surprisingly breezy read, thanks to his economical world-building and humor. Donwood ventured into longer stories with "My Giro" and "Wage Packet," which he released in 2006 on CD, as read by actor, writer, and artist Ric Jerrom.

Catacombs of Terror! (2002)

Despite going longform with his first and only novel, Donwood keeps this noir tale brisk through lots of action, succinct world-building, and a self-aware tone.

Holloway (2012)

Donwood's tree obsession continued expanding like ancient roots when, after spending the night in a holloway with writers Robert Macfarlane and Dan Richards, the trio put together a collection of poetry and artwork inspired by their adventure. Thinking that not many people would want a book about a tree tunnel, they printed 277 copies. When they realized the true size of the demand—around 15,000 people wanted one—Farber reached out and completed several mass printings.

Maybe Donwood was too close to it to give an accurate diagnosis, but *Holloway* is one of his most enchanting works, blending a real-life adventure memoir with drawings out of a dark fairytale. As a centerpiece, an emerald-green depiction of the holloway glows off the page.

21 Covers for J.G. Ballard

When considering the late J.G. Ballard's running themes of natural disaster, dystopian societies, alternate histories, and fetishization of technology in his work, it's no wonder he's Donwood's favorite author—science fiction or otherwise.

So when Donwood was approached by 4th Estate to create the covers for the reissues of all 18 of Ballard's novels, plus his autobiography and two short story collections, he leapt at the opportunity. His artwork was also shown at London's Lawrence Alkin Gallery from March 27–April 25, 2015.

Stylistically, the spacescapes and volcanic colors are the most similar to Donwood's work on *In Rainbows*, with many of them created through the similar methods of melting wax and igniting flammable liquids. The cover for *Millennium People* even uses an inverted and recolored version of the ominous etching from Donwood's *If You Lived Here You'd Be Home By Now* gallery—an image that also served as the single artwork for "Jigsaw Falling Into Place."

Six Inch Records

Attributing the idea to a drunken Christmas in 2006, Donwood randomly decided to found his own record label with his friend Richard Lawrence. Called Six Inch Records, it lasted less than three years, probably because Donwood and Lawrence painstakingly printed everything themselves using a 1965 Heidelberg platen press.

In keeping with the number three, the label also only produced three albums by three artists: Patrick Bell's *Travel Notes*, Max de Mara's *Classist*, and the Joy of Living's *The Beyond Within*. Each CD had a limited printing of 333 copies, sold for £6.66, and packaged in a six-inch square sleeve. But even that proved to be a lot for what was essentially a mom-and-pop operation, and once there was a release show and all of the copies were sold, Donwood and Lawrence shuttered operations (which may have been the plan from the start).

The most interesting project to come out of Six Inch Records actually materialized long after the short-lived label had gone extinct. For their self-titled EP released in 2016, the Joy of Living approached Donwood about once again distributing the album through Six Inch Records. While Donwood informed them that the label was no more, he was convinced after a few drinks (there's a pattern here) to be in their music video for "A Murmured Life." The concept was to shoot the band and Donwood—all dressed in animal masks—in black and white at the mudflats on the coast of Essex, an area known for its rushing currents, quicksand, and being used as a missile-testing site by the Ministry of Defence.

Thankfully, no one fell victim to any of these hazards, and Donwood even agreed to create the album art for *The Joy of Living*—a hazy ink rendition of the mudflats and the animal disguises (crowd, gull, fox, and rabbit) of the artists.

THE JOY OF LIVING

Album art for *The Joy of Living*'s self-titled LP.   *Author's collection*

26

"Bet You Think That's Pretty Clever, Don't You Boy?"

The Bends

Today, *The Bends* is remembered as a capital-M Masterpiece—the album where the world started taking Radiohead seriously. It showed audiences that the band amounted to more than just the guys who wrote "Creep." It showed that Radiohead could write a true album with relatively little filler, rather than an LP with only a handful of memorable songs.

But while Radiohead's second album always has been and always will be a superior product to their debut, both records fall under the category of fairly straightforward alt-rock. And process-wise, the band wasn't exactly reinventing their approach, as they would on everything from *OK Computer* onward. All of this made *The Bends*, at least at the time of its recording and release, a stepping stone rather than a full-on revolution. Phil Selway confirmed just as much in a 20th-anniversary interview with *Stereogum* on March 9, 2015, explaining that the band hadn't set out to make a classic.

"I think we were just very wrapped up in making the best possible record that we could at the time, and we didn't really look any further than that," he said.

What truly does set *The Bends* apart from *Pablo Honey*, outside of the stronger quality of the songs themselves, is a barrage of sonic flourishes outside the usual guitar-drums-bass-vocals setup. For the first time, Radiohead shaped a microverse of spaced-out, sometimes mechanized noise underneath many of the otherwise conventional songs. This soundscape would become louder with every subsequent album until it eventually swallowed the more traditional rock-band element of Radiohead on 2000's *Kid A*.

London's own John Leckie was instrumental in helping Radiohead discover this greater world within themselves. Having built a prestigious career as both an engineer and producer at Abbey Road Studios, he had already worked on storied albums by XTC, the Stone Roses, the Fall, and many others. As Ed O'Brien told *The Big Takeover* in 1995, the band was excited by the prospect of a relaxed, non-engineering producer who just let musicians do their thing. Then

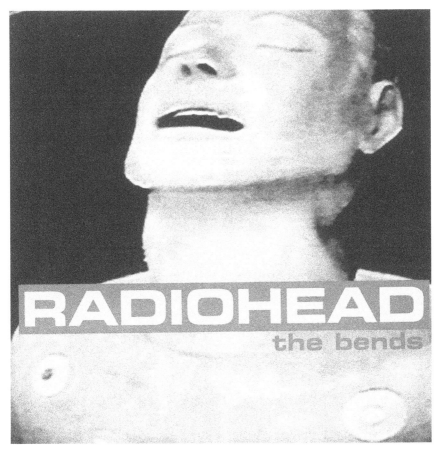

Album art for *The Bends*.   *Author's collection*

again, perhaps Leckie's secret is that he knows how to be hands-off while still pushing artists in new and exciting directions.

Seeing as Leckie was everyone's first choice, EMI executive Keith Wozencroft passed along a copy of *Pablo Honey*, as well as a demo of songs under consideration for the next album, to him in the summer of 1993. Though Leckie wasn't all that taken by Radiohead's debut, he saw promise in the directness of the newer material.

Shortly after he agreed to produce *The Bends*, the band hit a snag. Leckie had been asked to produce *Carnival of Light*, the third album from Radiohead's old Oxford acquaintances Ride. Although Ride were originally supposed to work with George Drakoulias, he had abandoned the project, leaving them in a pinch. Radiohead agreed to move the start of recording *The Bends* from January to February 1994 so that Leckie could work on both projects.

After a productive month of January rehearsals at the band's Canned Applause studio, Radiohead started recording in earnest at RAK Studios in

London. Tensions soon began to arise from a lack of faith in the songs, some of which predated *Pablo Honey*. Because the band had gotten so comfortable playing them on tour, they found themselves struggling to inject them with new life. According to co-manager Chris Hufford and Leckie, though, many of the album's problems were internal and self-imposed, caused by the pressure for the music to live up to the success of "Creep" and EMI wanting an October 1994 release date. Arguments arose over what the lead single should be, and Yorke began to freak out—the strain of great expectations and his own ego starting to clash with everyone else.

By the band's own admission, they also hadn't quite figured out how to navigate their interpersonal conflicts yet. This would eventually come to a head during an eight-date Mexican tour in October, when they exploded at one another, letting out all of the frustrations they had suppressed for years.

"We're friends and everything, but because of maybe our upbringing and the school that we went to, we don't tell each other our problems" O'Brien later said, though no one in Radiohead has elaborated on what exactly was discussed in Mexico.

Although Radiohead would come to work out their communication problems, they still had a lot of growing to do during the *Bends* sessions. Leckie picked up on this, and two months into recording, encouraged an increasingly anxious Yorke to step away and record some songs with just his voice and acoustic guitar. This resulted in a breakthrough with "Fake Plastic Trees," which was followed by a short European tour in May and a jaunt through Japan, Hong Kong, Australia, and New Zealand throughout the first half of June. Fully recharged, everyone then reconvened at the Manor Studio in Oxfordshire—starting an extravagant pattern of recording in old English mansions—before the group went on to put finishing touches at Abbey Road Studios in London.

In a modern context, none of this sounds all that remarkable in the history of Radiohead. But *The Bends* deserves credit for introducing the tension, mid-recording tour, and location-hopping to Radiohead's recording process, all of which would become par for the course as soon as the next album rolled around.

While *The Bends* wasn't ready in time for EMI's desired October 1994 release date, Radiohead decided to unveil six new songs—none of which would make their way onto the album—in conjunction with lead single "My Iron Lung" on September 26, 1994. As was the money-grubbing custom at the time, EMI distributed four different versions of the single on two CDs, cassette, and vinyl—each with a slightly different tracklist. All seven tracks would eventually appear in one place, along with the acoustic version of "Creep," as the eight-track *My Iron Lung* EP.

EMI's worst fear came true when "My Iron Lung" underperformed, peaking at #24 in the United and Kingdom and receiving little airplay. The single didn't fare much better in the United States, where it sold around 20,000 copies. This sent EMI into a panic regarding the sound of *The Bends*. Although Leckie had already begun mixing several of the album's tracks, the label insisted it be sent to *Pablo Honey* producers Sean Slade and Paul Q. Kolderie in Boston for a remix that involved a distinctly American coat of stadium-rock polish.

Three of *The Bends'* 12 songs still ended up with Leckie's mixes, and even then, it's hard to tell who did what. Slade, Kolderie, and Leckie have all described Radiohead cycling through multiple versions of every song. In some cases, the adjustments were almost indetectable.

Whatever the specifics of Slade and Kolderie's involvement, their contributions further tie Radiohead's second album to its predecessor. Both *Pablo Honey* and *The Bends* are big '90s-rock records with soaring guitars, heavily reverberated vocals, and lots of distortion. The latter just brings out more of Radiohead's future identity, from more adventurous sonic embellishments to lyrics that lean further into imagery and abstractions rather than straightforward platitudes. While Yorke sometimes falls into the habit of viewing romantic hardship through a woe-is-me lens, there are still some deeper observations and subject matter at play. His words aren't as evocative as they would be on *OK Computer*, but hey, evolution takes time.

The Songs

"Planet Telex"

The Bends states its grander ambitions with the opening seconds of "Planet Telex." After a short burst of lunar wind, a staggering, almost trip-hop drum beat in the vein of "Airbag" backs a series of mellow piano chords.

While the instruments themselves are nothing out of the ordinary (the piano had already been used sparingly on *Pablo Honey*), Radiohead was now getting into the habit of manipulating sounds rather than just playing them. The drumbeat is actually a loop of three different sections from the initial version of "Killer Cars"—the same version that appears on the "Just" single (though the rhythm sounds significantly slowed down).

As for the piano, Yorke has recalled asking Leckie to run the instrument through a noise gate and four vintage Roland Space Echo units. Leckie remembers it differently, suggesting that it was a delay on a Yamaha SPX90, which was further tinkered with on the console's EQ filters. Either way, the copy-and-paste move was a precursor for a style that would come to rule the band's recording methods on *Kid A*, *The King of Limbs*, and other future Radiohead albums.

The futuristic outlook and richer textures are a welcome pairing with the lyrics, which, while nowhere near the embarrassing lows of *Pablo Honey*, still aren't anything to write home about. Yorke seems to be describing existential dread or the futility of institutions or some other larger-than-life force outside of one's control—something he would nail on *OK Computer* by adding more imagery and details.

Here, though, it's the instrumentation and Yorke's own vocal performance (recorded while he was crouched in a corner after a drunken night out) that give "Plane Telex" a sense of surrealism. That, and even the title. Originally called "Planet Xerox," the band had to change it to "Telex" after Xerox refused to clear the use of their brand name. Although there are several companies with the trademarked name Telex, the song title likely refers to a global network of tele-printers. Since the name comes from the system rather than a business name, the chances of getting sued were far less likely.

"The Bends"

The album's title track dates back to before the *Pablo Honey* sessions, and it's puzzling why Radiohead didn't include it on their first album. Even an early, slowed-down version recorded in 1992 has more dynamic shifts than anything on the band's debut.

Where most Radiohead tracks from that time had two sonic tricks—get louder or get softer—"The Bends" is an endless source of surprise. Yes, there are the big, soaring chords that form the song's backbone. But whenever Yorke sings about wanting to be happy, most of the instruments drop out, with one of Radiohead's three guitarists filling in the dead air with tiny accents. Oh, and Jonny Greenwood plays a recorder.

The rinky-dink instrument is barely audible in the final studio version, but the guitars are louder and more metallic—a case for Radiohead relying on a three-axe-attack more often, even if it amounted to a lot of hot air on *Pablo Honey*.

Fans, critics, and even Radiohead themselves have alluded to "The Bends" possibly being about the band's rapid ascent to fame, which is strange given that the earliest known demo of the song was recorded several months before "Creep" was released as a single. Yorke has since admitted that he can't remember what the song is actually about—something he views as a good thing when considering the melodramatic nature of some of the lyrics.

The line that has always stood out is Yorke wishing it was the '60s, although he has insisted that he meant it as a joke. However, another poor-me lyric, "We don't have any real friends," did spring from the members of Radiohead actually not having all that many acquaintances back home, partly due to their insular nature and partly due to always gigging.

These clashing sensibilities (along with a live version of the song being released as "The Benz" on the French single for "Creep") make for a strange mixture of earnestness and comedy. Couple all of that with imagery of ex-girl-friends, gunboats, and airplanes (the latter another precursor to *OK Computer*), and the lyrics of *The Bends* are a bit of a mess. Luckily, it's hard to understand what Yorke is singing under all of the joyful guitar noise—even the quiet parts.

"High and Dry"

The second single from *The Bends* dates even further back than the title track. In the late '80s, Thom Yorke performed a higher-octave, cowpunk version of "High and Dry" with his college band, Headless Chickens, at the University of Exeter. A few years later, Radiohead recorded a demo of the song in early 1993 at Courtyard Studio.

Surprisingly, that's the version that made its way onto the album, despite not even being completed during the *Bends* sessions. While the band hated the sound of "High and Dry" when they recorded it with their live sound engineer, Jim Warren (thus giving him engineering and production credit on one track of *The Bends*), they dug it up for another listen at the behest of Hufford and Wozencroft.

Hindsight is 20/20, and the second time around, Radiohead loved "High and Dry" so much that they opted not to re-record it, although Slade and Kolderie did remix it. Perhaps the song's nakedness made it stand out from the other tracks on *The Bends*. Primarily driven by three simple acoustic chords, there's enough room to hear the most minute sonic details—blanket-warm percussion thanks to Selway having just replaced the skin of his bass drum; Jonny backing the verses with tearful guitar notes played with a nail file.

And for once, the self-loathing in the lyrics is digestible—deserving of empathy, even. On *Pablo Honey*, Yorke's criticisms of himself came off as another bid for attention. They were histrionic in how they equated themselves with cosmic catastrophe. But on "High and Dry," he does away with sun metaphors and over-the-top despair for something more akin to quiet realism. According to an interview with *Billboard* on February 17, 1996, Yorke combined his troubles with an old girlfriend with his mixed feelings on fame and failure.

He pours his doubts into a handful of different scenarios, such as riding a motorcycle and breaking several mirrors. The line "You'd kill yourself for recognition" rings especially true, with Yorke finally acknowledging his own desperate need for attention—something he never did on *Pablo Honey*'s more self-critical songs.

In true Yorke fashion, he's since come back around to hating "High and Dry." Radiohead hasn't played it live since January 21, 1998, and Yorke told *Pitchfork* on August 16, 2006, that he was strong-armed into including it on the album. Maybe "High and Dry"'s massive success as a single (it peaked at #17 on the UK Singles chart and #18 on *Billboard*'s Alternative Songs chart in the United

States) caused him to grow weary of it, or maybe he simply no longer identifies with the solemn young man who wrote it.

"Fake Plastic Trees"

Yorke recorded the falsetto-laced vocals for "Fake Plastic Trees" after seeing a Jeff Buckley concert, and that beauty comes across in his performance.

This is what people usually point to when discussing the third single from *The Bends*: its delicacy, and how it competes against elegiac synthesizers and a crescendo of strings arranged by Jonny. Bringing the band's career full circle, they were played on multiple tracks by session cellist Caroline Lavelle and John Matthias, an old bandmate of Yorke's from Headless Chickens who contributed viola and violin. The whole affair is sad, majestic, and absolutely worthy of a Buckley namecheck.

But "Fake Plastic Trees" is also incredibly ugly—the first song on *The Bends* where Yorke truly gets weird. He starts off by describing a plastic watering can that a girl uses on a fake Chinese rubber plant. He keeps widening his lyrical scope, creeping outward to reveal an entire miniature biosphere—the shopkeepers, the surgeon the girl lives with, the girl herself—that is artificial. Unlike so many other songs, rubber and polystyrene (yes, Yorke actually uses the scientific term) is used not to represent fakeness, but sadness. The song paints images of people who want to feel, but don't have the ability to. In that way, "Fake Plastic Trees" manages to ache, even as the imagery remains grotesque.

And to think, it could have easily been devoid of the proper emotionalism. In April 1998, Ed O'Brien described the original vision of the song to *Guitar World* as a bastardization of Guns N' Roses' "November Rain," the strings taken to ridiculous heights by a perpetual swell of electric guitars. In the same interview, Yorke revealed that Kolderie inadvertently made the song more vulnerable by bringing in the guitars at the wrong place—a little under three minutes in, and only for 30 seconds or so.

Kolderie's mistake was the final piece needed for making "Fake Plastic Trees" organic rather than bombastic—however accidentally. On June 12, 1995, Yorke told *The Denver Post* that the band had spent months trying to get everything to fit together, especially the keyboard notes. According to him, they were played on the same Hammond organ at Abbey Road Studios that Paul McCartney used on *Magical Mystery Tour* (Leckie has disputed this, saying that it was at RAK on a rented Hammond). The number of strange sounds available was overwhelming.

Then there was the vocal. Cut during the first session at RAK, Yorke only got it right after several failed attempts and his breakdown that prompted the rest of the band to leave the studio. He recorded a bare-bones guiding track featuring just himself and his acoustic guitar—the stripped away aesthetic finally allowing him to get it right.

Perhaps the vocal simplicity laid a foundation that encouraged Radiohead to be more judicious with their ambition. While some of the fuss around "Fake Plastic Trees" could be attributed to the band's usual second-guessing, some of it could be the result of them subconsciously not wanting to overshadow Yorke's powerful performance. Their obsessiveness paid off when "Fake Plastic Trees" became *The Bends'* highest-charting stateside single, peaking at #11 on *Billboard*'s Alternative Songs chart in the United States. Back home, it peaked at #20 on the UK Singles chart.

"Bones"

Of all the songs on *The Bends*, "Bones" is the most opposite of "Fake Plastic Trees" in both sound and the recording process. A fuzzed-out rocker, Radiohead laid it down at the Manor in just one or two takes, depending on the interview—on the same day as the final version of "The Bends," no less.

Even if it had taken as long to record as "Fake Plastic Trees," it would be hard to suck out the joyful marrow of "Bones." Kick-started by a rippling effect generated from Jonny's tremolo pedal (the sound is similar to the opening of "Planet Telex"), the song's engine lies in a busy bassline from Colin. For the verses, the guitars of Jonny, Yorke, and O'Brien arrive in briefly sustained bursts, allowing the majority of the melody to flow from Colin's Music Man Sterling. "The National Anthem" aside, it's unusual for the melody of a Radiohead song to come from the bass guitar, thus giving "Bones" a giddy bounce. Never mind that Yorke is lamenting the effects of old age, despite him being only 25 when it was recorded.

"(Nice Dream)"

Written sometime in 1992, "(Nice Dream)" isn't quite as old as "High and Dry," but relies on the same kind of acoustic simplicity. Yorke originally composed it as a four-chord waltz, which Jonny embellished with an arpeggiated intro and additional chord in the chorus. When getting to work at RAK, Leckie added his own touch—a recording of whale songs at the end to bolster the ethereality.

And that's "(Nice Dream)"'s problem. It's ethereal to the point of being wispy. The gentle strumming, the thinness of Yorke's vocal, and yes, those whale songs, all build toward a song devoid of power. Despite lyrics about a macabre dream of Yorke's (in it, an angel warns the human race about getting electrocuted by the entire ocean), the song never gets off the ground, except for when the distortion kicks in around the two-and-a-half minute mark.

Along with "Sulk," "The Bends," and "Just," "(Nice Dream)" was an early candidate for the album's lead single. And who knows? Given the eventual success of "High and Dry" and "Fake Plastic Trees," maybe listeners would have flocked to another quieter Radiohead number. But where those songs find a relaxed balance between gentleness and power, the floating aesthetic of "(Nice Dream)" feels forced.

"Just"

In April 1998, Yorke told *Guitar World* that "Just," with music written mostly by Jonny, came out of a friendly challenge to fit as many chords into a song as possible.

The final product has 13 by our count. That's not exactly venturing into prog-rock territory, but is still impressive given the radio-readiness of *The Bends'* searing seventh track. It's hard to know how all of Jonny Greenwood's jumping around remains so catchy unless you happen to be Jonny Greenwood, and even then, the answer likely isn't all that mathematical or even tangible.

By all accounts, the band had a blast recording "Just" during their winter rehearsal session, whittling it down from seven minutes to just under four minutes when it came time to record. The truncated complexity wasn't an issue, as it ended up being the first completed song of the RAK sessions.

This suggests that "Just" has some kind of animalistic spirit within—an energy that's always been easy for the band to tap into, despite all of its changes; an energy that begs Yorke to be forgiven for the somewhat snotty lyrics (according to a fan letter, he wrote it about an annoying acquaintance who kept trying to jump out a window at a party); an energy that landed it at the modest spot of #48 on the UK Singles chart and #36 in Scotland.

"My Iron Lung"

A screed against being labeled a one-hit wonder after the success of "Creep," it makes sense that Radiohead wrote "My Iron Lung" when they were in the middle of an especially painful tour cycle toward the end of 1993.

Yorke even goes as far as to reference "Creep," not just by comparing the band's biggest song to the titular medical device, but more literally with the lyric "This is our new song / just like the last one / a total waste of time." There's also a subtler connection to Radiohead's first single. In the process of railing against being perceived as just another pseudo-grunge band, they ended up penning their grungiest song to date.

Divided into two distinct sonic halves, "My Iron Lung" chimes like a nervous lullaby for the verses and goes absolutely apeshit on the chorus, with Jonny's solos the equivalent to constantly adjusting a set of rabbit-ear TV antennas.

"My Iron Lung" also absorbed noxious grunge energy through its recording process. Radiohead had made many unsuccessful attempts to record a studio version during the RAK sessions, which led to them opting for using an in-concert take recorded for *Live at the Astoria* in London on May 27, 1994. Since the *Bends* version of "My Iron Lung" retains everything from that performance except for Yorke's vocals, which were re-recorded, it remains stubbornly loose and ragged. Just like any good grunge song.

"Bullet Proof . . . I Wish I Was"

Once again venturing into the body-horror territory of "Bones," "Bullet Proof . . . I Wish I Was" examines the weakness of the human form. The lyrics read as minimalist sci-fi poetry as Yorke imagines his body being waxed and molded and longs to be made of sterner stuff.

Musically, though, it's far from the most interesting track on *The Bends*. The softened instrumentation—it's little more than Yorke's voice and acoustic strumming—matches the vulnerability of homosapien anatomy described in the lyrics, but that doesn't keep the bulk of the song from being boring. Like "(Nice Dream)" it only picks up when there's some added texture, courtesy of Jonny and O'Brien making ambient noises with their guitars.

"Black Star"

If only Radiohead were willing to record more songs in the same fashion as "Black Star."

During the RAK sessions, Leckie was away at a wedding, leaving his 23-year-old engineer Nigel Godrich in charge. Challenging themselves to finish and entire song before Leckie's return, Radiohead and Godrich recorded "Black Star" quick and dirty, with Jonny's guitar becoming especially frayed when it blasts in on the chorus.

While Radiohead often drag out recording by fretting over the playing, arrangement, and production on their songs, "Black Star" remains an anomaly for being completed Ramones-style: one (or maybe two or three) and done. It's curious why the band hasn't worked more frequently in such a ragged style, as the results ("Black Star," "My Iron Lung," "Bodysnatchers") tend to be wildly successful. If nothing else, the recording process worked toward cementing their permanent relationship with Godrich, who has produced every Radiohead release since.

"Black Star" also deserves special attention for its lyrics. Early on in Radiohead's career, Thom Yorke had a hard time blending the personal and the cosmic. A song like "You" off of *Pablo Honey*, for example, generically equates a relationship with drowning or being caught in a fire. In "Black Star," he subverts the notion of tying a breakup to natural disasters. "What are we gonna do?" he asks of the dissolution of a romance. "Blame it on the black star? Blame it on the falling sky?" For one of the first times in a Radiohead song, Yorke recognizes that romantic turmoil is nobody's fault but his own (and maybe his partner's).

"Sulk"

If "Black Star" makes a case for Radiohead recording more rapidly and organically, "Sulk" is the opposite side of the coin—a song that shows how overblown the band can get when they fuss too much over a composition.

The track was reportedly one of the most difficult to get right on *The Bends*, considered as a single during the RAK sessions, but not actually completed until the end of the band's time at Abbey Road. Radiohead's solution seemed to be layering on guitar after guitar, despite there not being a tangible hook. To make matters worse, Jonny apparently had to record his part while lying on the studio floor with a bad case of stomach flu.

But even if the recording sessions for "Sulk" had gone well, the cards were always going to be stacked against it because of the lyrical content. Yorke drew inspiration from a tragic shooting spree in the summer of 1987, when a 27-year-old man killed 17 people, including himself. Yorke addresses the shooter in the second person, criticising him for taking after his father and essentially being a crybaby.

The device itself is a bit much, and the idea of hurling insults at a mass murderer feels churlish and ineffective. It's not that Yorke should feel the need to sympathize with the shooter—it's just unclear how helpful a song like "Sulk" is in the aftermath of a tragedy. Maybe it could have been more effective if the melody was more memorable, the words were more eloquent, and Yorke's vocals were less whiny.

Radiohead themselves took a similar stance on the song even before they had finished recording. During the *Bends* sessions, it quickly became the band's least-favorite track on the album, and they haven't played it live since a gig at Town and Country Club in Leeds on November 1, 1995.

"Street Spirit (Fade Out)"

The Bends concludes with a natural bridge to *OK Computer*. It's not that "Street Spirit (Fade Out)" sounds particularly like anything on Radiohead's third album, but it shows an interest in reincarnation and the afterlife that's in line with "Airbag." On a more subtle note, it's also the first Radiohead song to feature a cinematic term in the title. The "Fade Out" can be seen as a precursor to track names such as "Exit Music (For a Film)" and "Motion Picture Soundtrack."

For the lyrics, Thom Yorke drew inspiration from Nigerian author Ben Okri's novel *The Famished World*, where the spirit world intersects with the mortal one. While Yorke veers into images of dying baby birds, most of the words have a positive outlook on death, recognizing that it may not be the end and that it's possible to still maintain a connection to one's former life. It's an idea that will always be more interesting than what Radiohead had to say about relationships on *Pablo Honey* (and some of *The Bends*), hinting at the richer thematic ground that would soon be covered.

Granted, it would be hard to peg the song as positive from just listening to the music. Centered around a synced arpeggio played by both Thom Yorke and Ed O'Brien, the instrumentation only gets more mournful as Jonny comes in with eerie synthesizers. Fittingly, Selway's drumming sounds like a funeral march. This creates a tension that positions death as not being a good thing or a bad thing. It's just something that is.

As Radiohead's interests and lyrics became more complex, the audience was more than willing to come along for the ride. "Street Spirit (Fade Out)" peaked at #5 on the UK Singles chart—the highest of any single from *The Bends*.

B-sides

In August 1994, Radiohead made a cassette of all the songs they had worked on for *The Bends* so far. Although many of them were rough mixes or unfinished, nine of the album's twelve tracks appeared on the tape in some form. The rest of the track listing was rounded out by a considerable number of B-sides, with the second side including all of the songs that would eventually appear together on the *My Iron Lung* EP.

Most of the non-*Iron Lung* B-sides are disposable—sometimes hardly even songs at all. Of course, there are some standouts here and there, as always seems to be the case with Radiohead's scrapped material.

"Maquiladora"

Appears on: CD1 of the "High and Dry" / "Planet Telex" single and the United States version of the "High and Dry" single

There's an alternate universe in which Radiohead's second album consists entirely of songs like "Black Star" and "Maquiladora," another quick and dirty number that's big on sloppy yet catchy guitar work. On top of the meaty central progression, there's a tiny hammer-down that almost serves as a half-second chorus. Any Radiohead fan looking for an even rougher version of the song should seek out On a Friday's 1990 demo compilation. Here, the lyrics are barely understandable.

Even on the studio version, it's hard to see what exactly Yorke is getting at with his words. The mentions of vehicles, interstates, and anxiety conjure images of the touring grind, as does the line "useless rockers from England." While the song would have felt a lot more upbeat than much of the material on *The Bends*, it possibly has a similar attitude toward fame. It was also the only B-side to be included on Radiohead's *Live at the Astoria* concert recording.

"Killer Cars"

Appears on: CD2 of the "High and Dry" / "Planet Telex" single and CD 1 of the "Just" single

For being a non-album track, "Killer Cars" has been obsessively reworked by Radiohead over the years. It first appeared as a live B-side on the 12-inch reissue of the "Creep" single, then popped up again in the *Bends* era.

While the standard electric version that appears as a B-side of "High and Dry" / "Planet Telex" deserves recognition for a tinny a cappella intro reminiscent of the Beach Boys, the earlier live take feels more charged due to the frenzied audience—a detail that also becomes absurd when reading the lyrics (it's darkly funny to hear such wild cheering to such a twisted song).

But the most widely beloved version among true Radiohead fans appears as a B-side to "Just." Dubbed the "Mogadon version," this John Leckie remix has a hypnotic quality due to its slower tempo and what sounds like an electric piano added to the mix. It also contains the drumbeat that the band sped up, looped, and used for "Planet Telex," showing that it's perhaps Radiohead's favorite version of "Killer Cars," too.

"India Rubber"

Appears on: CD1 of the "Fake Plastic Trees" single and the US version of the "High and Dry" single

If it's a head-scratcher why some version of "Killer Cars" never made its way onto a proper Radiohead album, it's a no-brainer why "India Rubber" was left on the cutting-room floor.

An experiment in the truest sense of the word, it's made up of little more than the band screwing around on their instruments. Painfully slow synthesizer notes permeate what's more or less a jam session, the lyrics about dogs and clowns never forming a cohesive image or story. The song's most fascinating trait is a demented loop of Jonny Greenwood laughing.

"How Can You Be Sure?"

Appears on: the US version of the "High and Dry" single

Another holdover from On a Friday's 1990 compilation demo, "How Can You Be Sure?" is the most kumbaya-sounding track to be released during the *Bends* era. And because it's one of the period's few B-sides to not be listed on the work-in-progress cassette, it's unlikely it was ever up for serious consideration as anything but a one-off.

While there's no way the in-the-pocket strumming and sunny vocal performance from Yorke would have fit in on the album, it's charming to hear the band play like they're huddled around a campfire. Backing vocals from Dianne Swann of the Julie Dolphin (who opened for Radiohead in fall of 1994) add extra warmth. Don't worry—the song's still about a drunk fuck-up.

"Talk Show Host"

Appears on: CD1 of the "Street Spirit (Fade Out)" single

Radiohead didn't allow "Exit Music (For a Film)" to appear on the *Romeo + Juliet* soundtrack, but they did hand over "Talk Show Host," giving larger exposure to one of their finest forays into trip-hop. The song grabs the listener with its delayed catharsis, the bulk of it inching along with organ and Yorke's vocals before the drums and bass launch it into clubbier territory. Throughout the lyrics, Yorke challenges a would-be lover to come and get him, sometimes veering into strange and violent imagery.

The trip-hop elements made it one of Radiohead's earliest candidates for remixing. Nellee Hooper added a richer soundscape, while the Black Dog remix messed with the tempo and added more muscular drums.

"Molasses"

Appears on: CD2 of the "Street Spirit (Fade Out)" single

Don't be fooled by the talk of genocide and natural disasters. The drunken harmonies, nonsensical rhyme schemes, and dopey guitar work all point to "Molasses" being a goof—and not an especially memorable one at that.

And that's fine. Because it was recorded during the same September 1995 sessions that produced the more substantial songs "Lucky," "Talk Show Host," and "Bishop's Robes," "Molasses" could just be the sound of Radiohead mucking around. Tacking it onto the final single from *The Bends* was harmless enough.

Conclusion

Today, both *The Bends* and *OK Computer* have achieved classic status. But unlike its successor, *The Bends* had a slow-moving journey toward global success.

Back in England, critical reception was glowing, the reviews praising Radiohead's wider scope and greater depth. The album peaked at #4.

The United States was a different story. It only peaked at #88, and many critics saw the band as leaning even further into the sad bastardisms they had begun exploring with *Pablo Honey*. Robert Christgau summed up the detractors' stance in his review for *The Village Voice*:

> Admired by Britcrits, who can't tell whether they're "pop" or "rock," and their record company, which pushed (and shoved) this follow-up until it went gold Stateside, they try to prove "Creep" wasn't a one-shot by pretending that it wasn't a joke. Not that there's anything deeply phony about Thom Yorke's angst—it's just a social given, a mindset that comes as naturally to a '90s guy as the skilled guitar noises that frame it.

But after the chart success of "Fake Plastic Trees" and Radiohead's subsequent tours with Alanis Morissette and R.E.M., more people began to take note of the marked evolution from *Pablo Honey*. The innovative music videos for "Just" and "Street Spirit (Fade Out)" also contributed to the buzz. A year after its release, *The Bends* went Gold, and would eventually crawl up to Platinum on January 27, 1999. This was after the universal acclaim of *OK Computer* made naysayers wonder if Radiohead's sophomore album was worth revisiting.

More important than any of *The Bends*' financial success, though, is how it firmly secured Radiohead's identity. No one knew it at the time, but they were on a path toward exploring more complex subject matter, and the new additions of Nigel Godrich and artist Stanley Donwood would be just as important to the band's aesthetic as the music itself. *The Bends* may not be as epic or innovative as some of Radiohead's later releases, but it's the moment where they truly came into their own not just as musicians, but artists.

27

"We Are Grateful for Our Iron Lung"

My Iron Lung EP

Radiohead's EPs have always been more compilations than proper extended plays, and *My Iron Lung* was no different. The title track had already been released as a single and would go on to appear on the band's forthcoming second album, *The Bends*. Likewise, the acoustic version of "Creep" had popped up several times, first as a UK B-side of the studio version and, more recently, on the *Itch* EP. The remaining six tracks were pulled from two different editions of "My Iron Lung"'s UK singles.

But despite its compilation status, *My Iron Lung* holds its own against Radiohead's studio albums, and not just because its marked the first time Nigel Godrich and Stanley Donwood's names appeared on the band's work. Aside from "Creep" being tacked on yet again (was Parlophone really *that* desperate to keep milking Radiohead's most popular song?), nothing on the record feels indisposable, unlike most of the other B-sides from the era. Any of the songs would have fit right in on *The Bends*, making it the only Radiohead EP that plays like an actual Radiohead EP built from the ground up—even though it wasn't.

"The Trickster"

Pablo Honey had already seen Radiohead playing around with loud/soft dynamics, but there was something in the production that made it sanitary and overly curated. On *My Iron Lung*, most of which was recorded during the same sessions as *The Bends*, producers Godrich and John Leckie corrected the course with rawness. During "The Trickster"'s many leaps in volume, the distortion crackles; the surge feels spontaneous.

Much of the power comes from Phil Selway's snare, dotted with intentional gaps that stay consistent throughout. This gives room for the rest of the band to vamp—sometimes syncing up the guitars, bass notes, and keys with the beat and at other times finding their own path.

my iron lung

Album art for the *My Iron Lung* EP.   *Author's collection*

Lyrically, "The Trickster" gets a leg up on much of the *Bends* material by veering away from interpersonal relationships and into abstraction. The title likely draws from the crafty, mischievous archetype found in mythology and folklore, and the sinister musicality makes a case for the listener being the victim of deceit.

"Lewis (Mistreated)"

Many fans have noted the same spritely energy between *Pablo Honey*'s "How Do You?" and "Lewis (Mistreated)." But once again, *My Iron Lung*'s third track transcends what came before it, thanks to how Radiohead fills in the gaps.

After the band gets quiet for the bridge, they jump back in with full-force harmonics and "dead notes" reminiscent of the pre-chorus of "Creep." The song's hook lies in how much everything is always changing—how Radiohead constantly leaps from alt-rock to punk and Pixies-esque noise pop, never staying on one sound long enough for it to become boring.

"Punchdrunk Lovesick Singalong"

"Punchdrunk Lovesick Singalong" certainly has its heavier, more metal moments (especially during the crescendos at the end), but it stands out from everything else on *My Iron Lung* for its wooziness and drawing inspiration from older genres. Organ blares recall psychedelia, and at one point, Jonny Greenwood's guitar takes on the tearful tone of Santo & Johnny's golden oldie "Sleep Walk." If one can get past some of the more cringe-worthy lyrics ("A beautiful girl can turn your world to dust"), it's a hypnotic blending of eras.

"Permanent Daylight"

A foreshadowing of the lyrical minimalism of *Kid A*, "Permanent Daylight" is the first Radiohead song to prove that the band doesn't need a ton of words to convey both beauty and doom. It's also the first-ever production credit for Godrich (with Radiohead or anyone else), who recorded both "Permanent Daylight" and *The Bends*' "Black Star" while Leckie was away at a wedding.

The song is a constant battle between majestically intertwining guitars and Selway's drums, each fill sounding like someone getting thrown down the stairs. When Yorke comes in with a single, heavily filtered verse, it's almost an afterthought—just another tonal addition and instance of him using his vocals as an instrument rather than a vehicle for poetry. No wonder the band premiered the song as an instrumental on June 3, 1993 at Barbue in Copenhagen, Denmark.

"Lozenge of Love"

Consisting only of vocals, dueling guitars, and some bass notes from Colin Greenwood added in for good measure, "Lozenge of Love" is *My Iron Lung*'s sole acoustic track (not counting the encore of "Creep"). For the first time on the EP, the band strips away the distortion to let the lyrics shine—a logical move considering they named the song after a line from a Philip Larkin poem and likely used the piece as inspiration for the lyrics.

Both the poem and the song find a first-person narrator holed up and lamenting the state of their romantic life. Each person experiences illness, restlessness, and, in Yorke's case, petulance. Where he relies on melodrama and self-pity ("I won't be around when you really need me," he pouts), Larkin shows a maturity when it comes to heartbreak, realizing that a breakup can be a source of strength as much as pain.

Yorke's bratty observations about romance were lyrical hallmarks back in Radiohead's early days, so it's not hard to get past them and enjoy the song for what it is: two minutes of pastoral beauty on an otherwise (wonderfully) loud EP.

Radiohead finished recording *The Bends* at Abbey Road Studios.   *Photo by portum/ Wikimedia Commons*

"You Never Wash Up After Yourself"

The guitars may not be acoustic, but Radiohead stay in the quiet zone for "You Never Wash Up After Yourself," an aesthetic that carries over into "Creep (Acoustic)." This gives the *My Iron Lung* EP a tidy structure: bookended by songs that have appeared or will appear elsewhere, with the meat made up of a loud half and a quiet half.

The central arpeggio sounds like the band's answer to the Animals' take on "The House of the Rising Sun," signaling a stage of both growth and regret. Lyrically, we're in gen-X despair territory once again, but Yorke leans so far into bluntness that it's almost poetic. Has there been a more effective line on a Radiohead deep cut than "I eat all day and now I'm fat"? Beforehand, he once again brings up the worms that appear on "The Trickster," giving *My Iron Lung* an informal ring structure.

28

"Crushed Like a Bug in the Ground"

The Bends Tour(s) / Live at the Astoria

As made clear by Grant Gee's documentary *Meeting People Is Easy*, touring hasn't always been Radiohead's strong suit.

It wasn't an issue of playing, but lifestyle. Or rather, not being cut out for all of the chaos and attention that comes with being on the road. Since the band had only gained a local following by the time they had signed to EMI, they hadn't exactly clocked in a marathon number of hours in vans and buses. As a result, the early tours of Radiohead had a strikingly similar narrative: the band puts out an album, plays nonstop in support of it, Thom Yorke has a breakdown, everyone pushes through, and they return home to recuperate until the next cycle begins. When examining these grueling sojourns, it's not as much about what was working for Radiohead as what was working against them.

Still, the band always seems to be up for more touring, which was even truer in those early days. Much of it had to do with their managers Chris Hufford and Bryce Edge, who insisted upon them not just touring Europe, but the wide-ranging expanses of North America. So many other British bands have scoffed at playing any city other than New York and Los Angeles, and their careers have suffered for it.

"Because they became so huge in Britain very quickly, bands like Happy Mondays and Stone Roses came to America with completely the wrong attitude," Ed O'Brien told *Mojo* in September 1997. "You have to keep touring."

The Bends: The Tour With Too Many Legs

At first, Radiohead's tour in support of their second album seemed to be a breeze. Then again, that's only because they mostly stayed so close to home. After two one-off dates in Riverside, California and Vancouver, the band stayed confined to the United Kingdom for February and most of March, 1995. Phil Selway was even able to drive back to his home in Oxford almost every night to see his wife Cait. There were a handful of problems here and there—the

Sheffield gig getting canceled due to Yorke's last-minute bout of stomach flu, for instance—but they were nothing compared to what awaited Radiohead on other continents.

First was a lengthy jaunt through the United States. While the first US leg of *The Bends* didn't officially start until May 26 at the Paradise in Boston, the band had spent the greater part of April hopping back and forth between countries, with many of the gigs played as acoustic sets by Yorke and Jonny Greenwood at promotional events. Here's a sample of Radiohead's hectic schedule at the time: March 29 and 30 in Canada, April 1–4 on the West Coast, April 5 in Illinois, April 6–9 on the East Coast, April 11 and 12 in Japan, April 19 back in England, April 20 in Sweden, and April 24 in France. Even with the break leading up to May 26, it was a lot.

Yorke didn't handle it well. Fluid had began building up in his ears from all of the flying, which led to him having to wear earplugs during performances—something he detested. At the Paradise show, he took out his frustrations on a group of attendees moshing at the front of the stage, going as far as to hit them with his guitar and demand they stop being so rough. When the band got to New York City for a May 29 gig, Yorke had a breakdown and pleaded with tour manager Tim Greaves to fly him home right away. His bandmates were able to talk him out of it.

As a means of giving Yorke some reprieve, Radiohead began renting rehearsal space on their days off so they could work on new material. This allowed them to start practicing and eventually performing several songs that would make their way onto *OK Computer*, including "Subterranean Homesick Alien."

The first US leg of *The Bends* ended at the Palace in Hollywood on June 15, and was immediately followed by six dates in Japan, another acoustic Yorke and Jonny show in Canada, then a string of American club shows that stretched all the way to July 27. Fortunately, the band got a second wind when their heroes R.E.M. asked them to be the opening act on the European leg of their *Monster* tour. The experience went so well that they extended the invitation to an additional run of dates back in the US.

All five members of Radiohead had been enormous fans of R.E.M. for quite some time—not just their music, but the way they handled their values and personal lives as the spotlight grew brighter. The fandom went both ways. The main reason R.E.M. picked Radiohead as tourmates was because *The Bends* was their favorite album of 1995 and they hadn't gotten to see the band perform any of its songs live yet.

Once Yorke got over his initial nervousness around R.E.M. frontman Michael Stipe (he even addressed him as "Mr. Stipe" at first), the two quickly forged a lifelong friendship. Stipe has often been a shoulder to lean on, offering insight as to how to deal with fame (something Yorke has always struggled with). Some of his advice even served as the inspiration for *Kid A*'s "How to Disappear Completely."

Poster for R.E.M.'s 1995 tour with Radiohead as the opening act.
Author's collection

The other members of R.E.M. were also keen to take on mentorship roles. As guitarist Peter Buck told Nick Johnstone for 1997's *Radiohead: An Illustrated Biography*, Radiohead was impressed with how R.E.M. would write new songs at soundcheck, then perform them live in the same night.

"I think that was maybe a little influential to them," said Buck. "Because next time I saw them, they had like five new songs in their set!"

Almost as soon as their time with R.E.M. ended on October 1 at Hartford, Connecticut's Meadows Arena, Radiohead booked an opening slot for another alternative giant, Minneapolis' Soul Asylum. Having dealt with their own fair share of hardships, from putting in 12 years as a band before finding mainstream success to frontman Dave Pirner's stint in a psychiatric hospital, they also proved to be mentors to Radiohead, if for a shorter term than R.E.M.

Radiohead's run of bad luck picked up again when Jonny suffered internal damage in one of his ears (to heal, he had to wear thick headphones while playing) and, at on the night of an October 5 gig in Denver, all of the band's gear got stolen from their hotel. Several shows had to be canceled as a result.

Once Radiohead had acquired new equipment, it was back home for another British tour, followed by the recording of "Lucky" for *The Help Album* (yet another *OK Computer* song that would be written during the *Bends* tour). Everything came to a head on November 25 at Munich's Alter Flughafen Riem, where Yorke passed out onstage three songs into the set—a combination of anxiety, general exhaustion and having gotten sick on the damp tour bus. By the time the holidays rolled around, Radiohead was more than ready for a vacation. After a final Yorke and Jonny set at KROQ's Almost Acoustic Christmas in Los Angeles on December 18, the band took a much deserved break from the road. Although they would reconvene to work on new material, they wouldn't play any shows until March 14 of the following year.

Live at the Astoria

On May 27, 1994, Radiohead recorded their performance at the now-demolished London Astoria for what would be their only concert officially distributed on home video. It was released on VHS on March 13, 1995 and on DVD over a decade later on November 21, 2005.

Live at the Astoria isn't just important for its anomalous status. It also captures Radiohead during a sweet spot in their early career. Having long finished the *Pablo Honey* tour, the band hit the road again in May 1994 as a reprieve from what they perceived to be unproductive recording sessions for *The Bends*. *Live at the Astoria* captures them on the cusp of finalizing their adventurous new songs during a much-needed break from the studio. It's the antithesis of the hellish post-recording tour they would embark on in less than a year. The musicianship is tight; the thrashing stemming from joy rather than frustration.

Outside of the still-horrendous single "Pop Is Dead" and future B-side/On a Friday remnant "Maquiladora," *Live at the Astoria*'s set consists entirely of songs from *Pablo Honey* and *The Bends*, the latter of which wouldn't be released for another 10 months. And because Radiohead had been playing them for so long, the eight *Pablo Honey* tracks make a case for *Live at the Astoria* being better than the actual album. Even a dud like "Vegetable" has enough added muscle to make it interesting.

The singles from *Pablo Honey* get the most explosive live treatment, as if the band was so confident in their popularity, they knew it didn't matter *what* they did to their hits. Yorke practically growls through "Creep," with the rest of the band blowing the chorus into the stratosphere with volume and fervor. Likewise, "Stop Whispering" gets an extended coda where all of Radiohead just loses it, piledriving the song's U2 sonics into something with more anger and distortion. By trying to destroy the *Pablo Honey* songs, Radiohead gave them new life and ended up creating their definitive versions.

NME ad for the Live at the Astoria tour date and other May 1994 Radiohead concerts.   *Author's collection*

Surprisingly, it's the *Bends* material that's weaker—if not as songs, then as performances. While the title track feels locked-in because it was already so old and
the take for "My Iron Lung" was good enough that the band used it for the album,
the other five cuts from the record feel hesitant. Everything's a little slower; a little
more polite than what would eventually make its way to the stage.

At the same time, that's what was necessary for Radiohead to figure the
songs out. Because they were still in the middle of recording *The Bends*, there's
an understandable lack of confidence in the arrangements. Even though many
of the songs had existed before recording began, the band has commented frequently on having to rediscover everything in the studio and make them fresh
again. The compositions are too delicate to be blown out of the water just yet.

"This Goes Beyond Me, Beyond You"

A Moon Shaped Pool

The recording of *A Moon Shaped Pool* was difficult, but for different reasons than usual. Where past Radiohead sessions were affected by insular, often self-made conflicts such as being overwhelmed by expectations and doing away with a traditional rock structure, the troubled nature of LP9 came from forces more external.

Everyone involved has declined to say too much about their hardships.

"There was a lot of difficult stuff going on at the time, and it was a tough time for us as people," Thom Yorke put it succinctly to *Rolling Stone* on May 31, 2017. "It was a miracle that that record got made at all."

"I don't want to talk about it anymore, if that's all right," O'Brien adds. "I feel like the dust hasn't settled. It was a hard time."

What we do know is this: In the middle of recording sessions, which took place sporadically at La Fabrique Studios near Saint-Rémy-de-Provence in southern France between 2014 and 2016, Yorke and his partner of 23 years, Rachel Owen, publicly announced their separation. The announcement came on August 15, 2015, and on December 18, 2016, Owen died of died of cancer, a little over six months after *A Moon Shaped Pool*'s May 8 release date. Radiohead would dedicate their 2017 reissue box set *OK Computer OKNOTOK 1997 2017* to her memory.

Another tragedy occurred when, while recording the strings for "Burn the Witch," producer Nigel Godrich's father Vic died.

"I literally left him on a fucking table in my house and went and recorded," he told *Rolling Stone*. "And it was a very, very emotional day for me. He was a string player as well, so it was one of those things where it felt like he would want me to go and just do this."

Because seven of *A Moon Shaped Pool*'s 11 songs had either been teased or played live long before recording began, it's impossible that most of the album's lyrics were directly inspired by either of these events. But the general air of loss, separation, and acceptance permeate the record. When deciding how

Album art for *A Moon Shaped Pool*.   *Author's collection*

the arrangements should sound, the band and Godrich were likely conveying how they felt at the time through the music. When viewed through that context of personal tragedy, *A Moon Shaped Pool* is achingly beautiful—to the point where it can be devastating and difficult to listen to. It's not an exactly a somber album, but a work where sorrow can unexpectedly rise from the depths at any moment, finding spaces to settle between arrangements that are somehow both lush and spare at the same time.

For all the darkness surrounding *A Moon Shaped Pool*, the recording environs were remarkably peaceful. On an assignment for *The Times Literary Supplement* on May 18, 2016, writer Adam Thorpe visited his friend Colin Greenwood at La Fabrique, which was a pigment mill in the 19th century. It's telling that his write-up consists mostly of descriptions of the picturesque surroundings. A country lane takes visitors past olive branches and vineyards to the courtyard and the three-story structure. Inside, a trove of broken-in luxury and comfort awaits, from period furniture to Turkish rugs, opulent fireplaces, and a music library with the world's largest vinyl collection. Although Radiohead had made somewhat of a habit of recording in old, luxurious buildings by that point, this was probably the first one that didn't feel haunted.

The most majestic element of *A Moon Shaped Pool* was actually the one part not recorded at La Fabrique at all. In November 2015, Jonny Greenwood convened with the London Contemporary Orchestra (LCO) at RAK Studios to add string parts and female choral vocals, as conducted by Hugh Brunt. Greenwood had previously collaborated with the LCO on his soundtrack for Paul Thomas Anderson's 2012 film *The Master*. The band was impressed with their contributions to *A Moon Shaped Pool*, with Yorke hailing it as a breakthrough—the moment where the album could start navigating grief without getting lost in the despair.

The Songs

"Burn the Witch"

If the anti-group think lyrics of *A Moon Shaped Pool*'s opener sound reminiscent of the *Hail to the Thief* era, that's because that's when the song first revealed itself in public. Radiohead had started working on it during the *Kid A* sessions, but fragments of its lyrics appeared on one of Stanley Donwood's map grids in *Hail to the Thief*'s booklet.

The band would continue to workshop it for *In Rainbows*, but could never get it to sound quite right. On June 24, 2006 Yorke even played a lightning-quick portion of the chords to the crowd at Berkeley's Greek Theatre, then stopped and said the band would one day play "Burn the Witch" in full when they had an orchestra.

While Radiohead could have probably gotten an orchestra for *In Rainbows*, it didn't happen until *A Moon Shaped Pool*, and true to Yorke's words, it's hard to imagine "Burn the Witch" without it. Unlike earlier Radiohead songs with strings, the LCO makes up the core, driving the composition by playing their instruments with the sticks of their bows instead of the sides with the hair. As if resisting the intimidating lyrics, "Burn the Witch" remains stubbornly adrenalized—the strings taking on new emotional shades whenever Phil Selway switches from cymbal and snare to the deeper sound of his floor toms.

Due to the five-year wait between *The King of Limbs* and *A Moon Shaped Pool*, "Burn the Witch" was likely going to sell well no matter what, but a creative marketing campaign drummed up even more support. A week before the album's release, select fans who had previously ordered Radiohead merchandise received an ominous card in the mail. Beneath a printing of one of Donwood's marbled-water paintings that would make up the album art were the lyrics "Sing the song of six-pence that goes 'burn the witch' / We know where you live." Although Radiohead's name appeared nowhere on the card, most fans knew what was up.

After an exclusive record-store physical release (a 7-inch paired with the band's unused James Bond theme, "Spectre"), "Burn the Witch" peaked at #9 in the US, and by the end of 2016, would be the year's 26th best-selling vinyl single in the UK. The cherry on top was a nomination for Best Rock Song at the 59th

Annual Grammy Awards. Ironically, it lost to a song with almost the exact same title as an earlier Radiohead release, David Bowie's "Blackstar" (their "Black Star" was broken up into two words).

"Daydreaming"

As one of only four songs on *A Moon Shaped Pool* to not have existed before the album's release, it's easy to connect lyrics of "Daydreaming" to Yorke's separation from Rachel Owen. That's especially true of the final garbled series of backmasked vocals. When played in reverse, it's revealed that Yorke is saying "half of my life." When he separated from Owen in 2015 at age 47, they had been together for 23 years—just about half of his life.

Whether knowingly or not, the band conveys the shift in Yorke's personal life by weaving a handful of subtle transitions into "Daydreaming." The pitch-corrected bells of the opening gradually get overtaken by a reflective piano sonata.

For a while, it's mostly just the piano and Yorke's voice, with the bells tinkling every few seconds in the background. The strings of the LCO arrive with a painfully slow crescendo, and take on an animalistic tone at the end, emitting growls thanks to the cellists tuning down to an unusually low level.

The band has said that after many false starts, roughly 80 percent of *A Moon Shaped Pool* was recorded after a sudden breakthrough. "Daydreaming" could very well have been the turning point. In an interview with *Fact* magazine on May 27, 2016, cellist Oliver Coates recalled that day of the recording sessions:

"I remember laying down the cello at the end of 'Daydreaming' and Thom said, 'That's it—that is the sound of the record.'"

Though more downtrodden and avantgarde than "Burn the Witch," the song still managed to chart at #12 in the US on *Billboard*'s US Hot Rock Songs and #74 on the UK Singles Chart.

"Decks Dark"

After the one-two gut punch of "Burn the Witch" and "Daydreaming," "Decks Dark"—the second of *A Moon Shaped Pool*'s four brand-new tracks—functions more as a breather than a memorable song. Backed by soft beatbox percussion, the piano twinkles until Colin gradually adds muscle with a bass line. Even then, it's all vibe, regardless of Yorke's sinister lyrics about people fleeing from some mysterious force above.

"Desert Island Disk"

The best thing about "Decks Dark" is that its final bass-drum thump segues into "Desert Island Disk," which Yorke premiered acoustically in Paris during a concert on December 4, 2015 that coincided with the landmark UN Climate Change Conference.

The song doesn't appear to be directly about climate change, the lyrics instead describing the sense of renewal one feels after getting over a relationship that's ended. When considering the greater context of *A Moon Shaped Pool* and the fact that Yorke premiered "Desert Island Disk" live a few months after he and Owen had separated, it could very well be about them.

The music reflects this idea of a new day, the acoustic strumming breezy and filled with plenty of wide-open space. The pockets get filled by mounting synth effects, but never enough for the relaxed tone to get overwhelmed by weirdness.

As for the title, *Desert Island Discs* is also a BBC Radio 4 show where each guest has to pick eight recordings, a book, and a luxury item they would take with them if stranded on a desert island. How this connects to the Radiohead song is unclear. Maybe the feel-good nature of "Desert Island Disk" made Yorke think of a sun-dappled island somewhere in the Caribbean.

"Ful Stop"

If "Desert Island Disk" represents the confidence that can come with being newly single, "Ful Stop" represents the regret. Yorke fluctuates between beating himself up over his mistakes and asking his lover to give him another chance.

As the most aggressive and brooding song on *A Moon Shaped Pool*, the instrumentation of "Ful Stop" matches Yorke's self-loathing. Two ominous bass notes and drums—played by both Selway and Portishead's Clive Deamer—start off muffled, then become slowly and painfully clear, as if the narrator is entering a club where they're about to betray their significant other.

Radiohead began playing and recording "Ful Stop" at soundchecks as far back as 2012 before sporadically weaving it into their actual setlists, so Yorke clearly didn't write the song in the immediate aftermath of his separation from Owen. However, that's not to say that their relationship couldn't have served as inspiration—he could have been documenting whatever mistakes were made in real time.

"Glass Eyes"

Of all the songs on *A Moon Shaped Pool*, "Glass Eyes" sounds the most classical—the strings of the LCO rising in mournful swells around Yorke's piano. Outside of the warped false starts of the intro, there are few effects; few spots where tradition gets interrupted by technology. Jonny once lamented how most rock bands who employ a string quartet or orchestra end up aping "Eleanor Rigby," but "Glass Eyes" finds Radiohead, like the Beatles before them, turning to classical music for traditional purposes.

And despite Greenwood's past misgivings, it works quite well, the calmness juxtaposing nicely with what seems to be a description of a panic attack.

"Identikit"

Before the release of *A Moon Shaped Pool*, Radiohead held off on playing "Burn the Witch" in full live because they felt it needed an orchestra. They could have applied the same restraint "Identikit." Only instead of strings being the most prominent factor, it would be a female backing choir.

"Identikit"'s performances throughout numerous shows during the 2012 *The King of Limbs* tour were by no means bad, but upon hearing the version that made its way onto *A Moon Shaped Pool*, the earlier takes feel skeletal. On top of being better rounded out by Jonny's spidery guitar line and Colin's underlying, full-bodied bass, the choir elevates the distinct shift that swoops in around the two-minute mark. "Broken hearts, make it rain," they sing with celestial glory—a musical prayer that asks for strength in the face of infidelity.

Radiohead found such strength in subsequent performances of "Identikit." O'Brien joined Yorke on the "broken hearts" refrain to give it more oomph, and while the band didn't bring a choir with them on the road, they could at least sample one and rely on the audience for help.

"The Numbers"

To coincide with the monumental UN Climate Change Conference, Pathway to Paris hosted a concert at Le Trianon on December 4, 2015, with performances by Thom Yorke, Patti Smith, and Yorke's bandmate in Atoms For Peace, Flea from the Red Hot Chili Peppers. One of Yorke's new songs, "Desert Island Disk," seemed to have little to do with climate change. Not so for the second song he played, "The Numbers."

Originally titled "Silent Spring," "The Numbers" isn't quite a lament, but a call to arms—a promise that human beings are "of the earth" and that they will do what's necessary to reclaim her glory. For a band who has written so much about the decline of civilization, Radiohead is surprisingly optimistic here.

Like the Paris performance, the studio version of "The Numbers" has a backbone of acoustic guitar, with the rhythm section of Selway and Colin implanting extra cartilage for support. But the most distinct addition on *A Moon Shaped Pool* is a flurry of sleigh bells that keeps fluttering in and out, as if winter is fighting to survive while the planet warms. Three-and-a-half minutes in, the LCO joins the rebellion, their arrival reminiscent of another artist's song produced by Godrich: Beck's "Paper Tiger," from his 2002 album *Sea Change*.

It would be impossible to truly replicate the strings live without the LCO, but there's yet another version of "The Numbers" that's worth seeking out. On

October 5, 2016, Radiohead posted a video to their YouTube account of Yorke and Jonny sitting in the hills of Tarzana, California. The minimalist footage features them playing the song with nothing except their guitars and a tropical beat from a Roland CR-78 drum machine. The director? None other than filmmaker Paul Thomas Anderson, who also helmed the official video for "Daydreaming."

"Present Tense"

About a month earlier on September 5, Radiohead posted another CR-78 video in collaboration with Anderson. In it, Yorke and Jonny play "Present Tense" while seated around a campfire at night. With just their guitars and the drum machine, it's catchier than what made its way onto the album.

On *A Moon Shaped Pool*, "Present Tense" buckles under too many bells and whistles, including multi-tracked backing vocals from Yorke, thus obscuring the relatively simple lyrics that seem to describe being caught in the middle of a flailing relationship (it's interesting that, on the album, Radiohead depicts romance in various stages). Such simplicity is better served by the CR-78 performance, as well as Yorke's solo acoustic take at the UN Climate Change concert. He premiered the song live in a similar fashion during a solo gig at the Latitude Festival in Southwold, England's Henham Park on July 19, 2009, having sound-checked it with the band since 2008.

"Tinker Tailor Soldier Sailor Rich Man Poor Man Beggar Man Thief"

Another new song written specifically for the album, the lyrics of "Tinker Tailor Soldier Sailor Rich Man Poor Man Beggar Man Thief" are reminiscent of Yorke's "seduction songs" from *In Rainbows*. However, it would have probably been relegated to the album's second disc—a coda rather than an instant classic.

Driven by a synth line and minimalist drum beat, the track remains hookless throughout. Even when the strings come in, it never gets past shuffling its own feet. Unsurprisingly, Radiohead has only played it live five times total as of this writing, apparently abandoning it after a July 26, 2016 performance at Madison Square Garden.

"True Love Waits"

After "Present Tense" and "Tinker Tailor Soldier Sailor Rich Man Poor Man Beggar Man Thief," there's no denying that, for all its orchestral and emotional strengths, *A Moon Shaped Pool* takes a dip in its back end. All is forgiven with closer "True Love Waits."

By 2016, the song had become the stuff of Radiohead legend. They premiered it live all the way back on December 5, 1995 at a stop at the Luna Theatre in Brussels, Belgium during the *Bends* tour. Regretful yet playful in its original incarnation, it featured Yorke on vocals and acoustic guitar, with Jonny adding lighthearted synth arpeggios in the middle.

The band would rely on these kinds of spacy effects when they recorded several versions of "True Love Waits" for both *OK Computer* and *Kid A/Amnesiac*, none of which were ultimately used. According to O'Brien's online diary, the vocal melody had remained relatively the same throughout, with the chords and effects underneath in constant flux.

The following year, "True Love Waits" finally did make its way onto an album, but it was a live album, meaning that the version that closes out *I Might Be Wrong: Live Recordings*, was the solo acoustic take that fans had already been hearing for years. Still, it was nice to finally have some kind of polished rendition on record.

It's telling that, for its first official appearance on a Radiohead studio album, the band went with a simplicity—little more than a piano arrangement. Throughout its nearly five-minute runtime, we get some bonfire-like crackling underneath, some additional twinkling from a second piano, and a handful of bass notes, but it largely remains just voice and keys.

It works so well that it's hard to imagine Radiohead churning out multiple experimental takes of the song. Maybe it's because the lyrics are so tragic and evocative, describing someone who will do anything to keep their lover from leaving. After Yorke promises to dress a certain way and wash their partner's swollen feet, he paints love as something that waits in the attic and survives off of "lollipops and crisps"—a force that literally feeds off of people and leaves them drained.

It bears repeating that Yorke wrote these lyrics at least 11 years before *A Moon Shaped Pool* came out, well before he and Rachel Owen separated. The "lollipops and crisps" line actually originated from a real-life story that had nothing to do with romance—an article that Yorke had read about a couple who went on vacation and left their child to survive off of junk food.

But like every other relationship song on *A Moon Shaped Pool*, Radiohead recorded "True Love Waits" in an arrangement that reflected the grief in their own lives at the time. One can't help but think of Yorke and Owen's separation and the latter's eventual death—or even the death of Godrich's father—when hearing those devastating piano notes and Yorke's pleading vocal. It's heartbreaking; sometimes impossible to sit through, but for all the right reasons—the album's final statement about losing someone close and learning to move on.

B-sides

"Ill Wind"

"Spectre" is *A Moon Shaped Pool*'s only proper B-side in the traditional sense, released as part of the "Burn the Witch" 7-inch single sold exclusively at independent record stores. But anyone who ordered the special physical edition of *A Moon Shaped Pool* got a second disc that paired the unused James Bond theme with "Ill Wind," a bossa nova track that wouldn't have been out of place on *In Rainbows*.

It starts out with the warmth of Radiohead's seventh album, but quickly gets overtaken by chilly, synthesized arpeggios. Even the lyrics describe coldness and distance: "Keep your cool / Do not give into emotion." While the track's subdued danciness makes it more memorable than "Desert Island Disk," the album version of "Present Tense" and "Tinker Tailor Soldier Sailor Rich Man Poor Man Beggar Man Thief," its ultimate mechanization would have made it stick out like a sore thumb had it been included on *A Moon Shaped Pool*.

A Moon Shaped Pool Live

Since 2007, it's become customary for Radiohead to put out their albums with little notice. *In Rainbows*' announcement came ten days before its release; *The King of Limbs* five days.

The band took this to a greater extreme with *A Moon Shaped Pool*, which came with no announcement at all. Instead, select fans received the mysterious "Burn the Witch" leaflets in late April 2016, and on the night of May 1, Radiohead disappeared from the internet. Sort of. The band's website and social media gradually faded to white, effectively erasing everything that had appeared beforehand. Although the site and Radiohead's social channels eventually returned, none of the content from before the great vanishing reemerged.

On the night of May 2, the blankness was replaced by a clip of a stop-motion bird—the opening shot of th "Burn the Witch" music video, which, along with the single itself, was available the following day on May 3. On May 6, "Daydreaming" dropped as a second single with its accompanying music video, and on May 8, the album hit streaming services and was available to purchase in full. But Radiohead wasn't about to launch headfirst into a traditional press cycle.

"We weren't in a position to really talk about it when it came out," O'Brien told *Rolling Stone*. "We were quite fragile, and we needed to find our feet."

They did so not through extensive interviews, but through touring. At the 2016 shows immediately following the release of *A Moon Shaped Pool*—a tour that extended into the release of the *OK Computer OKNOTOK 1997 2017* box set, with more dates announced in 2018—there was a sense of pure summer joy onstage; of the band exorcising the hardships of their personal lives through kinetic movement. With Clive Deamer joining once more, there were also two drummers, perpetually crossfading projections, and lots of dancing. At Radiohead's headlining Lollapalooza set on July 29, Yorke was especially giddy, owning his improvised awkward-dad choreography and ecstatically yelping gibberish phrases between songs.

But the tour was not without controversy. On July 19, 2017 Radiohead was set to play Park HaYarkon in Tel Aviv, Israel. They had performed there eight times before, and the country was instrumental to their early success, having been the first place where "Creep" became a smash hit.

The Tel Aviv gig was heavily opposed by artists who had taken part in the Boycott, Divestment and Sanctions movement (BDS), a campaign that promotes boycotts against Israel until equal rights are granted to Palestinians facing oppression in the country. Among BDS' stipulations are for Israel to withdraw from its occupied territories, removing the separation barrier from the West Bank, and equal rights for all of the country's Arab-Palestinian citizens.

Tour poster for Radiohead's controversial Tel Aviv gig in 2017.   *Author's collection*

Over 50 artists, including Sonic Youth's Thurston Moore and Tunde Adebimpe of TV On the Radio (whose first album riffed on Radiohead with the title *OK Calculator*), signed a petition urging Radiohead not to play in Tel Aviv, with Roger Waters being the most vocal critic.

Yorke had addressed the controversy earlier with both a Twitter statement and June 2 interview with *Rolling Stone*, where he stated that he strongly opposed cultural bands of any sort and was angered by so many artists he admires telling him how to think and what to do.

"The person who knows most about these things is Jonny," Yorke said. "He has both Palestinian and Israeli friends and a wife who's an Arab Jew. All these people to stand there at a distance throwing stuff at us, waving flags, saying, 'You don't know anything about it!' Imagine how offensive that is for Jonny. And imagine how upsetting that it's been to have this out there. Just to assume that we know nothing about this ... It's fucking weird. It's such an extraordinary waste of energy. Energy that could be used in a more positive way."

His comments only poured gasoline on the fire being spat by his various critics, but Radiohead still went on to play the show, which went off without a hitch. As reported in *The Guardian*, the crowd was diverse, and Yorke addressed the controversy with a simple statement: "A lot was said about this, but in the end we played some music."

Conclusion

Since it wasn't released all that long ago, it's not immediately clear how *A Moon Shaped Pool* will hold up in the greater Radiohead legacy. In 2016, it received a "Universal Acclaim" designation on Metacritic, landing on the year-end list for a number of notable pop-culture sites, including *Pitchfork*, *Rolling Stone*, and *The New York Times*. It also peaked at #1 in nine countries, including the United and States and United Kingdom, and has sold more than a million copies worldwide (in 2016, that may as well be Triple-Platinum). And it goes without saying that it got nominated for Best Alternative Music Album, with "Burn the Witch" nabbing a Best Rock Song nomination. The former lost to David Bowie's *Blackstar* and the latter lost to his song of the same name.

But how will *A Moon Shaped Pool* eventually stand up to the rest of Radiohead's discography? While it doesn't have quite as much filler as *Hail to the Thief*, its three throwaways prevent it from reaching the straight-up impeccability of *In Rainbows*. Then again, it will likely—and rightfully—be remembered for its beauty and heavy emotional weight. As the fading piano of "True Love Waits" brings *A Moon Shaped Pool* to a close, it's hard to argue with the album's last word.

30

"Now Self-Employed"

Unconventional Distribution

In Rainbows—A Deeper Dive

Pay-What-You-Want: A Brief History

When Radiohead made their seventh studio album, *In Rainbows*, available for preorder as a pay-what-you-want download on October 1, 2007, they were far from the first musical act to adopt such a model.

Christian singer Keith Green did something similar all the way back in 1980 when he made his third album, *So You Wanna Go Back to Egypt*, available for whatever price the listener wanted at shows or through a mail-order coupon. Green and his wife Melody mortgaged their home so they could privately finance the album, and he even made his concerts free. The practice continued for two more records until he died in a plane crash on July 28, 1982.

On the other end of the musical spectrum, New York punk mainstay Jeff Rosenstock founded Quote Unquote Records in 2006, the "First Ever Donation Based Record Label." Although everything is offered as a free download, listeners can choose to contribute to any amount they'd like to the label.

In addition to predating *In Rainbows*, Green and Rosenstock's use of the pay-what-you-want model is far more comprehensive than Radiohead's. After all, Radiohead only turned to it for a single album, and the option of a free download was only available for two months. On December 10, it was removed in preparation for a wider release of physical editions of the album. The all-encompassing Discbox edition shipped on December 3, with a staggered CD and vinyl release of the standard edition throughout the rest of the month and into the next year. It also went live as a digital purchase on both iTunes and the Amazon music store.

Two months. That's it. And yet the brief time period didn't matter, nor did the fact that Radiohead weren't the first artists to try something like this by a long shot. What did matter was their status. While Green and Rosenstock both have their own sizable followings in their respective worship-music and punk communities, neither artist is exactly mainstream. In today's streaming-rampant world, it's easy to forget just how shocking it was in 2007 for a platinum-selling, Grammy-winning rock band to release an entire album for free.

Backlash

While fans were generally over the moon about Radiohead's latest distribution model—enjoying how it allowed people around the world to experience *In Rainbows* at the exact same time, with no advance singles or reviews—there was still a considerable amount of backlash. Surprisingly, most of it came from other musicians. On June 4, 2009, Kim Gordon of Sonic Youth expressed her distaste to *The Guardian*.

"It seemed really community-oriented, but it wasn't catered towards their musician brothers and sisters, who don't sell as many records as them," Gordon said. "It makes everyone else look bad for not offering their music for whatever." *The Guardian* itself had taken a similar stance on October 19, 2007, when it published an editorial penned by Will Hodgkinson titled "Thanks, Radiohead, for making it ever hard for new acts to survive." Lily Allen, Gene Simmons of KISS, and Oasis' Liam Gallagher all joined the chorus of naysayers via a November 14, 2007 article in *Rolling Stone*.

Of all the musicians to speak out against *In Rainbows*' formatting, Nine Inch Nails' Trent Reznor was the most specific. He didn't have issues with the pay-what-you-can model itself; on the contrary, he didn't feel that Radiohead adhered to it enough, as told to the Australian Broadcasting Corporation in a March 2008 interview.

"If you look at what they did, it was very much a bait and switch, to get you to pay for a MySpace quality stream as a way to promote a very traditional record sale," he said, referring to the low 160kbps quality of *In Rainbows*' initial mp3 files. "There's nothing wrong with that, but I don't see that as a big revolution [that] they're kind of getting credit for."

Legacy

While Reznor does have a point regarding the audio quality and the length of time that the pay-what-you-want download of *In Rainbows* was available, the final part of his comment misses the point.

Radiohead's move was revolutionary precisely because they're Radiohead. Their stature alone was what brought visibility to the practice of pay-what-you-want. Sure, they could have gone about it more aggressively and paid closer attention to the technology. But they'll always be the first mainstream act to seek out that kind of agency with their music. If it had been Foo Fighters or Red

Hot Chili Peppers or R.E.M. or any other band at a similar level of fame, we'd be talking about them.

Yorke said just as much in *Wired* during a December 19, 2007 interview with the Talking Heads' David Byrne—the very man Radiohead has to thank for their band name.

"The only reason we could even get away with this—the only reason anyone even gives a shit—is the fact that we've gone through the whole mill of the business in the first place," Yorke said. "It's not supposed to be a model for anything else. It was simply a response to a situation. We're out of contract. We have our own studio. We have this new server. What the hell else would we do? This was the obvious thing. But it only works for us because of where we are."

Whether or not the band wanted to be a model for the rest of the industry, that's exactly what happened. Although it was already being conceived before the release of *In Rainbows*, the website Bandcamp launched the year after its release, allowing any musician on the planet to upload their music and sell it for however much they'd like. Yorke himself went on to use platform himself as one of the distribution channels for his surprise second solo album, *Tomorrow's Modern Boxes*.

Similarly, numerous hip-hop artists—from Big K.R.I.T. to Future to Ty Dolla $ign—have all released mixtapes as free downloads, with Chance the Rapper building a stratospheric career without ever selling a single record until 2019's *The Big Day*. As a lead-up to 2010's *My Beautiful Dark Twisted Fantasy*, Kanye West gave away a new song every week for 15 weeks as part of his GOOD Fridays series.

And while they haven't released their studio albums for free, Future, Beyoncé, Young Thug, and countless other rappers and pop stars have leaned heavily into the surprise-release model popularized by Radiohead. The music industry isn't making as much money as it used to, but artists both mainstream and independent have a hell of a lot more agency in the post-*In Rainbows* world.

Other Tactics

Although Radiohead hasn't released any other album using the pay-what-you-want model since *In Rainbows*, most of their career has been highlighted by nontraditional release strategies. There was the iBlip marketing campaign and decision not to try and shut down file-sharing services during *Kid A*; the erasing of social media that heralded *A Moon Shaped Pool*; and the out-of-the-blue album announcements that have accompanied everything since *In Rainbows*.

But there are still a handful of release/promotional strategies we haven't covered regarding Radiohead and Radiohead-related projects—ones that go beyond the simple surprise release and involve taking greater ownership of the material.

Live in Praha/Radiohead for Haiti

In 2010, Radiohead put their first concert films since 1995's *Live at the Astoria* in the hands of their fans. Or rather, their fans took the initiative and Radiohead helped with the final product.

The first show took place at the Výstaviště Holešovice exhibition hall in Prague, Czech Republic on August 23, 2009, a week before the end of the *In Rainbows* tour. Over 50 fans banded together to collectively film the show on Flip cameras, then over the next year, compiled the footage until they had a cut of the same concert from many different vantage points. The project got a dream-come-true boost when Radiohead stepped in to provide audio masters, resulting in a consistent sound quality. Titled *Live in Praha*, the film was released exactly a year from the original concert as a download, Blu-Ray, DVD, CD, and in various other formats—all of them free.

Radiohead for Haiti was a touch more formalized, with fan footage captured at the band's January 24 benefit show for Oxfam's response efforts to the 2010 Haiti earthquake. Dr. Inez Rogatsky had attended the concert, which took place at the Henry Fonda Theatre in Hollywood, and filmed a little bit of the show on her own. She soon connected with another fan named Andrea, who organized a mass compilation of footage from 14 audience members. The process took two to three months before all of the footage was handed to another fan named Devin, who started putting it all together. As with *Live in*

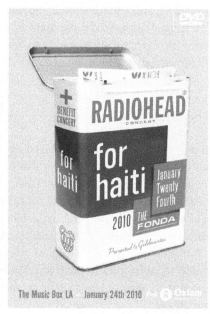

Poster for *Radiohead For Haiti*.   *Author's collection*

Praha, Radiohead approved its release—this time with the caveat that it would be for sale, and that all proceeds would go toward Oxfam. *Radiohead for Haiti* was distributed as a download on December 24, 2010, and by January 10, 2011, had already raised over $11,500.

Of the two films, *Radiohead in Praha* is the more exhilarating viewing experience. The crowd buzzes with an excitement that accelerates throughout the show, culminating in singalongs and camera-wielding fans who can barely contain their enthusiasm. The entire movie has an uneasy found-footage feel, as if everyone's poised to break into a mosh pit at any moment (something the band would probably hate).

Radiohead for Haiti is far more measured. Because the Hollywood concert was a high-priced benefit (tickets ranged from $475 to $2,000) and the audience consisted largely of wealthy attendees and celebrities, it resulted in a fairly subdued crowd. It's still an entrancing project, but only picks up as a film when the cuts get faster and more unhinged—the most prominent example being during a frothing performance of "A Wolf at the Door."

PolyFauna

Since it came out on February 11, 2014—exactly four years after the release of *The King of Limbs*—the PolyFauna app wasn't as much a promotional tool for Radiohead's eighth album as an extension of it.

Created by digital arts studio Universal Everything in collaboration with the band, Nigel Godrich, and Stanley Donwood, PolyFauna invites users into a number of alien landscapes, with only a tiny red dot as their guide. There's no end goal—it's more about exploring various worlds inspired by Donwood's artwork for *The King of Limbs*. Thorny red trees jut toward a giant spider web in the sky; a glowing moon illuminates a range of stark white mountains; electric eels squirm and shock beneath a gelatinous sea. All the while, isolated elements of *The King of Limbs* opener "Bloom" play, the different stem tracks corresponding to different locales.

In a February 12, 2014 interview with *NME*, Universal Everything founder Matt Pyke—who has also created the artwork for various musicians on Radiohead's beloved Warp records—revealed that the design process took about nine months. And while a second version of PolyFauna unveiled stems from *Tomorrow's Modern Boxes*, with other hidden Radiohead singles planned for the future, the app has since been removed from iOS and Android.

Tomorrow's Modern Boxes

With *Tomorrow's Modern Boxes*, Yorke didn't just use BitTorrent as a means of distribution—he created the album specifically for the platform.

Album art for Thom Yorke's second solo album, *Tomorrow's Modern Boxes*.   *Author's collection*

According to BitTorrent Chief Content Officer Matt Mason, the peer-to-peer sharing company drew inspiration from *In Rainbows* for their own version of the pay-what-you-can model called the BitTorrent Bundle. The concept is that artists of any stripe—filmmakers and authors as well as musicians—release new work as torrent files, allowing fans to unlock their content by providing an email address.

It was a Radiohead album that inspired the Bundle and it would be a member of Radiohead who modified it. Through the band's management, Mason met Nigel Godrich on Christmas Eve 2013. The two hit it off and discovered they had many of the same ideas regarding the future of music, including a distaste for Spotify and other streaming platforms that made it difficult for artists—new artists, especially—to make money.

Mason explained the concept of the Bundle to Godrich, and how he wanted to try out something called a paygate Bundle that year—where consumers could purchase an album through BitTorrent for a reasonably low price. Both Mason and Godrich—and eventually Yorke—still believed artists should make money from their creations. They just wanted to provide more agency and a more direct connection to fans.

As *Fader* pointed out to Mason in a September 26, 2014 interview, sites such as Bandcamp were already doing that very thing. While Mason praised Bandcamp, he explained that BitTorrent has a much larger audience of 170 million people every month (maybe even more today). When Yorke released *Tomorrow's Modern Boxes* on September 26, 2014, as the first paygate Bundle on BitTorrent for £3.69 (or $6), it was downloaded over 100,000 times in the first day alone. By February, that number had skyrocketed to 4.5 million.

While official sales figures have yet to be released, sites such as *Stereogum* and *Gigaom* posited that Yorke likely raked in somewhere around $20 million through the paygate Bundle. But in a November 29, 2015 interview with *La Republica*, he didn't view it as a completely successful business move. After all, it's not like it became the universal model for distributing music. Then again, Yorke, Godrich, and Mason have all stated that they don't believe there *should* be a universal model for distributing music.

"I wanted it to be an experiment," Yorke said in the interview. "It was a reaction to everything that was going on. People always and only spoke about Spotify. I wanted to show that, in theory, today one could follow the entire chain of record production, from start to finish, on his own. But in practice, it is very different. We cannot be burdened with all of the responsibilities of the record label. But I'm glad I did it, for having tried to."

Maybe the best way forward is a combination of different release methods. In keeping with the pattern established by *In Rainbows, Tomorrow's Modern Boxes* was eventually released through other channels, including a since-removed Bandcamp download, a standard CD and vinyl version from XL Recordings on December 8, 2017, and a deluxe vinyl version that came in an antistatic bag. It even hit Apple Music once it launched on June 30, 2015, and despite Yorke and Godrich's misgivings about the streaming service, anyone can find it today on Spotify.

OK Computer OKNOTOK 1997 2017

On the surface, *OK Computer OKNOTOK 1997 2017* doesn't seem all that remarkable—just another expanded box set of a landmark album. But for Radiohead, it represents a reclamation of their entire body of work.

Although the band left EMI/Parlophone after fulfilling their six-album contract in 2003, the label still retained the rights to their back catalogue. This resulted in EMI "Collector's Editions" of Radiohead's first six albums, released throughout 2008 and 2009 without the permission of the band. The members of Radiohead have been highly critical of the move, with O'Brien slamming it as a cash-grab on EMI's part in a March 19, 2009 interview with *RadioheadPeru*.

The most common critique is that none of the music was remastered and all of the material on the two-disc Collector's Editions had previously appeared elsewhere on EPs, singles, and live recordings. In EMI's defense, it was nice to have everything in one place for the first time. It's not like physical copies of Radiohead's singles are easy to come by, and even if they were, tracking them all down would be a pain in the ass.

Still, Radiohead and EMI didn't part on the best of terms, and the unsanctioned Collector's Editions must have stung. Vindication arrived on April 4, 2016, when, on Spotify and other streaming services, the band's back catalogue was suddenly listed as being owned by XL Recordings and not EMI or Parlophone. Radiohead had regained the rights to their first six albums.

While this meant that the Collector's Editions vanished from streaming services, Radiohead digitally redistributed most of their B-sides in their original singles format. "Coke Babies" is once again attached to "Anyone Can Play Guitar"; "Fast-Track" and "Kinetic" are with "Pyramid Song," etc. It also seems that the band has started reissuing their back catalog on their own terms, starting with the massive *OKNOTOK*.

Remastered with new artwork (the original *OK Computer* image being burned from the edges), the standard version contains the primary album on the first disc, plus a second disc with all of the already-existing B-sides of the era. In typical Radiohead fashion, fans could also order a deluxe boxed edition, packed with goodies such as the album on vinyl, a hardcover book of artwork, notes from Yorke, and a sketchbook loaded with concept art from Yorke and Donwood.

But the most fascinating aspect of the boxed edition is a cassette tape with various scratch tracks and experiments that were part of the genesis of the album and works that came later. Failed attempts at "True Love Waits," Yorke's early 4-track version of the bass line from "The National Anthem," and a weird "Space Echo" take of "Karma Police" are just a few of the many curiosities included. Even if most of the tape's contents don't warrant repeat listens, springing the extra cash for the deluxe set is a no-brainer for any Radiohead completist.

And even the most casual fan might be interested in the cassette tape, as it contains two *OK Computer*-era songs that no one knew existed. They come in addition to the inclusion of "I Promise," "Man of War," and "Lift" on the standard version's second disc. *OKNOTOK* marks the first time these songs have appeared on any official Radiohead release.

"I Promise"

Of the three finished unreleased tracks that appear on *OKNOTOK*, "I Promise" sounds like the least likely candidate for *OK Computer*, despite being played live several times throughout 1996.

But it would have been a standout track on *The Bends*, had Radiohead written it a little earlier. The acoustic strumming has a stargazing quality to it, countered by the directness found in Selway's military snare cadence, and the lyrics lean more on the cryptic side of Thom Yorke's songwriting. Is he promising to subject himself to pain for a love, an Orwellian government, or something else?

After a 21-year break from playing it live, Radiohead resurrected "I Promise" for their tour supporting *A Moon Shaped Pool*, performing it at least three times in support of the *OKNOTOK* box set.

"Man of War"

Radiohead has a long relationship with James Bond. From 1995–1997, they covered Carly Simon's theme for *The Spy Who Loved Me*, "Nobody Does It Better," at least 15 times live. Some of the shows in 1995 also featured performances of "Man of War" (originally titled "Big Boots," then "Man-O-War"), a song the band wrote as a sort of imaginary Bond theme.

While it's hard to imagine an opening sequence to a James Bond film scored by the lyrics "I'll bake you a cake made of all their eyes," the melodramatic piano and strings from the Royal Philharmonic Orchestra would be right at home in the world of 007. And thanks to a blazing Jonny Greenwood solo that permeates the final third of the song, "Man of War" still fits in with the best of *The Bends*- and *OK Computer*-era Radiohead.

But the band didn't include it on either of those albums, perhaps because they were holding out hope for its use in an actual Bond film. In March 1998, they at least came within spitting distance when they asked to include "Man of War" in another British spy movie, the film adaptation of *The Avengers* TV series. The documentary *Meeting People Is Easy* actually shows footage of the band and Godrich trying to lay down a new version of the song at Abbey Road Studios. Tensions were high during this period, which found the band in the middle of the *OK Computer* tour cycle, and the sessions were abandoned.

As much as Yorke's lyrics about big boots would have befitted Emma Peel karate-kicking villains in the face, it's probably the best that "Man of War" didn't make it onto the *Avengers* soundtrack. The film bombed at the box office and is widely recognized as one of the worst movies ever made.

A dream came true when Radiohead finally got asked to write the theme for the 2015 James Bond film *Spectre*. Unfortunately, "Man of War" was rejected since the band hadn't written it specifically for the movie, which led to them penning "Spectre"—also rejected, much to the chagrin of Godrich, who viewed the whole venture as a waste of time (Radiohead was still in the middle of recording *A Moon Shaped Pool*).

No matter. "Man of War" finally got a proper release on *OKNOTOK*, with a killer music video to boot. However, as of this writing, it still hasn't been played live since August 7, 2002.

"Lift"

On May 3, 2017, *The A.V. Club* ran an article with the headline "Radiohead once nixed a song for being too catchy, which is so perfectly Radiohead." The article is, of course, referring to "Lift."

Debuted at the Troubadour in West Hollywood on March 14, 1996, and played more than 30 times throughout that year (including on the band's opening stint for Alanis Morissette), "Lift" stands out for its stadium-ready optimism. Over breezy strumming that gives way to sunbursts of distortion, Yorke urges himself to come back down to Earth, out of the malfunctioning elevator of the title. "Today is the first day of the rest of your days," he sings with reassurance. At one point, he even refers to himself by his own name, an apparent nod to Major Tom from David Bowie's "Space Oddity."

While recording *OK Computer*, Radiohead was fully aware of "Lift"'s megahit potential—a trait they were reluctant to embrace.

"If that song had been on that album, it would've taken us to a different place, and probably we'd have sold a lot more records—if we'd done it right," O'Brien told BBC Radio 6 Music on May 3, 2017. "But when we got to the studio and did it, it felt like having a gun to your head. There was so much pressure." In Jonathan Hale's *Radiohead: From a Great Height*, he went as far as dismissing it as a "bogshite B-side."

It's easy to see why "Lift"'s shimmering aesthetic would have separated it from the rest of *OK Computer*. At the same time, there's also optimism to be found in Radiohead's third album. The "slow down" motif of closer "The Tourist" is similar to the reassurances of "Lift" and its final line to "lighten up, squirt." O'Brien's comments don't give the song or the band enough credit.

To be fair, Radiohead never completely shut the door on "Lift," either. Yorke and Jonny Greenwood have both assured fans that they hadn't lost track of the song over the years, and on July 22, 2002, they unveiled a reworked version of the song to an audience in Lisbon, Portugal. Its dirge-like pace—not to mention the absence of that big, soaring distortion—could have been an attempt to make it less anthemic. The band also supposedly attempted a rearranged version during the *Hail to the Thief* sessions, but it has yet to be released to the public.

In 2017, not long after O'Brien's interview, Radiohead finally bit the bullet and released the proper studio version of "Lift" on *OKNOTOK*. Maybe they felt that they no longer had to prove themselves as a band like they did back in 1997. Or maybe they had finally taken the advice of that final lyric and lightened up.

"Attention"

Released on the cassette tape of demos that came with the special edition of *OKNOTOK*, "Attention" is a gently strummed protest song that no one except Radiohead knew existed. Its unveiling probably won't set the world on fire, as it falls victim to the corniest cliches of the genre—a sing-songy intro and vaguely idealistic lyrics such as "the joy of the uprising."

"Are You Someone?"

The cassette's second previously unknown demo—tacked onto the end of side A—fares slightly better, its dour chords reminiscent of unplugged Nirvana. The lyrics also hit closer to home with first-person attacks on anyone who dares to feel (a theme that fits right in with the rest of *OK Computer*).

31

"I Trust I Can Rely on Your Vote"

Nigel Godrich

The George Martin to Radiohead's Beatles, Nigel Godrich has produced every single one of the band's releases since 1997's *OK Computer*. He isn't just someone who makes them sound good. He's a confidant, a source of moral support, someone who shares their sense of humor, and—in Thom Yorke's case with Atoms For Peace—an actual bandmate.

And that's just the tip of the iceberg when talking about Godrich's work with Radiohead. As he explained to the *Evening Standard* on July 6, 2016, it's hard to define what a producer actually does—so much that he dreads being asked the question at dinner parties.

"If pushed, the analogy would be with a film director; you have the control and the interface through technology of making a record," he said. "You have that vision and, depending on what kind of producer you are, you're the one who steers the ship and puts it all together." In other words, different albums have called for different things. The discover-as-we-go methodology of *A Moon Shaped Pool* was a much different process than something like *The Bends*, which had a rough outline before Radiohead entered the studio.

"Thom just doesn't work like he used to," Godrich told *Rolling Stone* on June 8, 2017. "He will write a song, or a piece of the song, and the idea is the last part of it is developed with everyone's input. If the focus isn't there, then it has to be my job to make it happen." In the end, he ended up assembling *A Moon Shaped Pool* by himself once everyone was finished recording.

While Godrich has said that he can only have one relationship with a musical act that's as deep and profound as his and Radiohead's, he's still had a distinguished career outside of the band, even working repeatedly with a handful of other artists as well. That being said, it's unlikely he'll be referred to as "Beck's right-hand" man or the "fifth member of Travis" anytime soon.

Childhood

Born on February 28, 1971 in the Westminster section of London to parents Victor and Brenda, Nigel Timothy Godrich already had studio work in his blood. His father was a studio engineer for the BBC with a laundry list of credits to his name. Vic Godrich's IMDb page contains several iconic British television shows such as *Doctor Who* and *Survivors*, with Vic his roles ranging from Sound Editor to Sound Supervisor and O.B. Sound.

While Nigel Godrich today plays guitar, bass, and synthesizers in Atoms For Peace and on various other artists' albums, he initially put aside his aspirations as a musician as his interest in recording equipment developed. As a child, he attended the William Ellis School in London before going on to study at the London's School of Audio Engineering. Afterward, he applied to nearly 100 studios in search of a job, including Abbey Road. On March 16, 2017, Godrich took to Twitter to share a polite rejection letter from then-General Manager Ken Townsend, dated February 12, 1990.

Godrich did eventually land a job at RAK Recording Studios, though not in the most interesting or glamorous of positions. His first professional role in the music industry wouldn't be that of producer or engineer, but tea boy.

"With a beeper in my pocket, I'd wait next to the kettle, ready to deliver my hot beverages," he once told the French magazine *Les Inrockuptibles*. "I wasn't even allowed in the studios, but I [would] hang there thinking, 'OK, it's only the first rung, but at least I'm on the ladder.'"

He soon got promoted to messenger, a position he held for three months thanks to his constant gabbing about recording equipment. His obsession didn't get him fired, but resulted in yet another promotion—this time to studio assistant. Godrich was finally in the room where he had always wanted to be.

Early Career

During Godrich's four years as a studio assistant, he began sharpening his skills as an engineer, trying out different techniques by recording his musician friends after hours. After four years, he got to put his sharpened skillset to good use when John Leckie tapped him to engineer Ride's latest album, *Carnival of Light*, which Leckie was producing.

It wasn't the first time Ride would enter the Radiohead story. When the band was still On a Friday and gigging around Oxford, the members of Ride were self-professed fans, which helped drum up local support. According to Jonny Greenwood, they even stopped to listen to he and Yorke when they were busking on the street.

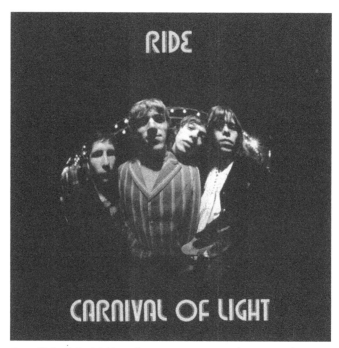

One of Nigel Godrich's earliest engineering credits was Ride's 1990 album Carnival of Light.   *Author's collection*

Unfortunately for both Leckie and Godrich, Ride's shift from shoegaze to psychedelia on *Carnival of Light* wasn't well received by anyone—fans, critics, even the band themselves. The album was released on June 20, 1994, and by the end of the year, the members of Ride had taken to calling it "Carnival of Shite." They broke up before their next album, *Tarantula*, even came out.

While *Carnival of Light*'s faults laid more in the overblown songwriting than the engineering or production, it wasn't going to put Godrich's work on the map for the outside world anytime soon. But his mentor must have seen something in him. Shortly after their work on *Carnival of Light*, Leckie asked him to work on a little album called *The Bends*.

Radiohead

Although Godrich was only supposed to serve as engineer, he and Radiohead recorded "Black Star" and a handful of B-sides together when Leckie was away at a wedding. Everyone liked the results so much that the quick take was included on the album, with Godrich receiving a single-track production credit on "Black Star" and some of the songs that appeared on the *My Iron Lung* EP.

When listening to "Black Star" alongside Godrich's future work with the band, its rough-and-tumble feel stands out from the trademarks that would soon be associated with his production. There are no orchestral touches, effects, or mechanized noises mixing in with traditional rock arrangements.

It didn't matter. Like Stanley Donwood, it was clear that Godrich fit in perfectly with Radiohead's humor, temperament, and aesthetic. They later asked him to produce the sessions that birthed "Lucky" and the B-sides "Talk Show Host," "Molasses," and "Bishop's Robes," and he's handled the production for every Radiohead release since.

In fact, the only time Radiohead did try to make an album without Godrich was somewhat of a failure. After a run of aborted sessions with Spike Stent on 2007's *In Rainbows*, they begged Godrich to come back. He did, and as Yorke told XFM on January 28, 2008, gave the band "a walloping kick in the arse."

Other Work

Of course, Godrich has completed plenty of non-Radiohead work as an engineer, producer, mixer, and composer. He remixed U2's 2001 single "Walk On," has lent his guitar work to two albums by Zero 7 (whose Henry Binns is a friend from his days at William Ellis School), and mixed most of Natalie Imbruglia's 1997 debut, *Left of the Middle*. It's funny to think that, for all of his accomplishments, Godrich's most widely-heard work is likely his mixing on Imbruglia's cover of "Torn," written by the short-lived, relatively unknown band Ednaswap.

There have also been random projects that have nothing to do with music. On April 9, 2013, Godrich and Thom Yorke participated in *Rookie Mag*'s "Ask a Grown Man" series, where they answered questions sent in by the publication's teen readers, most of whom are female. Both Godrich and Yorke address *Rookie Mag*'s fanbase with sincerity, offering empathetic tips on dating and self-worth while also sharing the insecurities they faced while growing up.

Godrich's most recent non-musical appearance was in 2015, when he cameoed as a stormtrooper in *Star Wars: The Force Awakens*. He even got a line, yelling "Hey!" when he encounters Han Solo, Chewbacca, and former stormtrooper Finn entering the Starkiller base to rescue Rey. Daniel Craig cameoed as a stormtrooper at another point in the film, meaning the two would have more to talk about than the "Spectre" debacle if they ever ran into each other on an elevator.

While there's not enough page space to cover all of Godrich's work (non-musical or otherwise), there are a few notable projects outside of Radiohead that call for a closer look.

Beck

Godrich will be forever associated with Radiohead, but they aren't the only musical act who he's worked with multiple times. He's also collaborated on three of Beck's studio albums—producing and mixing 1998's *Mutations*; producing, mixing, and engineering 2002's *Sea Change*; mixing the single "Girl" from 2003's *Guero*; and producing, mixing, and playing on 2006's *The Information*.

A testament to Godrich's diversity as a producer, each of the full-length albums finds Beck at a different sonic phase in his career. *Mutations* is the most ramshackle—loose, comfortable, and exploring a variety of genres in a down-home sort of way. *The Information* is a return to Beck's everything-in-the-blender, white-boy brand of hip-hop, with he and Godrich creating an entire universe of beats to build from. And *Sea Change* of course focuses on Beck the heartbroken songwriter—its 12 tracks written in the aftermath of breaking up with his fiancee at the time, Leigh Limon.

Godrich had also just gotten out of a breakup, leading both men to pour their own emotional turmoil into the album. That, coupled with Godrich's employment of strings on several tracks, make *Sea Change* the Beck counterpart to Radiohead's *A Moon Shaped Pool*. While he'll never have as prolific a relationship with Godrich, there's still a connection there that takes their work together beyond being merely transactional.

Travis

Radiohead has never aligned themselves with the Britpop movement, and yet so many of the bands to come out of it have been unfavorably compared to them—namely Coldplay, Snow Patrol, and Travis.

Of the three, Travis actually does have a tenuous connection in that three of their albums were produced or co-produced by Nigel Godrich. He handled sole production duties on the band's 1999 commercial breakthrough *The Man Who*, as well as 2001's *The Invisible Band*, and co-produced 2007's *The Boy With No Name* with Brian Eno and Mike Hedges. In all fairness to Travis' detractors, the comparisons aren't exactly unfounded, especially with Godrich at the boards. Though the music is more tuneful, jangly, and banjo-heavy than Radiohead, the delicate vocals of Fran Healy and upsurges of murky effects will always feel slightly reminiscent of *The Bends*.

Like Beck, Healy also has a relationship with Godrich that expands beyond the studio. In an August 16, 2013 retrospective on Travis' discography with *Drowned In Sound*, he recalls Godrich being frustrated during *The Invisible Band* sessions, feeling that the album wasn't up to the level of its predecessor.

"I really felt he was going to desert the record," Healy said. "Unbeknownst to us, Nigel was having his own dramas, and he wasn't getting any rest, so we were getting the brunt of it ... It got much better when we realised that."

Given the timeline, Godrich could have been going through the breakup that he drew from for Beck's *Sea Change*.

Godrich would be more immediately complimentary of Travis' most recent album, 2016's *Everything at Once*, produced by Michael Ilbard. He got to hear some of the band's work while he and Yorke were rehearsing at Healy's for some upcoming Atoms for Peace gigs in Japan.

"Nigel came in while we were recording and he said he thought it was great," Healy told *Music Radar* on June 7, 2016. "Now, Nigel is a really fussy fucker and he really wouldn't say it was good if he didn't think it was good!"

Pavement

Not all of Godrich's collaborations have been perfect matches. Pavement, for instance, didn't usually work with a producer. They were also on the verge of breaking up when Godrich asked if he could produce the band's fifth and final album, 1999's *Terror Twilight* (he and Radiohead had been fans of Pavement's third album, *Wowee Zowee*).

"He was cool," Pavement's primary songwriter and frontman Stephen Malkmus told *The Talkhouse Music Podcast* on February 16, 2017. "He was like 'I just want my percentage points, you don't even have to pay me a fee. I'm free and I've already made a lot of money and I want to work with you guys, so we'll carry this to the end.' We paid for the studio time of course, which started to get expensive. Because he had his own, uh, standards."

Those standards included wanting the band to push themselves more than they had been accustomed to; wanting them to fully bring out the radio friendliness that had always been apparent beneath the shambling nature of their music; wanting them to show more interest in recording than playing Scrabble, which they were prone to doing in the studio. One particular point of contention had to do with the tracklist.

"[Nigel] had a certain order that was with a difficult song first, like Radiohead's *OK Computer* that had a longer more challenging song to set the tempo," Malkmus told *The Talkhouse*. "Scott [Kannberg] in our band, and the other ones—not only did they not like that song, but they barely played on it. They wanted this easier song first, like the hit song. So Nigel was like 'I'm done with this. This is the wrong move. We made a stoner album and you're going halfway.' He's right probably."

While *Terror Twilight* is widely accepted as being Pavement's weakest LP, it's still loved by fans, especially when viewed as a bridge from their first four records to Malkmus's and Kannberg's solo careers that came afterward. The songs are slower and more meandering than the rest of Pavement's catalogue, but the catchiness is there—enough that it allows Pavement to be one of the few acts to pass critic Steven Hyden's "Five-Albums Test"—a barometer for greatness that requires a musical act to release five stellar albums in a row (Radiohead also passes).

After the *Talkhouse* podcast, many publications framed their headlines to make it sound as if Malkmus didn't enjoy working with Godrich. "Stephen Malkmus calls 1999's Terror Twilight 'overproduced," read a tweet from *Pitchfork*. Godrich retorted with "I literally slept on a friend's floor in NYC to be able to make that album" on Twitter. Malkmus quickly squashed any potential nerd-rock beef by tweeting at *Pitchfork*, "I love Nigel and can't even believe I got to record with him!!! Towering skills and fucking fun to hang with." Godrich got the final word by giving back the good vibes: "Love you too dear Stephen ... one of my fav people ... just wanted to point out what a lame headline that was ... :)"

The point is, *Terror Twilight* only sounds overproduced because the songs themselves are somewhat undercooked—though still undeniable in their hooks—when compared to the rest of Pavement's catalogue. And the band, very much by their own admission, just didn't have their hearts in it anymore.

And if nothing else, *Terror Twilight* brought Radiohead and Pavement directly into each other's spheres. One of the most charming stories from the sessions is when Jonny Greenwood entered RAK Studios not to work on a new Radiohead album, but to contribute harmonica to two of *Terror Twilight*'s songs, "Platform Blues" and "Billie." As observed by *The Quietus* during the recording sessions in 1999, Pavement bassist Mark Ibold marveled at Jonny's fervor from the control room above:

"He's blowin' the Oxford blues, man!"

The Strokes

Though characterized by clashing styles, Godrich's work with Pavement at least resulted in an appreciated final product. His collaboration with the Strokes didn't get nearly that far.

The band had brought him in to produce their second album, 2003's *Room On Fire*. Amusingly, the Strokes already had a minor connection to Radiohead. The band's rhythm guitarist is Albert Hammond, Jr., whose father wrote co-wrote the Hollies' "The Air That I Breathe"—the very song Radiohead had plagiarized with "Creep." As a result, Hammond Sr. gets a writing credit and royalty percentage.

Godrich's work with the Strokes didn't last long, as they found his production to be, in their words, "soulless." In one of his typically insufferable *Rolling Stone* interviews from that era, frontman Julian Casablancas answers a question about Godrich's departure with "Fuck you."

To Casablanca's credit, he's since mellowed out with his press appearances, and according to *Drowned In Sound*'s June 19, 2009 interview with Godrich, the two got along well during the abandoned sessions.

"The problem there was that me and Julian are just too similar," Godrich said. "We're both control freaks. He wanted to do it his way, I wanted to do it my way, and obviously that's the point of me being there ... We got on great. It was just one of those laughable things where it just doesn't work. I wanted them to change, and they didn't."

Roger Waters/Paul McCartney

Artists who have taken a more flexible mindset than Casablancas to Godrich's admittedly hard-nosed suggestions have often found success. Roger Waters, another notorious control freak, confessed that he had to teach himself to be quiet when Godrich produced his 2017 album *Is This the Life We Really Want?* (the two had previously collaborated on the 2015 live album *Roger Waters: The Wall*).

That must have been especially hard when Godrich started out the sessions by telling Waters how inaccessible some of his solo records were. But the Pink Floyd mastermind was more than game and ended up churning out his most acclaimed solo album outside of 1992's *Amused to Death*.

Another elder statesman, Paul McCartney, adopted a similarly open mind when Godrich produced his 13th studio album, 2005's *Chaos and Creation In the Backyard*. McCartney had originally wanted George Martin, who had retired in 2003. For a replacement, Martin recommended that Macca seek out Godrich. Suddenly, the sixth member of Radiohead was taking the place of the fifth Beatle.

Once again not pulling any punches for one of his musical heroes, Godrich asked McCartney to send away his touring band so he could play most of the instruments himself, hoping for the same direct and adventurous spirit as 1970's *McCartney* and 1980's *McCartney II*. Godrich also asked (or maybe ordered?) him to scrap his sillier, treacly songs in favor of more spiritual and philosophical compositions—the energy and introspection further mobilized by strings from the Millennia Ensemble, who would also appear on Radiohead's *In Rainbows*.

Despite McCartney almost firing Godrich at several points throughout nearly two-year stop-and-start recording process, the two soldiered through for what some critics have called McCartney's finest solo effort to date. *Chaos and Creation In the Backyard* sold over a million copies worldwide, with the song "Jenny Wren" winning Best Male Pop Vocal Performance at the 49th Annual Grammy Awards.

The previous year, the entire album was nominated for Album of the Year and Best Pop Vocal Album, with opener "Fine Line" nominated for Best Male Pop Vocal Performance and Godrich getting nominated for Non-Classical Producer of the Year.

Ultraísta

With Godrich on bass and synthesizers and Joey Waronker on drums, Ultraísta features two members of Atoms for Peace. Unsurprisingly, their only album to date, 2012's self-titled solo record, has all of that act's strengths and weaknesses. The electronic textures and Afrobeat influences make for decent background noise, but there's not a lot to grab onto in terms of actual songcraft, even with chilled-over vocals from Laura Bettinson.

Scott Pilgrim vs. the World: Original Score

The closest Godrich has ever gotten to a solo album, the score for *Scott Pilgrim vs. the World* finds him at his most playful, combining adventure themes with ambient swells and 8-bit arrangements that fit perfectly with the film's comic-book-video-game mashup aesthetic.

In the film, based on a series of graphic novels by Bryan Lee O'Malley, the title character competes in a battle of the bands against several other musical acts. The fictional bands' songs were written and performed by real-life musicians, with Beck penning the music for Scott Pilgrim's band Sex Bob-Omb. While most of Sex Bob-Omb's songs appear on the corresponding *Original Motion Picture Soundtrack*, a handful make an appearance on the *Original Score*, including one co-written by Godrich. That makes *Scott Pilgrim* Godrich's fourth collaboration with the hardest-working Loser in show business.

32

"I'm an Animal"

The King of Limbs

W hen Radiohead released their eighth studio album on February 18, 2011 after less than two years of recording, much of it consisted of looped beats—some of which were new and some of which were pulled from the band's past work. Jonny Greenwood went as far as to write his own sampling software—a sort of janky version of Ableton Live—to generate what the band would refer to as "blocks" of sound that could then be paired with somewhat minimalist lyrics, with the more nuts-and-bolts elements of rock 'n' roll filled in later.

The collage-like approach recalls a more primitive take on the band's recording process for *Kid A*, and as a result, there's definitely a recycled quality to the music. But like anything involving Radiohead, there's also a deliberation to it, a stubborn method behind all the repetitive madness. As Thom Yorke described to *NPR* on October 7, 2011, *The King of Limbs* is "an expression of wildness and mutation," an attempt to sonically embody the gnarled Savernake Forest that houses the ancient tree of the album's title. It was near this patch of woods that Radiohead recorded their last album, *In Rainbows*, while holed up in Tottenham House.

When viewed through that naturalistic lens, *The King of Limbs* becomes an environmentalist piece of pop culture, but that's not to say it's some blunt save-the-planet screed a la Neil Young's *Storytone*. As always seems to be the case with Radiohead, the meaning isn't blatantly ideological as much as ideology drawn from observation.

In other words, *The King of Limbs* is an album that recognizes the power of nature—how dwarfing and uncaring it is. That's a bold political statement in itself: Nature exists, it's wild, it's unknowable, it's majestic, and it will always be bigger and more powerful than us measly human beings. When navigating *The King of Limbs*' pulsing soundscapes, one gets the idea that nature *should* be saved from the ravages of pollution and climate change, but at the same time, it's aliveness reminds us that it will still be there long after we're gone. When humankind talks about saving the planet, they're really talking about saving

Album art for *The King of Limbs*.   *Author's collection*

themselves as a species. Earth may change and suffer from what we've done to it, but it will outlast us regardless.

That theme becomes especially apparent when Yorke occasionally examines his own relationship problems in the lyrics. His phrases surrounding lost or frayed love tend to slip into the songs rather briefly, then fade away quickly once the next musical element or image is introduced. It's as if Yorke's human-centric issues aren't all that important when compared to the all-encompassing scope of the trees, the ocean, the plants, the animals, the earth.

And in a way, they really aren't. It's the closest *The King of Limbs* gets to a tangible hypothesis: the complex, somewhat frightening idea of the natural world trumping our self-obsession as human beings.

To be fair, though, the album's detractors do have a point. The sonic palette of *The King of Limbs* is narrow, with subtle variations only becoming apparent after several listens. There's nothing as explicit as the switch from hard rock to slowed-down salsa on "Paranoid Android," for example, or the jump from electronic texture to full-punk assault on "2 + 2 = 5." One can see how some of the band's older fans would be frustrated at the stasis on LP8.

The Songs

"Bloom"

Although later songs on *The King of Limbs* zoom in on a specific animal, on the opening track, "Bloom," finds Thom Yorke describing an entire environment. His falsetto sounds almost frightened as he observes the various elements of the ocean, including both the water and the wildlife. When describing the floating tentacles of a jellyfish and the larger-than-life eyes of a sea turtle, one can imagine him as a little fish in an especially big pond. In the extended, unused lyrics found in the special newspaper edition of the album, added words describe fighting against the strong current.

Like "Weird Fishes/Arpeggi" on *In Rainbows* before it, the band counters Yorke's fear of his foreign surroundings by painting a dreamlike vision of the landscape, this time through a gorgeous piano loop and Phil Selway's muffled drums. His percussion sounds submerged, but never so much that the staggered snare loses track of the beat. With no jarring spikes in the structure, it's already clear that this an album more concerned with mood than grandiosity. Throughout *The King of Limbs*, the band locks into a groove, then explores the open air of it all.

"Morning Mr Magpie"

The majesty continues on "Morning Mr Magpie," accompanied by a growing sense of paranoia, thanks to Ed O'Brien's descending guitar line and a clatter of percussion held together only by a small cymbal hit. Just as "Bloom"'s bubbly wall of piano replicates the ocean, the jitteriness here recalls the bird of the title swooping through a forest, stealing the narrator's jewelry and perhaps something more important, too.

Interestingly, Yorke debuted "Morning Mr. Magpie" as an acoustic ballad on a 2002 webcast, which eventually made its way into the short-film collection *The Most Gigantic Lying Mouth of All Time*. Then titled "Morning M'lord," the somber arrangement, though fascinating and gorgeous, doesn't quite match the impressionistic lyrics, and it was vetoed for inclusion on every Radiohead album after that. With *The King of Limbs*, the band finally finds the appropriate nervousness to make the song fly, sing, and steal.

"Little by Little"

"Little By Little" is the first song on *The King of Limbs* to sneak in lyrics that hinge on a relationship. And for a moment, the forces of love actually seem to keep the forces of nature at bay. Even though the tittering guitar is similar to

"Morning Mr Magpie," the raised volume of Colin Greenwood's bass adds a false sense of security and relaxation.

All is not well, though. As the song progresses, the story devolves into romantic dispute, and a reversed guitar line ups the tension, as if the trees have begun blowing and the animals have started yowling to match the lovers' quarrel.

"Feral"

Everything ends sourly by the time "Feral" rolls around—a song that consists solely of the phrases "You are not mine / And I am not yours / And that's okay / Please don't judge me." It's easily the most minimalist—and thus the most polarizing—song on *The King of Limbs*; repetitive, otherworldly, and cavernous due to Selway's furious drum bursts and an echo filter placed over Yorke's voice. It's pleasing enough, but also ends before the song can truly burrow into the listener.

"Lotus Flower"

The trope of the breakup song fully melds with nature on "Lotus Flower." A running theme in Radiohead's work has always been not knowing how to react in the face of lust and/or romance, and here, Yorke tangles that dilemma with a series of plant metaphors.

As he alternates between wanting to embrace a new lover and wanting to run away from them, he describes the person both in terms of strangling weeds and newly blossoming flowers. As an added sonic bonus, he drops into his lower register (low for him, anyway) during the darker verses, then goes high with the elated choruses.

Maybe it's because of its straightforward subject matter, but more so than "Morning Mr Magpie," "Lotus Flower" works well as an acoustic ballad. That's how many fans first heard it when Yorke premiered it live with the Atoms for Peace, starting in 2009.

"Codex"

Everything slows down on "Codex," the only song on *The King of Limbs* that arrives with almost no percussion. This hacks away some of the preceding thorns and bramble, instead conjuring a nighttime scene by the lake in the lyrics. All is glassy calm. Instead of flailing, Yorke stays glued to his piano, fixated on sparse C major, Bb, Dm, F, Gm, and Am chords. One can almost hear the keys softly buzzing as he sings about dragonflies and flitting above the water.

Despite the melancholia, there's a sense of rebirth that becomes even more apparent when considering the title: "Codex" is derived from the Latin word "caudex," which means "tree trunk." Fittingly, it's the song that feels the most musically direct and decipherable on *The King of Limbs*—inviting and firmly rooted to the ground.

"Give up the Ghost"

On "Give Up the Ghost," the forest comes alive in a more literal sense, with bird-song underscoring the gentle acoustic strumming.

It also comes alive in a more supernatural sense, as Yorke pleads for a spirit not to haunt him. As peaceful as the arrangement is, the plea feels useless; the lyrics throughout *The King of Limbs* seem to point to him *always* being haunted. There's a reason why Stanley Donwood's crudely drawn trees on the cover look more like dead octopode or Lovecraftian deities rising out of a swamp. As if embodying these paranormal figures in both title and phrasing, "Give up the Ghost" is a perfect example of how to sound at ease and tortured at the same time. The rise of French horns at the end does nothing to calm things down.

"Separator"

Selway returns with full force on the closing track, "Separator," an exercise in restrained bombast that was originally titled "Mouse Dog Bird."

Not many drummers can draw such power from half-executed drum rolls. Perhaps he knew that if he went full-blast, Yorke's anxieties would explode out of his body, ruining the mystery of the album. So Selway holds back as Yorke returns to the frightened-fish metaphor of the opening track. This time, though, he insists it's just a dream, and when Jonny Greenwood's synthesized pan flute comes in (an instrument from the wild if there ever was one), it's easy to believe him. Even if Yorke's still asleep, there's a rise and fall at the end of *The King of Limbs* to let the listener know that they're finally out of the woods. For now.

B-sides

Unlike many of its predecessors, *The King of Limbs* didn't produce a wealth of B-sides. In fact, none of them were released as proper B-sides at all. The record's sole single was a promotional copy of "Lotus Flower," which only contained the radio edit and the album version. Every non-album track from *The King of Limbs* era (2009–2011) was distributed as its own release or, in the case of "The Daily Mail" and "Staircase," pulled straight from a *Live From the Basement Session.*

"Harry Patch (In Memory Of)"

When Harry Patch died on July 25, 2009, he was the last-surviving combat soldier of World War I, having fought in the trenches of France on the Western Front.

When the war ended, Patch didn't speak about it publicly until a 1998 documentary for BBC One. Following that, he began expressing anti-war sentiments to the press, including a December 4, 2005 interview on BBC Radio 4's *Today*. Thom Yorke happened to be listening, and was moved by his stance.

"If two governments can't agree, give 'em a rifle and let *them* sort it out," Patch told BBC. "The third war will be chemical. I don't want to see it."

Yorke wouldn't get to writing a song about Patch until a few weeks before his death, which he and Jonny recorded live at an alley during the summer of 2009. Perhaps as a way of honoring the past generation, "Harry Patch (In Memory Of)" consists only of Yorke's voice and a string section arranged by Jonny that sounds like a memorial, even though Patch was still alive when it was written. For the words, Yorke paraphrased several of Patch's interview quotes, making it one of Radiohead's most straightforward and literal songs.

When it came time to release "Harry Patch (In Memory Of)," the band made it available on their website for $1.68 (£1 for Brits), with all proceeds going toward the Royal British Legion. Just as touching, the song premiered 11 days after Patch's death on *Today*, the very show that aired his interview that affected Yorke so much in the first place.

"These Are My Twisted Words"

Despite predating album by a year-and-a-half, "These Are My Twisted Words" feels like a test run for *The King of Limbs*, from the sylvan album art to the sparse lyrics about the lost, wandering narrator to the mutative state of the music.

Like so many songs on *The King of Limbs*, the song locks into a mood and sticks to it, with Selway's motorik beat serving as the wooden skeleton. Spectral wails fade in and out, with Yorke's lyrics backed by a childlike echo.

Perhaps sensing that this was all a wildly different direction from *In Rainbows* (even though the song's title appeared on tour merch from that era), Radiohead or someone involved with Radiohead released "These Are My Twisted Words" on August 17, 2009 as a leaked torrent. Five days later, it appeared on the band's website as a zip file with cryptic phrases and interactive artwork of tree branches and thorns meant to be printed on tracing paper. Was the band testing the waters with their newfound aesthetic before fully committing to *The King of Limbs*?

"Supercollider"

With its fat synthesizer notes and crescendoing wail, "Supercollider" is somewhat of an outlier compared to the mellower tracks on *The King of Limbs*—darker, moodier, and more distant. Lyrically, it's somewhat different, too, chronicling a planet being formed in a cosmic soup instead of the water, trees,

Art for the "Supercollider" / "The Butcher" single.   *Author's collection*

or wildlife here on Earth. Not a bad Radiohead song by any means, but one can understand why it didn't fit in with the rest of the album.

None of "Supercollider"'s ethereality was present when Yorke debuted it live in full during the *In Rainbows* tour in 2008, but a shorter sample of the song can be heard as the intro for "Everything in Its Right Place" from an April 1 show of that year. The 26-second clip feels more in line with what would eventually get released as a single.

"The Butcher"

It makes since that, for a double-single pressing on Record Store Day 2011 (anyone who bought *The King of Limbs* could download it for free just three days later), "Supercollider" was paired with "The Butcher." Similarly brooding, it's driven by primitive drums and synth notes straight out of a *Castlevania* video game. The most abrupt change occurs around the two-minute mark, where the drums evolve into a more traditional rock trap kit, then become subdued once more.

Yorke's lyrics on "The Butcher" are also more abrasive than anything else on *The King of Limbs*, using phrases such as "little bitch" and "beauty will destroy your mind" to apparently offer up a critique of traditional, testosterone-soaked masculinity. Because the words are so clear, with no distortion or effects obscuring them, they do ring a bit melodramatic.

"The Daily Mail"

For the final two singles of the *King of Limbs* era, Radiohead turned not to the album, but their *Live From the Basement* recording. During that session, the band performed two unreleased songs, "The Daily Mail" and "Staircase," both of which had been road-tested by Yorke on 2010's Atoms For Peace tour and would be released as a digital double-single on December 9, 2011.

"The Daily Mail" goes back further than that, with portions of its scathing lyrics against the British tabloid of the same name appearing on Dead Air Space as far back as 2004. Back then, the song was referred to as "A Pig's Ear" or "Pigsee." Yorke played it as a piano composition at one of his own gigs, then during the solo section of one of the Atoms For Peace shows. But it didn't truly take off until Atoms For Peace attempted a full-band version, yanking the bitter piano of the first half into a heavily distorted assault during the finale. *Live From the Basement* took it one step further into maximalism with a horn section.

It's this version of "The Daily Mail" that works best. As sometimes happens when Yorke writes anti-establishment songs, the lyrics rely on passe imagery to rightfully criticize the tabloid, from the Rapture to lunatics running the asylum. These aren't quite so glaring when washed away by a grand finale.

"Staircase"

Yorke performed a guitar-and-vocal version of "Staircase" during his solo section of the Atoms For Peace tour. The gentleness and lack of a hook made it kind of a slog.

While it gets a little more mileage as a jittery piece of electronica on *Live From the Basement*, it can't hide that the song has no tangible element to latch onto. At least the lyrics, which describe whisking someone away on a helicopter, fit under Yorke's "seduction songs" umbrella. Better to have a shapeless song about love than a shapeless song about dystopia.

The King of Limbs Live

Though far from being a critical failure, *The King of Limbs* is easily the most polarizing of Radiohead's full-length albums. On the review aggregator site Metacritic, it clocks in at a 79, which doesn't sound too bad until looking at the band's next lowest score (*Amnesiac*, which has an 87). Among its most prominent detractors were Robert Christgau ("So much more fun than Eno these days," he wrote in a one-line review) and *NME*, who dubbed it "stylistically similar" to *In Rainbows*, "but not as good."

Fans and critics were far more receptive to the live versions of the songs, which weren't widely seen until June 24, 2011 during Radiohead's surprise appearance at the Glastonbury Festival. The break was due to Yorke wanting to continue work on Atoms For Peace and other studio projects, plus, the band had needed time to figure out to most effectively present *The King of Limbs'* songs in a live setting. They even had to enlist the help of a second drummer, Portishead's Clive Deamer, to help Selway round out the complex rhythms. Selway described the process as each percussionist alternating between playfulness and operating in the steadier fashion of a drum machine.

When unveiling their new live lineup and having to rely on a more traditional rock setup, *The King of Limbs'* songs suddenly took on more power—their hooks more visible. But outside of Glastonbury, a two-night stint at New York City's Roseland Ballroom, and a handful of late-night appearances on *Saturday Night Live*, *The Colbert Report*, and *Late Night With Jimmy Fallon*, Radiohead didn't tour extensively in 2011.

That meant, for many fans and critics, the *Live From the Basement* episode became the definitive version of *The King of Limbs*. There was already a consensus that the songs worked better live than on record, and the show's laid-back nature—jokes and studio chatter and tea breaks in between songs—reminded viewers that the electronically dense music was indeed created by humans.

Radiohead did eventually embark on a proper North American tour in February 2012, complete with their second drummer (who subsequently joined the band on its *A Moon Shaped Pool* tour) and an elaborate visual display. In front of an enormous floor-to-ceiling projection screen behind the band, video monitors hung in various diagonal positions—the two different types of projection surfaces blasting audiences with color in sync with the songs.

The tour was smooth sailing until its final date at Toronto's Downsview Park on June 16, 2012. Around 4 p.m., an hour before concert attendees were allowed into the venue, the stage's temporary roof collapsed, injuring three members of Radiohead's crew and killing their drum technician, 33-year-old Scott Johnson, who was struck by a falling video monitor. The band was traumatized by the experience and discussed never touring again. But after rescheduling their upcoming European dates, they decided to work through the tragedy together and made their first stop in Nîmes, France on July 10.

Radiohead stayed involved in the legal case surrounding the stage collapse, even as the investigation took upwards of a year. In June 2013, the Ontario Ministry of Labour leveled 13 charges against Live Nation, Optex Staging & Services

Inc, and stage engineer Domenic Cugliari, who was accused of miscalculating the weight of the stage roof and its various equipment attachments. It took another two years for the case to reach trial.

After even more delays (Optex not having a lawyer, the defense team requesting more time, etc.), the case was eventually dropped due to something called the Jordan ruling, a 2016 Supreme Court of Canada decision that states anyone charged with a crime must be tried within a reasonable timeframe.

When Radiohead returned to Toronto to play Scotiabank Arena on July 19, 2018, Yorke stopped the encore to address the situation.

"Six years ago, we wanted to do a show in Toronto," he told the crowd of over 19,000 people. "The stage collapsed, killing one of our colleagues and friends. The people who should be held accountable, are still not being held accountable. In your city."

Before playing "Karma Police," he led a minute of silence for Johnson. As *VICE Canada*'s Jill Krajewski noted in her review of the show, the lyric "arrest this man" took on a much more poignant meaning than usual.

Conclusion

Regardless of one's feelings towards *The King of Limbs*, there was no denying the apparent lack of ambition upon its release. As inventive as the romance-lost-among-nature theme is, the music itself takes a while to sink in its claws. In that sense, Christgau's tongue-in-cheek description is somewhat accurate. Because of its subtlety, this is Radiohead's most ambient collection of songs—music to cool out by rather than rock out to.

But as time has gone on, that's not a bad thing. As written in the year-end list of *Rolling Stone* (who dubbed *The King of Limbs* the fifth best album of 2011), it was "a record that grew all year—in your room and onstage." That aptly describes the subtleties that eventually bloom into fuller musical ideas with every listen. There's also the fact that, love it or hate it, *The King of Limbs* still sounds like nothing else in the Radiohead canon (*NME* be damned), and the wood-strolling contemplation is refreshing when stacked against the real-life tragic leanings of the band's next album, *A Moon Shaped Pool*.

At least the Grammy Awards recognized the power of the album, nominating *The King of Limbs* for Best Alternative Music Album, Best Boxed or Special Limited Edition Package, Best Short Form Music Video, Best Rock Performance, and Best Rock Song (the final three were all for "Lotus Flower").

Commercially, the contrasting viewpoints surrounding *The King of Limbs* didn't seem to hurt its sales. In the United States, it debuted at number-six on the *Billboard* 200, with eventual sales figures reaching up to 400,000 (downloads only). For retail copies, it sold 307,000, making it the first Radiohead album not to achieve Gold certification stateside. It did, however, make up for it in vinyl sales over in the UK, where it not only became the best-selling vinyl album of 2011, but accounted for 12 percent of all vinyl sales in the first half of the year.

Most important of all, the album marked another step in Radiohead's journey toward total control of their music. With *The King of Limbs'* release, the band founded Ticker Tape Ltd., a vanity label and subsidiary of XL Recordings that would distribute all of the band's music moving forward.

33

"You've Got Ventriloquists"

Covers of Radiohead

In all their 30-plus years as a band, Radiohead has never been all that interested in playing other artists' songs live. According to the comprehensive tour database setlist.fm and not including Thom Yorke and Jonny Greenwood solo compositions, they've only played 20 covers total throughout their career. Of those 20, only 3 have been played more than five times—Carly Simon's James Bond theme, "Nobody Does It Better" (16 times); Can's "The Thief" (10 times); and Larry Weiss's "Rhinestone Cowboy" (6 times).

Everything outside of that has been played sporadically, the only running theme being that Radiohead really likes covering Neil Young. "Cinnamon Girl," "After the Gold Rush," "On the Beach," and "Tell Me Why" have all gotten their due, sometimes during special studio performances and other times during Young and his late ex-wife Pegi's annual Bridge School Benefit, which ran from 1986 to 2016.

Even when Radiohead does play a cover, they don't tend to reinvent it like one would think. Their versions of "Rhinestone Cowboy," Tim Buckley's "Sing a Song For You," and Belly's "Untogether" are far from avantgarde. Rather, the band has preferred to deliver their covers in straightforward rock arrangements or with just Yorke on guitar and/or piano, sometimes with accompaniment from Jonny. They haven't yet given another musician's song the *King of Limbs* treatment, and haven't played a cover in public since their spur-of-the-moment "Tell Me Why" at the Hollywood Bowl on August 25, 2008.

But what about the reverse question? How often do other musicians cover Radiohead? The answer is all the time, and to comprehensively examine every last one would take up a fourth of this book. So let's set some parameters and only talk about what's been professionally recorded. That means, outside of this sentence, we won't get to spend a ton of time on some of the stellar live renditions of Radiohead songs (unless they made their way onto an album), such as Gnarls Barkley's vibrado-slapped rendition of "Reckoner" and Panic! At the Disco's appropriately theatrical version of "Karma Police." Such is life.

Tribute Albums

Christopher O'Riley

There's no shortage of albums dedicated entirely to filtering Radiohead's songs through a different genre. The *Rockabye Baby!* series put out a whole CD's worth of Radiohead lullabies, and *Music Box Mania* has two volumes of Radiohead songs played on the titular children's toy.

Christopher O'Riley's classical-piano treatment of Radiohead has a lot more substance than either of these gimmicky outings, casting a wide range of the band's songs in a pool of moonlit ivory. Throughout 2003's *True Love Waits* and 2005's *Hold Me to This*, he pulls from every one of Radiohead's albums

Album art for Christopher O'Riley's first album of Radiohead covers, *True Love Waits*.

Author's collection

up to that point, from deep cuts off of *Pablo Honey* ("I Can't") to little-known B-sides ("Cuttooth") and singles from the just-released *Hail to the Thief* ("2 + 2 = 5"). Even the first album's title track hadn't gotten a publicly released studio recording at that point.

The first album relies on Radiohead songs with more concrete melodies, making it more accessible and immediately recognizable. With *Hold Me to This*, O'Riley expanded his curation into more abstract compositions such as "Like Spinning Plates." Since there are no overdubs, some of the band's otherworldly textures get lost in the stately arrangements, but both albums go down easy and are worth seeking out for the fandom that went into them.

Vitamin String Quartet

The rotating musicians of the Vitamin String Quartet project have released literally hundreds of albums that tackle different artists from the rock and pop spectrum. In certain cases, such as Radiohead, musicians get multiple records dedicated to their music. To date, there's been a mixtape tribute, a "True Love Waits" / "Burn the Witch" single, and string quartet versions of the albums *OK Computer*, *Kid A*, and *In Rainbows* in their entirety.

The higher number of players allows the different quartets to find some of the nuances that a solo classical piano cannot, making each album a slightly more dynamic listen than the works of Christopher O'Riley. At the same time, some of Radiohead's more percussive tracks, such as "There there," lose some of their momentum when recreated by violins, a viola, and cello.

Various Artists—*Exit Music: Songs with Radio Heads* (2006)

Christopher O'Riley has various eras of Radiohead on his two tribute albums, but because the playing comes from one person working within a highly specific musical parameter, there's a unity to each of his projects.

Not so with *Exit Music: Songs with Radio Heads*. The tracks range from *Pablo Honey* all the way to *Amnesiac*, and because the featured artists are so wildly different, the results are severely scattershot. Shawn Lee's funk-lite version of "No Surprises" is insufferably corny, Meshell Ndegeocello and Chris Dave's "The National Anthem" may as well be smooth jazz in a dentist's office, and RJD2's leans so far into cheap-synth robot noises for "Airbag" that the song loses all of its gravity. Even with a handful of standout tracks—most notably a more colorful "Morning Bell" from Questlove and James Poyser's side project the Randy Watson Experience—*Exit Music* is best listened to on a song-by-song basis rather than in one sitting.

Easy Star All-Stars—*Radiodread* (2006)

It's unlikely that all or even most of the covers in this chapter have made it to Radiohead's ears. Easy Star All-Stars' reggae makeover of *OK Computer*, however, is the rare Radiohead tribute that's gotten the band's stamp of approval. At a 2006 concert, *USA Today* reported Thom Yorke telling the audience how much he loved the New York reggae collective's version of "Let Down," infused with joy by a feature from Toots & the Maytals. The melancholy guitar chimes become buoyant trombones; Yorke's despairing words sound more hopeful through the late Toots Hibbert's Jamaican patois.

That's the fun of listening to *Radiodread*: discovering how every one of *OK Computer*'s sonic tricks will get translated, whether it's the clanging, drop-D guitars of "Electioneering" getting replaced by soulful organ or the strings of "Climbing Up the Walls" becoming an echo-chambered brass section.

The special edition of *Radiodread* also features somewhat of an accidental callback to Radiohead's early years as On a Friday. Since the Easy Star All-Stars cover classic albums in a reggae/dub framework, it's become custom for each one to include a second side of dub remixes. On a Friday did the same thing on their 1986 demo tape.

The Arrogant Sons of Bitches— *This Is What You Get* (2006)

One of the musicians to predate Radiohead on the pay-what-you-want game of *In Rainbows* was Long Island punk veteran Jeff Rosenstock, who founded Quote Unquote Records, "The First Ever Donation Based Record Label."

One of the bands on Quote Unquote is Rosenstock's third-wave ska act the Arrogant Sons of Bitches, who, on November 1, 2003, played an entire set of Radiohead covers at the Downtown in Farmingdale, New York. In keeping with the Halloween spirit, they dressed as Radiohead and spoke in British accents during their stage banter, then released the album three years later on All Hallow's Eve.

While the playful dedication of the Sons' experiment is admirable, the full-on ska versions of Radiohead songs are, to put it bluntly, kind of annoying. So many of Yorke's lyrics are already so emotive, that when given an extra helping of punky snot from Rosenstock, they become abrasive. This is especially true of album closer "True Love Waits."

That's not a knock against Rosenstock, who's recorded and distributed plenty of wonderfully energized music over the years in his respective genres. But ska and Thom Yorke just don't go together. On a Friday fared no better when they wrote and recorded several ska songs themselves back in the late-'80s.

Various Artists—*Stereogum Presents . . . OKX: A Tribute to OK Computer* (2007)/*A Tribute to OK Computer* (2012)

In 2001, Vitamin String Quartet was the first musical act not fronted by Thom Yorke to record *OK Computer* in its entirety. Easy Star All-Stars followed in 2006, and 2007 marked the year that music publications would put begin putting their own spins on Radiohead's masterpiece.

First came *Stereogum*, who commissioned 12 different artists—several of whom *Stereogum* named Bands to Watch in the preceding year—to record one song apiece on *OK Computer* in celebration of its tenth anniversary. They even went the extra mile and got Death Cab For Cutie's Chris Walla to put an a cappella spin on the first section of "Polyethylene (Parts 1 & 2)" before it launches into a more faithful cover.

Album art for Stereogum Presents . . . *OKX: A Tribute to OK Computer* (2007)/*A Tribute to OK Computer*   *Author's collection*

All 12 artists put their own distinct stamps on the music, resulting in a tribute album that plays more like a mixtape, and that's part of *OKX*'s charm. Every listener is likely to have a different set of favorites. For this writer's money, Mobius Band's post-punk speed-up of "Subterranean Homesick Alien" is the most fun and Copenhagen's Slaraffenland take "Paranoid Android" to a most delicate place by subbing out Jonny Greenwood's jagged guitar solo with woodwinds. Of all the covers on the album, it's the song that sounds farthest from the original.

Vampire Weekend also deserve credit for adding playful synths to "Exit Music (For a Film)" while sacrificing none of the song's acidity. Their cover also marks the first time their music received wide distribution, as *OKX*'s July 2007 release date was still three months away from the band's debut single, "Mansard Roof." The only disappointment of *OKX* is David Cross adopting a voice that sounds like a Black stereotype for his character Samson Dalonoga, who recites the deadpan Macintosh SimpleText dialogue from "Fitter Happier."

In addition to the music, *OKX* came with individual track notes from each artist, along with original artwork created by Nicole Johnston and an introductory essay from Brandon Stosuy. *Stereogum* would put similar love and care into other tribute albums in the series, including works from Radiohead's friends R.E.M. and Björk, and Nigel Godrich's would-be collaborators the Strokes.

The German magazine *Musikexpress* took a similar approach to *Stereogum* for the 15th anniversary of *OK Computer*, once again soliciting 12 different acts to each record a different song from the album. The CD was available as an insert in the publication's July 15, and while the final product isn't quite as memorable or specifically curated as *Stereogum*'s, it actually holds together as a more cohesive work. There are far more electronic textures, with every group possessing an ethereality that helps connect all the tracks. Emika's "Exit Music (For a Film)" is Radiohead for a coked-out disco, Diagrams' multi-tracked, in-the-round vocals on "Airbag" score the morning after, and Sizaar caffeinates "Lucky" with cavernous beats from a drum machine.

Amanda Palmer—*Amanda Palmer Performs the Popular Hits of Radiohead on Her Magical Ukulele* (2010)

The quirky title and retro album art reek of cuteness, but Amanda Palmer transcends what could be an overly gimmicky concept by adding vocal depth to six different Radiohead songs, all from their first three albums.

Another strength of *Magical Ukulele*'s is its cache of tasteful musical accents. On its own, the ukulele can quickly become a precious instrument in the wrong hands. But because Palmer adds well-placed flourishes—downtrodden piano notes for the root notes on "High and Dry," for instance—it never becomes

Album art for *Amanda Palmer Performs the Popular Hits of Radiohead On Her Magical Ukulele*.   *Author's collection*

overbearing. It also helps that she refuses to slow down "Idioteque," as so many other uke players would be wont to do.

Radiohead—*TKOL RMX 1234567* (2011)

Technically, this double-disc whopper has Radiohead's name on it and is sourced mostly from *The King of Limbs*. But each of the 19 different electronic acts puts such a distinct spin on the material that they sound like different songs altogether. Reshaping would be a more accurate term than remixing.

According to Yorke, that was the point. As told to Atease on September 26, 2011, the band wanted the songs to mutate and branch out into different directions. If that's the criteria, then *TKOL RMX 1234567* is ultimately a success.

But it's also somewhat impenetrable. Although Lone adds more wildness to "Feral" and Mark Pritchard's able to transform "Bloom" into a jackhammering industrial cut that returns to the original's sylvan beauty by the end, so many of tracks depart from the source material to the point where they lack shape and melody.

The most egregious example is Illum Sphere's remix of "Codex," which roboticizes a small portion of the horn line while scrapping the piano sequence that forms the song's backbone. It would have been nice to see Illum Sphere retain at least some of the song's central hook while also exploring its other sonic spaces. Deadmau5 did that very thing with his own cover of "Codex," which was released just two months after *TKOL RMX*'s September 16 release date.

Reviews of *TKOL* were largely mixed, with *Pitchfork* calling it "listenable, but ultimately bloodless." Had Radiohead limited it two a single disc, perhaps with just one remix of each song (do we really need five different reinterpretations of "Bloom"?), the humanity could have shone through a little more.

Individual Songs

Brad Mehldau—"Exit Music (For a Film)" (1998)

Christopher O'Riley has gained fame for his classical piano covers of Radiohead, but Brad Mehldau was the first studio musician to take their songs to the ivory. Thanks to accompaniment from Larry Grenadier on double bass and Jorge Rossy on drums, he's able to squeeze more moods out of the composition than O'Riley, especially during an extended musical break. The jazz approach also foreshadows where Radiohead themselves would go with songs such as "The National Anthem" and "Pyramid Song."

Anthrax—"The Bends" (1999)

Though a touch heavier than the original, Anthrax doesn't add enough of their groove-metal muscle to this cover from their *Inside Out* EP to justify its existence. Harmless, and that's the problem.

Jamie Cullum—"High and Dry" (2002)

The no-frills arrangement and earnestness of "High and Dry" was always going to doom it to the singer-songwriter-cover circle of Hell. At least jazz-popper Jamie Cullum had the good sense to get Geoff Gascoyne to lay down some swinging bass underneath it for his 2002 major-label debut *Pointless Nostalgic*. The song even manages to boil a bit when Cullum comes in with an added piano motif.

Flaming Lips—"Knives Out" (2002)

Recorded live at KCRW on July 18, 2002 and released on the *Fight Test* EP in 2003, the Flaming Lips' cover of "Knives Out" drags due to its sauropod pace and Wayne Coyne's vocal performance, which never gets past aping Thom Yorke.

The cover does have a touching connection to the band who wrote it, however. After the June 16, 2012 stage collapse that resulted in the death of drum technician Scott Johnson, the Flaming Lips dedicated "Knives Out" to them during their own show in Toronto that night at the North by Northeast festival.

John Mayer—"Kid A" (2003)

John Mayer's curse will always be that he gets to show off his guitar chops way more in concert than he does in the studio. While it's given him a lot of grief from fans who view him as nothing more than a bubblegum singer-songwriter, he's also gotten plenty of street cred from those who know better. Fellow Radiohead fan Questlove drummed for him on the first track of his second album, 2003's *Heavier Things*, and he's collaborated several times with Frank Ocean.

Heavier Things' lead single, "Bigger Than My Body," showed that Mayer's musical tastes run deeper than many people think with a cover of "Kid A" that served as its B-side. He keeps it simple with just his voice and acoustic guitar, meaning that the song loses some of the twistedness of its words, but he manages to conjure the dark reaches of space whenever he goes into his lower register.

Robert Glasper Trio—"Maiden Voyage" (2006)

It's now clear that there are several jazz pianists included in this chapter, but Robert Glasper stands out for using Radiohead as a gateway to another artist.

On his 2006, debut, *Mood*, he and his jazz trio weave elements of "Everything In Its Right Place" into an interpretation of Herbie Hancock's "Maiden Voyage." True to the album's title, it's a fascinating experiment with moods, adding a street-corner darkness to the original Hancock composition, and at times even sounding like "Pyramid Song." Glasper and his trio performed a more straightforward yet equally resonant rendition of "Reckoner" on their 2015 album *Covered*, recorded at Capitol Studios.

El Lele de los Van Van—"High and Dry" (2006)

On the only cover of "High and Dry" that truly transforms the song, Cuban troubadour El Lele (real name Abdel Rasalps) lifts up the vocal melody with his bold tenor, all while the lilting piano and percussion cast off the arrangement on a Havana wind. The only strange choice is a muffled sample of the original's guitar solo that comes in on the chorus and clashes with the soft rise of trumpets.

Krystle Dos Santos—"Talk Show Host" (2009)

Soul singer Krystle Dos Santos is one of the lesser-known names in this chapter, and that shouldn't be the case. Over a boom-clap arrangement of one of

Radiohead's finest B-sides, she takes the resentment found in Yorke's original vocal and infuses it with righteous anger.

Yoshida Brothers—"The National Anthem" (2009)

The trick to any good cover of "The National Anthem" is nailing the bass line. For traditional Japanese musicians the Yoshida Brothers, that meant playing it with the three-stringed shamisen that makes up the backbone of Tsugaru-jamisen music. The reedy timbre provides a perfect counterbalance for guest singer Jesca Hoop's vocals and the thundering electronic elements that eventually take the song by storm.

Streetlight Manifesto—"Just" (2010)

For anyone jonesing for more ska-punk takes on Radiohead, Streetlight Manifesto tackled "Just" for the massive series of cover songs, *99 Songs of Revolution*. The results are slightly more tolerable, with Tomas Kalnoky's vocals coated in way less snot than Jeff Rosenstock's. The polished production helps, too. But at the end of the day, Radiohead and ska is still a horrible combination.

Punch Brothers—"Packt Like Sardines In a Crushd Tin Box" (2010) and "Kid A" (2012)

Bluegrass shouldn't work with Radiohead songs any more than ska, and yet the Punch Brothers were ballsy enough to tackle two of the band's most electronically based, abstract compositions: "Packt Like Sardines In a Crushd Tin Box" as a bonus track on 2010's *Antifogmatic* and "Kid A" on 2012's *Who's Feeling Young Now?*

The trick is that they never try and fit either song into a singer-songwriter or even a traditional backwoods mold. Instead, they use the strings of of mandolin, fiddle, banjo, guitar, and double bass percussively, both retaining and redefining the cybernetic beat of each song. For "Kid A," they don't even include any vocals, perhaps knowing that their instruments were a better substitute for Thom Yorke's electronically modified singing than anyone's actual voice.

The band's love for Radiohead goes even further in their live show, where they've been known to inventively cover other Radiohead songs such as "2 + 2 = 5" and "Paranoid Android."

Peter Gabriel—"Street Spirit (Fade Out)" (2010)

The only cover of "Street Spirit (Fade Out)" that's quieter than the original, with Peter Gabriel fluctuating between spoken-word and a higher pitch. Tender and skillful—as are most of the songs on his 2010 covers album *Scratch My*

Back—sure. But also a snore when nudged along by the weepy strings of the London Scratch Orchestra.

Regina Spektor—"No Surprises" (2010)

Outside of "Creep," "No Surprises" is the most-covered Radiohead song. And exactly one of them matters (no offense to Amanda Palmer).

Regina Spektor's version consists of just her voice, piano, and some faint strings, which doesn't make it all that different from the other 20 recorded covers out there. But she stands apart from so many lesser performers for being a master interpreter—the way she adds a random exhale during the instrumental break, the sudden high notes she peppers throughout the final verse.

Spektor also released "No Surprises" as an iTunes exclusive, with 100 percent of the proceeds going toward the Doctors Without Borders Emergency Relief Fund—a cause of which Radiohead would probably approve.

Korea—"Street Spirit (Fade Out)" (2010)

While Korea pressed their metal version of "Street Spirit (Fade Out)" to wax before the Darkness did, the latter band had been performing it for much longer. Unfortunately for Korea, the Darkness' faster, more operatic version will be burned into our brains forever, giving it more staying power than their sludgier, more sober take.

Deadmau5—"Codex" (2011)

"Sacred" isn't usually a word that comes to mind when thinking of progressive-house DJ Deadmau5 (a.k.a. Joel Zimmerman), and yet that's exactly how we'd characterize his cover of *The King of Limbs'* most meditative track. By keeping the central piano melody, he has plenty of room to play, but instead of adding a laptop's worth of bells and whistles, he keeps the arrangement sparse, finding half-evolved formations of life in synthesized brass and wah-wah effects. It's quite beautiful (another word not usually associated with Deadmau5).

But then again, why wouldn't he? The guy had his first dance to Radiohead's "All I Need" at his wedding. The band clearly means a lot to him.

The Darkness—"Street Spirit (Fade Out)" (2012)

Even at its quietest, Radiohead's music has an emotional weight that becomes even heavier when dressed up in hard rock. Case in point: the Darkness' chugging cover of "Street Spirit (Fade Out)," which they had covered for nearly a decade before including a proper studio recording on 2012's *Hot Cakes*. While it's hard to top the original, the Darkness' version is definitely more fun, especially when frontman Justin Hawkins drops from his absurdly powerful falsetto into a voice that sounds identical to Thom Yorke's on the song's final word, "again."

Blueprint—"Packt Like" (2012)

The drums stutter less in Blueprint's cover of "Packt Like Sardines In a Crushd Tin Box" (shortened to "Packt Like"), thus keeping it within the hip-hop trappings of his 2012 album *Deleted Scenes*. Outside of the clearer vocals, everything else sticks closely to the original, making "Packt Like" a decent enough vibe-heavy closer to the LP.

Calico Horse—"Idioteque" (2012)

If "Idioteque" loses some of its danciness as a slowed-down slice of California soft rock, it sure doesn't lose its creepiness. The harmonies are spooky in their own right, but is that distant tambourine being played by a ghost?

Jimmy Eat World—"Stop Whispering" (2013)

As a B-side to their 2013 single "Damage" (off of the album of the same name), Jimmy Eat World included a serviceable rendition of "Stop Whispering," which

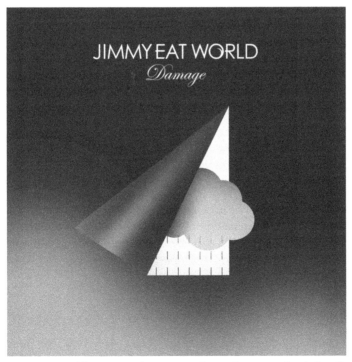

Jimmy Eat World's 2013 single "Damage" featured a cover of Radiohead's "Stop Whispering" as its b-side.   *Author's collection*

deserves inclusion here since they're one of the few bands to cover the song on record. It's a decent listen, though not all that different from the original. That's a shame when considering how adventurous Jimmy Eat World's covers have been in the past, most notably the Prodigy's "Firestarter" and Taylor Swift's "We Are Never Ever Getting Back Together."

Kendra Morris—"Karma Police" (2014)

Radiohead's more musically straightforward songs are sometimes the hardest to interpret. How does another musician make it distinct without completely ruining its foundation? In Kendra Morris' case, she added a twinge of rasp and some strategic bending of the notes for her covers album, *Mockingbird*. The addition of subtle blues-guitar accents ain't bad, either, nor is taking the glockenspiel out of "No Surprises" and applying it to *OK Computer*'s sixth track. Tasteful, though not exactly groundbreaking.

Leo—"Burn the Witch" (2017)

Leo Moracchioli (stage name Leo) never gets as heavy with "Burn the Witch" as he does on his 2016 cover of "Creep," and that's fine. The song's core string sequence already has enough momentum without getting smothered by a hogpile of distortion. He wisely goes into rougher vocals for the chorus, adding some refreshing loud-soft dynamics to *A Moon Shaped Pool*'s opener.

Various Artists—"Creep"

There are 63 recorded cover versions of "Creep." Yes, 63. Most of them are rigidly (and boringly) performed in the singer-songwriter tradition, either not diverting enough from the original or played on a piano or acoustic guitar. Here are six that break the mold.

J Church (1994)

When covering "Creep" as a B-side for their 1994 single "Kittens In a Coma," California punkers J Church applied Jonny Greenwood's pre-chorus dead notes to the entire song, armoring it with crunchy distortion, speeding it up, and calling it a day. The result is exhilarating—galloping, deliberate, and saddled with zero trace of whininess.

Korn (2007)

A flamenco-laced version of a Radiohead song played by a nu-metal band sounds like a recipe for disaster, but Korn exhibit their delicate side to great effect on their cover of "Creep." The nylon guitars are gorgeous, Jonathan Davis refuses to get heavy (even on the chorus), and, on the *MTV Unplugged* broadcast, there's a guy in a pig mask thumping on a cajón. Something about that last detail feels very Radiohead.

Karen Souza (2007)

Argentinian singer Karen Souza leans so hard into the vocal-jazz stylings of her cover that it overshoots irony and comes off as sincere. Unlike the original, the ending actually resolves.

I'm Not a Pilot (2010)

The middle of I'm Not a Pilot's cover of "Creep" is fairly standard—it's the minute or so before the full band comes in that's most interesting. Until then, the arrangement is driven solely by an electric cello line that's instantly recognizable without having to rely on any root notes.

Macy Gray (2012)

Aside from her smoky voice, Macy Gray's live version of "Creep" has stuck fairly close to the original. But when she cut a studio version for her 2012 covers album, she laced it with fuzzy bass and church organ, raising up its power throughout the entire song—not just the distorted chorus.

34

"Off the Diving Board"

Unreleased Radiohead Songs

If this chapter had been written before the 2016 release of *A Moon Shaped Pool*, it would be a lot longer. Of that album's 11 songs, 7 had already been circulating in live performances—some of them as far back as 1995. It's long been a common practice for Radiohead. Before the release of *Kid A*, the band made a point to play almost every one of its songs prior to the album's release.

Of course, there's still an LP's worth of tracks out there that have yet to find a home on a proper Radiohead album. With any luck, that will change in the near future for at least some of the below compositions. Note that these are just the songs that have been captured live, even if it's just a partial clip at a soundcheck. There are several more, such as "We Agree" and "Rubbernecks," that have been mentioned by the band either in interviews or on Dead Air Space, but without a publicly available recording (yet).

"Follow Me Around"

Although interview footage plays over a portion of it, "Follow Me Around" is one of the only Radiohead songs to be played full in Grant Gee's 1998 documentary *Meeting People is Easy*. It starts with Thom Yorke playing it solo on acoustic guitar at a soundcheck in Fukuoka, then climaxes when the rest of the band casually joins in, heightening the lyrics' paranoia about being shadowed by the government.

Since then, "Follow Me Around" has refused to die. A recording was at least tempted during the *Kid A/Amnesiac* sessions, fragments of its lyrics have popped up frequently on Dead Air Space, and Yorke played it as part of an actual performance at an acoustic gig in Toronto on October 17, 2000. This occurred after fans created a website, followmearound.com, and clamored for a proper live performance by the hundreds.

After another solo appearance during Yorke's performance at the UK's Latitude Festival on July 19, 2009, "Follow Me Around" finally got the full-band treatment once again—this time with Atoms For Peace. At the band's April

14, 2010 gig at Oakland's Fox Theater, Yorke randomly taught Flea the chords, resulting in a somewhat hesitant cover of the Radiohead gem.

Fortunately, it fell back into Radiohead's hands in on August 20, 2017, when Yorke and Jonny Greenwood performed it in Macerata, Italy at an earthquake benefit concert. Backed by a drum machine, the more subdued arrangement had a distinctly Middle Eastern vibe to it. The original still remains the most powerful version, and if Radiohead ever decides to record "Follow Me Around" for a studio album, they'll have plenty of arrangements to choose from.

Split Sides

In 2003, New York City's Merce Cunningham Dance Company commissioned both Sigur Rós and Radiohead to compose ethereal electronic music for a show titled *Split Sides*. Due to the company's improvisational nature (the show was to have a different sequencing each night) and Cunningham's method of choreographing with computer programs, it seemed like a perfect fit.

By all accounts, it was—unless you ask Radiohead. In awe of both the dance company and Sigur Rós' appropriately ethereal music, they felt that their own compositions weren't up to snuff. Although they performed live for the first show at Brooklyn Academy of Music, Sigur Rós handled most of the other dates, with Radiohead's music played through recordings or manipulations by other musicians.

Radiohead was apparently dissatisfied with their work to the point that they weren't going to release it at all. While it's never made its way to a proper album, the dance show finally came out on DVD in 2013.

As for the music itself, it's not horrible. But where Sigur Rós added innovative touches such as a xylophone-type instrument connected to pointe shoes, Radiohead ran through a collage of their most reliable tricks. Ambient textures shift back and forth between busy soundscapes, roboticized drum beats, and ice-age drones. About 16 minutes in, a moment of (perhaps unintentional) comedy arrives when Yorke stars meowing like a cat. It's nothing remarkable on its own, though maybe it was evocative when paired with avantgarde dance.

"Skirting On the Surface"

Yorke's solo shows and performances with Atoms For Peace have long been a dumping ground for unreleased Radiohead songs. Although "Skirting On the Surface" wasn't performed live until an October 2, 2009 at Los Angeles' Echoplex (once again during Yorke's solo section of the yet-to-be-named new band), fragments of its lyrics had appeared on Radiohead's website since the *OK Computer* sessions. They've performed it as a full band three times since then, all during the *King of Limbs* tour in 2012. Anchored by palm-muted guitar and the scraping duel percussion of Selway and Deamer, the arrangement lightens up Yorke's musings on mortality with a snakey groove.

"Ed's Scary Song"

The horror-movie vibes continue on this oddity that supposedly appeared on one of Radiohead's webcasts in the early 2000s—though in a much more campy fashion. While the rest of the band jams, O'Brien does his best Vincent Price impression and improvises narration about happy plants and speakers eating people alive. It's unlikely that this goof will appear on his long-awaited solo album, but you never know.

"I Froze Up"

Yorke premiered this by-the-numbers string of similes and metaphors on Radiohead's fourth webcast, which aired on December 18, 2002. It was just him and a Fender Rhodes piano, and when he played it live at a Green Party benefit on February 25, 2010, he kept the arrangement similarly sparse.

The only other time Yorke has played "I Froze Up" live was during his solo section at Atoms For Peace's April 10, 2010 gig at the Aragon Ballroom in Chicago. He revealed to the crowd that it was written around the time of *Kid A*, but given that he's only played it while by himself, it seems there's a better chance of it one day making its way onto a solo album or an Atoms For Peace record.

"Come to Your Senses"

For some of Radiohead's unreleased songs, all we have is a brief snatch of melody. That's the case with "Come to Your Senses," which was partially recorded during a soundcheck at the Greek Theatre in Berkeley on June 24, 2006. Although it's not even a minute long, the music has a banjo line from Jonny Greenwood that's unabashedly twangy. He's dabbled with more rustic musicality in his film scores, but even this tiny sliver of "Come to Your Senses" sounds like no other Radiohead song out there.

"I Lie Awake"

Sound-checked before Radiohead's performance at Malahide Castle in Dublin on June 6 2008, "I Lie Awake" only has a garbled 30-second clip to prove its existence. But its menacing guitar line and title link it to another Radiohead with somnambular imagery, "Go to Sleep."

"Wake Me"

Radiohead were really on a roll with sleep-themed songs in 2008. Similar to "I Lie Awake," "Wake Me" was recorded at a soundcheck by an inconspicuous fan from the Atease message board—this time at the Hollywood Bowl on August 24. Unlike "I Lie Awake," the 1:14 clip of "Wake Me" has a decent audio quality, allowing it to twinkle. The only musical element keeping it from being a soothing lullaby is a lurking guitar line that vibrates beneath everything else, then explodes during a cathartic climax.

It's worth noting that Radiohead has never officially confirmed the title, leading some fans to dub it "Dawn Chorus," a name that feels descriptive of the song's brightened second half.

"Riding a Bullet"

Although an extended six-minute recording exists of Radiohead sound-checking this unreleased track in Mansfield, Massachusetts on August 13, 2008, the rough quality makes it hard to hear what's going on. From what we can tell, it's a faster, guitar-driven track that wouldn't have been out of place on *The Bends*. The title—if that is indeed the title—would place it nicely alongside "Bulletproof . . . I Wish I Was."

"Open the Floodgates"

Yorke's solo section of the Atoms For Peace show at the Echoplex on October 2, 2009 was a treat for Radiohead fans. All but one song was a live premiere, and two have yet to be released on albums. The second was "Open the Floodgates," a melodically simple ballad with a piano line that wouldn't be out of place in a Carol King song. If Radiohead ever decides to record it as a full band, hopefully they'll treat it like they did "True Love Waits" and keep the arrangement minimal and gorgeous.

"Cut a Hole"

The most recent of Radiohead's unreleased tracks, "Cut a Hole" received its live debut at the American Airlines Arena in Miami on February 27, 2012. Haunted-house synths intertwine with imagery that depicts a long-distance relationship straight out of a horror movie. When Yorke sings about wishing he could emerge from a lover's phone, one can't help but think of *A Nightmare On Elm Street*, where the receiver becomes Freddy Krueger's mouth—wet tongue and all. Though lonely and atmospheric, the general creepiness of "Cut a Hole" would have made it a poor candidate for *A Moon Shaped Pool*.

35

"Motion Picture Soundtrack"

Jonny Greenwood

It's amusing to think that, in Radiohead's early years as On a Friday, Jonny Greenwood was merely viewed as Colin's little brother who always hung around rehearsals. But it soon became clear that, even at a young age, he was the most musically talented member of the band, which has led to a solo career that's astounding in its output and diversity.

Jonny certainly isn't the first lead guitarist to play a music-room's worth of other instruments, nor is he the first to venture into classical music. But when listening to his pummeling guitar work with Radiohead, especially on their first three albums, it's not the most obvious connector to his eventual foray into classical music. Then again, his classical work has an aggression not typically associated with the genre.

Despite once telling *Rolling Stone* that he hates guitar solos, Jonny has played a number of notable ones in Radiohead ("Paranoid Android" immediately comes to mind). But, true to his opinion, he's veered further and further away from guitar, expanding his musicality to the point of being somewhat of a mad scientist. Live, he's often hunched over, dark curtains of hair hanging over his face as he moves a ring across the wire of the ondes Martenot, teasing out notes that almost sound human.

Although he had developed an interest in the early electronic instrument as a teenager, he wouldn't use it on a Radiohead album until 2000's *Kid A*. Other electronic instruments in Jonny's wheelhouse include a barrage of modular synthesizers and the Kaoss Pad. Manufactured by Korg, the effects unit is featured heavily on a number of Radiohead songs, most prominently "Everything In Its Right Place," where Jonny used it to manipulate Thom Yorke's voice into something more fragmented and robotic. Live, Jonny often runs a portable radio through his effects pedals, meaning that, in concert, "The National Anthem" might crackle with anything from a Japanese news broadcast to trap music.

Jonny's love of technology goes beyond just instruments, pedals, and effects units. In addition to loving video games, he taught himself the ropes of the visual programming language Max. The suggestion came from Radiohead

Starting with *Kid A*, Jonny Greenwood began using Korg's Kaoss Pad heavily in Radiohead's music.
Photo by Yusuke SAKAI/Wikimedia Commons

producer Nigel Godrich, who was learning the software himself at the School of Audio Engineering. In an interview with Max's developer, Cycling '74, Jonny described its benefits.

"Encountering computers in recording studios was always a bit disappointing when we were starting out," he said. "I found that early music software really off-putting: cubase, logic, all those programs seemed desperate for you to write in 4/4 at 120 BPM and loop the first four bars. You were always being led down a certain route—despite the supposed limitless directions you could go in."

By learning Max, Jonny gained more agency by building his own delays, reverbs, and sequencers from the ground up. "Before, there was all this padding between the computer and me," he continued. "Now there was a blank screen as a starting point." The software has since figured heavily into songs such as "Glass Eyes," "Go to Sleep," and the majority of *The King of Limbs*. Even before then, he was using simple machine code to build primitive computer games as a child.

In many ways, Jonny's relationship with various sounds and instruments reflects the arc of Radiohead as a whole. His alternating love and skepticism of technology ties to the themes of *OK Computer*, his embrace of electronics made

Kid A what it is, and his desire to have more agency in the band's music coincides with their increasingly independent distribution systems. Yorke may be the voice of Radiohead, but Jonny's the heart. It's sometimes a synthetic heart, but a heart nonetheless.

Childhood

Jonathan Richard Guy Greenwood was born November 5, 1971, in Oxford. As a boy, he had a musical adeptness well beyond his older peers—in both taste and talent. While his first record was Squeeze's "Cool For Cats" single on pink vinyl, he also enjoyed jazz and classical music from an early age, unlike his eventual bandmates, who were drawn more to post-punk and New Romantic music in the early days.

It also helped that, during long car rides, Jonny and Colin Greenwood's mother Brenda would cycle through four cassettes that were outside of the masculine rock framework: a collection of Simon and Garfunkel covers, Mozart's horn concertos, and the soundtracks for *Flower Drum Song* and *My Fair Lady*. In his program notes for his 2005 composition for the BBC Concert Orchestra, "Popcorn Superhet Receiver," Jonny recalled being fascinated by how the music with blend with the hum of the car engine.

"I found that if I concentrated hard enough, I could hear the music from the cassettes still playing in the background," Jonny wrote. "I'd do this for hours, until I could nearly hear every detail fighting to be heard through the drone of the car." It's an apt description of "Popcorn Superhet Receiver," as well as many Radiohead songs.

Around the age of four or five, Jonny began playing the recorder at the same time Colin began playing guitar. Jonny learned his instrument much faster than Colin, then proceeded to learn *Colin's* instrument much faster than Colin. Although the two have always gotten along and enjoyed each other's company, the color-blind Jonny insists that his older sibling would (somewhat playfully) take out his jealousy by mixing up his crayons.

While many consider the recorder to be a child's instrument, Jonny took it quite seriously all the way into adulthood, even playing it on the title track of "The Bends."

"Instead of stealing cars and having a good time as a teenager, I was literally playing recorders until the age of 18, with no shame," he told *NPR*'s *All Things Considered* on August 4, 2016. "I wish I'd had a drug habit."

Instead of getting into trouble, he began hanging around On a Friday's rehearsals at Abingdon School. Because Jonny was so quiet, none of the other band members outside of Colin knew how truly talented he was (at this point, he was playing viola in the Thames Valley Youth Orchestra). After a year of his perseverance, they finally let him play harmonica, then keyboards, then—once they became Radiohead—just about everything.

College Years

It's not surprising that, of everyone in Radiohead, Jonny was the only one to actually study music—in addition to psychology—at university. Not that it lasted very long.

While attending Oxford Polytechnic College in 1991, On a Friday signed their record deal with EMI just three weeks into Jonny's first semester. Torn between devoting himself full-time to the band or finishing his education, it was his mentor and tutor who convinced him to leave and pursue a once-in-a-lifetime opportunity.

This influential figure was supposedly the inspiration for the character of Charlie Kay in Hanif Kureishi's 1990 novel *The Buddha of Suburbia*. Anyone who's read the novel shouldn't be surprised at his advice for Jonny—in the book, Charlie is a failed glam-rocker who takes a leap into the punk scene.

Collaborations Outside of Radiohead

Junun

During one of Radiohead's stops in Israel, the band heard another group of musicians playing in the Negev desert. While Jonny admitted to *IndieWire* on July 10, 2018, that the band wasn't very good, he was impressed by one song. But they weren't even the ones who wrote it.

Jonny eventually tracked down the composer, Shye Ben Tzur. Though raised in Israel, he developed a lifelong passion for classical Indian music after seeing a performance by Indian musicians Hariprasad Chaurasia and Zakir Hussain. This eventually led to him writing in the tradition of Qawwali, a type of exuberant Sufi devotional music.

"It's very trance-oriented," Tzur described to *IndieWire*. "The lyrics are all very passionate and they talk about the relation between the human and the divine."

When Jonny and Tzur decided to create an album together in 2015 (titled *Junun*), they set some strict parameters: all of the musicians would be Indian and from the state of Rajasthan, and any string instruments used would be native to there as well. Under the engineering skills of Godrich, they would also do away with the high fidelity that's so rampant in world music.

Album art for *Junun*.   *Author's collection*

"When lots of Westerners go to India they make music with lots of respect, but sometimes it feels a bit like there's *too* much respect," Jonny told *IndieWire*. "People can be too wary—too wary to make anything that captures the real roughness of some of this music, especially the way the brass bands play when they're following processions and weddings down backstreets and the like."

As with so many Radiohead albums, Jonny and Tzur picked a recording setting that would foster such authenticity. It turns out the Maharaja of Jodhpur is a fan of Tzur's music, and he invited them to set up shop in his massive 15th-century fort, Mehrangarh. A large space beneath the fort gave the entire album a natural reverb.

Across its 13 tracks—all of which were written by Tzur, produced and played by Jonny and their 15-member ensemble (dubbed the Rajasthan Express)—*Junjun* bounces with the exuberance its creators sought out to achieve. In addition to Qawwali, there are traces of Hindu maharajas, which were sung by Muslim vocalists. This highlights the multicultural aspect of *Junun*: North Indian music written by an Israeli, produced by an Englishman, and played by an Indian ensemble made up of both Hindus and Muslims.

As Tzur noted to *IndieWire*, North Indian music doesn't rely on chords the way most Western music does. This leaves more space; more room for being playful and highlighting the brass—brought to India by the British and used in various ceremonies—and nagara percussion (similar to a kettledrum). Jonny, who added his own eccentricities (drum machines, computers, and his beloved ondes Martenot) favorably compared the music to the ecstatic nature of James Brown. The album's so fun, it's easy to forget that Tzur's lyrics are so intensely spiritual.

Film Work

Bodysong

Simon Pummell's 2003 documentary *Bodysong* was a perfect film for Jonny to work on as his first soundtrack. It shows the human life cycle through a series of otherwise unrelated images with no dialogue, covering a vast expanse of moods and themes.

This gave Jonny plenty of room to experiment, and the final result plays like a greatest hits of all his sonic moods up to that point. "Moon Trills" turns to an orchestra to capture the majesty of conception, the distorted jazz of "Clockwork Tin Soldiers" conveys the monotonous carnage of war, and the opening of the triptych "Bode Radio/Glass Light/Broken Hearts" ponders death via abstract electronica. In a personal connection to Jonny's own life, Colin plays bass on the sinister "24 Hour Charleston."

Paul Thomas Anderson

While Jonny, Tzur, Godrich, and the Rajasthan Express were making *Junjun*, film auteur Paul Thomas Anderson traveled to Mehrangarh to make a documentary about the recording process. It wasn't the first time he had worked with Jonny.

Their initial collaboration was 2007's *There Will Be Blood*. Already a fan of Jonny's work on *Bodysong*, Anderson had listened to Jonny's classical composition "Popcorn Superhet Receiver" while adapting the screenplay rom Upton Sinclair's novel *Oil!* Jonny agreed to compose his first narrative score, and ended up using elements of "Popcorn"'s unsettling orchestral swells in the track "Henry Plainview."

Most of the score has this same off-kilter menace. Despite being mostly driven by an orchestra that would have fit in with the film's 1898 setting, there's little majesty to be had in *There Will Be Blood*'s music. Instead, the classical instruments sound warped, ratcheting up their tension as protagonist Daniel Plainview corrupts his own soul in his pursuit for oil and wealth. The soundtrack—with artwork from Jonny's wife, Sharona Katan (partially and appropriately created with oil paints)—was praised for its groundbreaking us of the orchestra, although the snippets of already-existing music (including "Popcorn Superhet Receiver," "Convergence" from *Bodysong*, and classical compositions by Arvo Pärt and Johannes Brahms) prevented it from getting nominated for an Oscar.

Jonny would use the London Contemporary Orchestra to more traditional effect on Anderson's next film, 2012's *The Master*. The unsettling swells are still there, but they often melt into uplifting arrangements that fit in with the film's post-World War II era, including posthumous vocals from Ella Fitzgerald, Jo Stafford, and other singers from the time period. That's not to say the central relationship between a troubled veteran and an L. Ron Hubbard-like religious leader is especially wholesome, but there's not the same kind of overt greed and consumption found in *There Will Be Blood*.

Anderson's following film, 2014's *Inherent Vice*, takes place in 1970, meaning the soundtrack is rounded out by songs from the likes of Neil Young, Can, and the Marketts—all of which help illustrate the movie's laid-back LA beach vibes. But being based on a Thomas Pynchon novel, *Inherent Vice* also spans several genres, most notably film noir. For this grimmer, internal side, Jonny once again turned to a traditional orchestra, this time reveling in sadness and introspection rather than menace.

The most noteworthy song for Radiohead fans on *Inherent Vice* is "Spooks," a strange surf-rock instrumental that the band premiered in Copenhagen on May 6, 2006 and briefly considered for the *In Rainbows* sessions. While that never came to fruition, Jonny slowed it down for *Inherent Vice* and got Radiohead's neighbors Supergrass to perform it.

"It's good, but not very rh!" he tweeted to *Pitchfork* on October 6, 2014.

Jonny finally received an Oscar nomination for his work on an Anderson film with 2017's *Phantom Thread*. Unsurprisingly, it's his most sincere score, sonically conveying the passion of a complicated romance between a controlling fashion designer and his muse.

"If this was even vaguely ironic or tongue-in-cheek, everything would be lost," Jonny told the *Los Angeles Times* on February 22, 2018. To bring his swooning compositions to life, he enlisted the help of usual suspects the London Contemporary Orchestra and the Royal Philharmonic Orchestra, with solo contribution from pianist Katherine Tinker and himself (Anderson apparently wanted to retain the style of Jonny's piano-playing from the original demos he had recorded on his iPhone).

Norwegian Wood

The romance at the center of 2010's *Norwegian Wood* (based on the 1987 novel by Haruki Murakami) is plagued by suicide, institutionalization, and other tragic events. While Jonny's soundtrack—performed by the Emperor String Quartet and BBC Concert Orchestra—is appropriately mournful, its somber nature also makes it his hardest film work to get through. The only respite comes from the inclusion of three more Can songs.

We Need to Talk About Kevin

Consisting mostly of transmissions and ambient drones, the soundtrack for *We Need to Talk About Kevin* is by far Jonny's most subtle film composition. Seeing as the film revolves around a mother dealing with the aftermath of her son going on a killing spree at his school, the subject matter didn't need a lot of additional media piled on top of it.

Due to its sparseness, *We Need to Talk About Kevin* is the only one of Jonny's film scores to not be released as an official soundtrack.

"There were a few pretty steel-strung harp things, but the rest of it was mostly laptop-generated stuff broadcast to and recorded from an old LW radio," he told *Uncut* in November 2012. "It's good in the film, but not exactly *Raiders of the Lost Ark* on its own."

You Were Never Really Here

Perhaps wanting to get a proper soundtrack released for his music on one of her films, Jonny contacted *We Need to Talk About Kevin* director Lynne Ramsay in 2016 to see what she was working on. As luck would have it, she was about to get started on a film adaptation of Jonathan Ames's novel *You Were Never Really Here*. A crime thriller about a hitman who rescues victims of human trafficking, the film called for a noir soundtrack that still felt understated and contemporary.

While Jonny still employed strings from the London Contemporary Orchestra, the most distinct sound from *You Were Never Really Here* comes from what he referred to in *NME* on March 6, 2018 as "big fat synthesizers." They feel more modern and cutting than the intentional romanticism of some of Jonny's recent work with Anderson. It's the closest his music has sounded to Vangelis's score for *Blade Runner*.

Classical Work

At this point, Jonny Greenwood is almost as revered as a classical composer as he is for his work in Radiohead. In addition to holding residencies with the

BBC Concert Orchestra and the Australian Chamber Orchestra, he's performed live versions of his soundtrack for *There Will Be Blood*, and created brand-new original compositions such as "Water."

Of course, Jonny's notoriety comes from deviating from the usual behavior of a classical composer.

"It's all about trying to play classical music in slightly different venues with a slightly less uptight atmosphere than is usually found in concerts," he told BBC Radio 5 on October 10, 2014, speaking of his live program that included selections from *There Will Be Blood*, Johann Sebastian Bach, Henry Purcell, and Iannis Xenakis.

Throughout the rest of the article, Jonny goes on to describe how classical music doesn't need to sound exactly the same every night. He stresses the importance of keeping the atmosphere somewhat loose, similar to a rock show, with a bar, dim lighting, and setlists decided at the last minute.

"In one of Mozart's early letters, he's boasting about one of his concerts to his father and is saying, 'It's amazing,'" he continued. "'The audience heard the first few bars and they liked the idea so they started clapping,' and it had that kind of excitement about it, which has kind of been squeezed out by the reverence and silence with which most classical concerts are done in now."

36

"Working Out Chaotic Things"

Fan Theories

For most of their career, Radiohead has dropped assorted Easter Eggs throughout their music, usually in the artwork. And because they've rarely commented on these cryptic messages, the codes, hidden images, and locked grooves have only fanned the flames of fans speculation.

In some ways, Radiohead obsessives are right to always be on the lookout for new information. When many listeners received mysterious "Burn the Witch" leaflets in the mail, it heralded the release of *A Moon Shaped Pool*. Seemingly random phrases in liner notes have become lyrics on future works, and when a Reddit user believed the pathways on the cover of *OK Computer* to be the eastbound junction of I-84 and I-91 in Hartford Connecticut, they were right.

The flipside is that many Radiohead fans think that *everything* the band puts out has a hidden agenda. Make no mistake—Radiohead are the type of artists who think long and carefully about their visual identity, marketing, and the overall cohesion of their albums. But that doesn't mean every last thing they touch has a deeper meaning. And yet some fans can't seem to help themselves. Some fans can't seem to stop over-analyzing every. Little. Thing.

The biggest example of this can be found in something called "01 and 10", the king cobra of Radiohead conspiracy theories. The basic gist is that *In Rainbows* was recorded as a direct response, comment, or extension to *OK Computer*, and as such, the albums are meant to be played together as one long album. Each album side should start with *OK Computer*, then alternate with the *In Rainbows* tracks all the way until the end, meaning the final sequence looks like this:

1. "Airbag"
2. "15 Step"
3. "Paranoid Android"
4. "Bodysnatchers"
5. "Subterranean Homesick Alien"
6. "Nude"
7. "Exit Music (For a Film)"
8. "Weird Fishes/Arpeggi"
9. "Let Down"
10. "All I Need"
11. "Karma Police"
12. "Fitter Happier"
13. "Faust Arp"
14. "Electioneering"

15.	"Reckoner"	19.	"Jigsaw Falling Into Place"
16.	"Climbing Up the Walls"	20.	"Lucky"
17.	"House of Cards"	21.	"Videotape"
18.	"No Surprises"	22.	"The Tourist"

The relative simplicity of this tracklist has origins that are much more complicated. It started with the 2007 release of *In Rainbows*, which, as recognized by many Radiohead fans around the world, involved several uses of the number 10. There were 10 tracks, it came out on the tenth day of the tenth month, and in the 10 days leading up to its unveiling, fans were sent a series of nine messages all scrawled with the letter "X," which many interpreted to represent the Roman numeral for 10.

One astute (or unhealthily obsessed) listener ran with the 10 theme on the now-defunct site Puddlegum. After realizing that *OK Computer* predated *In Rainbows* by 10 years, they pointed to one of *OKC*'s working titles, *Ones and Zeroes*, then tied it to the binary numeral system.

"If *OK Computer* is represented by 01 and *In Rainbows* is represented by 10, then we have 01 and 10," they wrote on Puddlegum. "In binary code, 01 and 10 complement each other." And thus, the "01 and 10" playlist was born. According to the Puddlegum post, the combination of the two albums results in seamless transitions and the dovetailing of similar themes.

While it's a fascinating theory, it's also riddled with inconsistencies and problems, the most glaring one being that the playlist doesn't even flow together all that well. Outside of the countdown blips at the end of "Airbag" directly launching us into the opening clatter of "15 Step," the songs rarely transition into each other, and the sequencing is a bit of a slog. *OK Computer* and *In Rainbows* are similarly paced with their peaks, valleys, beginnings, and conclusions. So when listened to in the "01 and 10" framework, there are a lot of repeat moves and false starts.

For example, we get the two brief oddball songs, "Fitter Happier" and "Faust Arp," right next to each other. We get two of the slowest songs, "Nude" and "Exit Music (For a Film)," right next to each other. We get one appropriate album closer, "Videotape," immediately followed by another appropriate album closer, "The Tourist," which suddenly takes the power of finality away from both of them. While some might view all of this as an expansion of the arc that's already there, it just elongates everything to point of being boring.

As for the album's respective lyrics connecting to one another, it would be easy to make that argument for any Radiohead album. Like any writer, Thom Yorke has his pet themes and subject matter that he's always been interested in writing about—technology, dystopia, control, romantic obsession, breakups, etc. To act like it's some revelation that he explores similar topics on two different albums feels self-congratulatory.

But if taken with a healthy grain of salt, geeky theories like "01 and 10" can be a lot of fun, and in the world of Radiohead fandom, there's no shortage of them. So in the spirit of the original Puddlegum post, here are 10 more Radiohead conspiracy theories—some of which have actually proven to have some plausibility.

Kid A Predicted 9/11

In many of his pop-culture essays, Chuck Klosterman presents a theory, acknowledges that it's ridiculous, but then goes down a rabbit hole with his writing that suggests he actually believes it. It's what makes his writing so entertaining—this mixture of examining a topic logically while still writing himself into a froth.

One of his most notorious examples of this appeared in his 2005 book *Killing Yourself to Live: 85% of a True Story*, where he posits that Radiohead predicted 9/11 with their 2000 album *Kid A*. His reasoning is that the sequencing parallels the events of that tragic day—the mood and title of "Everything In Its Right Place" capture the normal New York City before the planes hit, the aggression of "The National Anthem" signals the actual attack, etc.

Knowing Klosterman's writing, part of him is probably poking fun at the general preposterousness of most Radiohead fan theories. And yet another part of him seems like he desperately wants to believe that Radiohead actually foreshadowed one of the deadliest terrorist attacks in the world. In reality, *Kid A*, like most great albums, has a range of moods that could be applied to any extraordinary day throughout history. Thom Yorke's lyrics had gotten so cryptic by that point that it's easy to bend them to one's own personal interpretation.

Kid A Is About *Amnesiac*

One of the most fertile hunting grounds for Radiohead conspiracy theories is Reddit, where, in 2013, one user by the name of zhgguy put forward the belief that *Kid A* is about *Amnesiac*. Their main piece of evidence comes from a Yorke quote where he compared *Amnesiac* to someone being caught in a forest fire and *Kid A* to someone standing outside the fire.

"Think about it thematically: *Kid A* and *Amnesiac* both deal with Thom's depression, but in different ways," zhgguy wrote.

The problem is, Yorke has never confirmed that either album is about his depression. While Radiohead have commented on the larger themes found in each album, they've never described either work as chronicling the personal struggles of their frontman. It seems especially unlikely given his lyric-writing process at the time, which involved pulling different phrases out of a hat and combining them together.

There's no denying the connection between the two albums, as they were recorded during the same sessions. But the depression angle is a stretch, as is zhgguy's hypothesis that the "A" in *Kid A* stands for "Amnesiac" (the album title came from the band's nickname for a sequencer).

Radiohead Play Occupy Wall Street

More of a hoax than a bona fide conspiracy theory, the first week of the famed protest movement buzzed with rumors that Radiohead would play a show at Zuccotti Park on September 30, 2011. Seeing as the band's collective politics have always leaned left and they were in New York for a two-night run at the Roseland Ballroom, a gig in support of Occupy Wall Street seemed probable.

Of course, it didn't happen, despite being confirmed by the Occupy Wall Street Arts and Culture Committee and several notable publications, including *Gawker* and *Gothamist*. Around 3,000 people descended upon Zuccotti—some of them regular protesters, some of them fans who just wanted to see the band— for a 4 p.m. performance, only to have their hopes dashed when Radiohead didn't show up. The band did, however, issue a statement to support the movement while also revealing that the rumor was just that—a rumor. The plus-side was that it brought increased visibility to the movement, and at 5:30 p.m., the army of attendees participated in a silent march to 1 Police Plaza (it actually ended at 1 St. Andrew's Plaza).

According to the hoax's engineer, writer and activist Malcolm Harris, that was exactly the point. In a December 14, 2011 *Gawker* essay titled "I'm the Jerk Who Pranked Occupy Wall Street," he revealed that the whole thing was an attempt to get more people gathering at Zuccotti Park.

"This was a little over a week into the occupation, before the mass arrests on the Brooklyn Bridge, and it still wasn't clear whether the whole thing would catch on," he wrote. "Someone suggested we should get Radiohead to play a free concert—they were in town for a couple small shows and fans were ready to sell pounds of flesh for tickets. The band wouldn't even have to play the thing, people just had to think they were going to."

All it took from Harris was the creation of a gmail account under the name of Radiohead's manager Bryce Edge. Once he "confirmed" they were playing, the hoax spread like wildfire, thanks to general buzz and tweets from celebrities like Russell Simmons. When it all proved to be false, the hoax was quickly overshadowed by other more substantial events of the protest. While the ethics of Harris's prank are debatable, the act seems to have at least played a role in bringing more attention to Occupy Wall Street.

Karma Police Inspired a British Surveillance Program

In 2008, the Government Communications Headquarters (GCHQ) in the United Kingdom initiated a mass surveillance program called KARMA POLICE. Operated with little to no regulation, its goal was to monitor online activity and create a web-browsing profile for every visible user on the internet, as described in a September 25, 2015 whistleblower article in *The Intercept*.

It's unclear whether the GCHQ took inspiration from the song while creating KARMA POLICE or if they merely used the song as a codename. Either way, it's troubling that they would associate the song in any way with an organization that clashes so repugnantly with Radiohead's politics. Also, the Karma Police in the song are framed as being an villainous shadow organization. That the GCHQ would so willingly align themselves with a group straight out of a George Orwell novel—for the purpose of committing acts straight out of a George Orwell novel, no less—is equally disturbing.

The King of Limbs Has Two Parts

At 37:34, 2011's *The King of Limbs* is Radiohead's shortest album by a long shot. Maybe that's why fans were so ready to believe that a second disc would arrive shortly after its release.

The theory began to circulate after several supposed clues surfaced. First, orders of the album from Radiohead's website were labeled TKOL1, leading some fans to believe there would be a TKOL2. From there, it snowballed, as Radiohead conspiracy theories tend to do, with some listeners pointing out that the final track's title ("Separator") and closing lyric ("If you think this is over, then you're wrong") hinted that there was more to come.

There wasn't. On April 14, 2011, Ed O'Brien explained to BBC Radio 6 Music that, while the band had started work on other songs that weren't included on the album, none of them were finished, outside of the "Supercollider" / "The Butcher" single released that year for Record Store Day. He also said that there would be no plans to put out any of that music in the future.

A Moon Shaped Pool Is in Alphabetical Order

This theory happens to be ... completely true! But unfortunately for all the tinfoil hats out there, Jonny Greenwood has already explained why *A Moon Shaped Pool*'s tracklist is in alphabetical order. Apparently, the band was constantly debating over the sequencing, and descending from "Burn the Witch" all the way down to "True Love Waits" flowed well and seemed as good a solution as any.

There's just one problem. As several Redditors have pointed out, many of the songs have a seamless transition to the next track—the final piano twinkle of "Decks Dark" carrying over to "Desert Island Disk," the tape loop at the end of "Tinker Tailor Soldier Sailor Rich Man Poor Man Beggar Man Thief" underscoring "True Love Waits." Did Radiohead add that connective tissue after deciding the final tracklist, or was there some bigger, secret plan at play?

Radiohead Covers "Gasolina"

During show at Berkeley's Greek Theatre on April 17, 2017, Yorke wigged out with his trademark spastic dance moves while performing "Myxomatosis." One week later, a savvy YouTube user overdubbed the footage with audio of Daddy Yankee's "Gasolina." The edit is near-flawless, making it appear that Radiohead is covering the massive reggaeton hit while the crowd goes wild.

Surely enough, fans of both songs thought Radiohead actually *did* cover "Gasolina," even though the theory was debunked by *NPR*, *Fader*, and elsewhere.

For his part, Daddy Yankee appreciated the joke, almost getting duped himself.

"When I saw the video, I was like, 'Is that real?!'" he said in a May 9, 2017 interview with *Rolling Stone*.

Silence on Dawn Chorus Day

On May 1, 2016—the day that all of Radiohead's social media vanished—Reddit user bornjoke connected it to International Dawn Chorus Day. Held annually on the first Sunday of May, it invites people around the world to rise early and listen to the early-morning birdsong (the dawn chorus).

However, Rachel Carlson's 1962 environmental science book *Silent Spring* describes the birds on her property going silent after pesticides had killed so many of them off. Since rumors had circulated at that point that Radiohead's new album would explore environmentalism, bornjoke believed that the silencing of the band's social media represented the silencing of the birds.

There are a few important things to note here: 1) As bornjoke pointed out in their original post, tweets are represented by a bird. 2) The original title of "The Numbers," *A Moon Shaped Pool*'s most environmentally-minded song, was "Silent Spring." 3) A yet-to-be-released Radiohead song that fans have dubbed "Wake Me" has also been referred to as "Dawn Chorus." 4) When Radiohead reemerged on social media a day later, they did so with the opening shot from the "Burn the Witch" music video—a shot of a bird.

"Imagine waking up one day and the songs of the birds are no longer there because how humans treated the planet killed them all off," bornjoke wrote. "We take them for granted. And now Radiohead is trying to show us what that would be like in a very small way."

So if Radiohead was creating a metaphor for the possible extinction of birds, did their eventual return to social media and a new album released just a week after everything disappeared signify some kind of hope? Yorke has been upfront about not wanting to treat the fight against climate change with a fatalistic point of view, and "The Numbers" posits that collective humanity can indeed make a change and save the planet. bornjoke could very well be onto something.

Ed O'Brien Only Sings His Own Name

Ed O'Brien has long been celebrated among Radiohead fans for providing powerful backing vocals during the band's live performances, especially in the long-lost gem "Lift". But what if, instead of singing an ethereal wordless syllable during the chorus, he was actually belting "Ed"?" Sorry, make that "EEEEEEEEEEEEEEEEEEEEED."

It's been a running joke among Radiohead superfans for years. After all, "Lift" is also the only Radiohead song where Yorke refers to himself by name. But on May 12, 2017, Nate Rogers of *Flood Magazine* took the theory one step closer by suggesting that O'Brien only sings his name on *every* Radiohead song. Rogers then shows live clips of "Karma Police," "Just," and "Weird Fishes/Arpeggi."

Rogers ends the article by detailing O'Brien's eventual expansion of his lyrical vocabulary. On both *The King of Limbs* and *A Moon Shaped Pool*, he doesn't say his name once, and in live performances of "Identikit," he gets to sing the repeated background hook that gives the album its title. If we're being completists, Rogers forgets to mention one other crucial track where O'Brien gets to say much more than his name: the studio bootleg "Ed's Scary Song," where he improvises an entire spoken-word monologue in the style of Vincent Price.

Of course, the *Flood Magazine* article is meant to be as much of a joke as the original "Lift" observation, but that doesn't change the fact that, once you read it and watch the clips, you can't unsee or unhear Ed O'Brien only singing his own name.

A Moon Shaped Pool Is Radiohead's Last Album

In Oscar Hudson's 2017 music video for "Lift," Thom Yorke encounters several images from Radiohead's past videos while riding in an elevator.

According to Reddit user harvestLuca, Radiohead explored a similar theme over a year earlier with the music video for "Daydreaming." In a post from 2016, harvestLuca parallels many of Yorke's travels to older Radiohead imagery—he floats through a grocery store just like in "Fake Plastic Trees," finds himself in a parking garage that resembles a space from an *OK Computer* photo shoot, and ends up facing snowy mountains similar to the artwork from *Kid A*.

Once harvestLuca opened the floodgates, other Reddit users started finding increasingly far-reaching parallels, with several fans suggesting that maybe *A Moon Shaped Pool* would be their last album. If the "Daydreaming" theory was true, that meant there was a sense of everything coming full-circle, a hypothesis driven home by the circular album art and the song's lyrics. What if Yorke wasn't bidding farewell to an old lover, but an entire fanbase? Other clues suggested by Redditors included the opening and closing words of the album ("stay" and "leave") and the special edition of *A Moon Shaped Pool*, of which every copy contained a piece of master tape from a past Radiohead album.

While Radiohead usually refrains from commenting on fan theories, Jonny Greenwood gave harvestLuca's thoughts some creedence when he shared the side-by-side comparisons on social media. However, that could have been him confirming (or simply getting a kick out of) the "Daydreaming" theory.

As for the bigger question of whether or not *A Moon Shaped Pool* marks Radiohead's last album, it seems unlikely. As of this writing, their current tour is lasting well into the end of the year, and they only recently obtained the rights to their back catalogue. It's reasonable to think they'll keep releasing reissues of their pre-*In Rainbows* output, similar to *OK Computer OKNOTOK 1997 2017*.

Finally, Ed O'Brien told *Rolling Stone* on June 8, 2017, that he would like to see Radiohead thrive as a band well into old age.

"You see that joy Leonard Cohen got," O'Brien said. "If we were to do it, it would have to be authentic."

Selected Bibliography

Books

Randall, Mac. *Exit Music: The Radiohead Story* (updated edition). Milwaukee: Backbeat Books, 2012.

Magazine and Newspaper Articles

Borow, Zev. "Difference Engine." *Spin* Nov. 2000.

Brantley, Ben. "Review: 'Old Times,' Where the Past Is a Dangerous Place." *The New York Times* Oct. 6, 2015.

Cavanagh, David. "I Can See the Monsters." Q Oct. 2000.

Cohen, Warren. "With Radiohead's *Kid A*, Capitol Busts Out of a Big-Time Slump. (Thanks, Napster.)." *Inside* Oct. 11, 2000

Fricke, David. "Bitter Prophet." *Rolling Stone* June 26, 2003.

Fullerton, Jamie. "Radiohead: Exclusive Interview Part 2." *NME* Apr. 10, 2007.

Kent, Nick. "Happy Now?" *Mojo* June 2001.

Reynolds, Simon. "Walking On Thin Ice." *Wire* July 2001.

Online Articles and Interviews

Battan, Carrie. "Thom Yorke and Jonny Greenwood Collaborate With DOOM for Compilation." *Pitchfork* Oct. 26, 2011. pitchfork.com/news/44417-thom-yorke-and-jonny-greenwood-collaborate-with-doom-for-compilation/

Battan, Carrie. "Watch the Flaming Lips Play 'Knives Out' to Support Radiohead After Stage Collapse." *Pitchfork* June 18, 2012 pitchfork.com/news/46886-watch-the-flaming-lips-play-knives-out-to-support-radiohead-after-stage-collapse/

Brandle, Lars. "Radiohead's 'In Rainbows' Looms For U.K. No. 1." *Billboard* Jan. 2, 2008. billboard.com/articles/news/1046947/radioheads-in-rainbows-looms-for-uk-no-1

Breihan, Tom. "Lloyd Banks Samples Radiohead." *Stereogum* Nov. 8, 2011. stereogum.com/873232/lloyd-banks-samples-radiohead/mp3s/

Cariad Records. "The Joy of Living and Stanley Donwood—Interview." January 2016. http://cariadrecords.com/thejoyoflivinginterview.html

Caruso, Vincent. "10 Years Ago: Radiohead Come Through the Darkness on 'In Rainbows.' *Diffuser* Oct. 10, 2017. diffuser.fm/radiohead-in-rainbows/

COS Staff. "Rachel Owen, longtime partner of Thom Yorke, passes away from cancer."

Consequence of Sound Dec. 19, 2016. consequenceofsound.net/2016/12/rachel-owen-longtime-partner-of-thom-yorke-passes-away-from-cancer/

Dombal, Ryan. "Radiohead-Approved, Fan-Shot Concert Movie Released." *Pitchfork* Sep. 2, 2010. pitchfork.com/news/39935-radiohead-approved-fan-shot-concert-movie-released/

Ehrlich, David. "Radiohead's motion picture soundtracks." *The Dissolve* July 22, 2014. thedissolve.com/features/exposition/669-radioheads-motion-picture-soundtracks/

France-Presse. "How Pink Floyd's Roger Waters refound his fire at 72." *The Nation* May 22, 2017. nationmultimedia.com/news/life/music/30315906

Frank, Aaron. "Radiohead's Artist Stanley Donwood's New Work Pictures L.A. in Flames." *LA Weekly* Apr. 27, 2012. laweekly.com/arts/radioheads-artist-stanley-donwoods-new-work-pictures-la-in-flames-2373614

Geslani, Michelle. "Radiohead's Philip Selway releases Let Me Go soundtrack: Stream/Download." *Consequence of Sound* Sep. 15, 2017. consequenceofsound.net/2017/09/radioheads-philip-selway-releases-let-me-go-soundtrack-stream-download/

Geslani, Michelle. "Watch Thom Yorke, age 21 and with a totally 90s haircut, perform experimental music." *Consequence of Sound* July 15, 2015. https://consequenceofsound.net/2015/07/thom-yorke-rare-footage-2/

Giles, Jeff. "Why Radiohead's 'Videotape' is Deceptively Brilliant." *Diffuser* Aug. 7, 2017. diffuser.fm/radiohead-videotape/

Gross, Judah Ari. "Before Radiohead conquered the world, it was already Israel's darling." *The Times of Israel* July 19, 2017. timesofisrael.com/before-radiohead-conquered-the-world-they-were-already-israels-darling/

Helman, Peter. "Thom Yorke Shares New MF Doom Remix, Promises More Radiohead Shows in 2017." *Stereogum* Sep. 7, 2016. stereogum.com/1897816/thom-yorke-shares-new-mf-doom-remix-promises-more-radiohead-shows-in-2017/mp3s/

Hewitt, Ben. "It's Not Blueberry Pie: Phil Selway Talks About His Solo Album." *The Quietus* Sep. 29, 2010. http://thequietus.com/articles/05035-phil-selway-interview-familial-radiohead

Hill, Scott. "Sonic Youth Slams Radiohead's *In Rainbows*' Model." *Wired* June 8, 2009. wired.com/2009/06/sonic-youth-slams-radioheads-in-rainbows-model/

Hogan, Marc. "19 Unreleased Radiohead Songs That Could Be on Their Next Album." *Pitchfork* Mar. 4, 2016. pitchfork.com/thepitch/1044-19-unreleased-radiohead-songs-that-could-be-on-their-next-album/

Holland, Taylor. "Thom Yorke Photobomb Goes Viral." *Plus Tard* Nov. 13, 2010. taylorholland.blogspot.com/2010/11/thom-yorke-photobomb-goes-viral.html

Jones, Lucy. "'Hail to the Thief' is 10—Revisiting Radiohead's Underrated Masterpiece." *NME* June 7, 2013. nme.com/blogs/nme-blogs/hail-to-the-thief-is-10-revisiting-radioheads-underrated-masterpiece-768588

Jones, Lucy. "Stanley Donwood On the Stories Behind His Radiohead Album Covers. *NME* Sep. 27, 2013. nme.com/blogs/nme-blogs/stanley-donwood-on-the-stories-behind-his-radiohead-album-covers-766325

Kaye, Ben. "Radiohead producer Nigel Godrich had a very important speaking role in Star Wars: The Force Awakens." *Consequence of Sound* Jan. 28, 2016. consequenceofsound.net/2016/01/radiohead-producer-nigel-godrich-had-a-very-important-speaking-role-in-star-wars-the-force-awakens/

Kaye, Ben. "Radiohead's OK Computer reissue is dedicated to Thom Yorke's late wife, Dr. Rachel Owen." *Consequence of Sound* June 22, 2017. consequenceofsound.net/2017/06/radioheads-ok-computer-reissue-is-dedicated-to-thom-yorkes-late-wife-dr-rachel-owen/

Kellmurray, Beth. "Is Radiohead's '01 and 10' Indie Rock's Greatest Easter Egg Hunt of All Time?" *Diffuser* Apr. 3, 2015. http://diffuser.fm/radiohead-01-and-10/

Kreps, Daniel. "New Radiohead Song 'Spooks' Appears In 'Inherent Vice' *Rolling Stone* Oct. 14, 2014. rollingstone.com/movies/movie-news/unreleased-radiohead-song-spooks-appears-in-inherent-vice-193202/

Kreps, Daniel. "Thom Yorke Talks 'Amok' Leak, Photobombing In Reddit Q&A." *Spin* Feb. 8, 2013. spin.com/2013/02/thom-yorke-nigel-godrich-atoms-for-peace-reddit-interview-amok-photobomb/

Leas, Ryan. "On A Friday: Radiohead In The '80s." *Stereogum* Mar. 9, 2015. stereogum.com/1785797/on-a-friday-radiohead-in-the-80s/franchises/radiohead-week/

Malan, Jamie. "Watch early footage of Thom Yorke's college band play 'High and Dry.' *AXS* July 15, 2015. www.axs.com/watch-early-footage-of-thom -yorke-s-college-band-play-high-and-dry-61023

McKinnon, Matthew. "Everything In Its Right Place." *CBC* July 24, 2006. cbc .ca/news/entertainment/everything-in-its-right-place-1.587693

Menta, Richard. "Did Napster Take Radiohead's New Album to Number 1?" *MP3Newswire.net* Oct. 28, 2000. mp3newswire.net/stories/2000/radio head.html

Michaels, Sean. "Radiohead benefit gig raises £350,000 for Haiti." *The Guardian* Jan. 26, 210 theguardian.com/music/2010/jan/26/ radiohead-benefit-gig-haiti

Mincher, Chris. "Radiohead's Thom Yorke and Ed O'Brien." *The A.V. Club* July 1, 2008. music.avclub.com/radioheads-thom-yorke-and -ed-obrien-1798214319

Nelson, Michelle. "Radiohead On A Friday Demo Cassettes Going for $50K On eBay." *Stereogum* Nov. 5, 2012 stereogum.com/1192021/ radiohead-on-a-friday-demo-cassettes-going-for-50k-on-ebay/top-stories/

Nicholson, Katie. "'I feel so let down by Canada': Radiohead and drum tech's parents demand answers in his Toronto death." *CBC* Nov. 29, 2017. cbc.ca/ news/canada/radiohead-drum-technician-death-1.4422702

NME Blog. "Stanley Donwood On Radiohead's 'The Universal Sigh' Newspaper. *NME* Apr. 4, 2011. nme.com/blogs/nme-blogs/stanley -donwood-on-radioheads-the-universal-sigh-newspaper-775089

Nonesuch Journal. "Nonesuch Journal Exclusive: An Interview With Jonny Greenwood." *Nonesuch* Dec. 6, 2007. nonesuch.com/journal/ nonesuch-journal-exclusive-an-interview-with-jonny-greenwood

Orange, Michelle. "10 Brief Blasts of Radiohead In Pop Culture." *IFC* Apr. 10, 2009. ifc.com/2009/04/10-brief-blasts-of-radiohead-i

Reilly, Dan. "The 21-Year History of Radiohead's 'True Love Waits,' a Fan Favorite Two Decades in the Making." *Vulture* May 10, 2016. vulture .com/2016/05/history-radiohead-true-love-waits.html

Richards, Will. "A Brief History of . . . Headless Chickens." *DIY* July 14, 2015. http://diymag.com/2015/07/14/a-brief-history-of-headless-chickens

Runtagh, Jordan. "Radiohead's 'Pablo Honey': 10 Things You Didn't Know." *Rolling Stone* Feb. 22, 2018. rollingstone.com/music/music-features/ radioheads-pablo-honey-10-things-you-didnt-know-201729/

Savage, Mark. "Radiohead approve release of fans' charity concert DVD." *BBC News* Jan. 10, 2011. bbc.co.uk/news/entertainment-arts-12151914

Schatz, Lake. "Lana Del Rey says Radiohead copyright infringement law-suit is 'over.'" *Consequence of Sound* Mar. 26, 2018. consequenceofsound.net/2018/03/lana-del-rey-says-radiohead-copyright-infringement-lawsuit-is-over/

Scheim, Benjamin. "The History of Thom Yorke On Other People's Songs." *Pitchfork* May 6, 2016. pitchfork.com/thepitch/1139-the-history-of-thom-yorke-on-other-peoples-songs/

Schultz, Christopher. "A Brief History of Rappers Sampling Radiohead." *Spin* Nov. 9, 2011. spin.com/2011/11/brief-history-rappers-sampling-radiohead/

Sigur Rós. "Split Sides—Merce Cunningham Dance Company." sigur-ros.co.uk/band/disco/split.php

Singh, Amrit, "Thom Yorke Photobomb Goes Viral 3 Years Later." *Stereogum* Nov. 8, 2010. stereogum.com/569822/thom-yorke-photobomb-goes-viral-3-years-later/top-stories/

Soghomonian, Talia. "Radiohead, 'The King Of Limbs—The Conspiracy Theories Begin." *NME* Feb. 20, 2011. nme.com/blogs/nme-blogs/radiohead-the-king-of-limbs-the-conspiracy-theories-begin-778356

Spata, Christopher. "'Walking Dead' Actor Starred In a '90s Radiohead Video." *Complex* Dec. 31, 2014. complex.com/pop-culture/2015/01/walking-dead-radiohead-fake-plastic-trees

Strauss, Matthew. "Thom Yorke Plays New Songs, Performs With Patti Smith and Flea at Pathway to Paris." *Pitchfork* Dec. 4, 2015. pitchfork.com/news/62390-thom-yorke-plays-new-songs-performs-with-patti-smith-and-flea-at-pathway-to-paris/

Taylor, Chris. "Plan B Sample Refused By Radiohead." *Gigwise* July 1, 2006. gigwise.com/news/19173/plan-b-sample-refused-by-radiohead

Yoo, Noah. "Watch Deadmau5 Dance to Radiohead at His Wedding." *Pitchfork* Aug. 15, 2017 pitchfork.com/news/watch-deadmau5-dance-to-radiohead-at-his-wedding/

Young, Alex. "Location of Radiohead's OK Computer artwork has been discovered." *Consequence of Sound* May 9, 2017. consequenceofsound.net/2017/05/location-of-radioheads-ok-computer-has-been-discovered/

Young, Alex. "Radiohead's back catalog purchased by XL Recordings: Report." *Consequence of Sound* Apr. 4, 2016. consequenceofsound.net/2016/04/radioheads-back-catalog-purchased-by-xl-recordings-report/

Young, Alex. "Radiohead sue Lana Del Rey, alleging she ripped of 'Creep.'" *Consequence of Sound* Jan. 7, 2018. consequenceofsound.net/2018/01/radiohead-sue-lana-del-rey-alleging-she-ripped-off-creep/

Young, Alex. "Watch Thom Yorke perform 'High and Dry" with his pre-Radiohead band Headless Chickens." *Consequence of Sound* July 13, 2015. consequenceofsound.net/2015/07/watch-thom-yorke-perform-high-and-dry-with-his-pre-radiohead-band-headless-chickens/

Audio and Video Interviews and Documentaries

"The Beatles' Apple Records: 40 Years Later." *NPR All Things Considered* May 14, 2008.
The Culture Show. Thom Yorke. *BBC 2* Oct. 21, 2006.
Explore Radiohead's Music Video For "Karma Police." Pitchfork Mar. 21, 2017

Websites

Citizeninsane.eu
Discogs.com
Greenplastic.com—Green Plastic Radiohead
IMDb.com
Metacritic.com
Setlist.fm
Songfacts.com
WhoSampled.com

Index

CPSIA information can be obtained
at www.ICGtesting.com
Printed in the USA
BVHW061134050221
599326BV00005B/7